Sovereignty Referendums in International and Constitutional Law

İlker Gökhan Şen

Sovereignty Referendums in International and Constitutional Law

Springer

İlker Gökhan Şen
Faculty of Law
Anadolu University
Eskisehir
Turkey

ISBN 978-3-319-36574-9 ISBN 978-3-319-11647-1 (eBook)
DOI 10.1007/978-3-319-11647-1
Springer Cham Heidelberg New York Dordrecht London

Softcover reprint of the hardcover 1st edition 2015

Printed on acid-free paper

Springer is part of Springer Science+Business Media (www.springer.com)

Preface

This book offers a systematic legal analysis of referendums on sovereignty issues and is based on my Ph.D. dissertation from the University of Zurich, Faculty of Law which was approved on 11 December 2013. The concern for authenticity has led me to prefer a facsimile publication except for certain formal modifications of the text. This is the main reason for the exclusion of certain referendums held in 2014, such as the ones in Crimea, Scotland and Catalonia. Putting aside the challenge of updating, these subsequent developments have, fortunately, reconfirmed my belief from the very beginning of this project that the use of referendums is growing in the resolution of sovereignty conflicts in international and national politics. I hope this book will serve as a useful reference for researchers in international and constitutional law who have a scholarly interest in the subject of sovereignty referendums.

Eskisehir, Turkey — İlker Gökhan Şen

Acknowledgements

I would like to take this opportunity to express the deepest appreciation and gratitude to my Ph.D. supervisor Professor Dr. Andreas Auer, who has shown the attitude and the substance of an experienced scholar, a mentor and a friend. Without his supervision and constant help, this thesis would not have been possible.

I am immensely grateful to those who gave much help during my visits to the Center for Research on Direct Democracy (c2d) attached to the University of Zurich in Aarau. Uwe Serdült, Fernando Mendez and Vasiliki Triga provided me a convenient and comfortable workplace. I am also indebted to the Dumont Family: Martina, Raymond, Louis and Isabelle for hosting me in their home several times during my visits to Aarau.

I would like to express my special thanks to Prof. Dr. James Hanlon, Elif Akalp, Edward Mcquaid and Mark Daniel for their invaluable help in the improvement of the English of the preliminary drafts of my thesis. Also, I wish to thank Antoine Barret and Saleh Chowdhury for their support in the course of writing the sections relevant to France and the UK.

Also, I wish to express my thanks to the academic and administrative staff of the Anadolu University Faculty of Law. I owe much to Prof. Dr. Nüvit Gerek, Assoc. Prof. Dr. Ayşe Tülin Yürük and Prof. Dr. Ufuk Aydın for providing me a positive and a convivial working environment since I started my academic career in 2001.

I am particularly indebted to Prof. Dr. Erdal Onar, who has supported me in every stage of my academic life.

Special thanks are due to my family and my friends. I owe much to my parents Bülent and Nevin, my sister Sibel, my friends Nathalie Boillat, Esin and Hakan Ferhatoğlu, Bülent Yücel, Kasım Akbaş, Gizem Koçak, Barış Toraman, Duygu Özer Sarıtaş for their full support and encouragement during the period of preparation of this dissertation.

Abbreviations

CNMI	Commonwealth of Northern Mariana Islands
CNRT	National Council of Timorese Resistance
COFA	Compact of Free Association
CPA	Comprehensive Peace Agreement
CSCE	Conference of Security and Cooperation in Europe
DCP	Derived Constituent Power
DOM	Département d'Outre Mer
ECtHR	European Court of Human Rights
EEC	European Economic Community
ELA	Estado Libre Asociado
EU	European Union
FAS	Freely Associated States
FLNKS	Front de libération nationale kanak et socialiste
FSM	The Federated States of Micronesia
GA	General Assembly
ICCPR	International Covenant on Civil and Political Rights
ICRC	International Committee of the Red Cross
IGAD	Inter-Governmental Authority on Development
INTERFET	International Force in East Timor
LRSLS	Law on the Referendum on State Legal Status
MINURSO	United Nations Mission for a Referendum in Western Sahara
NC	National Council
NCC	National Consultative Council
NCP	National Congress Party
NIA	Northern Ireland Act
NPP	New Progressive Party
OAU	Organization of African Unity
OCP	Original Constituent Power
ODIHR	Office for Democratic Institutions and Human Rights

OSCE	Organization for Security and Co-operation in Europe
PDP	Popular Democratic Party
PIP	Popular Independence Party
POLISARIO	Popular Front for the Liberation of Saguia-el-Hamra and Rio de Oro
PQ	Parti Québécois
RPCR	Rassemblement pour la Calédonie dans la République
SADR	The Saharawi Arab Democratic Republic
SEA	The Single European Act
SPLM/A.	Sudanese People's Liberation Movement/Army
SSRA	Southern Sudan Referendum Act
TOM	Territoire d'Outre Mer
TTPI	Former Trust Territory of the Pacific Islands
UDHR	Universal Declaration of Human Rights
UK	United Kingdom
UN	United Nations
UNAMET	The United Nations Mission in East Timor
UNAMIS	The United Nations Advance Mission in the Sudan
UNIF	Front Bersama Pro-Otonomi Timor-Timor
UNIRED	United Nations Integrated Referendum and Electoral Division
UNISFA	United Nations Interim Security Force for Abyei
UNMIS	United Nations Mission in the Sudan
UNMISS	United Nations Mission in the Republic of South Sudan
UNTAET	United Nations Transitional Administration in East Timor
USA	United States of America
USSR	Union of Soviet Socialist Republics
WWI	World War I
WWII	World War II

Contents

Chapter 1
Introduction

Abstract This book is a product of the belief that there is a convincing justification for a systematic legal analysis of the referendums on sovereignty issues. With more than 300 referendums that have been held since the late eighteenth century, there are now abundant data in international and constitutional law for a comparative analysis on sovereignty referendums, which mostly derive their philosophical foundations from liberal values such as nationalism, democracy, popular and national sovereignty and self-determination. Thus, this first introductory chapter highlights this point of departure and provides a brief summary and plan of the book.

Referendums on sovereignty issues have been a prominent feature of the international political and legal landscape since the late eighteenth century. Up to now, more than 350 referendums have been held on sovereignty since 1791.[1] This number accounts for a considerable portion of the total referendums that have been held in the world so far. Butler and Ranney highlighted this point by observing that referendums on "territorial" issues constitute one of the four groups of subjects that commonly appear in referendums. If one includes some of the constitutional referendums (another group of referendums as reported by Butler and Ranney) that have been associated with these territorial issues, the number of referendums on the subject of sovereignty makes up almost half of all world referendums.[2] This far-reaching presence of territorial issues in the practice of direct democracy is not a coincidence. It shows that sovereignty referendums have been a widespread element used throughout different historical periods of democratisation, nation building and state creation.

Nationalism, democracy, popular and national sovereignty and self-determination had been the founding concepts in the formation of nation states. These values

[1] According to the data retrieved from the Center for Research on Direct Democracy: www.c2d.ch. This number may vary depending on the inclusiveness of the working definition of sovereignty referendums. For instance, Laponce noted an approximate number of 190 sovereignty referendums (Laponce 2010, p. XII); according to Sussman, this number is around 240 (Sussman, G. When the demos shapes the polis – The use of referendums in settling sovereignty issues. http://www.iandrinstitute.org/Studies.htm. Retrieved 5 May 2007).

[2] Butler and Ranney (1994), p. 2.

İ.G. Şen, *Sovereignty Referendums in International and Constitutional Law*,
DOI 10.1007/978-3-319-11647-1_1

appeared during the same course of events, and it should be noted that they overlap and/or support each other in meaning and content. At the beginning of the twentieth century, nationalism and democracy were generally perceived as synonymous concepts in the West. This may be sensed in Renan's allegory[3] defining the nation as "a daily plebiscite". The nation state was considered as the political expression of the will of the people. The association of these two doctrines was provided by the fact that they were both directed against multinational monarchies as a common enemy. As to the principle of national self-determination, the right of the people to form an independent state or to choose which state to belong to appeared as the product of revolutionary theories asserting that the people had a fundamental right to make a constitution and choose its own government.

This study deals with the sovereignty referendums that have been used within the process of nation building and state creation and where the Renanian metaphorical "daily plebiscite" of self-constitution of a nation has become a reality.

The first question in this respect may be this: what is sovereignty? This and other concepts such as national and popular sovereignty, democracy and self-determination should be clarified before starting a study of referendums that involve sovereignty in its various aspects. The concept of sovereignty may be considered in political and legal terms. Politics may be further considered in the descriptive and normative sense of political legitimacy. In the former sense, it involves the conceptual explanation of acquisition and consolidation of a political power in a polity, whereas in the latter it explores the question of how political power should be acquired and what its limits are. In legal terms, sovereignty is tied to independence of states according to international law and to state competence to make and execute laws in terms of constitutional law.

The point of departure for understanding the concept of sovereignty and the relevant referendums is the historical process of birth of the modern nation state. The emergence of the nation state in the nineteenth century created a set of values that made profound changes in the nature of the relationship between territories, peoples and their rulers. Although the origins of the modern nation state can be traced back to the sixteenth century, which is regarded as the breakdown of the medieval era, its theoretical underpinnings grew in prestige in the domestic and foreign policies of the Western world with the advent of American independence and the French Revolution—the latter also being the stage upon which the preliminary experiences of sovereignty referendums occurred. The fundamental guiding principles like popular sovereignty, democracy and self-determination of the French Revolution were decisive in the renouncement of the war of conquest by France and the pledge by the new regime that the consent of the people concerned would be secured before any territorial alteration could be made. This era being the first historical stage of sovereignty referendums, four subsequent and different historical periods may then be discerned, encompassing an increasing momentum

[3] Renan, E. What is a nation. http://ig.cs.tu-berlin.de/oldstatic/w2001/eu1/dokumente/Basistexte/Renan1882EN-Nation.pdf. Retrieved 10 November 2012.

of state creation and constitution making in which sovereignty referendums were held in greater numbers.

These five different eras of sovereignty referendums are described in the third chapter. The first two historical stages included the referendums that were held following the French Revolution, and in the second half of the nineteenth century particularly concerned, the creation of Italy. The third and fourth periods of territorial reconfiguration and state creation following the two successive World Wars and relevant referendums are also mentioned in this context. The fifth group of referendums was held during the process of post-communist state creation and democratisation at the end of the twentieth century.

The significant presence of sovereignty referendums in history explains why so many authors have something to say on this subject, especially political scientists, philosophers and lawyers. The following sections in the third chapter aim to survey the relevant literature offering a brief but holistic account from differing perspectives. The main purpose of this research is to study sovereignty referendums from a legal perspective. Therefore, following a synopsis on the sociological, philosophical and moral or—in other words—meta-juridical aspects, Part I concludes with the main outline of our legal perspective on which we shall build Part II.

In the second part, the legal appraisal of sovereignty referendums will be considered from aspects of international and constitutional laws, as sovereignty and self-determination have both international and domestic dimensions. That may be considered in material and formal perspectives. The material dimension refers to the content or the subject matter of the vote concerned, and the formal dimension indicates its legal basis. In international law, the question of state creation may be observed as the central theme included within the subject matter of any sovereignty referendum. From a formal perspective, the legal status of referendums in international treaties and international customary law will be assessed in the light of historical experiences from the earliest to the most recent periods. The presence of sovereignty referendums in contemporary international law is not a random practice arising from some political expediency. Rather, its legal status in international treaties and international customary law has been gradually and determinedly consolidating itself until the present day.

In constitutional law too, sovereignty referendums have both formal and material aspects. In its material context, the concept of sovereignty is central theme to constitutions and constitution making. In other words, if we refer to the final authority to make and execute laws in a polity when we use the term sovereignty, then the sovereignty becomes the basic condition that should be secured before any constitution may be made. Formally, the question of the legal status of sovereignty referendums may be considered within the larger framework of constitutional change, boiling down to two questions: (1) the legal evaluation of constitution-making activity (constituent power) in a state and (2) the overall picture of sovereignty referendums in comparative constitutional law.

Having dealt with these two questions, we will go on to tackle in-depth cases: France, the United Kingdom, Canada (Quebec), and the United States of America. France has a rigid and written constitution, and it is the home of the doctrine of territorial inviolability. Yet it is also the historical inventor of sovereignty referendums and their relevant underlying principles in Europe. This puts France in a distinctive position. While being the creator of sovereignty referendums, France shows a strong tendency to control the questions of decolonisation—and the referendums held for this purpose—in the limits of its constitutional system. The approval of its 1958 Constitution led to the decision of colonies whether or not to remain as part of France. Further decolonisation issues and relevant procedures also involved referendums in Algeria, Mayotte and New Caledonia. The description of these cases and ensuing debates offer substantial insights as to the political impact and legal appraisal of these referendums in terms of constitutional law in a written constitution.

The case of the UK, in contrast to France and to other cases having written constitutions, is relevant to the discussions of the role of the sovereignty referendums in the context of an unwritten constitution, where the difference between constitution and politics is considerably blurred. Referendums in the UK may be considered as forming a constitutional convention and challenging seriously the principle of parliamentary sovereignty.

Canada and the US offer useful insights to assess the legal value of referendums in a common law context, albeit within a written constitution. Particularly, the secession opinion of the Canadian Supreme Court regarding Quebec explicitly refers to the unwritten rules of the Canadian Constitution regarding the legal value of the referendums. In a similar manner, the US rhetoric of consent of the governed has been the overriding theme in constitutional politics. The referendums and surrounding debates both in the realms of politics and judiciary of the overseas territories will be studied, Puerto Rico being the most recent case.

Chapter 7 is dedicated to a comparative study of common legal problems of sovereignty referendums. The first section deals with fair and impartial referendum administration. From this perspective, the administration of a referendum includes every action required to secure a legitimate referendum. These actions might include census; preparation of electors list through the registration of the voters; guaranteeing of freedom of speech, freedom of assembly and right to vote; counting of votes; declaration of results; resolution of legal disputes; and the daily administration of the referendum area during a fixed period before and after the referendum.

Another common legal issue of the sovereignty referendums is the problem of the quorum, whether there is a need to require an enhanced majority for the final result. According to a first view, enhanced majority may impair the credibility of a referendum since it enables minorities to block the democratic decision process. According to the contrary view, a fairly set level of enhanced majority secures the protection of minorities against the tyranny of the majority.

Equally important is the question as to who should be entitled to vote. This problem lies at the heart of almost all of sovereignty referendums creating an abundant amount of data in comparative constitutional law and international law. Indeed, the question of voter qualification involves the need for two equally legitimate principles of democracy and self-determination, the principle of universal suffrage and securing the genuine wish of the populations concerned. This question will be assessed within the framework of cases, most particularly those of Western Sahara, Puerto Rico, South Sudan and New Caledonia.

Additionally, in this chapter the question of the designation of the voting units will be tackled. Finally, the last section of the chapter handles the issue of formulation of the ballot question, which is of crucial importance in ensuring a legitimate and credible referendum. It has three aspects. Firstly, the wording should be clear and free of ambiguity to allow the voters to cast informed votes. Secondly, the voters should not be forced to vote for more than one option, which may be dissimilarly put in the one ballot question—this is the single subject rule. Finally as a third issue, the ballot should not be prepared in a way that supports the maintenance of the *status quo*.

By exploring in detail a diversity of ideas, cases contexts and issues, the global aim of this study is to achieve a better empirical and legal understanding of the sovereignty referendums, in international and national politics and law. This research therefore aims to provide the students, researchers and all other readers who may be interested in the subject with a comprehensive survey of the sovereignty referendums, as they have developed both in modern political-legal theory and actual practice of modern international law.

References

Butler, D., & Ranney, A. (1994). Practice. In D. Butler & A. Ranney (Eds.), *Referendums around the world: The growing use of direct democracy*. New York: Macmillan.

Laponce, J. (2010). *Le référendum de souveraineté: comparaisons, critiques et commentaires*. Quebec: Les Presses de l'Université Laval.

Part I
Theorising the Sovereignty Referendums

Chapter 2
Introduction to the Theory of Sovereignty Referendums

Abstract There is a growing literature on the topic of referendums and sovereignty, which can be classified according to numerous overlapping dimensions, such as constitutional law, international law, political science and political philosophy. Furthermore, this literature is becoming increasingly sophisticated in terms of the methods it employs and the potential for interdisciplinarity. This chapter is an introductory note on the basic concepts, theoretical framework and methodoloy used. A more detailed account of the theoretical aspects, methodology and discussions of philosophical views and empirical observations will appear in the subsequent chapters. It starts with the assertion that sovereignty referendums have been principal elements in the territorial reconciliations at different points in history. Furthermore, the chapter gives a definition of the concept of sovereignty referendum and reviews different terms such as "plebiscite" and "self-determination referendums", which are used to mean the same concept. The remaining of this chapter briefly reviews the seminal literature, which concludes that the topic of sovereignty referendums may be the subject of several disciplines, most particularly, of politics and law.

In this part, we aim to explore the various concepts that appear in the laws and politics of sovereignty referendums. The many different stages of sovereignty referendums have occurred during the major transformations and realignments of the world map. In these processes, the pivotal issue has been the legitimacy of the acquisition or the possession of territories by various states. In other words, the common concept in these periods of state formation has been the challenges that have occurred against the legitimacy of territorial adjustment or preservation. Different actors, in times of great change, have attempted to overcome this challenge by means of referendums. The concept of legitimacy as its central theme has interacted with the notions of sovereignty, self-determination, nationalism and democracy within the law and rhetoric of sovereignty referendums. By considering these notions, Part I aims to study the basic concepts and their theoretical underpinnings, which we shall refer to in the following chapters.

The common theoretical underpinning of all sovereignty referendums is their legitimating power: allowing the people to express their consent in the process of

İ.G. Şen, *Sovereignty Referendums in International and Constitutional Law*,
DOI 10.1007/978-3-319-11647-1_2

determination of a political unit. According to Auer's definition, sovereignty referendums are popular consultations pertaining to territorial modifications, the independence of states, the self-determination of a decentralised community or adhesion of a state to a supranational organisation.[1] There are also other differing terms used to define the concept of "sovereignty referendums",[2] namely, "self-determination referendums"[3] and, more commonly, "plebiscite".[4]

The term plebiscite is a Latin expression, created by the unification of two separate words: *pleb* and *scitum*. The former refers to the social strata having political rights in the Roman civilisation, whereas the latter means decree. Plebiscite therefore means the decree approved by the plebs.[5]

Gawenda discerns four separate connotations of the word plebiscite. In the first, there are the plebiscites of Roman law signifying, as mentioned in the preceding paragraph, the practices of direct democracy during the Roman era. Second, there are the plebiscites taking place within the domestic politics of states. These encompass all the different sorts of referendums that are held, either according to the constitution or legislation of a state or ad hoc by the governments without any prior legal base. Gawenda coins the term "social plebiscite" (*plébiscite social*), as a third type of plebiscite, indicating questionnaires held by the private research institutions. Fourth, as to the "plebiscite of international law" (plebiscite in its strictest sense), the term is used as a synonym for sovereignty referendums.[6] The use of the term plebiscite, both in literature and in legal documents, evokes a considerable amount of ambivalence. The "plebiscite" therefore is one of the most problematic and controversial concepts in the terminology of both law and political science. This inconsistency mainly stems from the fact that diverse authors in literature attribute various meanings to the term. For certain authors, plebiscite and referendum are synonymous words and may be used interchangeably.[7] Others tend to use the expression to connote votes not taken in a free way or under unfair political conditions. They refer to farcical referendums where dictators or other sorts of despotic regimes use the device to legitimise their authoritarian policies. Under these conditions, the democratic principles such as free campaigning or the secrecy and open tabulation of the vote are not observed. Among these diverse authors, for instance, Uleri says, "Plebiscite could…denote any kind of popular vote…where there is no real possibility to compete in a free and fair way".[8]

---

[1] Auer (2007a), p. 262; Auer (2007b), p. 58.

[2] Auer (1997), p. 28; Laponce (2010); LeDuc (2003), pp. 101–124.

[3] Dobelle (1996); European Commission For Democracy Through Law. "*Opinion on the Compatibility of the Existing Legislation in Montenegro Concerning The Organization of Referendums With Applicable International Standards*". Opinion No: 343/2005, Council of Europe, Strasbourg, 19 December 2005. Para. 33.

[4] Wambaugh (1920, 1933), Farley (1986) and Gawenda (1946).

[5] Berger (2004), p. 63; Barnhart (1995), p. 576; Ernout and Meille (1967), p. 514.

[6] Gawenda (1946), pp. 13–14.

[7] Eule (1990), p. 1587; Bogdanor (1981), p. 143.

[8] Uleri (1996), p. 4.

Accordingly, for Zoller, a plebiscite is a degenerate form of referendum.[9] The reasons for such a negative connotation may be found from examining the historical experiences of referendums. Indeed, many dictators have had recourse to use a distorted form of referendum, such as Napoleon in France, Hitler in Germany and Mussolini in Italy.[10] Also, there are other scholars who differentiate between referendums and plebiscites, the former referring to votes held on policies or issues, the latter involving votes on political leaders, i.e., a sort of vote of confidence given by the people. Dezso also made such a distinction, discerning democratic and anti-democratic plebiscites where De Gaulle's use of the referendum in France was an example of democratic plebiscites. [11] Thus, in this case, the plebiscites do not necessarily have to be undemocratic but may still have "a slightly negative connotation".[12]

This short survey of literature shows us that the term plebiscite has many diverse connotations in diverse contexts and resources and thus is prone to ambiguity. Indeed, "There are many different systems of classification that categorise the types of referendums, indeed as many as there are authors".[13] Adding to this plethora of typology another ambivalent term like "plebiscite" will not serve in any way to a greater conceptual understanding of the referendums that are examined in this study. Taking this into account, and to avoid confusion, we opt to endorse the term "sovereignty referendums" for the purpose of this study rather than the term "plebiscite", unless it appears in a direct quotation from legal documents or literature.

An initial observation about the state of literature regarding sovereignty referendums may be that the study of referendums on sovereignty issues is not the sole preserve of a single discipline. The dominant approaches are law and political science, to which one could add political philosophy. Even within the two dominant fields there are disciplinary divisions, which roughly boil down to whether the focus is on domestic versus international aspects. This is because the concept of a sovereignty referendum naturally implies, both internal and external, i.e., the national and international aspects of sovereignty. In law it tends to break down into constitutional law approaches[14] on the one hand and international law approaches on the other.[15] The political science approach seeks to answer the question of whether the referendum device is a preferable option in the resolution of sovereignty issues. This is in fact associated with a broader question of the

[9] Zoller (1999), p. 365.

[10] Uleri (1996), p. 4; Dezso (2001), p. 264.

[11] Dezso (2001), p. 265.

[12] Suksi (1993), p. 11.

[13] Dezso (2001), p. 264.

[14] Auer (1996) and Beaud (1994, 1997).

[15] Beigbeder (1994), Farley (1986), Wambaugh (1920, 1933), Sureda (1973) and Rudrakumaran (1989).

impact of referendums in the polities where they are used. This question may be dealt with by a focus either on domestic politics[16] or on international relations.[17]

Likewise, we may discern three approaches to referendums: explanatory, normative and legal. The explanatory (or descriptive) approach to any social phenomenon often deals with the causes and consequences of any social process or event that takes place in diverse contexts. In the context of sovereignty referendums, one may consider the description of referendums from a historical perspective, and additionally several works may be cited in an attempt to answer questions such as the timing, the reasons, the role of the political parties, voter behaviour and, most importantly, the impact of these referendums in the course of the various resolutions of sovereignty issues for which they are held.[18] From a normative viewpoint, the question concerns the moral duty to hold referendums whenever a change of sovereignty is in question. Finally, from a legal perspective, referendums may be studied in the light of a variety of legal resources, namely, court decisions, constitutions and international legal documents.[19]

With respect to the legal aspects of sovereignty referendums, Wambaugh's two successive treatises stand as seminal examples.[20] Evidently, these works from the interwar period are outdated, and they are open to criticism that they were no more than the historical records of the referendums lacking a thorough legal analysis. However, by raising some of the basic issues and compiling the historical material, the two works have served a community of scholars working on the topic since. Other examples of mapping the field can be identified, such as Gawenda's legal analysis of the referendums held until WWII[21] or Sureda, who directly addressed the sovereignty referendums held in the post-war decolonisation process and offers a detailed legal analysis of the referendums held in British Togoland and Cameroons, Gibraltar and Somali.[22] More recently, Farley reformulated some of the basic legal issues as set out by Wambaugh in a more systematic manner, with a more precise language and with reference to some of the more recent referendums.[23] One of the most recent and up-to-date legal surveys from an international law perspective has been provided by Beigbeder, whose work remains a reference point on the role of UN involvement.[24] In addition to these works, we could also mention some of the articles that deal with particular issues of sovereignty referendums such as customary international law[25] and questions concerning the eligibility of voters and

[16] Bogdanor (1981, 1994), Ginty (2003), Goodhart (1981), Morel (2007) and LeDuc (2003).

[17] Rourke et al. (1992).

[18] Balsom (1996), Bogdanor (1981, 1994), Brady and Kaplan (1994), Butler and Ranney (1994a), Gallagher (1996), Goodhart (1981), Rourke et al. (1992) and Uleri (1996).

[19] Pavkovic and Radan (2007), p. 171.

[20] Wambaugh (1920, 1933).

[21] Gawenda (1946).

[22] Sureda (1973).

[23] Farley (1986).

[24] Beigbeder (1994).

[25] Rudrakumaran (1989).

the wording of the question.[26] In addition to these studies, certain number of works may be mentioned that focus on sovereignty referendums in a specific country. For instance, Dobelle and Amiel have both focused on the legal regime underpinning French-related decolonisation referendums.[27]

These works, as outlined above, being the first point of departure, this thesis is devoted to a study of sovereignty referendums from a legal perspective. On the other hand, the relationship between the explanatory and normative theories with legal theory remains to be answered before deciding on the methodology. To this end, one may refer to Luhmann's system theory, according to which politics and law are considered as two different social systems. According to this conception, social systems are like living organisms, in the sense that they produce and reproduce the components that constitute the system itself. These systems operate as if they are related to each other yet remaining reciprocally distinct. In this process, each system treats the other systems as their environments. Every system (as the environment) sends communications and demands to the other systems. These systems are "autopoetic": they are "cognitively open", i.e., they allow transfer of information and thus may adapt to demands from the environment. However, they are also closed, that is, this adaptation may only be realised if, and only if, the system translates the new information in its own terms. This is made by the bipolar-binary code specific to each system, which is "legal/illegal" in law. In politics, it may be defined as "holding/non-holding of the political authority" from a sociological perspective, or it may be "good/evil" or "justified/non-justified", from a moral one.[28] Also, each system sends communication to the other systems by means of their binary codes.

The historical experience of sovereignty referendums may be observed according to this pattern. In politics, referendums may be associated with the success/failure of (1) the resolution of a sovereignty conflict, (2) the acquisition of political power, or (3) secession or state creation. In political philosophy (morality), the doctrinal accounts such as the consent of the governed and social contract theories may be read by reference to the justified/non-justified title to sovereignty. Needless to say, in law, referendums may be found in the procedural patterns, which determine the legality or illegality of the possession of a territory. Referendums are the key components in each of these systems, and all these systems communicate and make demands as regards the right to a piece of territory.

Following this outline, in the following chapters we will first determine the location of sovereignty referendums within the environments of politics. Then we will go on to draw the framework of this study from a legal point of view. Finally, we will offer a typology by considering the legal and political elements that have surrounded sovereignty referendums throughout history.

---

[26] Héraud (1983).

[27] Dobelle (1996) and Amiel (1976).

[28] Michailakis (1995), pp. 325–332.

References

Amiel, H. (1976). La pratique française des plébiscites internationaux. *Revue générale de droit international public*, (80), 425–501.

Auer, A. (1996). Le référendum constitutionnel. In A. Auer (Ed.), *Les Origines de la Démocratie Directe en Suisse* (pp. 79–101). Bale, e.t.c: Helbing et Lichtenhahn.

Auer, A. (1997). Rapport introductif: Le Référendum Européen: Définitions reperes historiques et jalons d'étude. In A. Auer & J.-F. Flauss (Eds.), *Le Référendum Européen: Actes du colloque international de Strasbourg, 21–22 février 1997*. Bruxelles: E. Bruylant.

Auer, A. (2007a). National referendums in the process of European Integration: Time for change. In A. Albi & J. Ziller (Eds.), *The European Constitution and National Constitutions: Ratification and beyond*, (pp. 261–271). The Netherlands: Kluwer Law International.

Auer, A. (2007b). La démocratie directe comme piège et comme chance pour l'Union européenne. In A. Flücgiker, A. Auer, & M. Hottelier (Eds.), *Etudes en l'honneur du Professeur Giorgio Malinverni Les droits de l'homme et la constitution* (pp. 57–75). Genève: Schulthess.

Balsom, D. (1996). The United Kingdom: Constitutional pragmatism and the adoption of the referendum. In M. Gallagher & P. V. Uleri (Eds.), *The referendum experience in Europe* (pp. 209–225). Houndmills, e.t.c: Macmillan Press Ltd.

Barnhart, R. K. (Ed.). (1995). *The Barnhart concise dictionary of etymology*. New York: Harpercollins.

Beaud, O. (1994). *Puissance de l'Etat*. Paris: PUF.

Beaud, O. (1997). Propos sceptiques sur la légitimité d'un référendum Européen ou plaidoyer pour plus de réalisme constitutionnel. In A. Auer & J. F. Flauss (Eds.), *Le Référendum Européen* (pp. 125–180). Bruxelles: Bruylant.

Beigbeder, Y. (1994). *International monitoring of plebiscites, referenda and national elections: Self-determination and transition to democracy*. Dordrecht/Boston: Martinus Nijhoff.

Berger, A. (2004). *Encyclopedic dictionary of Roman law*. Union, NJ: Lawbook Exchange.

Bogdanor, V. (1981). Referendums and separatism: II. In A. Ranney (Ed.), *The referendum device* (pp. 143–158). Washington/London: American Enterprise Institute for Public Policy Research.

Bogdanor, V. (1994). Western Europe. In D. Butler & A. Ranney (Eds.), *Referendums around the world: The growing use of direct democracy* (pp. 24–97). New York: Macmillan.

Brady, H. E., & Kaplan, C. S. (1994). Eastern Europe and the former Soviet Union. In D. Butler & A. Ranney (Eds.), *Referendums around the world: The growing use of direct democracy* (pp. 174–218). New York: Macmillan.

Butler, D., & Ranney, A. (1994). Practice. In D. Butler & A. Ranney (Eds.), *Referendums around the world: The growing use of direct democracy*. New York: Macmillan.

Dezso, M. (2001). Plebiscites and referendums. In A. Auer & M. Bützer (Eds.), *Direct democracy: The eastern and central European experience* (pp. 264–270). Aldershot, e.t.c: Ashgate.

Dobelle, J.-F. (1996). Référendum et droit à l'autodétermination. *Pouvoirs, 77*, 41–60.

Ernout, A., & Meille, A. (1967). *Dictionnaire étymologique de la langue latine*. Paris: C. Klincksieck.

Eule, J. N. (1990). Judicial review of direct democracy. *Yale Law Journal, 99*, 1503–1589.

Farley, L. T. (1986). *Plebiscites and sovereignty: The crisis of political illegitimacy*. London: Westview Press.

Gallagher, M. (1996). Ireland: Referendum as a conservative device. In M. Gallagher & P. V. Uleri (Eds.), *The referendum experience in Europe*. Houndmills, e.t.c.: Macmillan Press Ltd.

Gawenda, J. A. B. (1946). *Le plébiscite en droit international*. Fribourg: Imprimerie St. Paul.

Ginty, R. M. (2003). Constitutional referendums and ethnonational conflict: The case of Northern Ireland. *Nationalism & Ethnic Politics, 9*(2), 1–22.

Goodhart, P. (1981). Referendums and separatism: I. In A. Ranney (Ed.), *The referendum device*. Washington/London: American Enterprise Institute for Public Policy Research.

Héraud, G. (1983). Démocratie et autodétermination. In G. Luke, G. Ress, & M. R. Will (Eds.), *Rechtsvergleichung, Europarecht und Staatenintegration: Gedächtnisschrift für Léontin-Jean Constantinesco*. Berlin [etc.]: C. Heymann, cop.

Laponce, J. (2010). *Le référendum de souveraineté: comparaisons, critiques et commentaires*. Quebec: Les Presses de l'Université Laval.

LeDuc, L. (2003). *The politics of direct democracy: Referendums in global perspective*. Ontario, e.t.c: Broadview Press.

Michailakis, D. (1995). Review essay: Law as an autopoietic system. *Acta Sociologica, 38*, 323–337.

Morel, L. (2007, November). The rise of politically obligatory referendums: The 2005 French referendum in comparative perspective. *West European Politics, 30*(5), 1041–1067.

Pavkovic, A., & Radan, P. (2007). *Creating new states: theory and practice of secession*. Aldershot: Ashgate.

Rourke, J. T., Hiskes, R. P., & Zirakzadeh, C. E. (1992). *Direct democracy and international politics: Deciding international issues through referendums*. London: Lynne Rienner Publishers.

Rudrakumaran, V. (1989). The "Requirement" of plebiscite in territorial rapprochement. *Houston Journal of International Law, 12*, 23–54.

Suksi, M. (1993). *Bringing in the people*. Dordrecht: Kluwer.

Sureda, A. R. (1973). *The evolution of the right of self-determination. A study of United Nations practice*. Leiden: Sijthoff.

Uleri, P. V. (1996). Introduction. In M. Gallagher & P. V. Uleri (Eds.), *The referendum experience in Europe* (pp. 1–19). Houndmills, e.t.c: Macmillan Press Ltd.

Wambaugh, S. (1920). *A monograph on plebiscites (with a collection of official documents)*. New York: Oxford University Press.

Wambaugh, S. (1933). *Plebiscites since the world war: With a collection of official documents*. Washington: Carnegie Endowment for International Peace.

Zoller, E. (1999). *Droit Constiutionnel* (Vol. 2). Paris: PUF.

Hénaud, C. (1985). Démocratie et autodétermination. In [illegible] (Eds.), [illegible]. Berlin: [illegible] Heymann.
Lagacé, [illegible] (2010). *Le référendum de souveraineté* [illegible]. Québec: Les Presses de l'Université Laval.
LeDuc, L. (2003). *The politics of direct democracy: Referendums in global perspective*. Ontario: Broadview Press.
[illegible], D. (1995). Review essay: Law as an autopoietic system. [illegible]
[illegible], L. (2007). [illegible] The use of [illegible] referendum in [illegible] comparative perspective. [illegible]
[illegible], [illegible] & [illegible], P. (2006). [illegible]
Rourke, J. T., Hiskes, R. P., & Zirakzadeh, C. E. (1992). *Direct democracy and international politics: Deciding international issues through referendums*. Boulder: Lynne Rienner Publishers.
[illegible], W. (1996). The [illegible] [illegible]

Chapter 3
Sovereignty Referendums in the System of Politics

Abstract This chapter begins with a description of the historical background of sovereignty referendums. The significant presence of sovereignty referendums in the history of the modern state explains why so many authors have something to say on this subject, especially political scientists, philosophers and lawyers. The following sections in this chapter aim to survey the relevant literature, offering a brief but holistic account from different perspectives to offer a synopsis of the sociological, philosophical and moral or—in other words—meta-juridical aspects of the sovereignty referendums.

3.1 Occurrence of Sovereignty Referendums in a Historical Context

3.1.1 Historical Overview: Practices Since the French Revolution

The germ of the idea and practice of consulting the inhabitants of a territory may be dated back to medieval times. Gonsollin notes that the first genuine popular consultation was held in Geneva.[1] In 1420 when the Duchy of Savoy decided to annex Geneva, the inhabitants of the city reacted by holding a referendum, after which the annexation was rejected unanimously. The significance of this referendum was that it was conducted by universal male suffrage, which was very progressive for the era.[2] Another experience may be observed, when in 1552 the cities of Metz, Toul and Verdun decided to stay as a part of France.[3]

We may further trace the initial and rudimentary practices of popular consultations regarding the foundation of a community, from the early seventeenth century, when the American Ancestors (the Pilgrim Fathers) founded their early colonies.

[1] Gonssollin (1921), p. 31.

[2] Farley (1986), p. 29.

[3] Rourke et al. (1992), p. 31.

İ.G. Şen, *Sovereignty Referendums in International and Constitutional Law*,
DOI 10.1007/978-3-319-11647-1_3

From the first colony (New Plymouth) henceforth, colonies were founded by means of the "plantation covenants": compacts signed by the entirety of the adult and male population. In the beginning, these communities were purely religion based. The plantation covenants were used to found new church congregations of puritans who had emigrated from Britain. However, it did not take long for this religion-based conception of formation of a political unit to evolve into a prototype for the democratic foundation of a political community. In this way, the "Fundamental Orders of Connecticut" was a document prepared for the foundation of Connecticut. It was created by the people who had withdrawn from Massachusetts and is noted as the first written constitution in history to be ratified directly by the people.[4]

Despite these preliminary experiences, the French Revolution is still considered as the starting point for sovereignty referendums. The theory underlying the popular consultation about its political status had been formed during the French Revolution. The guiding principles of the French Revolution such as popular sovereignty, democracy and self-determination urged France to renounce the war of conquest and the employment of force against the liberty of the people as the main framework of its foreign policy.[5]

From this point on, sovereignty referendums may be examined in five main periods.[6] The first period begins with the French Revolution, where resolving territorial problems through referendum as both principle and procedure first appeared. The union of Avignon, the Comtat Venaissin, Savoy and Nice with France were realised through referendums. When representatives of the Papal States Avignon and the Comtat Venaissin submitted their will for unification with France, the French Assembly compelled the representatives of these states to consult the people in the given areas. It was only after these popular consultations that the French Assembly decided to annex the aforementioned provinces.

The second period of referendums started with the process of the unification of Italy in the nineteenth century. The process of unification of Italy through referendums started in 1848, with a referendum in Lombardy to join the Kingdom of Sardinia and was completed in 1870 with the adhesion of Rome.[7] Also in this period, the return of the Saint-Barthélemy Islands from Sweden to France (1877) and the independence of Norway from Sweden (1905) were realised by means of a referendum. In this period, one should note that not every country was eager to use referendum in its territorial settling. The United States is a striking example of that

---

[4] Auer (1996), p. 85.

[5] Wambaugh (1920), p. 5; Farley (1986), p. 30.

[6] Laponce (2001), pp. 38–40.

[7] In the Lombardy referendum, the voters were asked whether to realise the immediate union with Sardinia. The result was almost unanimously in favour of the immediate union. After the first referendum in Lombardy, similar votes followed in Venetia, Parma and Modena for joining the Sardinian Kingdom. These regions were then incorporated into the Kingdom of Sardinia through the laws enacted by the Sardinian Parliament. Then referendums were held in Tuscany and Emilia Sicily, Naples, Umbria and Marches (Wambaugh 1920, pp. 14 and 61–65).

point. No referendum was held during the acquisition of Florida (1819), California (1848), Texas and New Mexico.[8]

After the First World War, a new third phase of sovereignty referendums began. Inspired by the Wilsonian principle of self-determination, referendums were provided by the Paris Peace Treaties for ending the war with Germany and Austria (Treaty of Versailles and Treaty of St. Germain). In this period, referendums were held in Schleswig, Allenstein and Marienwerder, Upper Silesia and Sopron. There were also "attempted plebiscites" that could not be held due to the lack of agreement between the parties on the basic terms and conditions of the referendum. These areas include Teschen, Spisz and Orava (Poland and Czechoslovakia), Vilnius (Poland and Lithuania), Tacna and Arica (Peru and Chile). Also, the transfer of some other regions, as may be seen in the case of Alsace-Lorraine, did not follow a referendum.[9]

The fourth wave of referendums comprises those held during the decolonisation process after the Second World War. By 1945, more than 750 million people were subject to a foreign power. Africa, the Middle East and Asia were all territories of colonialist European countries. The most significant consequence of the Second World War was the emergence of independent states outside Europe in large numbers.

Soon after its establishment, the United Nations took an active role in reshaping the political map of the world. The colonial territories of the defeated countries (Italy, Germany and Japan) were put under the Trusteeship System of the United Nations. The Trust Territories would be administered by the USA, the UK or France on behalf of the UN. The United Nations Trusteeship Council was established in order to check the compliance of the administering authorities with the rules and principles of the trusteeship system as set out in the UN Charter. The trusteeship was different from the mandate system of the League of Nations in that it was defined as an explicit transitional period to independence.[10]

In light of the foregoing, it may be observed that virtually all of the post-Second World War referendums were related to the independence of territories under colonial rule. In this era, the right to self-determination of the people gained its utmost prestige, especially within the UN and in parallel with the decolonisation process. Several sovereignty referendums were held, under the UN's auspices in Africa, Asia, the Pacific Islands and Latin America. In this period, metropolitan states also applied referendums in the process of ceding their colonies. In these cases, certain referendums were based on the internal legal order of the country concerned. France is a model example of this category, where Algeria (1961–1962), for instance, gained its independence by means of referendums organised by France.

It should be noted that European Referendums, which have been held since 1970s, differ from those of the decolonisation processes. By European Referendum,

[8] Dobelle (1996), pp. 41–60.

[9] Regarding Alsace Lorraine, it was argued by the French government that given the continuous protests of the population since the region had been occupied by Germany, there was no need for a referendum (Beigbeder 1994, pp. 80 and 81; Wambaugh 1933, p. 17).

[10] Farley (1986), p. 37.

one is referring to any popular consultation relating to the European integration process. These referendums were the result of the domestic legal-political orders of each country concerned. The European Union, as it is today, is a result of a series of international treaties, whereby each member or candidate state has incorporated the given treaties into the respective domestic laws inherent within their constitutional orders; some of which oblige or provide for popular approval.[11]

Lastly, the collapse of communism and the ensuing process of post-Cold War reordering of the political map of the world unleashed a series of referendums in Eastern Europe and Central Asia. This period was comprised of referendums held during the dismantling of the USSR and the former Yugoslavia. The striking feature of these referendums is that they alone spurred the events of a new era, while all past referendums had been selectively used to solve problems that were left over after wars and international negotiations. From a legal point of view, though, the recognition of new states was not merely based on these referendums. The Soviet Union was dissolved, for instance, based on the mutual consent between Moscow and its constituent republics. As to Yugoslavia, the guidelines for the recognition of emerging states were developed during a peace conference held during the civil war. In those cases where the international community did not recognise the secessionist groups as new states, the relevant referendums remained obsolete. This was the case, for instance, for the referendums held in South Ossetia (1992)[12] to secede from Georgia and in Trans-Dniester (1991)[13] to secede from Moldova.

Despite their limited legal effects, the political impact of these referendums has undeniably been of great importance. According to White and Hill, "the referendums were instrumental in accelerating the collapse of communist rule and confirming the breakup of the federal Soviet Union". In particular, the Ukrainian independence referendum was the "death blow" of the Union. Consequently, "The legal status of these referendums may have been uncertain and the results non-binding, but politically their impact was devastating for the Union".[14] Referendums were used both as forums for public mobilisation and as the formal justification of the secession in USSR and Yugoslavia. Thus, one may safely conclude that referendums gained a considerable status as an effective political tool in the course of post-communist state creation.[15] This leads us to focus on the legitimating power of referendums in sociological terms, which will be discussed in detail in the following section.

---

[11] Auer (2007), pp. 262–264; Gallagher (1997), pp. 73–76; Rideau (1997), pp. 87–113.

[12] http://www.c2d.ch/detailed_display.php?lname=votes&table=votes&id=57548&continent= Europe&countrygeo=165&stategeo=11429&citygeo=&level=2&recent=1. Retrieved 14 March 2013.

[13] http://www.c2d.ch/detailed_display.php?lname=votes&table=votes&page=1&parent_id=&sublinkname=results&id=57652. Retrieved 14 March 2013.

[14] White and Hill (1996), pp. 158, 159 and 167.

[15] For example, see Gönenç (2002), p. 352; Brunner (2001), pp. 220 and 221. For particular cases, Estonia: Ruus (2001), pp. 51–53; Lithuania: Krupavicius and Zvaliauskas (2001), p. 124.

3.1.2 Role and Functions of the Referendums Securing the Sociological Legitimacy of a Change of Sovereignty

When we consider the use of sovereignty referendums in sociological terms, we imply the aim of overcoming a political impasse caused by controversy over relevant sovereignty issues. A survey of literature on this topic reveals that political actors resort to these referendums to overcome internal party conflicts. A fundamental change in the constitution, territory, or state power is indeed different from decisions of everyday politics. Thus, politicians may find themselves in a dilemma where favouring either alternative may equally risk their political popularity. When this risk of losing popularity happens to a governing political party, it often culminates in an internal party split that may then only be overcome by recourse to a referendum. This was the case, for example, in 1975 when the governing Labour Party put to referendum the issue of whether the United Kingdom (UK) should remain in the European Community that it had joined in 1973.[16]

Morel divides the motives of the executives in their use of referendums into four categories: "mediation", "agenda", "legislation" and "legitimation".[17] Mediation refers to the above-mentioned role of referendums in the resolution of internal party or coalition splits within the government. In this context, referendum is seen as 'a means by which governments escape responsibility for a specific decision, by transferring it to the people'. In Western Europe, European Integration has been the common theme, which may be subsumed under this category. In addition to the one held in the UK, we may also mention the referendums in Norway (1973) and Finland (1994) in this context.

With respect to the agenda function, governments tend to promise to hold a referendum in the future, in order to remove a divisive issue from the political and electoral agenda. The typical motive for the announcement of such a referendum is the decoupling of a related sovereignty question from a forthcoming electoral campaign, which in the case of a debate may reveal divisions within a party. In other words, in contrast to mediation referendums, agenda-removing referendums are those that are promised to be held before an apparent party or coalition division comes into existence. The referendum in Sweden on European Community membership (1994) served for just this purpose. In other cases, referendums may be promised by political parties to alleviate distrust or fear among the electorate. For example, during the electoral campaign in 1976, the Parti-Quebecois declared that it would submit the issue of Quebec's secession to a referendum if it came to power. This was done in order to appeal to the part of the electorate who did not support the secession of Quebec.

There is also a legislative aim in the use of referendums: the government calls a referendum on a piece of legislation, which might not be adopted or would meet

[16] Bogdanor (1994), p. 38; Qvortrup (2005), p. 103.

[17] Morel (2007), pp. 1045–1050.

certain objections in the standard parliamentary procedure. This mostly applies to minority governments where, in a parliamentary system, the executive does not control the majority of the parliament. For example, in Denmark, the minority government of the time used the referendum of 1986 for the approval of the Single European Act, right after it had been rejected by parliament.

As to the legitimating function of referendums, it may be best observed in the case of France, where the political crisis that had emerged during the process of decolonisation could be overcome via referendums. Two referendums on the independence of Algeria (January 1961 and April 1962) may be categorised as such. In this case, the referendums not only helped to defuse the issue in the face of a recalcitrant parliament but also served as irrefutable evidence for the popular legitimacy of a bitter and fraught decision over the future of the nation's territory. The referendum served here as a "crisis-solving" device, as well as alleviating the popular opposition against these politically divisive sovereignty decisions.

It may be argued that these categories are not mutually excluding, and they may indeed be observed to be overlapping in various degrees within the context of different sovereignty referendums. On the one hand, sovereignty referendums may be seen as an instrument of elite bargaining, but on the other hand, "they give political actors the political legitimacy to pursue change and potentially alter status quo institutions".

Thus, all of these diverse motives for the use of referendum boil down to one element: securing the legitimacy of taking politically hard decisions on sovereignty. The concept of legitimacy should be understood in its descriptive or sociological sense at this point.

The sociological method to legitimacy took its roots from Weber's conception of legitimacy. According to the Weberian approach, legitimacy is the "active belief by citizens, that particular claims to authority deserve respect or obedience".[18] This view implies that the viability of a political regime or a state may solely rest on the "supportive states of mind"[19] or the "sentiment and conviction"[20] of the people over whom the political power claims authority.

Bearing this basis in mind, the legitimating role of referendums, in sociological terms, may be considered within a process of "persuasion through arguments" to justify a new title to territory.[21] Justification in that sense has "objects" (the sovereignty) for which the arguments are put forward and "audiences" to whom these arguments are addressed. Rational justification, and thus legitimating a shift

[18] Fallon Jr (2005), p. 1795; For Weber, "The basis of every authority, and correspondingly of every kind of willingness to obey, is a belief, a belief by virtue of which persons exercising authority are lent prestige". Legitimacy of an order rests on "the prestige of being considered binding" (Weber 1978, p. 263).

[19] Easton (1957), pp. 391–400.

[20] Schaar (1981), p. 22.

[21] Arendt (1954). See also: Ball (1991).

of sovereignty over a territory, aims at the "approval" and "endorsement" of it by the addressees.[22] In this context, the addressees involve both the people who live on the territory under question and the international community whose endorsement is vital for the future viability of the new territorial possession.

In this sense, referendums fulfil a double function: the first is the "subjectively binding force" over the relevant people, justifying their obedience to the new political authority. The other is its "publicly symbolic declaratory force", which serves as an evidence of legitimacy to the international community.[23]

3.1.2.1 People as the Audience

If a political actor claims sovereignty over or on behalf of a people, it should first persuade that people about its legitimacy. From a Weberian perspective, this may be explained by reference to two interrelated concepts: power and domination (authority). Power in this context denotes "carrying out one's will despite resistance", and domination means "uncritical" and "unresisting" compliance with a given command.[24] Hence, whereas the former connotes an involuntary compliance by the people to a political power, the latter involves a voluntary one. From this perspective, power turns to authority to the extent that it is perceived as rightful by the people, or put in other words, "authority is legitimised power".[25]

According to this line of thought, the capacity to govern a territory rests on the acceptance of the rightfulness of sovereignty in public opinion. Referendums have been referred to as the most appropriate means to legitimise a new entitlement over a territory. Wambaugh explained this point when she commented on the referendums held during nineteenth-century state formation:

> History would seem to prove that, in questions of territorial sovereignty public opinion bases its opinion on an unexpressed major premise; namely, that no title acquired either through treaty, conquest or occupation or based on economic, racial or historical arguments, or arguments of military necessity, is valid, no matter how many centuries it has run, unless it has behind it the consent of the majority of the inhabitants of the territory.[26]

This idea may also be sensed in more recent observations. Butler assumes that "Basic changes in territorial boundaries, or sovereignty or structure of government, will be respected more readily when it has been incontrovertibly demonstrated that they command the support of a majority of the voting population".[27] Thus, by

[22] Morris (1998), pp. 108 and 125; See also Bobbio (1989), p. 81.

[23] Beetham (1991), pp. 12, 18, 19 and 91.

[24] Weber (1978), p. 53.

[25] Bealey (1999), pp. 189 and 190.

[26] Wambaugh (1920), p. 31.

[27] Butler (1981), p. 76.

involving the people in the process, referendums may be said to provide the most efficient tools in the persuasion of a related people of a fundamental change in the structure of territory or state competence.

Referendums also play a significant role in the legitimating of new power-sharing arrangements, particularly in post-conflict situations. In any transition from conflict to peace, creation or restoration of the legitimacy of the governing authority constitutes the most important task for the relevant political actors. In this context, the support of the community to the new regime is a decisive element. During peace talks, negotiators must seek public endorsements at certain points, sometimes on more than one occasion. This stems from the plain fact that the legitimacy of the new post-conflict government is the key factor in determining whether the post-transitional political regime will succeed or fail. The referendum device is one of the most commonly used tools in this process.[28]

Considering, for example, the problem of Northern Ireland, the referendum at the end of the process of the Good Friday Agreement of 1998 fulfilled such a function. The simultaneous referendums held in Northern Ireland and the Republic of Ireland aimed, for the most part, to alleviate the fears of the Protestants as to the effects of the new agreement. The outcome of the referendum was 71 % in favour in Northern Ireland,[29] whereas it produced an even larger majority in the Republic of Ireland of around 94 %.[30] Furthermore, the referendums also helped to refute the long-standing claim of the Irish nationalists that Northern Ireland had been created against the wishes of the majority of the population of the island of Ireland as a whole. The claim that the partition of Ireland into two jurisdictions was illegitimate was thus undercut by means of these referendums.[31]

Likewise, in the case of the Cyprus conflict, the aim of the 2004 referendum was explained to be a correction of a "historical error": "The 1960 constitutional settlement had been imposed by Ankara, Athens and London on the Greek-Cypriots, to their evident discontent". The referendum would serve to be evidence of the free endorsement of new constitutional arrangements by Greek and Turkish Cypriots.[32]

3.1.2.2 The International Community as the Audience

The audiences of legitimacy in international relations are the "international law agencies", "potential allies" and "world opinion" to whom states have an obligation

---

[28] Reilly (2003), p. 174.

[29] http://www.c2d.ch/detailed_display.php?lname=votes&table=votes&page=1&parent_id=&sublinkname=results&id=37800. Retrieved 12 March 2012.

[30] http://www.c2d.ch/detailed_display.php?lname=votes&table=votes&page=1&parent_id=&sublinkname=results&id=38937. Retrieved 12 March 2012.

[31] Guelke (2003), pp. 60 and 61.

[32] Carras (2009), p. 59.

to persuade and convince about the legitimacy of their territorial possessions.[33] In this sense, "the legitimacy of states is thought to depend on recognition by other states".[34]

The use of referendums as legitimating tools within international relations may be gleaned since the very earliest experiences. The renouncement of the forceful annexation of territory by the post-revolutionary France was, to a certain extent, induced by the concern to alleviate the international criticism and distrust against the revolutionary government. The new government, in an attempt to build trust and legitimacy in the eyes of European states, sought to create a pacifistic image for the new revolutionary regime. The principle of non-conquest was thus accepted and embodied in the constitution in 1791 by the French Constitutional Assembly. A similar observation may be made for the referendums held during Italian unification. Italian statesmen resorted to referendums as the legitimating means against the Holy Alliance to realise unification and maintain independence. The choice of this method was due to the fact that there was no other way to establish a title against the opposition of the various European courts, which could evoke treaties and the principle of legitimacy in support of the dispersed city states and against unification. The use of referendums was interpreted as the wisdom of the Italians, who managed successfully to overthrow the efforts of the Holy Alliance, and the opposition of the Northern Powers.[35]

More recently, in the international sphere, referendums were used as the principal instruments in the process of post-communist state creation. In the course of the break-up of the Soviet Union and Yugoslavia, the seceding units, in almost all cases, demanding for international recognition sought to legitimise their claim to statehood by referring to the fact that their declaration of independence was approved by the will of the majority of the people living in the territory of the purported state. The referendum was the most common device resorted to for the ascertainment of this will.[36]

Regarding the particular question of the dissolution of Yugoslavia, in all four of the republics a referendum was held on independence. Croatia, Slovenia and Macedonia all mentioned the result of referendums as evidence in favour of their recognition. Bosnia and Herzegovina had not had a referendum when their application for recognition was made. This led to the negative opinion of the Arbitration Commission of the Conference on Yugoslavia (the Badinter Arbitration Commission) regarding Bosnia and Herzegovina's recognition as a new state. The given reason for such an opinion was that "the will of the peoples of Bosnia and Herzegovina" concerning the secession and independence had not been

[33] Poggi (1978), pp. 90 and 91.

[34] Morris (1998), p. 103.

[35] Wambaugh (1920), pp. 5–10.

[36] Raic (2002), p. 424.

established.[37] It was only after a vote in support of independence from Yugoslavia when Bosnia and Herzegovina was internationally recognised as a new state.[38]

Thus, the case of Bosnia and Herzegovina supports the view that the international community takes the referendum as an appropriate argument for the recognition of new states. In this particular case, the international community saw the referendum as a legitimating tool for secession and extended international recognition to Bosnia only after this referendum. Of the 63.4 % of the population who voted, 99.4 % voted in favour of independence. In fact, the Serbian electorate boycotted the vote. Yet despite this boycott, the referendum result meant that the vote of 62.7 % of the total electorate of Bosnia and Herzegovina in favour of independence was deemed sufficient for the legitimacy of secession. Consequently, the Badinter Commission's recommendation in relation to Bosnia and Herzegovina was thus construed: "to elevate the holding of a referendum to the status of a basic requirement for the legitimization of secession".[39]

3.2 The Doctrine of Consent and Other Underpinning Principles of Sovereignty Referendums

Sovereignty referendums typically appear when a change of the possessor of sovereignty is at issue. They serve as both the means and ends in the achievement of political goals as underlined by concepts such as national-popular sovereignty, self-determination and democracy. The emergence of sovereignty referendums in history is "inextricably linked to the emergence of the ideas of sovereignty, popular sovereignty, nationalism and self-determination, which are linked to the emergence of the centralized state".[40] Thus, in this context, one should note the normative shift over time for the explanation of sovereignty over territory, in terms of the modern nation state.

On the most fundamental level, this question may be considered by reference to the concept of "will" and its relationship to political legitimacy. According to the "will" basis, the legitimacy of political power originates from a will, which is inherently superior to political power. This superior will may be either God or people, and accordingly, if this legitimacy comes from God to people, then one may speak about the "pyramidal conception" of legitimacy. Whereas, when legitimacy emanates from the will of people, it is an "ascending conception".[41] Thus, it may be

[37] "*Opinion No. 4 on International Recognition of the Socialist Republic of Bosnia – Herzegovina by the European Community and its Member States*". The full text of the Commission's Opinions No 4–10 may be found at Türk et al. (1993), pp. 74–91.

[38] Raic (2002), p. 292.

[39] Pavkovic and Radan (2007), p. 229.

[40] Sussman G, When the demos shapes the polis – the use of referendums in settling sovereignty issues. http://www.iandrinstitute.org/Studies.htm. Retrieved 5 May 2007, p. 3.

[41] Bobbio (1989), p. 84.

said that the first historical appearance of sovereignty referendums is found in the process of a normative shift, taking the legitimating power from the will of God to the will of the people.

This fundamental change of the normative underpinnings of the justification of political power leads us to consider the legitimacy in its normative sense, in which case the theory tends to justify the existence of political power in moral terms. The question here, from a perspective of political philosophy, is how state power is ought to be acquired in the first place. The relevant string of thoughts may be categorised under the conception of "consent-based" legitimacy.[42]

The consent-based legitimacy arguments hold that the sovereignty of a political power may be justified on the sole condition of the consent of those who are subject to it. In this way, the consent of the governed, in American Constitutional history for example, has been the overriding rhetoric as the underlying principle of a legitimate government. In Hamilton's words, "The fabric of the American Empire *ought* to rest on the solid basis of THE CONSENT OF THE PEOPLE. The streams of national power ought to flow immediately from that pure, original fountain of all legitimate authority".[43] Even before this in 1638, Hooker remarked, for the first time written in American History, "The foundation of authority is laid in the free consent of the people".[44] The notion of consent is also the key element in social contract theories. For the classical social contract theorists, such as Hobbes, Locke and Rousseau, "political authority is legitimate only in so far as it is conditional upon the wills of the consent of the subject to it".[45] In this sense, the concept of the consent of the governed is located at the heart of social contract theories as the legitimating medium for political power.[46]

The basis of consent as a legitimating rhetoric may be sensed in the related political principles of sovereignty, democracy and self-determination. These concepts may be listed as the fundamental political principles, which constitute the philosophical basis of sovereignty referendums, the concept of the consent being the central theme, in each of them.

As Krasner put it, since Bodin, all theories of sovereignty were outgrowths of 'a desire to provide an intellectual rationale for the legitimacy of some.....source of authority within the state'.[47] According to Lutz, sovereignty has a dual implication with respect to authority. In this way, the word sovereign implies the supremacy of political power, as well as "excellence, such that the supreme power is characterised by superior qualities that make it better than the normal supreme power".[48] In a similar manner of thinking, we may detach the content and the

---

[42] Fallon Jr (2005), p. 1797.

[43] Hamilton ([1787–1788] 1982), pp. 123–132.

[44] Quoted in Borgeaud ([1895] 1989), p. 11.

[45] Smith (1991), p. 391.

[46] Stanley (1991), pp. 478–492.

[47] Krasner (1999), p. 11.

[48] Lutz (2006), pp. 33 and 34.

source of sovereignty. In this way, the former implies its legal substance or political connotation, whereas the second denotes the subject of the power holder. In this second case, the question is: to whom does the sovereignty belong? Accordingly, the source of sovereignty may be the monarch in his capacity as the possessor of a "divine right", the state as a juridical person or the people within the context of popular sovereignty, each of which has been resorted to, as a legitimating medium in the rhetoric on political power, in the course of history.[49]

Democracy, undoubtedly, is another value that is on a par with and interrelated to other underlying concepts and norms, such as self-determination, consent of the governed and national sovereignty. The idea of civic or political nationalism, which tends to unify a society under one nation, emphasising a common sense of political identity regardless of racial, ethnic and religious origin, is closely associated with this sense of democracy. The logical linkage of political/civic nationalism and democracy may be sensed in the Declaration of the Rights of Man and Citizen, adopted by the revolutionary French Assembly: "The principle of sovereignty resides essentially in the nation; no body of men, no individual can exercise authority that does not expressly emanate from it". Liberal theorists, such as John Stuart Mill and Giuseppe Mazzini, defended the idea that nationalism was the corollary of democracy and freedom, serving to liberate the oppressed nations under imperial regimes. These ideas inspired the nineteenth-century nation-building and independence movements, and also in the post-WWI political environment, the US President Woodrow Wilson's assertions on self-determination.[50]

In the contemporary context of international world order, democracy has become an undeniable norm, a *sine qua non* for legitimating the state power that states, ostensibly at least, have to endorse. Franck reminds us that the legitimacy of a state's power may be solely claimed on the ground of "democratic entitlement". The democratic validation of a government, which may only be secured through free and fair elections, is the only means by which states may claim that they enjoy the consent of the governed. "Democracy; thus, is on the way to becoming a global entitlement, one that increasingly will be promoted and protected by collective international processes".[51] This may be sensed in the International Covenant on Civil and Political Rights (Art. 25):

> Every citizen shall have the right and the opportunity, without any of the distinctions. . .and without unreasonable restrictions:
>
> (a) To take part in the conduct of public affairs, directly or through freely chosen representatives;
> (b) To vote and to be elected at genuine periodic elections, which shall be by universal and equal suffrage and shall be held by secret ballot, guaranteeing the free expression of the will of the electors.

[49] Merriam ([1900] 1999), pp. 55–72 and 85–129.

[50] Lakoff (2001), pp. 101–110; Cobban (1969), p. 132.

[51] Franck (1992), p. 46.

The principle of self-determination is the third notion that constitutes the moral underpinning of sovereignty referendums. The emergence of the doctrine as a political principle may be dated back to the French Revolution and the American Declaration of Independence. In this context, democracy and nationality are the two designative elements in the theory of self-determination.[52] As mentioned above, France, after the Revolution, resorted to this principle in the guiding of its international relations, and post-revolutionary referendums were held based on this principle. Thereafter, the doctrine of self-determination, along with that of popular sovereignty, replaced the "divine right of monarchs" as the "legitimating ground for the change of sovereignty".[53] With respect to nationalism, the doctrine of self-determination locates state sovereignty within the ideology of nationalism, where notions of "nation" and "people" interact together in the nation-building process. In this case, sovereignty, as it belongs to the nation and/or people, displays a "symbolic importance within civic nationalism".[54]

The appearance of the concept of self-determination as an "operative principle", in international relations, owes much to the Bolshevik Revolution and the process of peace settlements at the end of the First World War.[55] Since then, this principle has been widely used in the rhetoric of international actors in times of fundamental changes to the world map. In this context, President Wilson is venerated as the "Father of Modern self-determination". He suggested that national aspirations and the consent of the people should be respected in post-war territorial settlements. Wilson defended "the right of every people: to choose the sovereign under which they shall live; to be free of alien masters, and not to be handed about from sovereignty to sovereignty as if they were property".[56] Wilson's assertions were the basic normative underpinnings of the referendums held in the post-WWI context.

One of the most controversial issues in political theory is whether self-determination entails the right to secession. Certain writers categorically reject this idea. According to Higgins, the right to self-determination must always be secondary to the right to territorial integrity, which is the fundamental guarantee of the international legal system.[57] Vyver argues:

> the right of peoples to self-determination does not include a right to secession. Not even in instances where the powers that be act in breach of minority's legitimate expectations.... The right to self-determination is almost invariably mentioned in conjunction with the

[52] Cobban (1969), p. 130; Thornberry (1993), p. 105.

[53] Wambaugh (1920), pp. 1–4.

[54] Lynch (1997), p. 43.

[55] Crawford (2006), p. 108.

[56] Wilson's war message to Congress quoted in Castellino (2000), p. 17; see also Pomerance (1976), pp. 2 and 18.

[57] [Rosalyn Higgins, "Judge Dillard and the Principle of self-determination" 23 ***VJIL*** (1983) 387–394], cited in Castellino (2000), p. 30.

territorial integrity of States, and reconciling the two principles in question necessarily means that self-determination must be taken to denote something less than secession.[58]

Regarding the proponents of secession, Buchanan distinguishes two broad groups of moral theories. According to "Remedial Right Only Theories", an ethnic group should be allowed to secede only under strict conditions, such as the case of being subject to serious injustices and human right violations, so that secession should be deemed as an "appropriate remedy of last resort". In the second group, there are "Primary Right Theories", which are more permissive. Strict conditions, such as the existence of severe injustices, are not required to assign certain groups the general right to secede.[59]

Furthermore, Primary Right Theories boil down to two major groups of arguments. The first is the "plebiscitary right theories", also called "individual autonomy arguments" or "choice theories of secession". The second is the "ascriptive" (Nationalist) theories, also referred to as the collective autonomy argument.[60] In both cases, referendums are referred to as the tools for demonstrating the "sovereign choice made by the majority of a population".[61]

The plebiscitary right theories (or choice argument) typically suggest that if a territorially concentrated majority expresses a wish to secede in a referendum, it may have the legitimate right to secede. According to this line of thought, the relevant people do not have to share a common characteristic (such as same language, same religion or common past) or have to be exposed to injustice in order to have the right to secede. A sole majoritarian preference shown via referendum is sufficient to legitimise secession.[62] In this case, referendums are used by the majority of the people for their "withdrawal of consent" from the state or government of which they are a part.[63]

This theory was used mostly for the advancement of a method of recursive secessions to be applied in regions, where two or more ethnic groups are so

[58] Van der Vyver (2003–2004), p. 427.

[59] Buchanan (1997), pp. 34 and 35. In fact, the primary right theory is rather speculative, given the dominant statist tendency in international law. However, the remedial right theory has a considerable support in the literature. Remedial secession theories rest on the Friendly Relations Declaration that may be construed as the following: the territorial integrity of states might be observed if, and only if, they conduct "themselves in compliance with the principle of equal rights and self-determination of peoples...and thus (possess) of a government representing the whole people belonging to the territory..." These theories still favour the territorial integrity and sovereignty of the state, but with one possible exception that certain minorities suffer from serious violations of fundamental human rights. Yet the scope and nature of the violations that may legitimate the secession are controversial. See, for a further discussion, Tancredi (2006), pp. 171–207 and Murswiek (1993), p. 25.

[60] Moore (2010), p. 86.

[61] Coppieters (2010), p. 249.

[62] Moore (2010), p. 86.

[63] Pavkovic (2000), p. 486.

complexly intermingled that a single referendum could not resolve the issue. Harry Beran explained this approach:

> If the issue of changing political borders arises in a polity, there is usually disagreement as to whether a change should be made. At the time of the breakup of the former Yugoslavia there was a majority in favour of secession from Yugoslavia in Croatia; but in the portion of Croatia known as Krajina, inhabited mostly by Serbs, there was a majority against secession. The reiterated use of the majority principle seems to be the only method of resolving such conflicts that is consistent with the voluntary association principle. According to this method, a separatist movement can call for a referendum, within a territory specified by it, to determine whether there should be a change in this territory's political status, e.g. whether it should secede from its state. If there is a majority in the territory as a whole for secession, then the territory's people may exercise its right of self-determination and secede. But there may be people within this territory who do not wish to be part of the newly independent state. They could show, by majority vote within their territory, that this is so, and then become independent in turn, or remain within the state from which the others wish to secede. This use of the majority principle may be continued until it is applied to a single community (i.e. a community which is not composed of a number of communities) to determine its political status.[64]

The basic arguments of this theory may be found as practical elements in the case of the creation of the canton of Jura, where a series of "Russian-doll type referendums" were held in a timeline of 8 years. In this process, after a referendum on the decision of creation of a separate Canton, the minority who had voted against the creation of Jura was given the opportunity to hold additional referendums. These additional referendums were held at two separate intervals until the borderline communities had decided between Bern and Jura.[65]

In the second group, there are the ascriptive (nationalist, collective autonomy or national self-determination) arguments, which may be sensed in the nationality principle of the nineteenth-century, in post-WWI Europe, in the post-WWII decolonisation and in the process of post-communist state creation. According to this view, the secession is justified in terms of the collective autonomy of the nation or people. Such autonomy gives the relevant people the prerogative to decide as a group to associate or dissociate to and from any other alien element. A common shared identity is the key component in the making of the nation in this context. In this respect, referendums are marked as one of the tools for "testing" the subjective elements of shared national identity or political community.[66]

Both Wilson and Lenin, who believed that the notion of self-determination suggested the emancipation of peoples and nations from external oppression, domination and exploitation, endorsed this group of arguments. Wilson's indication

---

[64] [Harry Beran, "A Democratic Theory of Political Self-Determination for a New World Order", in Theories of Secession, ed. Percy Lehning (London: Routledge, 1998), 38–39], cited in Wellman (2010), pp. 24 and 25.

[65] Laponce (2001), p. 48.

[66] Moore (2010), p. 86.

of referendum as a legitimate device for the solution of the territorial disputes after WWI may be mentioned as a significant example of this line of thought.[67] Lenin's assertions inspired, for the most part, the post-WWII decolonisation movement and the referendums held in this context:

> This demand for political democracy implies complete freedom to agitate for secession and for a referendum on secession by the seceding nation. This demand [...] is not equivalent of a demand for separation, fragmentation and the formation of small states. It implies only a consistent expression of struggle against all national oppression.[68]

The basic tenets of popular sovereignty and liberal constitutionalism induced not only referendums on secession and other sorts of territorial conflicts but also the referendums on the transfer of national powers to supranational organisations, notably in the European Integration. For Setala, the philosophical underpinnings of these referendums may be inferred from the representative theory of political legitimacy, where "Transferring...law making power to some supra national organisation which is beyond the control of the citizens requires the approval of these citizens".[69]

Considering the explanations made so far, we may safely conclude this section by asserting that the notions of consent-based legitimacy may be found in every historical experience of sovereignty referendums, involving diverse issues such as secession, decolonisation, post-war and post-conflict state creation and formation of supranational organisations.

3.3 Normative Deductions from Empirical Observations

Given the fundamental stakes involved in sovereignty issues, the questions to be asked in this section revolve around whether it is appropriate to consult the people and let them decide directly. This could have been considered in the first point of departure for the more normative strand of the literature, which has been already discussed above. The debates on the advisability of referendums, however, detach from the above-mentioned discussions since they tend to focus on the utility and efficiency of referendums in the resolution of sovereignty conflicts rather than on a mere moral duty. Essentially, the debate pits republican/participatory theorists,[70]

---

[67] Raic (2002), p. 221.

[68] [V.I. Lenin, The Socialist Revolution and the Right of Nations to Self-Determination (Theses), in: V.I. Lenin, COLLECTED WORKS, 1964. p. 143, p. 146.] Quoted in Raic (2002), p. 185.

[69] Setala (1999), p. 94. (Quoting John Locke Second Treatise, para. 41: "The Legislative cannot transfer the power of making laws to any other hands. For it being but a delegated power from the People, they who have it cannot pass it to others".)

[70] "*Toute loi que le peuple en personne n'a pas ratifiée est nulle*; *ce n'est point une loi*" (Rousseau 1762, p. 68); "...for a democratic polity to exist it is necessary for a participatory society to exist, i.e. a society where all political systems have been democratised and socialization through participation can take place in all areas" (Pateman 1970, p. 42); "Participation, after all, enhances

who view coherent and politically active demos as a prerequisite for a healthy democracy, on the one side, and, on the other side, pluralists/elitist theorists,[71] who to varying extents worry that the referendum is not suitable for increasingly culturally diverse societies of a modern polity.

3.3.1 *For the Referendum*

3.3.1.1 Referendums Maximise Legitimacy

Perhaps the most convincing argument in favour of referendum is its efficiency in the legitimation of sovereignty decisions. From a moral point of view, it may be argued that the consent of the governed may best be achieved by way of the direct intervention of the people. Additionally from a sociological point of view, the people regard the decisions taken by referendum "as the most authoritative" because referendums are considered as the "least mediated of all expressions of popular will".[72] Thus, one may assess the key role of referendums in representative democracies as the following: the legitimacy of decisions of great importance, that is "constitutional" and "territorial issues", may best be achieved by way of referendums.[73]

From this perspective, one may argue that the very act of consulting the people can stimulate a deliberative process of opinion formation, potentially leading to a more enlightened outcome. Habermas explained this point by stating that "the modern legal order can draw its legitimacy only from the idea of self-determination: citizens should always be able to understand themselves also as authors of the law to which they are subject as addressees". Habermas defends a model of procedural democracy, a theory built on a "discourse principle".[74] Basically, the discursive model endorses the active participation of citizens in lawmaking with a deliberative method, by which "the legal community constitutes itself" through a "discursively achieved agreement". This method, for Habermas, secures the legitimacy since, "at every level of opinion,—and will formation, and law—and policy making, there obtain the structures to facilitate full communicative interaction leading to general assent".[75] Habermas' discursive scheme provides interplay between state, its lawmaking and executing organs, and civil society. From a

the power of communities and endows them with a moral force that non participatory rulership rarely achieves" (Barber [1984] 2003, p. 8.).

[71] For the relevant discussion, see Butler and Ranney (1994), pp. 11–14. However, even the skeptics of direct democracy, like Schumpeter, conceded the convenience of referendums regarding "the most important decisions" of a polity (Schumpeter [1984] 2003, p. 5).

[72] Butler and Ranney (1994), p. 15; see also Cronin (1999), pp. 12–17 and 41–42; Calligan (2001), p. 111.

[73] Hamon (1995), p. 50.

[74] Habermas (1996), pp. 448–450.

[75] McCormick (1997), p. 737.

sociological point of view then, the participatory democratic model of discourse principle opens the way for active participation in lawmaking, and this may provide the participants with the feeling of being influential in the taking of important political decisions. In this way, by allowing the citizens to be the authors of the laws that will apply to them, the discursive procedure establishes the grounds for legitimacy in terms of sociological acceptation. Thus, through a "discursive process" the active citizens may deliberate and come to a consensual agreement as to the validity of the resolution of a sovereignty conflict.[76]

3.3.1.2 Division Solving Function of the Referendums

As mentioned above, in representative systems, referendums may function as a "division solving" instrument, or they may be used to bypass a recalcitrant legislature in the resolution of politically salient sovereignty questions.[77] Bogdanor, in his analysis of referendums in Western Europe, noted that sovereignty referendums, the subject of which is highly sensitive and divisive, may be politically palatable where political parties fail to handle such problems.[78]

Indeed, Denmark, the UK, Sweden, Finland, Norway and France have all used the referendum device to defuse political, particularly legislative, deadlocks caused by sovereignty problems. The common subject matter of these particular sovereignty referendums was that of European Integration. There are also other types of sovereignty referendums, e.g., in Denmark, the sale of the West Indies to the US was put to a consultative referendum to overcome the parliamentary deadlock. Likewise in the UK, the decisions on devolution and the status of Northern Ireland were the subject of referendum. In France, a referendum helped to overcome the political crisis caused by the question of Algeria.[79]

3.3.2 Against the Referendum

3.3.2.1 Voter Incompetence

One of the widest assumptions held by the opponents of direct democracy is the incompetence of the voters. In this perspective, one reason advanced by the sceptics

[76] Habermas (1975), p. 104.

[77] Morel (2001), pp. 53–57; for a more recent evaluation from the same author, see Morel (2007), pp. 1041–1067.

[78] Bogdanor (1994), p. 89. The author elsewhere noted that "A referendum can be used to defuse a political issue by taking it out of the hands of extremists. This is what the Scottish referendum did in 1979. It defused the devolution issue in the only way possible" (Bogdanor 1981, p. 6).

[79] For, Denmark see Svensson (1996), pp. 42–46; for the UK: Balsom (1996); for France: Morel (1996).

of referendum is the ordinary citizens' lack of interest in politics and their reluctance to participate.[80] This observation can justifiably be verified by a high level of absenteeism in the polities where the referendum is an active component of the political system; Switzerland is a good example of this.[81] Accepting this hypothesis in the case of sovereignty referendums, however, requires a second consideration given the fundamental importance of the ballot question. Indeed, it can be reasonably argued that a referendum on a sovereignty issue may attract more attention and greater participation by voters than a referendum over an ordinary political decision would. The Swiss referendum on the joining of the EEA may be mentioned in this context, where the turnout was around 78 %, a percentage that is much higher than the average turnout of voters. This example also reminds us that the political campaign preceding a sovereignty referendum will be very intense, which may contribute to the mass mobilisation of the electorate.[82]

Moreover, it is assumed that the ordinary voters do not have sufficient cognitive ability to understand and to evaluate the ballot question, let alone to vote reasonably and consistently with their long-term interests.[83] For example, Magleby reports that voters' cognitive deficiency has sometimes caused them to misunderstand the ballot question and to vote in a manner diametrically opposed to their aims. This fact alone caused him to be pessimistic about the intelligence of an ordinary voter, and thus he said: "The expectations of the proponents of direct legislation that voters would read and study ballot propositions and then cast informed ballots have been substantially disproved".[84] This and other similar observations typically lead to an assertion that experts rather than ignorant people should take important political decisions.

One of the reasons for voters' cognitive deficiency in referendums may be that the voters in referendums do not have the key cognitive assistance as they do in most other elections. Indeed, in parliamentary or presidential elections, the candidate's party affiliation saves the voters from a painstaking analysis of the candidate's political past, personality, skills, etc. This is the main difference of the referendums, where the voters have to understand and evaluate the content, legal ramifications and advantages/disadvantages of their yes or no votes. This shortcoming may be overcome by providing effective cognitive cues to the voter. This leads us to consider an educative campaign and the leading role of political parties, which will be discussed in more detail in Chap. 7.

---

[80] Budge (1996), p. 76.

[81] Kobach (1994), pp. 137 and 138.

[82] In this context, Kriesi notes: "The exceptional participation in the vote on the EEA Treaty is related to the fact that this vote was preceded by an extraordinarily intensive campaign-by far the most intensive campaign of the entire period covered by this study and probably the most intensive campaign in the history of Swiss direct-democratic voting". (Kriesi 2005, p. 116).

[83] See, for a review and an evaluation of the American voters, Cronin (1999), pp. 60–89; Magleby (1984), pp. 122–144, 166–179 and 197–198.

[84] Magleby (1984), p. 198.

3.3.2.2 The Tyranny of Majority and the Destabilising Effect of Referendums

Another argument against the referendum device is that the lack of a representative body as a filter would lead to unwise and hasty decisions. In comparison to representative decision-making, referendums do not offer a deliberative process, and this may lead to the tyranny of the majority.[85]

German lawyers of the late nineteenth century such as Hotzendorf, Geffker Stoerk and Francis Liever were against the use of referendums because they subjected the minority to the decisions of a simple majority without any protection.[86] After the Second World War, the United Kingdom were opposed to using referendums in the process of decolonisation. For most British politicians, referendums were not compatible with the representative nature of the political system of the colonies. They did not seem to provide fair protection for different ethnic groups within the same territory. A body of representatives elected by the people should decide upon the status of a people in a territory. This was thought to be more advantageous than referendums by offering a more deliberative process.[87]

The difficulty with secession referendums by a simple majority is that it forces a minority of people (which may be as high as 49 %) to change their political affiliation, their citizenship and the area of jurisdiction of their government.[88] In a secession referendum,: Independence referendum each person's citizenship in the contested region is at stake. For this reason, some argue that the vote should be unanimous: the consent of every single person in a region should be obtained for a secession to take place.[89] The conundrum that the referendum causes in ethnically divided societies is that the decision of a stark sovereignty preference through a bare majority renders the whole process a zero-sum game. A threshold of '50 per cent plus one' for victory or defeat serves, by no means, to defuse the conflict. Reilly notes[90]:

> Despite hollow claims that the 'will of the people' must prevail, it is only the most obtuse interpretation that would recommend building peace in this way. Majoritarian devices like plebiscites are typically blunt instruments that obscure as much as they reveal. As a device for resolving deep-rooted sociopolitical conflicts, they are a particularly poor choice for one simple reason: in a yes/no vote, one side will always lose. Unlike in ordinary elections, in which an issue may be debated and reconsidered every few years, plebiscites – particularly on highly charged issues such as self-determination or statehood – tend to be one-offs. There are no second chances, no face-saving ways to sugar-coat the pill and no creative options such as power-sharing arrangements that build in some voice for the losers. Losers, in such circumstances, often perceive themselves to be losers for ever.

---

[85] Budge (1996), pp. 60–83; Cronin (1999), pp. 90–99; Butler and Ranney (1994), p. 19.

[86] Quoted in Wambaugh (1920), pp. 20–25.

[87] He (2002), p. 67.

[88] On this see: Wellman (2010), p. 25.

[89] Buchanan (2007), p. 377.

[90] Reilly (2003), p. 180.

Reilly saw the danger in the irreversible nature of referendum and in the "short-circuit" effect to any effort and process of political dialogue for the accommodation and management of ethno-national conflicts. In fact, referendums in general may have the effect of elevating tensions and may hinder both the people and political elites from reaching a compromise by pushing them towards extreme positions. This particular effect of referendums becomes even greater, owing to the highly emotional nature of self-determination issues. Indeed, in many cases, the majority sees such referendums as a historical point in their national emancipation and sees the minority as possible traitors. The minority, on the other hand, tends to view the results as a threat to their security and their survival. This, for Reilly, is one of the basic reasons that many sovereignty referendum experiences were followed by inter-ethnic violence or even by civil war.[91]

We may note another anti-referendum argument in ethnically divided societies as follows: referendums may have an alarming effect that may turn into "an ethnic census, a head count of rival groups". In this perspective, Bogdanor noted the danger of using this majoritarian instrument in ethnically divided societies.[92] This may cause the mobilisation of voters around all-or-nothing positions and strengthen the hands of extremist political hubs. This may even cause strife and polarisation in those societies that, in the pre-referendum stage, were not so divided.[93]

This may be observed in the referendums in the former Yugoslavian context, which were said to push "the region closer towards war". The independence referendums "not only fragmented Yugoslavia, they radicalised the anti-independence Serb minorities, particularly in Croatia and Bosnia".[94] Likewise, Brady and Kaplan described the independence referendums held in the former Yugoslavia as the "battle cries of highly mobilised and desperate populations, rather than as instruments of deliberative democracy".[95]

A situation similar to the above may be observed in East Timor. There was an explosion of violence and bloodshed right after the announcement of the results of the 1999 East Timor referendum. This provides as an explicit example of the potential detrimental effects of holding a referendum before essential sovereignty issues have been discussed or resolved. In the referendum, 78.5 % voted in favour of independence, whereas 21.5 % rejected the independence option and decided to remain a part of Indonesia. Following the declaration of the result of the referendum, sporadic violence broke out caused by this annoyed minority with the active support of the Indonesian military. In the case of Kosovo, the referendum proposal on independence, which was held during the peace talks in Rambouillet, France, in early 1999, was widely seen as the "game breaker" that moved Serbia's strategic choices away from the negotiating table and towards ethnic cleansing. Similarly, as

[91] Reilly (2003), p. 179.

[92] Bogdanor (1994), p. 89; Butler (1981), p. 6.

[93] Reilly (2003), p. 180.

[94] Reilly (2003), p. 180.

[95] Brady and Kaplan (1994), p. 206.

regards the Palestinian conflict, the pledge by former Israeli Prime Minister Ehud Barak to hold a referendum on the Israeli–Palestinian Peace Accords was considered to be one of the reasons for the polarisation of the region and the undermining of the peace progress.[96]

The divisive effects of referendums may be observed even in the most benign conditions. Moore said: "The 1995 Quebec referendum on sovereignty revealed and exacerbated cleavages in Quebec". More than 90 % of the votes of the English-speaking and alien population were estimated to be for the "No" side. This not only revealed that the purported "civic Quebec project" was a failure, but it also aggravated the hostility of the French-speaking majority against the rest of the population. This may be sensed in the words of the then Quebec Prime minister Parizeau, who said that the defeat in the referendum was largely due to the "money and the ethnic vote". The money was understood by the rest of Canada as referring to the English-speaking population, whereas the ethnic vote was referring to the immigrant population.[97]

The stable multinational democracy of Canada owed much to an accommodation of the elite. According to this method, the prime ministers of the different provinces met with the federal government behind closed doors to come to an agreement on the central–provincial relations. Yet this method of reaching a constitutional agreement met with its first challenge when in 1990 during the talks with the federal government, the Quebec government stated that it would put any constitutional package to a referendum. This move by Quebec generated similar demands in the other provinces and made constitutional change extremely difficult. The difficulty here again involved the absolutist "all-or nothing" nature of referendums, leaving no room for deliberation and discouraging the parties from reaching a compromise.[98]

3.4 "Wanting It Both Ways"[99]: A Synthesis

The explanations made so far lead us to consider the ways by which we can maximise the advantages while minimising the disadvantages of the referendum device. Indeed, there are as many sufficiently convincing arguments in defence of referendums as there are against. As Wambugh put it:

> As long as we have democracy, the plebiscite is here to stay. It is not that democracy considers the plebiscite a perfect tool: on the contrary it appears at present to be extremely critical of it. There is, however, no perfect method of establishing national boundaries. . .Therefore it seems certain that we shall keep the plebiscite as a tool in the

[96] Reilly (2003), pp. 179 and 180.

[97] Moore (2001), p. 67.

[98] Moore (2001), p. 91.

[99] Butler and Ranney (1994), p. 21.

> workshop of political science...Democracy cannot, however be served by faulty plebiscites. If we are to keep the tool we must learn how to use it. Therefore we must study those plebiscites already held so that we may discover our errors as well as perfect our technique for the future.[100]

So what may the "errors" be that should be evaded? In fact, Wambaugh's comment consisted of an overall reflection of the legal issues necessary for a fair referendum. This will be evaluated in detail in the seventh chapter. Here, we may limit ourselves to thinking about the possible ways in which political wisdom may palliate the flaws of the referendum device. In this perspective, Bogdanor asserts that for a referendum to serve as an effective and efficient tool in solving sovereignty disputes, it should be applied only in "clearly circumscribed situations". The value of a referendum is limited and consequently cannot resolve all prevailing conflicts, but "it can articulate a submerged consensus".[101] LeDuc notes in the same way that peaceful secessions are the results of a dual process: an accumulation of negotiations among the elites and the ratification of the achieved agreement in a referendum.[102] These comments may lead to the following conclusions: first, the parties should reach a compromise on the key points concerning the conflict before a referendum is held; second, referendums on sovereignty conflicts should have a well-founded legal base or at least a commitment of the parties to the issue.

3.4.1 Referendums Should Not Be Used Hastily in the Initial Phase

As mentioned above, the opponents of the use of referendums in the resolution of sovereignty conflicts highlight the majoritarian nature and destabilising effect of referendums, where they can be very divisive devices in the setting of an ethnonational conflict.

In this context, we can allude to the cases of South Africa and Northern Ireland, where the political leaders rejected the option of premature referendums, preferring patient and carefully steered negotiations. In both of these cases, referendums were used as the final stage of public approval of a lengthy and much-debated constitutional package.[103] In a similar way, the case of the Jura's separation from Berne may be recalled. In this case, the creation of canton of Jura in Switzerland was realised in a timeline starting from early 1960s and ending in 1978 when the canton of Jura was officially created. The process started with commissions of inquiry and

---

[100] Wambaugh (1933), p. ix.

[101] Bogdanor (1981), p. 144.

[102] LeDuc (2003), p. 102.

[103] Reilly (2003), p. 179.

ended by a series of referendums starting from 1974, which may be defined as an "unhurried but systematic pace of Swiss reform processes".[104]

Similarly, the French approach to the decolonisation of New Caledonia may be mentioned. This French overseas territory had been troubled by violent strife between the indigenous Kanak peoples and the French-origin Caldoche settlers in the 1980s. This bitter dispute was ended by the 1988 peace agreement, the Matignon Accord that provided for a 10-year transitory period, including educational and infrastructural assistance to the marginalised Kanak peoples, before a referendum could be held. This 10-year period supported the economic and political development of the region, and it also created a more congenial atmosphere for a peaceful discussion on the alternatives to full independence. The extension of the timeline for the resolution of the conflict allowed some space for the formation of new ideas and the transformation of the extremist non-negotiable positions to more consensual political stances.[105]

By way of contrast, the negative effect of hasty referendums may be presumed by reference to the referendum on the unification of Cyprus. This referendum was held before reaching a consensus at an elite level on such fundamental issues as the return of the refugees, the restitution of their property, the withdrawal of foreign troops and the status of the Turkish settlers. The "No" vote of the Greek part of the island was largely due to this dispute. Moreover, the majority saw the UN and the EU, which had in fact the principal role throughout the process, as intruding foreign organisations.[106] This shows the importance of reaching a consensus on the most important matters and the legitimacy of the procedure itself before a conclusive referendum can be held. There is also the referendum in East Timor, which may be referred to in this context. In contrast to the case of New Caledonia, a rushed independence referendum in East Timor was held before a phase of staggered autonomy was considered. One of the reasons for the ensuing post-referendum ethnic violence was the hasty nature of this referendum. In fact, a transitory period was proposed by the then President Habibie in early 1999, but it was rejected by the international community on the ground that the right to self-determination of the East Timorese people called for an immediate vote.[107]

3.4.2 *The Vetoing Effect of Referendums*

The above-mentioned experiences also remind us of the vetoing effect of referendums. This effect stems from the conservative character of the referendum device. In particular, radicals and socialists, who feared the mass public refusal of their

[104] Laponce (2001), pp. 47 and 48.

[105] Reilly (2003), pp. 181 and 182.

[106] Rudolph (2006), p. 85.

[107] Reilly (2003), s. 182.

progressive political agendas, mentioned this as a relevant argument in the beginning of the twentieth century. According to this view, referendums may thwart political and social development, in that they enable narrow-minded voters to block progressive legislation. Earlier in 1890, Dicey cast doubt on the prospect of women gaining voting rights, foreseeing that Swiss voters would block the necessary constitutional amendment, a presumption that was proved correct by history.[108] This assumption rests, in part, on voters' tendency to "when in doubt vote no". That is to say, "voters will support the status quo unless they are given clear arguments for changing it".[109]

In other words, in the case of an uncertainty regarding the future impacts of each preference in a referendum, it is the *status quo* that prevails. What is more, this tendency is reinforced by the nature of the politics of the popular vote: the voters who are in favour of change may probably be divided with respect to secondary questions, while on the other hand, supporters of the *status quo* are inherently monolithic. Consequently, while some of the voters who demand change may support a proposed legislation, others would abstain. In the face of the indivisible no voters, this division would defeat the proposal to the advantage of the *status quo*.

On the other hand, thanks to this conservative character, referendums may turn out to be a handy strategic tool for the states in the overcoming of secessionist groups. For Lynch, "the simple reason for the failure of secession in the West is that it requires majority support, usually expressed through a referendum".[110] Indeed, as Goodhart notes, "the call for a referendum has generally come from those who are most anxious to preserve the unity of their country".[111] In the same way, Dion asserts that the secessionists have "never managed to split a well-established democracy" since they always fail in achieving and maintaining "the magic number of 50 per cent support" in a referendum or an electoral race.[112] In the light of these explanations, it can be fairly argued that in the case of a secessionist conflict, the proponents of the *status quo* may prefer to opt for a referendum (unless there is a clear and visible support in favour of secession), with a greater prospect of defeating the proponents of change.

---

[108] Cited in Qvortrup (2005), p. 59.

[109] Cronin (1999), p. 85. In Australia, constitutional referendums on the extension of the federal government have consistently met with voters' resistance. This is explained by the peoples' sceptical attitude to the federal government and general tendency to refuse any extension of its competences (Qvortrup 2005, p. 74). See, for a review on the referendums on Australia and New Zealand, Hughes (1994), pp. 154–173.

[110] Lynch (2005), pp. 503 and 504.

[111] Goodhart (1981), p. 139.

[112] Dion (1996), p. 270.

3.4.3 The Difficulty with Unilateral Referendums

Historical evidence shows that the unilateral referendums that were held to override the explicit requirements of the international community have been inconclusive. That was the case when Tyrol (1921) and Salzburg (1921) voted to join Germany. These referendums were held disregarding the international prohibition of the unification of Austria and Germany. Consequently, despite the outcome in favour of adhesion to Germany, these referendums were declared invalid by the Allies.

After the Second World War, France sought to maintain its colonial possessions with the help of referendums against the anti-colonial sentiment in the international community. The "empire wide" referendum (1958), held in the overseas colonies at the same time with Metropolitan France, aimed at keeping its colonial territories under its sovereignty. However, over the course of time only a handful of small entities have remained under the sovereignty of France, and among those, the status of New Caledonia[113] and Mayotte[114] is a continuing subject of controversy in international law.

The post-communist context offers sustainable evidence in line with the preceding pattern of the international community's reaction to unilateral referendums. During the process of the break-up of Yugoslavia and the Soviet Union, independence referendums were held in Abkhazia (1999) and South Ossetia (2007) in Georgia and Nagorno-Karabakh in Azerbaijan (1991) and a referendum on the adhesion of Trans-Dniestr to Russia from Moldova (2006). None of these referendums were recognised either by the central state authorities or the international community. The principle of *Uti Possidetis* prevailed over regional secession demands, which in the post-communist context meant that international recognition would be limited to the titular constituent republics of the USSR or states in ex-Yugoslavia.[115] These cases suggest that the international community opts for a remedial, or at best an "ascriptive", type of justification for secession rather than the pure plebiscitary one. Referendums, in this context, should be seen not as a self-referring and conclusive device but rather as a complimentary tool within the more

---

[113] A/RES/42/79: The UN General Assembly Resolution of 4 December 1987, on the "*Question of New Caledonia*".

[114] A/RES/3291 (XXIX): The UN General Assembly Resolution of 13 December 1974 "*Question of Comoro Archipelago*"; A/RES/31/4: The UN General Assembly Resolution of 21 October 1976, on the "*Question of the Comorian island of Mayotte*"; A/RES/32/7: The UN General Assembly Resolution of 1 November 1977 on the "*Question of the Comorian island of Mayotte*" A/RES/36/105: The UN General Assembly Resolution of 10 December 1981 on the "*Question of the Comorian island of Mayotte*"; A/RES/41/30: The UN General Assembly Resolution of 3 November 1986, on the "*Question of the Comorian island of Mayotte*".

[115] Pazartzis (2006), pp. 364 and 365; in the particular cases of Republika Srpska and Transnistria, the EU refused to recognise the outcomes of the referendums arguing that there had been no massive human rights violations against the populations of these territories that could justify the attempted secessions at the expense of the principle of territorial integrity (Coppieters 2010, p. 250).

complex pattern of state creation, in which the interaction of power struggles, historical claims and arguments of ethnicity are in play. Coppieters noted this fact while commenting on the secession of Montenegro from the State Union of Serbia and Montenegro: "The choice argument may be powerful only in cases where secession can be peacefully negotiated and where a referendum can take place in accordance with constitutional law".[116]

On the other hand, even if it is true that these unilateral secession referendums did not achieve their initial objectives, they were far from being a zero-sum game. The case of the Aaland Islands is a seminal example. After WWI when Finland gained its independence from Russia, residents of the Aaland Islands submitted a petition to the Swedish King demanding their adhesion to Sweden. This first petition was then known as the "first plebiscite".[117] Finland opposed it promptly, arguing that the Islanders did not have a right to secede because the frontiers of Finland had been fixed prior to independence since 1556 as the Duchy of Finland, and as a result the Aaland Islands were under the jurisdiction of Finland. In 1919, the residents circulated another petition. The result of this "second plebiscite" restated the wish of the residents to join Sweden. When the case was brought before the Council of the League, it asked the International Committee of Jurists for their view, which may be summarised as follows: the question at hand did not refer to 'a definitively established political situation with a dependence exclusively upon the territorial sovereignty of' Finland, and the "state was not fully formed or undergoing transformation or dissolution". "Under such circumstances, the principle of the self-determination of peoples (could) be called into play" and the resolution of the dispute should not be "left by International Law to the domestic jurisdiction of Finland".[118]

Yet the Council of League endorsed the argument of Finland stating that the sovereignty of the Aaland Islands belonged to Finland. However, it conferred to the Island a considerable degree of autonomy, which the other regions, notably the Swedish-speaking areas, did not have. Even if it were true that the Islanders could not achieve what was foreseen by the referendum, they did acquire a privileged status within the jurisdiction of Finland. The said referendum, it may be argued, had a decisive influence on the decision of the Council of League.[119] Similarly, as mentioned in the preceding paragraph, the European governments were resolutely opposed to any further divisions of the territories that became the successors to Yugoslavia and the USSR. On the other hand, these referendums were instrumental in securing the internal self-determination: "The OSCE and its participating States

[116] Coppieters (2010), p. 251.

[117] Wambaugh (1933), pp. 515–518.

[118] "Report of the the International Committee of Jurists entrusted by the Council of the League of Nations with the task of giving an advisory opinion upon the legal aspects of the Aaland Islands question". http://www.ilsa.org/jessup/jessup10/basicmats/aaland1.pdf. Retrieved 15 January 2013; see also Castellino (2000), p. 19.

[119] Sureda (1973), p. 117.

have called upon the parties to negotiate a special status for the secessionist regions, supporting the allocation of autonomy for these regions".[120]

In terms of constitutional law, i.e. the relationship between a region and the central state, the case of Quebec is unique. The Supreme Court of Canada recognised the legal value of a referendum as a legitimate way to demonstrate the wish of the population to secede and as the initiator of a negotiation process, which may result in secession. The Court held: "The federalism principle, in conjunction with the democratic principle, dictates that. . .the clear expression of the desire to pursue secession by the population of a province would give rise to a reciprocal obligation on all parties to Confederation to negotiate constitutional changes to respond to that desire".[121] "The key element" in the secession decision of the Supreme Court of Canada was that it acknowledged the constitutional duty of the federal government "to negotiate secession following a clear majority vote on a clear question".[122]

Thus, the power of unilateral referendums in terms of their sociological legitimacy may not be denied. Such unilateral referendums may prove to be a strong strategic tool in the hands of groups seeking legitimacy for their cause, and which may create the momentum that makes the maintaining of the *status quo* impossible. These referendums may influence the decisions and behaviour of statesmen, the international community and the judiciary. However, the legal value and the nature of unilateral referendums are always uncertain. This is because they lack the vital element of enforcement due to the absence of the formal agreement of the parties, each of which may have varying degrees of power concerning the fulfilment of the referendum and its outcome.

References

Arendt, H. (1954). What is authority? http://la.utexas.edu/users/hcleaver/330T/350kPEEArendtWhatIsAuthorityTable.pdf. Retrieved 17 December 2014.

Auer, A. (1996). Le référendum constitutionnel. In A. Auer (Ed.), *Les Origines de la Démocratie Directe en Suisse* (pp. 79–101). Bale, e.t.c: Helbing et Lichtenhahn.

Auer, A. (2007). National referendums in the process of European integration: Time for change. In A. Albi & J. Ziller (Eds.), *The European Constitution and National Constitutions: Ratification and beyond* (pp. 261–271). Netherlands: Kluwer Law International.

Ball, T. (1991). Power. In D. Miller (Ed.), *The Blackwell encyclopaedia of political thought* (pp. 397–399). Oxford: Blackwell.

Balsom, D. (1996). The United Kingdom: Constitutional pragmatism and the adoption of the referendum. In M. Gallagher & P. V. Uleri (Eds.), *The referendum experience in Europe* (pp. 209–225). Houndmills, e.t.c: Macmillan Press Ltd.

[120] Pazartzis (2006), p. 368.

[121] *Reference re Secession of Quebec*, [1998] 2 S.C.R. 217, para. 88.

[122] Monahan (2000), p. 8.

Barber, B. R. ([1984] 2003). *Strong democracy participatory politics for a new age*. London: University of California Press.

Bealey, F. W. (1999). *The Blackwell dictionary of political science*. Oxford: Blackwell.

Beetham, D. (1991). *Legitimation of power*. London: Macmillan.

Beigbeder, Y. (1994). *International monitoring of plebiscites, referenda and national elections: Self-determination and transition to democracy*. Dordrecht, Boston: M. Nijhoff.

Bobbio, N. (1989). *Democracy and dictatorship: The nature and limits of state power* (trans: P. Kennealy). Cambridge: Polity Press.

Bogdanor, V. (1981). Referendums and separatism: II. In A. Ranney (Ed.), *The referendum device* (pp. 143–158). Washington, London: American Enterprise Institute for Public Policy Research.

Bogdanor, V. (1994). Western Europe. In D. Butler & A. Ranney (Eds.), *Referendums around the world: The growing use of direct democracy* (pp. 24–97). New York: Macmillan.

Borgeaud, C. ([1895] 1989). *Adoption and amendment of constitutions in Europe and America* (trans: C. D. Hazen). Littleton, CO: F.B. Rothman.

Brady, H. E., & Kaplan, C. S. (1994). Eastern Europe and the former Soviet Union. In D. Butler & A. Ranney (Eds.), *Referendums around the world: The growing use of direct democracy* (pp. 174–218). New York: Macmillan.

Brunner, G. (2001). Direct vs. representative democracy. In A. Auer & M. Bützer (Eds.), *Direct democracy: The Eastern and Central European experience* (pp. 215–227). Aldershot, e.t.c: Ashgate.

Buchanan, A. (1997). Theories of secession. *Philosophy & Public Affairs, 26*(1), 30–61.

Buchanan, A. (2007). *Justice, legitimacy, and self-determination: Moral foundations for international law*. Oxford: Oxford University Press.

Budge, I. (1996). *The new challenge of direct democracy*. Cambridge, e.t.c: Polity Press.

Butler, D. (1981). The world experience. In A. Ranney (Ed.), *The referendum device*. Washington, London: American Enterprise Institute for Public Policy Research.

Butler, D., & Ranney, A. (1994). Theory. In D. Butler & A. Ranney (Eds.), *Referendums around the world: The growing use of direct democracy*. New York: Macmillan.

Calligan, B. (2001). Amending constitutions through the referendum device. In M. Mendelsohn & A. Parkin (Eds.), *Referendum democracy: Citizens, elites and deliberation in referendum campaigns* (pp. 109–124). Houndmills: Palgrave.

Carras, C. (2009). The international relations aspect of the Annan Plan. In H. Faustmann & A. Varnava (Eds.), *Reunifying cyprus : The Annan Plan and beyond* (pp. 55–67). London: I.B. Tauris.

Castellino, J. (2000). *International law and self-determination: The interplay of the politics of territorial possession with formulations of post-colonial "National" identity*. The Hague: Martinus Nijhoff.

Cobban, A. (1969). *The Nation State and National self-determination*. New York: Thomas Y. Crowell Company.

Coppieters, B. (2010). Secessionist conflicts in Europe. In D. H. Doyle (Ed.), *Secession as an international phenomenon: From America's Civil War to contemporary separatist movements* (pp. 237–258). Athens, GA, USA: University of Georgia Press.

Crawford, J. (2006). *The creation of states in international law* (2nd ed.). Oxford: Clarendon Press.

Cronin, T. E. (1999). *Direct democracy: The politics of initiative referendum and recall*. Cambridge, MA: Harvard University Press.

Dion, S. (1996, April). Why is secession difficult in well-established democracies? Lessons from Quebec. *British Journal of Political Science, 26*(2), 269–283.

Dobelle, J. -F. (1996). Référendum et droit à l'autodétermination. *Pouvoirs, 77*, 41–60.

Easton, D. (1957, April). An approach to the analysis of political systems. *World Politics, 9*(3), 383–400.

Fallon, R. H. Jr. (2005, April). Legitimacy and the constitution. *Harvard Law Review, 6*(118), 1787–1853.

Farley, L. T. (1986). *Plebiscites and sovereignty: The crisis of political illegitimacy*. London: Westview Press.

Franck, T. M. (1992, January). The emerging right to democratic governance. *The American Journal of International Law, 86*(1), 46–91.

Gallagher, M. (1997). The referendum in Europe. In A. Auer & J.-F. Flauss (Eds.), *Le Référendum Européen: Actes du colloque international de Strasbourg, 21–22 février 1997* (pp. 69–79). Bruxelles: E. Bruylant.

Gönenç, L. (2002). *Prospects for constitutionalism in post-communist countries*. Hague: Martinus Nijhoff.

Gonssollin, E. (1921). *Le plébiscite dans le droit international actuel*. Paris: Libr. Générale De Droit & De Jurisprudence.

Goodhart, P. (1981). Referendums and separatism: I. In A. Ranney (Ed.), *The referendum device*. Washington, London: American Enterprise Institute for Public Policy Research.

Guelke, A. (2003). Negotiations and peace processes. In J. Darby & R. MacGinty (Eds.), *Contemporary peace making: Conflict, violence, and peace processes* (pp. 53–64). Gordonsville, VA, USA: Palgrave Macmillan.

Habermas, J. (1975). *Legitimation crisis* (trans: T. McCarthy). Boston: Beacon Press.

Habermas, J. (1996). *Between facts and norms: Contributions to a discourse theory of law and democracy* (trans: W. Rehg). Cambridge, MA: MIT Press.

Hamilton, A. ([1787–1788] 1982). The federalist no: 22. In *The federalist papers* (pp. 123–132). Westminster, MD: Bantam Dell Publishing Group.

Hamon, F. (1995). *Le référendum: étude comparative*. Paris: LGDJ.

He, B. (2002). Referenda as a solution to the national-identity/boundary question: An empirical critique of the theoretical literature. *Alternatives, 27*, 67–97.

Hughes, C. A. (1994). Australia and New Zealand. In D. Butler & A. Ranney (Eds.), *Referendums around the world: The growing use of direct democracy* (pp. 154–173). Washington, DC: AEI Press.

Kobach, K. W. (1994). Switzerland. In D. Butler & A. Ranney (Eds.), *Referendums around the world: The growing use of direct democracy* (pp. 98–153). Washington, DC: AEI Press.

Krasner, S. D. (1999). *Sovereignty: Organized hypocrisy*. Princeton, NJ: Princeton University Press.

Kriesi, H. (2005). *Direct democratic choice: The Swiss experience*. Plymouth: Lexington Books.

Krupavicius, A., & Zvaliauskas, G. (2001). Lithuania. In A. Auer & M. Bützer (Eds.), *Direct democracy: The Eastern and Central European experience* (pp. 109–127). Aldershot, e.t.c: Ashgate.

Lakoff, S. (2001). Democracy. In A. J. Motyl (Ed.), *Encyclopedia of nationalism: Fundamental themes* (Vol. 1, pp. 101–110). San Diego: Academic Press.

Laponce, J. A. (2001). National self-determination and referendums: The case for territorial revisionism. *Nationalism and Ethnic Politics, 7*(2), 33–56.

LeDuc, L. (2003). *The politics of direct democracy: Referendums in global perspective*. Ontario, e.t.c: Broadview Press.

Lutz, D. S. (2006). *Principles of constitutional design*. Cambridge: Cambridge University Press.

Lynch, P. (1997). Sovereignty and the European Union: Eroded, enhanced, fragmented. In L. Brace & J. Hoffman (Eds.), *Reclaiming sovereignty* (pp. 42–61). London: Pinter.

Lynch, P. (2005). Scottish independence, The Quebec Model of secession and the political future of the Scottish National Party. *Nationalism and Ethnic, 11*(4), 503–532.

Magleby, D. B. (1984). *Direct legislation: Voting on ballot propositions in the United States*. Baltimore: John Hopkins University Press.

McCormick, J. P. (1997, September). Review: Habermas' discourse theory of law: Bridging Anglo-American and continental legal traditions? *The Modern Law Review, 60*(5), 734–743.

Merriam, C. E. ([1900] 1999). *History of the theory of sovereignty since Rousseau*. Union, NJ: Lawbook Exchange.

Monahan, P. J. (2000, February). *Doing the rules an assessment of the Federal Clarity Act in light of the Quebec secession reference*. C.D. Howe Institute. http://www.cdhowe.org/pdf/monahan-2.pdf. Retrieved 01 Feb 2011.

Moore, M. (2001). *Ethics of nationalism*. Oxford: Oxford University Press.

Moore, M. (2010). Ethics of secession. In D. H. Doyle (Ed.), *Secession as an international phenomenon: From America's civil war to contemporary separatist movements* (pp. 76–94). Athens, GA, USA: University of Georgia Press.

Morel, L. (1996). France: Towards a less controversial use of the referendum? In M. Gallagher & P. V. Uleri (Eds.), *The referendum experience in Europe* (pp. 66–85). Houndmills, e.t.c: Macmillan Press Ltd.

Morel, L. (2001). The rise of government initiated referendums. In M. Mendelsohn & A. Parkin (Eds.), *Referendum democracy: Citizens, elites and deliberation in referendum campaigns* (pp. 47–66). Houndmills: Palgrave.

Morel, L. (2007, November). The rise of politically obligatory referendums: The 2005 French referendum in comparative perspective. *West European Politics, 30*(5), 1041–1067.

Morris, C. W. (1998). *An essay on the modern state*. Cambridge: Cambridge University Press.

Murswiek, D. (1993). The issue of a right of secession reconsidered. In C. Tomuschat (Ed.), *Modern law of self-determination* (pp. 21–39). Dordrecht, Boston, London: Martinus Nijhoff.

Pateman, C. (1970). *Participation and democratic theory*. Cambridge[e.t.c]: Cambridge University Press.

Pavkovic, A. (2000). Recursive secessions in former Yugoslavia: Too hard a case for theories of secession? *Political Studies, 48*, 485–502.

Pavkovic, A., & Radan, P. (2007). *Creating new states: Theory and practice of secession*. Aldershot: Ashgate.

Pazartzis, P. (2006). Secession and international law: The European dimension. In M. G. Kohen (Ed.), *Secession: International law perspectives* (pp. 355–373). Cambridge, e.t.c: Cambridge University Press.

Poggi, G. (1978). *The development of the modern state: A sociological introduction*. Stanford, CA: Stanford University Press.

Pomerance, M. (1976, January). The United States and self-determination: Perspectives on the Wilsonian conception. *The American Journal of International Law, 70*(1), 1–27.

Qvortrup, M. A. (2005). *A comparative study of referendums: Government by the people* (2nd ed.). Manchester: Manchester University Press.

Raic, D. (2002). *Statehood and the law of self-determination*. Leiden: Brill Academic Publishers.

Reilly, B. (2003). Democratic validation. In J. Darby & R. MacGinty (Eds.), *Contemporary peace making: Conflict, violence, and peace processes* (pp. 174–183). Gordonsville, VA, USA: Palgrave Macmillan.

Rideau, J. (1997). Les référendums nationaux dans le contexte de l'intégration européenne. In A. Auer & J.-F. Flauss (Eds.), *Le référendum européen: actes du colloque international de strasbourg, 21–22 février 1997* (pp. 81–113). Bruxelles: E. Bruylant.

Rourke, J. T., Hiskes, R. P., & Zirakzadeh, C. E. (1992). *Direct democracy and international politics: Deciding international issues through referendums*. London: Lynne Rienner Publ.

Rousseau, J. -J. (1762). *Du contrat social ou Principes du droit politique*. Official Website of Université de Quebec a Chichoutimi. http://classiques.uqac.ca/classiques/Rousseau_jj/contrat_social/Contrat_social.pdf. Retrieved 09 Oct 2013.

Rudolph, J. R. (2006). *Politics and ethnicity: A comparative study*. Gordonsville, VA, USA: Palgrave Macmillan.

Ruus, J. (2001). Estonia. In A. Auer & M. Bützer (Eds.), *Direct democracy: The Eastern and Central European experience* (pp. 47–62). Aldershot, e.t.c: Ashgate.

Schaar, J. H. (1981). *Legitimacy in the modern state*. New Brunswick: Transaction Books.

Schumpeter, J. A. ([1984] 2003). Excerpt from: Joseph Schumpeter, capitalism, socialism, and democracy. New York: Allen & Unwin, 1976. In R. A. Dahl, I. Shapiro, & J. A. Cheibub (Eds.), *Democracy sourcebook* (pp. 5–11). Cambridge, MA, USA: MIT.

Setala, M. (1999). *Referendums and democratic government*. New York: Palgrave Macmillan.

Smith, G. W. (1991). Political obligation. In D. Miller (Ed.), *The Blackwell encyclopaedia of political thought* (pp. 378–382). Oxford: Blackwell.

Stanley, J. (1991). *Social contract*. In D. Miller (Ed.), *The Blackwell encyclopaedia of political thought* (pp. 478–492). Oxford: Blackwell.

Sureda, A. R. (1973). *The evolution of the right of self-determination. A study of United Nations practice*. Leiden: Sijthoff.

Sussman, G. When the demos shapes the polis – The use of referendums in settling sovereignty issues. http://www.iandrinstitute.org/Studies.htm. Retrieved 5 May 2007.

Svensson, P. (1996). Denmark: The referendum as minority protection. In M. Gallagher & P. V. Uleri (Eds.), *The referendum experience in Europe* (pp. 33–50). Houndmills, e.t.c: Macmillan.

Tancredi, A. (2006). A normative 'Due Process' in the creation of states through secession. In M. G. Kohen (Ed.), *Secession: International law perspectives* (pp. 171–207). Cambridge, e.t.c: Cambridge University Press.

Thornberry, P. (1993). The democratic or internal aspect of self-determination. In C. Tomuschat (Ed.), *Modern law of self-determination* (pp. 101–138). Dordrecht, Boston, London: Martinus Nijhoff.

Türk, D. (1993). Recognition of states: A comment. *European Journal of International Law, 4*, 66–71.

Van der Vyver, J. D. (2003–2004). The right to self determination and its enforcement. *ILSA Journal of International and Comparative Law, 10*, 421–436.

Wambaugh, S. (1920). *A monograph on plebiscites (with a collection of official documents)*. New York: Oxford University Press.

Wambaugh, S. (1933). *Plebiscites since the world war: With a collection of official documents*. Washington: Carnegie Endowment for International Peace.

Weber, M. (1978). (trans: E. Fischoff et al.). In G. Roth & C. Wittich (Eds.), *Economy and society: An outline of interpretive sociology* (Vol. I, II vols). Berkeley: University of California Press.

Wellman, C. (2010). The morality of secession. In D. H. Doyle (Ed.), *Secession as an international phenomenon: From America's Civil War to contemporary separatist movements* (pp. 19–36). Athens, GA, USA: University of Georgia Press.

White, S., & Hill, R. J. (1996). Russia, the former Soviet Union and Eastern Europe: The referendum as a flexible political instrument. In M. Gallagher & P. V. Uleri (Eds.), *The referendum experience in Europe* (pp. 153–170). Houndmills, e.t.c: Macmillan Press Ltd.

Chapter 4
Sovereignty Referendums in the System of Law

Abstract This chapter aims to build a general, theoretical and conceptual framework, which will be used in the following chapters. In law, sovereignty referendums may be studied from the point of international law/constitutional law perspectives on the one hand and according to material/formal aspects on the other. This chapter starts with a brief explanation of the legal nature and legal status of sovereignty referendums in international and constitutional laws. The material aspect (i.e., subject matter) of sovereignty referendums simultaneously involves the issues of state creation and constitution making. In the following sections of this chapter, there will be a systematic analysis of the legal nature of two fundamental elements, which exist in both the processes of state creation and constitution making, i.e., sovereignty and self-determination. The chapter further explains the formal approach (i.e., legal basis) to the sovereignty referendums. The final section offers a classification based on formal and material dimensions of the sovereignty referendums.

This chapter aims to build a general theoretical and conceptual framework, which will be used in the following chapters. In law, sovereignty referendums may be studied from a point of international law/constitutional law perspectives on the one hand and according to material/formal aspects on the other. This chapter starts with a brief explanation of the legal nature and legal status of sovereignty referendums in international and constitutional laws. The material aspect (i.e., subject matter) of sovereignty referendums simultaneously involves the issues of state creation and constitution making. In the following sections of this chapter, there will be a systematic analysis on the legal nature of two fundamental elements, which exist in both processes of state creation and constitution making: sovereignty and self-determination. The chapter further explains the formal approach (i.e., legal basis) to the sovereignty referendums. The final section offers a classification based on formal and material dimensions of the sovereignty referendums.

İ.G. Şen, *Sovereignty Referendums in International and Constitutional Law*,
DOI 10.1007/978-3-319-11647-1_4

4.1 Sovereignty Referendums in International and Constitutional Law

When we examine sovereignty referendums from a perspective of international law, we may observe both material and formal aspects. Materially, it may be asserted that all sovereignty referendums have the common theme of state creation (or existence of states). From a formal point of view, the question of the legal status of sovereignty referendums may be considered: their status in international treaties, as well as the assessment of the question as to whether referendums are part of the international customary law. In this context, we will be guided by the question, where do referendums stand in the legal framework of state creation?

Also in constitutional law, the question may be studied from both formal and material viewpoints. From a material point of view, the common theoretical underpinnings of the issues voted for in sovereignty referendums may be discussed from a perspective of constitutional theory. In this context, one may argue that the issue of sovereignty is discernible to varying degrees in all the actions of constitution making. Moreover, in sovereignty referendums, this issue appears in its most crystallised and distinct form. Formally, there may be two issues: (1) the legal evaluation of the constitution-making activity and the constituent power, (2) the status of sovereignty referendums in comparative constitutional law. In this framework, the question of the legal regulation of constitutional changes may be mentioned. By and large, the issue calls for a theoretical survey regarding constitution making under revolutionary conditions, as well as a report on the existing provisions of the constitutions of the world on sovereignty referendums.

The internal (constituent power) and international (state creation) aspects of sovereignty are constantly interacting. Along this line of interaction, one may discern two main sorts of the occurrence of constituent power: one that pertains to the international personality of a polity and one that does not. From the perspective of international law, sovereignty referendums involve the former. In this context, we may list the elementary themes that underpin the legal nature of sovereignty referendums in terms of international law as follows: (1) concept of statehood, (2) acquisition of territory, (3) territorial changes, (4) changes in the international status of states, (5) extinction of states, (6) merger of territories and states. As far as the international personality is concerned, constituent power may generate three different types of "changes in the condition of states". First, it may well happen that constitutional changes occur in such circumstances as regime change and constitutional revolutions, which do not affect the international personality and identity of states. Even in these cases, a loss of territory or territorial changes may appear. The second group of changes may generate a change in the international status of the states without their complete annihilation. The entrance of states into real unions, a partial loss of independence such as the partial transfer of sovereignty to another state or an international organisation and accession under the international protection of another state may be mentioned as examples. Last, there may be changes that cause the "extinction" of states. A state loses its international personality when it merges with other states, when it blends into a new state or when it falls apart so that its whole territory is partitioned between two or more new states. Thus, not all the constitutional revolutions affect the identity and continuity of states. There is no doubt, however, that an interruption of the continuity of a state eliminates the basis of its constitution. When a state becomes extinct as an international person, its whole legal order collapses and it is assumed by international law that it is the successor state that determines the applicable local law.[1]

From these explanations, we may infer that sovereignty referendums are found at the intersection between state creation and constitution making. This observation leads us to consider the common concepts that exist in both processes, which from a material point of view constitute the basic elements of sovereignty referendums, namely, sovereignty and self-determination. An overall understanding of the legal nature of these concepts will offer us the general basis of reference for the subject matters that are put to vote in any referendum under this study.

4.2 Exploring the Subject Matter of Sovereignty Referendums: The Material Approach

4.2.1 Sovereignty as the Subject Matter

As stated above, sovereignty referendums are at the intersection of state creation and the process of building a constitution. Therefore, such referendums have simultaneously both international and domestic aspects, where the sovereignty as a political and legal concept may be considered both from internal and external dimensions. We may find the reason for this dimensional separation by examining the historical pattern of state formation, found particularly in Europe—in which cases we may infer that European states emerged through a dual process. The internal dimension of state formation was the consolidation of central power at the expense of feudal lords, whereas external dimension was the protection of one's territory against foreign enemies. This process has resulted in the fact that sovereignty, as the theoretical foundation of the modern state, has now both international and domestic (or constitutional) aspects. For this reason, the concept of sovereignty is simultaneously associated with the very existence of the state and its constitution. In this perspective, sovereignty may be defined to be the basic condition for the existence of the constitution of every state, or when put conversely, the constitution as the supreme law presupposes the state.[2]

From a legal point of view, external sovereignty was initially formulated by the Peace of Westphalia in 1648. Three basic principles emerged, setting the basic

[1] Oppenheim (1996), p. 219.

[2] Beaud (1994), p. 209.

tenets of modern public international law and interstate relations: (1) the notion of independence that entails the immunity of a state from external intervention in organising its territory and system of government, (2) the legal equality of states in public international legal order, (3) unanimity in taking international decisions, allowing a state to oppose international decisions against its will.[3]

As it is understood today, the notion of sovereignty in international law may be defined as follows: "sovereignty equals independence and consists of the bundle of competences which have not already been transferred through the exercise of independent consent to an international legal order".[4] Thus, in international law, the notion of state sovereignty implies the quality of the state to be recognised by other states as an equal member of international society, free from the control of another state.[5]

As to the internal aspect of sovereignty, its meaning and content evolved in tandem with the developments in the conceptions of democracy, nationalism and federalism. According to Krasner, "The intellectual history of the term sovereignty is most closely associated with domestic (internal) sovereignty. How is public authority organized within the state? How effectively is it exercised?"[6] The notion of indivisibility and the unlimited features of mediaeval and monarchical sovereignty were challenged, firstly by American independence, which brought the concept of popular sovereignty, and secondly by the French Revolution, which transformed the title of the sovereign from monarch to nation. In this way, the source of the legitimacy of political power shifted from the "divine-right" to the government—being "based on the social contract of free and equal individuals".[7]

Furthermore, American federalism brought the idea of "dual sovereignty": comprising the union and its component states. According to this concept, the people of the United States hold total sovereignty of the state. This sovereignty, though, is exercised on the basis of a functional division of power between the federal institutions and the states. Accordingly, the monolithic nature of the notion of indivisibility of sovereignty was challenged at the beginning of the twentieth century by scholars such as Leon Duguit, H. Hugo Krabbe and Harold Laski, who argued that sovereignty is pluralistic and therefore that state power is held and shared by various political, economic, social and religious groups.[8]

Additionally, developments since the Second World War have been challenging the concept of exclusive and unlimited sovereignty of the state in both the external and internal sense. Externally, the emergence of regional supranational organisations, resulting from regional political-strategic interdependencies, has led to significant transfers of sovereignty from individual states to organisations such as the

[3] Farley (1986), p. 7.

[4] Carty (1997), p. 101.

[5] Castellino (2000), pp. 95–97; Krasner (1999), pp. 15–25.

[6] Krasner (1999), p. 11.

[7] Finer (1961), p. 223; Merriam ([1900] 1999), p. 33.

[8] Cited in Lapidoth (1992), p. 333.

European Union.[9] As to the internal context, ethnic and regional cleavages, challenging the national states, have generated a debate about the sharing or division of the sovereignty of the central state.[10]

So far, we have offered a synopsis on the evolution of the concept of sovereignty in the system of politics and political philosophy. In the systems of law, the concept may be defined as follows: in international law as a legal term, "sovereignty" refers "not just to omnipotent authority, but the totality of powers that States may have under international law".[11] By the same token, from a perspective of constitutional law, a sovereign may do "whatever is not excluded by the" constitution.[12]

However, it is important to note that sovereignty is not a static concept in any of the systems that we have been examining. The dynamic nature, i.e. the ongoing demand for changes to the limits of sovereignty, from both international and internal environments, may be considered as the foremost reason for contemporary sovereignty conflicts. In this context, the mutual claims for self-determination by the various, antagonistic, linguistic, ethnic and religious groups are the causes of "contested and fundamentally irreconcilable claims of sovereignty".[13] In this context, we should examine the legal nature of this "contested sovereignty", which appears as the main subject matter in any sovereignty referendum. Lynch discerns three dimensions of sovereignty in terms of the legitimacy of political power[14]: (1) the "state dimension", (2) the "Constitutional dimension", (3) the "popular dimension".

Within the context of the state dimension, sovereignty entails three subsidiary elements. Firstly, the "territorial element" delineates the physical boundaries of state power. Secondly, the "functional element" represents the whole of the state power within the confines of its territory, whereas, thirdly, the "external element" corresponds to the independence of states in international law. In the context of the second dimension—the "constitutional dimension"—sovereignty is "the location of political power within the polity", as it is provided by the written or unwritten constitution. Finally, from the perspective of the "popular dimension" (popular), sovereignty reformulates the main premise of the consent-based legitimacy: "the authority of the state derives from the consent of the political community".

From the above, we may infer two main aspects to the concept of sovereignty in its relation to sovereignty referendums. The first aspect refers to the content of sovereignty: the final lawmaking power in a polity and independence from international or internal alien elements. The second aspect is all about the people or the nation as the legitimate source from which sovereignty emanates. While the first aspect is the basic element in the subject matter of any sovereignty referendum, the

9 For the discussion of sovereignty in terms of the European Union, see Lynch (1997).

10 Lapidoth (1992), pp. 335–336.

11 Crawford (2006), p. 33.

12 Lutz (2006), p. 68.

13 Hopkins (1997), pp. 62–73.

14 Lynch (1997), p. 43.

second aspect is a reformulation of the consent-based legitimacy in the foundation or change of any sort of sovereignty, which then culminates in the moral obligation to hold a sovereignty referendum. In other words, it involves the basic moral obligation that only people, acting as the sovereign, may decide on their sovereignty. In short, these two aspects of mutually interacting sovereignty constitute the normative basis as well as the subject matter of referendums.

4.2.2 Self-Determination in Modern International Law

Also, with regard to the concept of self-determination, we may discern the external and internal aspects of it. External self-determination is the right of a people to determine their future international status and to liberate themselves from foreign domination, whereas internal self-determination is the "selection of the desired system of government".[15]

Rosas distinguishes five elements of self-determination as a legal principle[16]:

> The right of a people of an existing State to determine freely their status without *outside* interference
> The right of a people, which has been subjugated, to *foreign* occupation or domination to free itself from occupation or domination
> The right of a people including a colonial people, to secede from a state and set up their own State or join another State
> The right of a people to determine its *constitution* (*pouvoir constituant*), including an autonomous status within the confines of a bigger state
> The right of a people to govern, that is, to have a democratic system of government.

The first three elements could be taken as external self-determination, while the last two may represent the internal aspect. Thus, internal self-determination includes, among other aspects, freedom for a minority from oppression by the central government, extending to the right to autonomy.

Accordingly, Suksi notes that while the external aspects of self-determination refer to sovereignty and nation building, the internal aspect comes closer to constituent power (*pouvoir constituant*).[17] On the other hand, we should note that internal self-determination and external self-determination are not two separate rights but only different aspects of the same right. Indeed, each element of self-determination may display both aspects depending on the way we look at it. For example, the right to independence from foreign intervention may be interpreted as the right to be independent within the internal affairs of the people. In the same way, the right to autonomy may be seen, from an international law perspective, as a remedy for secession and/or a preference of the people to remain within the limits

---

[15] Pomerance (1982), p. 37 in Kimminich (1993), p. 88.

[16] Rosas (1993), p. 230.

[17] Suksi (1996), p. 237.

of a bigger state (in return for a promised autonomy), rather than gaining independence.[18]

There are also other perspectives in the assessment of the legal content of the principle of self-determination. Chen Lung-Chu divides the claims to self-determination into two basic categories. The first category includes the establishment of a new political unit, i.e., independence and secession. The second category involves those claims outside the remit of creating a new political unit, such as the "claims to be free of external coercion" or the "claims of a group within an entity to such special protection as autonomy". Furthermore, from a broader perspective we may identify "five themes around which the claim to self-determination is advanced: *Human rights* for the individual level; *minority rights* for the sub-national level; *national independence* for the national level; *regional integration* for the regional level and a *global central guidance system*".[19] Further, we may study the legal nature and status of the right to self-determination, according to whether they are inside or outside of the decolonisation context.

Decolonisation: In terms of decolonisation, the UN Charter contains two separate legal frameworks that identify the eventual political units of self-determination: the Trusteeship System (Chapter XII, Articles 75–85) and Non-Self-Governing Territories (Chapter XI, Articles 73–74). Firstly, under the trusteeship system different countries from the Allied Powers would exercise sovereignty over certain non-self-governing territories by acting as trustees. Within their capacity as the administering authority, these countries had the duty to "promote the political, economic, social, and educational advancement of the inhabitants of the trust territories, and their progressive development towards self-government or independence as may be appropriate to the particular circumstances of each territory and its peoples and the freely expressed wishes of the peoples concerned" (Article 76). secondly, the UN Charter, under Chapter XI, lays the basic principles in relation to Non-Self-Governing Territories, "whose peoples have not yet attained a full measure of self-government" (Article 73). Chapter XI covers all those territories that have been integrated into another state without the free decision of its people and whose people do not enjoy the same rights as the rest of the population, having an inferior status within the constitutional system of the administering state. When compared with Chapter XII that regulates trust territories, the formulation of Article 73 is rather ambivalent with respect to the rights of external self-determination. In the first place, the obligations of the colonial states are less stringent than those of the administering powers under the trusteeship agreement. While the trusteeship system provides for a strict scrutiny of the administering power by the UN, there is no institutionalised supervision of the states, which exercise sovereignty over the non-self governing territories. Second, in contrast to Article 76, there is no explicit reference to the right of self-determination in Article 73. The trusteeship system speaks of independence as the objective, whereas the corresponding right of the

[18] Rosas (1993), p. 231; Kimminich (1993), p. 87; Eide (1993), pp. 139–176.

[19] Cited in Kimminich (1993), p. 87.

non-self governing territories was confined to "self-government". Finally, as to the methods utilised to achieve these goals while under the trusteeship system, "the freely expressed wishes of the peoples concerned" should be taken into account; Article 73 vaguely speaks of the "obligation" of administering states, "as a sacred trust", to "take due account of the political aspirations of the peoples". This "vague" and "hesitant" formulation of Article 73 resulted from the concerns of the UK and France to provide safeguards for their own colonial possessions.[20]

Thus, these regulations alone were not sufficient in themselves to create a firm legal substance to liberate the colonised people as a whole. Accordingly, in the early post-war era, "the question of whether self-determination was a legal right or principle (still remained) a divisive issue".[21] Further steps had to be taken that could create further rights for people in these colonial countries and impose duties upon the administering powers.[22] Indeed, over the course of time, the above-said dual international mechanism remained ineffective in saving the colonies of the Allied Powers, as the UN had developed an interpretation that eradicated the differences within the legal substance of each subsequent legal regime. The first breakthrough step in this process was the Declaration on the Granting of Independence to Colonial Countries and Peoples (Resolution 1514 in 1960 by the General Assembly). The wording of the declaration was plain: it proclaimed the right of self-determination of "all peoples".[23] A following UN resolution laid further criteria for the eventual units of self-determination. According to Resolution No 1541, the administering power had the obligation to transmit information regarding a territory (as provided by Chapter XI of the Charter), if the territory in question was "geographically separate and ethnically and/or culturally distinct from the country administering it". In the same document, three options were offered to the non-self governing territories within the framework of their right to self-determination. The territories could constitute themselves as a sovereign independent state, associate freely with an independent state or be annexed to an independent state already in existence.[24]

Outside Decolonisation: The legal nature of the right to self-determination outside of the colonial context is controversial.[25] This ambiguity, in fact, stems

[20] Fastrenrath (2002), pp. 1089–1091; see also Rauschning (2002), pp. 1110–1113.

[21] Crawford (2006), p. 108.

[22] Tomuschat (1993), pp. 1–5; Eckert (1999–2000), pp. 67–72.

[23] A/RES/1514 (XV): The UN General Assembly Resolution of 14 December 1960, on the "*Declaration, on the Granting of Independence to Colonial Countries and Peoples*". According to Castellino (2000, p. 23), "One of the important results of the Declaration is that it included self-determination as a fundamental human right..."

[24] A/RES/1541: The UN General Assembly Resolution of 15 December 1960, on "*Principles which should guide members in determining whether or nor an obligation exists to transmit the information called for under Article 73 e of the Charter*".

[25] Quane (1998), pp. 558–571; Dobelle (1996), p. 48; Crawford (2006), p. 122. The earliest appearance of the issue of legal nature of self-determination was in the Aaland Islands case before

from the contradictory theoretical implications of the principle, which provide a legitimating rationale for the creation of states, as well as present a threat to their territorial integrity.[26] We may sense this conundrum in the contradictive expressions of diverse legal documents. International Covenants on Human Rights hypothetically conferred the right of self-determination to *all* peoples without any preconditions, such as being colonised or oppressed.[27] Consequently, this forthright language raised concerns among the international community in terms of the stability of existing borders. Therefore, pursuant to this document, the General Assembly approved, by wide consensus, the "Declaration on Principles of International Law Concerning Friendly Relations and Co-operation among States in Accordance with the Charter of the UN".[28] This declaration included a more cautious approach by providing a "safeguard clause" that prohibited, in the use of the right to self-determination, "any action which would dismember or impair, totally or in part, the territorial integrity or political unity of a sovereign and independent State".

Therefore, considering this inconsistency, it can hardly be argued that in international law, self-determination (outside the colonial context) can be taken as a firm and operative legal rule and substantive in terms of state creation. It may only serve as a secondary supportive norm along with effectiveness.[29] The right to self-determination therefore does not automatically entail the right to secession. In this way, Tancredi, commenting on the dissolution of the former Yugoslavia, stated that "what the EC member states recognized was not the right to create new States exercising secessionist self-determination, but simply the inevitability of a *de facto* process which was already under way".[30] In the same vein, Pazartzis noted that the *ex post facto* acknowledgement by the international community of the dissolution of the former Yugoslavia and Soviet Union could not be construed as recognition of the right to secession.[31]

Thus, the legal nature of the right to self-determination is always prone to controversy because it is full of "indeterminacy".[32] On the other hand, when we

the League of Nations, in which the populations of the Islands opted for joining to Sweden rather than Finland, during the course of Finland's independence from Russia. In this case, the dominant view, among international lawyers as stated by the Commission of Jurists, was as follows: "The recognition of the principle of self determination in a number of international treaties (could not) be considered sufficient to put it upon the same footing as a positive rule of the Law of Nations", Crawford (2006), p. 109.

[26] For a further discussion, see Murswiek (1993), pp. 21–39.

[27] Castellino (2000), p. 32.

[28] A/RES/2625: The UN General Assembly Resolution of 24 October 1970, on the "*Declaration on Principles of International Law Concerning Friendly Relations and Cooperation Among States in Accordance with the Charter of the United Nations*"; Castellino (2000), p. 34; Crawford (2006), p. 118.

[29] Crawford (2006), p. 128.

[30] Tancredi (2006), p. 185.

[31] Pazartzis (2006), p. 365.

[32] Koskenniemi (1994), p. 260.

look at the principle from a negative perspective, international law is rather decisive. Indeed, the positive aspect of self-determination, that is, its legitimating power for the groups demanding secession, is unclear.[33] On the contrary, its negative or defensive aspect (people's right to veto any change on the international status of their territory) may be somewhat operative, and referendums play substantive roles in this respect. As noted above, the international community constantly referred to referendums during the recognition of the post-Yugoslavian states. Likewise, in Southern Rhodesia, the referendum on the constitution by which the white minority government declared independence was not "recognised internationally".[34] The unilateral declaration of independence met with the collective non-recognition of the international community. In this way, we may conclude that "an entity may not claim statehood, if its creation is in violation of an applicable right to self-determination".[35]

4.3 Formal Approach to Sovereignty Referendums: Legal Base and Regulation of the Referendums

The formal approach to sovereignty referendums particularly involves its legal basis. In terms of constitutional law, this involves the constitutional or legislative provisions that provide and regulate referendums. In international law, the legal basis may be either international treaties or customary law. Additionally, the discussions on the formal legal evaluation of sovereignty referendums involve the legality of state creation from the perspective of international law and the legality of constituent power in terms of constitutional law.

The ramifications of these discussions on international and constitutional laws will be analysed in detail in the following part. Suffice it here to mention the antithetical views of naturalist and positivist law theories on the validity of legal norms (and therefore the entirety of the whole legal order). According to naturalists, legal norms are valid only to the extent that they satisfy high standards of morality and/or justice. Positivists, on the other hand, see morality as something beyond the scope of law, a meta-legal concept.[36] For the positivist view, "all law is source-based, and anything which is not source-based is not law".[37]

Therefore, if there is no written legal base for referendums, the positivist view refuses to evaluate them from a juridical perspective. Natural law theories, on the

[33] According to Pazartzis (2006, p. 289), "The international community has no interest in favouring or opposing secession; its legal system does not contain any norm which prohibits or authorizes it".

[34] http://africanelections.tripod.com/zw.html#Rhodesia. Retrieved 11 November 2012.

[35] Crawford (2006), p. 131.

[36] Beaud (1997), p. 132.

[37] Marmor (2002), p. 105; Murphy (2007), p. 35.

other hand, refer to consent-based legitimacy arguments and confer the relevant moral norms a legal value, even if they are not posited in the constitutions, international treaties or any other legal documents. For naturalists, law is already immanent in nature, and at its most extreme, naturalist theory sees the lawmaking activity as limited to inferring the law from nature and promulgating it. According to Thomas Aquinas, lawmaking is "ordinance of reason", that is, the main source of law is human reason. What is significant for natural law theory is that it sees the validity of legal norms in their satisfaction of moral standards.[38] According to this conception, only people, as the genuine holders of sovereignty, hold the right and competence to discuss and alienate their sovereignty. Referendums therefore are the only means that confer the "legality" of the *de facto* incidences of state creation and constitution making.[39]

When we consider the question from a positivist perspective, we should be reminded of the fact that sovereignty referendums are votes held in a process where the main source of the law itself is being created—the state and/or its constitution. In this context, one may refer to Kelsen, who defines a legal order in which a basic norm, a constitution constitutes the "unity" of a group of norms. In this legal order, the validity of a single legal norm is measured according to its conformity to a "higher" norm, where the basic norm as the highest norm is "the common source for validity of all norms that belong to the same order".[40] Most of the sovereignty referendums are held (and in certain cases without a legal base) during the collapse or creation of this legal order, rendering the legal evaluation of the process problematic.

We may mention Luhmann's perspective at this point, where the issues of state creation and constitution making belong to two separate but interacting systems: law and politics. It may be that the domains of creation of state and its constitution are simultaneously occupied by these systems, what Luhmann calls as "structural coupling".[41] We may also argue that due to this structural coupling, the borders of law with other systems are rather blurred, this being the most visible in the cases of judge-made law and customary law. As regards the role of judges in the creation and/or interpretation of legal rules, one may contrast the difference between the Anglo-American concept of "Rule of Law" and the Continental European *Rechtstaat-Etat de droit*. In this perspective, rule (or supremacy) of law entails certain fundamental principles of justice, which may not be violated even by the highest lawmaking authority. The substantive (material) content of these principles are very well grounded over the centuries in British legal and political culture, thereby leaving no room for a claim of relativity. This is thanks to the evolutionary

[38] Aquinas notes, in this line of thinking, that "a legal norm fails to be valid if it goes against the human reason, regardless of the fact that it has been adopted by the state". Quoted in Murphy (2007), pp. 38–45.

[39] See, for a relevant discussion, Gözler (1997), pp. 285–368.

[40] Kelsen ([1967] 2002), p. 195.

[41] Çataloluk (2012), pp. 55 and 101–111.

formation of the unwritten English Constitution and its substantial interpretation and construction through case-based common law. In this sense, the limitation of state power in England is inductive, where the substantial basics of each rule are unquestionably determined by court decisions.[42]

We may also observe a relevant debate between Hart and Dworkin regarding the constitutional and statutory interpretation. In Hart's positivist model, positive law is constructed by a "core" and an outer circle of "penumbra". The core of law is then certain and "determinate", whereas "penumbra" is uncertain or indeterminate. While interpreting certain laws, the core is self-evident and automatically applied as a matter of fact, thereby leaving no room for moral argument. In contrast to the core, the penumbra invites ambiguity, in which case judges have to leave the sphere of law and enter that of morality, where each case can be judged by means of their own subjective values. Dworkin challenges this view by asserting that in every case where judges are to interpret laws, there is always one "right answer" "already immanent in law". Thus, in contrast to Hart's view that judicial choice or discretion is alien to law, Dworkin maintains that settlement of "hard cases" entails judgments that are "based on legal principles".[43]

In accordance with these discussions, legal positivists are divided into two groups with respect to their perception of the relationship between law and morality: exclusive and inclusive. Exclusive positivists think that law should be identified and understood without making even a minimum degree of reference to moral values. In their view, "Justification of law by a moral order is irrelevant".[44]

On the contrary, the inclusive positivists do not refrain from criticising existing legal norms on moral grounds. In their view, a legal norm or decision may be valid without necessarily being legitimate, and "legitimate law is merely that law which happens to have the right moral content, where the standards of rightness are the standards of morality". For the inclusive positivists, therefore, liberalism sets the standards to be met by laws in order to be deemed as legitimate. In other words, "the liberal morality hovers above the positive law – a by and large, universal and eternal set of standards that provide us with the criteria for evaluating particular and changing positive laws".[45]

These underpinnings may be sensed in certain key court decisions regarding referendums. In France, the Constitutional Council refrained from making a constitutional review of a piece of legislation providing for the direct election of the

[42] Berman (1991), pp. 44–45; Dicey ([1902] 2010), pp. 179–201; we should note that this distinction is only historical. As a common wisdom, in modern Western societies, one could hardly argue that there is such a rapport of inferiority or superiority in terms of liberty, democracy and protection of fundamental rights. As Rosenfeld (2001, p. 1328) put it, "...today's Rechtstaat has became inextricably tied to constitutional democracy framed by fundamental substantive values, and its legality has become subjected to a set of substantive norms embodied in constitutional justice".

[43] Dyzenhaus (1997), pp. 6–7; see also Marmor (2002), pp. 102–124.

[44] Kelsen ([1967] 2002), p. 68.

[45] Dyzenhaus (1997), p. 10.

president on the ground that it had been approved by the referendum. The Council in this case decided that it did not have the power to control the constitutionality of those laws adopted by the referendum. For the Council, in contrast to the laws adopted by parliament, laws adopted within a referendum were the "the direct expression(s) of the sovereignty of the people". This was an erroneous decision, however, firstly, because there was no provision in the French Constitution prohibiting the Council from reviewing laws adopted in a referendum. Secondly, in practice it produced counter-effects as regards the philosophical tenets on which it was based. The problem was that the French Constitution provides two ways of changing constitutional provisions: one by a joint session of the houses of parliament and the other by referendum, dependent on the initial parliamentary approval of the proposed modification (Article 89). President De Gaulle ignored this provision and submitted the proposal directly to a referendum by invoking Article 11 of the French Constitution of 1958. This gave him the competence to put to referendum any governmental bill concerning the organisation of the public authorities. This decision opened the way for the President to submit any proposal purposing to change the Constitution (institution of the direct election of the President) directly to a referendum, thus circumventing parliamentary debates.[46]

The Supreme Court of Canada, in its Quebec Secession Reference, went beyond the text of the constitution and created "a theory of positive obligations" by referring to the "underlying constitutional principles". For the Court, "these principles may give rise to very abstract and general obligations, or they may be more specific and precise in nature. The principles are not merely descriptive, but are also invested with a powerful normative force, and are binding upon both courts and governments".[47] In view of these statements, the Court decided that despite its unilateral nature, the referendum favouring the secession of Quebec would impose an obligation on Canada and the provinces to enter into negotiations.[48] According to Radan, this decision "indicates that the fundamental legitimising principle that informs the rules of constitutional law regulating process of secession is that of consent...The key mechanism for finding out whether a community desires to secede is the referendum..."[49] In short, this decision leads us to suppose that the legal evaluation of referendums does not only include a listing of the related explicit legal provisions but also reflects on the underlying constitutional principles such as democracy, sovereignty of the people and self-determination.

[46] Stefanini (2004), pp. 52–59.

[47] *Reference re Secession of Quebec*, para. 54.

[48] Chartrand (2003), p. 107.

[49] Radan (2010a), p. 71.

4.4 Classification of Sovereignty Referendums

Broadly speaking, sovereignty referendums may be classified from a material or formal point of view. Formal criterion helps us to consider whether a referendum is held pursuant to a legal basis or not. In this way, a referendum may be either *de jure* or *de facto*. The legal base of referendums may originate from either international or constitutional law. Material criterion may be noted in the typology of referendums according to their subject matter. In this section, we aim to present a summary and survey of the literature concerning the classification of sovereignty referendums.

Scelle distinguishes three types of *plébiscites*. The first two types are distinguished according to the time of the popular consultations: *plébiscites de ratification* are the referendums *a posteriori*, which are held after the conclusion of a cession, for the confirmation of annexations or transfers of territory already decided or even implemented by the unilateral or bilateral decisions of governments. The term *plébiscites de determination* is used for referendums *ex ante*, those that are held before the completion of the cession. In contrast to the former, these referendums may have an actual legal validity if the terms and conditions of their execution are fair and sincere. The third type is based on the actor having the competence to start the process. Sovereignty referendums may take the form of *plé biscites d'initiative*, if they are held on the initiative of the populations concerned. Scelle maintains that—by reference to popular initiatives in several constitutions—if the populations were provided the opportunity to start a process about eventual change within the status of their territory, this might be the genuine medium for the expression of their right to self-determination.[50]

Amiel made his classification from two different dimensions: according to the degree of participation of the people and to the legal nature of the consultations. According to the degree of participation, popular consultations may be direct or indirect. If a consultation is direct, the relevant people of that territory directly express their preference by voting on the question related to the issue at hand. In the case of indirect consultation, an assembly specially designed and mandated for that purpose is chosen by universal suffrage. As a representative method, it may be deemed less satisfactory when compared to the legitimating effect of direct democracy. However, this method may prove to be convenient, to the extent that chosen representatives may pay greater attention to the wishes of their constituents.[51] Further, Amiel opposes those referendums held according to international law (*Le plébiscite international proprement dit*) and all secession referendums (*plébiscite de sécession*). Secession referendums are not subsumed under international referendums according to French state practice, where independence referendums during decolonisation have always been held according to internal law.[52]

[50] Scelle ([1932–1934] 1984), pp. 277–278.

[51] Amiel (1976), p. 452.

[52] Amiel (1976), p. 459.

Similarly, Gawenda contrasted sovereignty referendums held according to internal law to those referendums taking place under international law. He used the terms *Le plébiscite unilatéral d'importance international* for the former and *Le plé biscite du droit international* for the latter. Gawenda's group of referendums, studied under the title *Le plébiscite du droit international,* included popular consultations held under bilateral and multilateral international treaties. [53]

Unilateral referendums are divided into three groups: in the first category, there are *ex post plébiscites,* dating back to the middle ages. This category includes the rudimentary practices of the middle ages, such as the annexing of the cities of Metz, Toul and Verdun by France. The historical importance of such consultations was that they were the initial experiences providing a check on the absolute power of the monarch concerning territorial issues.[54] Second, *de facto* referendums (*Le plé biscite de fait*) include those referendums held by governments or secessionist groups in the course of state creation during revolutions. Examples to be mentioned in this category are the post-revolutionary referendums held by France for the adhesion of the papal territories of Avignon and Comtat Venaissin; referendums pertaining to the Italian unification, the separation of Norway and Sweden, the adhesion of Vorarlberg to Switzerland; and the referendum held in the Aland Islands for secession from Finland. Last, occupation referendums (*Le plébiscite d'occupation*) comprise those consultations held in territories under the military control of a foreign state during an occupation in order to legitimise the annexation of that territory.[55]

Sussman's classification offers useful insights for a typology from a material viewpoint. He divides sovereignty referendums into six categories[56]: (1) "Independence Referendums" are used to "celebrate the independence of nation states"; (2) referendums that are held in regions to decide on joining another state are called "Upsizing/Incorporation" referendums; (3) the referendums held to resolve border disputes are defined as the "Border Referendums"; (4) the term "Status Referendum" is used to define referendums that are used "in managing relations between colonies and colonial powers and trustee territories and UN trustees"; therefore, most of the referendums held within the framework of decolonisation are termed as such; (5) the referendums on "Transfer of Sovereignty" refer to the referendums held on transfer of state competences either to supranational (i.e., European Union) or sub-national level (i.e., devolution in the UK); (6) finally, there are "Secession/ Downsizing Referendums", which facilitate secession or cession of territories. Here, the central state or a colonial power uses a referendum to gain public support within its domestic politics, prior to giving away a piece of territory in a decolonisation process.

[53] Gawenda (1946), pp. 19 and 54.

[54] Gawenda (1946), pp. 19–22.

[55] Gawenda (1946), p. 37.

[56] Sussman G, When the demos shapes the polis – the use of referendums in settling sovereignty issues. http://www.iandrinstitute.org/Studies.htm. Retrieved 5 May 2007

When we consider this literature survey, we may note that the classification of referendums may involve three elements: legal base, subject matter and the historical and political context in which the referendums are held. One should recall that there is no perfect typology and that each one is prone to include overlapping elements. On the other hand, a typology is necessary to distinguish the diverse interactions of these three elements, each of which may produce their own legal problems. We may summarise our classification for the purpose of this study as follows.

Accession and Border: Referendums held to decide about the incorporation of a region into a state may be termed accession referendums: referendums to resolve territorial disputes between two states and those that were founded in the cession treaties of the nineteenth century may be included in this category. If the territorial dispute in question is between two neighbouring states, then the related referendum may be termed as a border referendum. In this context, post-WWI referendums had all the features of a border conflict resolution.

Unification: The distinctive feature of a unification referendum is that more than one entity is merged into a separate state. As a result, after the unification referendums, all the entities lose their previous international personality and a new state is born out of the process. The most typical examples in this category were the two consecutive referendums held in the states of Australia (1898 and 1900) in order to establish the federation and, a more recent example, the Reunification referendum in Cyprus (2004).

Status (Decolonisation): The term status referendums may be used for referendums held within a decolonisation context when independence is not an option (Mayotte 2000 and 2009) or, politically, is highly unlikely (Puerto Rico). This term is quite useful for those referendums that do not involve a single question such as the question of independence or adhesion to another state. Instead, in these cases a set of legal rules, a constitutional reform package or an international treaty is put to referendum. Therefore, referendums in the context of decolonisation are held to determine the international status of trust territories and non-self-governing territories. For instance, in the referendums held in Palau (1992), the Federated States of Micronesia (1983), Puerto Rico (1967, 1991, 1993, 1998 and 2012) and the Marshall Islands (1983), various sovereignty arrangements were proposed in one ballot, namely, free association, becoming a state of the USA, or Commonwealth Association and independence. In the same way, in the referendum held in the Faroe Islands (1946), the voters were asked whether they wanted independence or adhesion to Denmark. Similarly, in the Cocos Islands (1984), there were three alternatives: Free Association with Australia, Independence or Adhesion to Australia. Given that the overwhelming majority of status referendums are held in the context of decolonisation, we may also name them as "decolonisation referendums". This term will be used, including "status referendums", throughout this study.

One common feature of this category is the presumed intent of the colonial/administering state to continue its relationship with the related territory, but with altered status patterns. In the Gibraltar referendum (1967), the voters were asked whether they wanted to retain their links with the UK. Central states may propose improvements to the constitutional status of the breakaway territories, namely, greater autonomy, extension of competences to the advantage of regional units or the elimination of discriminatory status *vis-a-vis* the metropolitan state. At this point, it is hard to limit these referendums to just one subject, where there is an overall structural constitutional change in the relations between the central state and the related territory or a change in the constitutional status of the territory. Such was the case in most of the French referendums. As an example, the 1958 referendum was held to gain approval of the constitution, and for the colonial possessions of France it meant whether or not they were to remain as a part of France with a renewed constitutional status. In Wallis and Futuna (1959), the referendum was held on a change of the status of these territories from protectorate to overseas departments. In the same way, with the agreement of Paris (2000), it was foreseen that the status of Mayotte would be moved from a *collectivité territoriale* to a *collectivité départementale*.

This category may also include those referendums that aim to preserve the *status quo* outside of the decolonisation context. The common feature of such referendums, along with decolonisation, is their intent to maintain links between the disputed territory and the central state. The political context and wording of the question determine this type, i.e., it is held by the central states and asks the people if they want to remain a part of these states. The legal ramification, however, is unclear since a rejection or "no" vote does not necessarily mean independence. The "border poll" held in Northern Ireland in 1973 may be considered an example of this, as the British Government held this vote in order to overcome the regional reactions arising after a suspension of the local parliament. Similarly, the "all union" referendum (1991) held by Gorbachev to keep the USSR together was another example of these status referendums. In Moldova, a referendum (1994) was held for the "Conservation of independence and Territorial Integrity". This was in order to counter-argue "the view among some nationalists that it would be better to 'reunify' with Romania" and "the need to restore Moldovan sovereignty over the breakaway region of Trans-dniestria".[57]

Transfer of Sovereignty: Referendums on the transfer of sovereignty may be either supranational or sub-national. Supranational referendums concern international treaties, which stipulate a transfer of power to a supranational organisation. Referendums held in several European countries during the integration process of the EU may be seen as the major examples. The subject of a sub-national referendum is the creation of a sub-national autonomous area. This category comprises the referendums on devolution in the UK. In Spain, the 1978 Spanish Constitution included a transitory provision allowing three historic nations, Catalonia, Galicia and Basque Country, to acquire a status of greater autonomy. In order to gain this status, it was provided that a referendum should take place in these regions.

[57] Wheatley (2008), p. 25.

Subsequently, all three historic nations used this right in 1979 and gained their autonomy status.[58]

Sub-national Territorial Modification: This category of referendums may be found mostly in the constitutions of federal states that specify the legal framework of territorial alterations or division of federal units into one or two separate parts. In fact, these referendums may involve issues that are explained in the case of international referendums. Secession of a territory from a federal unit to form a new one may be compared to independence referendums, or referendums on the territorial exchanges between two units may be deemed akin to the border or adhesion referendums. Nevertheless, the nature of its legal framework, that is, national constitutional law, leads us to subsume them under a different category.

The procedure of creation of the Canton of Jura may be highlighted in this context[59]:

> The first (referendum) was an amendment to the Bernese cantonal constitution which the people of the canton of Berne accepted on March 1, 1970. This amendment provided for a three-step cascade of (referendums) in Jura. In the first vote of June 23, 1974, the majority of voters (52 %) in the seven Jurassic districts of the canton of Berne opted for the formation of the new Canton. In those four out of the seven districts in which a majority had voted against the formation of a new canton, additional (referendums) became possible. In the second (referendum) of March 16, 1975, the three southern districts (with the exception of the district of Laufen) decided to stay with the canton of Berne. In the third round of referendums of September 7, September 14 and October 19, 1975, the borderline communities were allowed to opt out of their district.

The final voting was held for the required amendment of the Federal Constitution in September 25, 1978.

Independence: This group of referendums includes the ones that are held on an eventual secession of a territory. Three types of such referendums may be distinguished: (1) *De facto* unilateral referendums held by secessionist groups; (2) *De Jure* independence referendums held in the territories subject to decolonisation. In this case, the international law confers the related territory the right to independence within the international legal framework on decolonisation. Referendums held by France in Algeria and the referendum in East Timor (1999) may be noted in this context. Also, the future referendum in New Caledonia to be held between 2013 and 2018 may be included in this category[60]; (3) *De jure* independence referendums that are outside of the colonial context, as specified by an international agreement or the constitution of the central state. Referendums held during the accession of Montenegro to independence (2006) and the one that led to the independence of South Sudan (2011) are two significant examples.

---

[58] Rourke et al. (1992), pp. 112–150.

[59] Wildhaber (1995), pp. 49–50.

[60] For the details, see Chap. 6, Sect. 6.2.4.2.

References

Amiel, H. (1976). La pratique française des plébiscites internationaux. *Revue générale de droit international public*, 425–501.

Beaud, O. (1994). *Puissance de l'Etat*. Paris: PUF.

Beaud, O. (1997). Propos sceptiques sur la légitimité d'un référendum Européen ou plaidoyer pour plus de réalisme constitutionnel. In A. Auer & J. F. Flauss (Eds.), *Le Référendum Européen* (pp. 125–180). Bruxelles: Bruylant.

Berman, H. J. (1991). The rule of law and law-based state (Rechtstaat) with special reference to Soviet Union. In D. D. Barry (Ed.), *Toward the "Rule of Law" in Russia?* New York: M.E. Sharpe.

Carty, A. (1997). Sovereignty in international law: A concept of eternal return. In L. Brace & J. Hoffman (Eds.), *Reclaiming sovereignty*. London: Pinter.

Castellino, J. (2000). *International law and self-determination: The interplay of the politics of territorial possession with formulations of post-colonial "National" identity*. The Hague: Martinus Nijhoff.

Çataloluk, G. (2012). *Hukuk Sistemi ve Autopoiesis*. İstanbul: Onikilevha.

Chartrand, P. L. A. H. (2003). Canada and the aboriginal peoples: From dominion to condominium. In L. Seidle & D. Docherty (Eds.), *Reforming parliamentary democracy* (pp. 99–128). Montreal, QC, Canada: McGill-Queen's University Press.

Crawford, J. (2006). *The creation of states in international law* (Vol. 2). Oxford: Clarendon Press.

Dicey, A. V. (2010). *Introduction to the law of the constitution* (6th ed.). Lexington: Elibron Classics [1902].

Dobelle, J.-F. (1996). Référendum et droit à l'autodétermination. *Pouvoirs, 77*, 41–60.

Dyzenhaus, D. (1997). *Legality and legitimacy: Carl Schmitt, Hans Kelsen and Hermann Heller in Weimar*. Oxford: Clarendon Press.

Eckert, A. E. (1999–2000). Free determination or the determination or the determination to be free?: Self-determination and the democratic entitlement. *UCLA Journal of International Law and Foreign Affairs, 4*, 55–79.

Eide, A. (1993). In search of constructive alternatives to secession. In C. Tomuschat (Ed.), *Modern law of self-determination* (pp. 139–176). Dordrecht, e.t.c: Martinus Nijhoff.

Farley, L. T. (1986). *Plebiscites and sovereignty: The crisis of political illegitimacy*. London: Westview Press.

Fastrenrath, U. (2002). Chapter XI. Declaration regarding non-self-governing territories, Vol. II. In B. Simma, H. Mosler, A. Randelzhofer, C. Tomuschat, & R. Wolfrum (Eds.), *The charter of the United Nations* (pp. 1089–1097). Oxford, NY: Oxford University Press.

Finer, H. (1961). *The theory and practice of modern government*. London: Methuen.

Gawenda, J. A. B. (1946). *Le plébiscite en droit international*. Fribourg: Imprimerie St. Paul.

Gözler, K. (1997). *Le pouvoir de révision constitutionnelle*. Villeneuve d'Ascq: Presses universitaires du Septentrion.

Hopkins, S. (1997). The search for peace and a political settlement in Northern Ireland: Sovereignty, self-determination and consent. In L. Brace & J. Hoffman (Eds.), *Reclaiming sovereignty* (pp. 62–79). London: Pinter.

Kelsen, H. ([1967] 2002). *Pure theory of law* (trans: Knight, M.). Union, NJ: Lawbook Exchange.

Kimminich, O. (1993). A "federal" right of self-determination? In C. Tomuschat (Ed.), *Modern law of self-determination* (pp. 83–100). Dordrecht, e.t.c: Martinus Nijhoff.

Koskenniemi, M. (1994). National self-determination today: Problems of legal theory and practice. *International and Comparative Law Quarterly, 43*, 241–269.

Krasner, S. D. (1999). *Sovereignty: Organized hypocrisy*. Princeton, NJ: Princeton University Press.

Lapidoth, R. (1992). Sovereignty in transition. *Journal of International Affairs, 45*(2), 325–346. Winter.

Lutz, D. S. (2006). *Principles of constitutional design*. Cambridge: Cambridge University Press.

Lynch, P. (1997). Sovereignty and the European Union: Eroded, enhanced, fragmented. In L. Brace & J. Hoffman (Eds.), *Reclaiming sovereignty* (pp. 42–61). London: Pinter.

Marmor, A. (2002). Exclusive legal positivism. In J. Coleman, S. Shapiro, & K. E. Himma (Eds.), *The Oxford handbook of jurisprudence and philosophy of law* (pp. 104–124). Oxford: Oxford University Press.

Merriam, C. E. ([1900] 1999). *History of the theory of sovereignty since Rousseau*. Union, NJ: Lawbook Exchange.

Murphy, M. C. (2007). *Philosophy of law: Fundamentals*. Malden, MA: Blackwell Publishing.

Murswiek, D. (1993). The issue of a right of secession reconsidered. In C. Tomuschat (Ed.), *Modern law of self-determination* (pp. 21–39). Dordrecht/Boston/London: Martinus Nijhoff.

Oppenheim, L. F. L. (1996). In R. Jennings & A. Watts (Eds.), *Oppenheim's international law* (9th ed., Vol. 1, 2 vols). London: Longman.

Pazartzis, P. (2006). Secession and international law: The European dimension. In M. G. Kohen (Ed.), *Secession: International law perspectives* (pp. 355–373). Cambridge, e.t.c: Cambridge University Press.

Quane, H. (1998, July). The United Nations and the evolving right to self-determination. *International and Comparative Law Quarterly, 4*, 537–572.

Radan, P. (2010a). Lincoln, the constitution, and secession. In D. H. Doyle (Ed.), *Secession as an international phenomenon: From America's civil war to contemporary separatist movements* (pp. 56–75). Athens, GA, USA: University of Georgia Press.

Rauschning, D. (2002). Chapter XII international trusteeship system. In B. Simma, H. Mosler, A. Randelzhofer, C. Tomsuchat, & R. Wolfrum (Eds.), *The charter of the United Nations a commentary* (Vol. II, pp. 1099–1128). Oxford, NY: Oxford University Press.

Rosas, A. (1993). Internal self-determination. In C. Tomuschat (Ed.), *Modern law of self-determination* (pp. 225–252). Dordrecht, e.t.c: Martinus Nijhoff.

Rosenfeld, M. (2001). The rule of law and the legitimacy of constitutional democracy. *Southern Califorina Law Review, 74*, 1307–1352.

Rourke, J. T., Hiskes, R. P., & Zirakzadeh, C. E. (1992). *Direct democracy and international politics: Deciding international issues through referendums*. London: Lynne Rienner Publ.

Scelle, G. ([1932–1934] 1984). *Précis du droit des gens. Principes et systématique*. Vol. 2. Paris: CNRS.

Stefanini, M. F.-R. (2004). *Le controle du référendum par la justice constitutionnelle*. Paris: Economica.

Suksi, M. (1996). Finland: Referendum as a dormant feature. In M. Gallagher & P. V. Uleri (Eds.), *The referendum experience in Europe*. London/New York: Macmillan/Stjames.

Tancredi, A. (2006). A normative 'Due Process' in the creation of states through secession. In M. G. Kohen (Ed.), *Secession: International law perspectives* (pp. 171–207). Cambridge, e.t.c: Cambridge University Press.

Tomuschat, C. (1993). Self-determination in a post-Colonial World. In C. Tomuschat (Ed.), *Modern law of self-determination*. Dordrecht, Boston, London: Martinus Nijhoff Publishers.

Wheatley, J. (2008). C2D working paper series direct democracy in the commonwealth of independent states: The state of the art. http://www.c2d.ch/files/C2D_WP28.pdf. Retrieved 10 Oct 2012.

Wildhaber, L. (1995). Territorial modifications and breakups in federal states. *The Canadian Yearbook of International Law, 33*, 41–74.

Part II
Sovereignty Referendums: A Legal Analysis

Chapter 5
Sovereignty Referendums in International Law

Abstract In this chapter, there will be an analysis of the sovereignty referendums from the perspective of international law. The question of what makes a referendum international may be gauged from both the material (subject matter) and the formal (legal basis) viewpoints. In terms of the former, international referendums are those in which outcomes produce ramifications in international law, or in other words, the issue voted for is a problem to be solved within the confines of international law. In this context, the issue of creation and/or existence of states is located at the most fundamental level of the process of sovereignty referendums. Formally, a referendum may be categorised as international if the legal base of a referendum is provided by international law or if international organisations are partially or totally involved in the referendum. This chapter also focuses on the following issues: the status of the sovereignty referendums in international treaties, as well as the assessment of the question as to whether referendums are part of international customary law. Finally, this chapter discusses the international monitoring and/or administration of sovereignty referendums by focusing on the cases of Western Sahara, East Timor, South Sudan, Cyprus and Montenegro.

5.1 General Framework

A referendum is assumed to be an element of international law if (1) the subject matter of the vote is an international law issue; (2) the legal source of the referendum is an instrument of international law, which may be a treaty or the act of an international organisation; (3) there is a certain presence of international actors within the implementation of the referendum.[1]

Whether these three criteria are equally indispensable to subsume the sovereignty referendums under international law may generate opposing views. Amiel, for example, limited himself to a material definition: "*Le plébiscite international s'entend de toute vote relatif a l'annexion ou la sécession d'un territoire*".[2] In the

[1] Laghmani (1998), p. 200.

[2] Amiel (1976), p. 428.

İ.G. Şen, *Sovereignty Referendums in International and Constitutional Law*,
DOI 10.1007/978-3-319-11647-1_5

same way, Luce said, "*Il ne peut...y avoir plébiscite que lors des mutations territoriales sont envisagées*".[3] Certain other authors tend to require the entirety of these criteria in order to consider a referendum in terms of international law. It is held that not only a referendum should have international subject matter, but it should also involve international elements in the proceedings of it. According to Laghmani, if the self-determination-related referendums are held purely pursuant to internal law, they are the mere facts contrary to the principle of self-determination.[4] Gawenda notes that unilateral referendums, held by post-revolutionary governments and secessionist national or ethnic groups, were not based on any international treaty and that they were not implemented within the framework of international law. Therefore, these *de facto* referendums may not constitute a condition for the validity of any territorial change.[5]

For de Visscher, the term *plébiscite international* should be reserved for referendums held pursuant to an international obligation provided by bilateral or multilateral treaties or by the decision of an international organisation established by a treaty. For him, referendums that are held as a result of an act of internal sovereignty, either constitutional or statutory, do not fall within the category of international referendums. In this vein, he excludes national constitutional provisions that require referendums for the ratification of international treaties—given that they are merely internal preparatory acts in the process of the foundation of an international legal instrument. Thus, for de Visscher, a perfect prototype of a *plébiscite international* should be (1) decided by a multilateral treaty, (2) organised by an international institution and controlled by a committee, whose members are from among the nationals of states not directly concerned in the territorial issue at stake.[6]

5.2 Subject Matter

Sovereignty referendums entail the question of international personality, of a polity: that is, "the capacity to be the bearer of rights and duties under international law". States are not necessarily the only, but the oldest and most commonly agreed possessors of international legal personality. Thus, in terms of international law, the issue of creation and/or existence of states is located at the most fundamental level of the process of sovereignty referendums—while interacting with a variety of associated legal and political questions that are on the surface. This leads us to the question of "statehood", about which criteria is commonly referred to the

[3] Luce (1958), p. 9.

[4] Laghmani (1998), p. 200.

[5] Gawenda (1946), pp. 36–37. Accession of Papal territories of Avignon and Comtat Venaissin, Italian unification, separation of Norway and Sweden, Accession of Vorarlberg to Switzerland, Aland Islands.

[6] de Visscher (1986), p. 144.

formulation laid down by the Article I of the Montevideo Convention on the Rights and Duties of States: the state as a person of international law should possess the following qualifications: (1) a permanent population, (2) a defined territory, (3) an effective government.

Defined Territory: Defined territory is the geographical and physical basis of a state—"the spatial dimension of state activities",[7] which is delimited against the external world and on which "the exclusive control", i.e. the state sovereignty, is exercised. The defined territory, as an object of international law, is an indispensable element in the formation of states since international law presumes the sovereignty of a state only with respect to and within its territory.[8]

From a territorial perspective, referendums may be used to resolve the question of legitimate acquisition of territory.[9] First among these we can consider cession. A historical account of territorial change shows that cession is the most common form of territorial acquisition that is accompanied by referendums. Cession may be defined as the transfer of sovereignty over state territory by one state to another. The "consent" of the ceding state is a prerequisite in this process, and it is certified via bilateral or multilateral treaties. With the advent of democratic norms, referendums became a complementary element of such treaties from the nineteenth century, when the consent of the inhabitants of the ceded territory was required.[10]

Two other traditionally mentioned sorts of territorial acquisition are today of historical value: "occupation" and "subjugation". The former denotes an effective possession of a territory, which does not belong to any state, whereas the latter denotes the forceful annexation of a territory following a successful war of conquest. Needless to say, acquisition of a territory through subjugation or occupation may not be deemed as legal, given the categorical rejection of it by contemporary international law. In this way, use of force is not allowed "against the territorial integrity and political independence of any State",[11] nor "any territorial acquisition resulting from the threat or use of force shall be recognized as legal".[12] These rules today are considered to have the character of *jus cogens,* excluding all related

[7] Cassese (2001), p. 55.

[8] "State territory is that defined portion of the globe which is subjected to the sovereignty of the state... It is the space within which state exercise its supreme and normally exclusive authority" (Oppenheim 1996, p. 564). "The legal competence of states and the rules for their protection depend on and assume the existence of a stable, physically delimited, homeland" (Brownlie 2003, p. 106).

[9] Traditionally, five distinct modes of territorial acquisition are distinguished: cession, occupation, subjugation (conquest), accretion and prescription.

[10] "Absolute monarchism of pre-nineteenth century has caused the cessions to be done in a private law conception, by which the territories were handed over from one sovereign to the other as if they were mere real estates". Crawford (2006), p. 684.

[11] The U.N. Charter, Art. 2(4).

[12] A/RES/2625: The UN General Assembly Resolution of 24 October 1970, on the "*Declaration on Principles of International Law Concerning Friendly Relations and Cooperation Among States in Accordance with the Charter of the United Nations*".

methods of territorial acquisition.[13] These maxims render the referendums held to legitimise such actions *a fortiori* illegal.

On the other hand, the concept of "belligerent occupation" or occupation in a general sense should be distinguished from the preceding two concepts. This concept and its relationship with the sovereignty referendums are discussed below. The term indicates an effective establishment and exercise of authority by a state on the territory of another.[14]

Referendums may be observed in the case of territorial disputes, in certain cases accompanied by occupations. Disagreement on the possession of a territory between two or more states generates territorial disputes, and they are, by no means, struck out of the records of international law.[15] Brownlie predicts a considerable increase in the saliency of such issues, indicating the large numbers of already existent, albeit "dormant", territorial disputes around the globe. This is particularly true for Asia and Africa, where the course post-colonial state formation has left successor states with the unresolved legal and political issues.[16] We may discern three different types: the legitimacy of possession or occupation of a territory by a state, which may be contested (Western Sahara, East Timor); the legitimacy of claimed international status of territories, which may be contested in the U.N. (Mayotte, Cyprus, New Caledonia); finally, a territorial dispute that may be in the form of a border dispute, if it emerges between neighbouring states that respectively claim sovereignty along the same border's territory (Kashmir, between Pakistan and India).

Permanent Population: Whereas territory is the physical basis, the criterion of permanent population is represented by the sociological and demographic aspects. "If states are territorial entities, they are also aggregates of individuals", and these individuals should form a "reasonably stable political community" to establish the state.[17] A permanent population is thus necessary for statehood that will be in control of the defined territory.[18] In fact, this element of state formation corresponds to the issue of the subject of constituent power in constitutional law. From this perspective, sovereignty referendums serve double functions with respect to the defined population: firstly, a referendum voted for positively by overwhelming numbers may be used as a self-referential argument—that the so-called people have committed a collective act of self-determination, i.e., it serves as a proof of the

[13] Oppenheim (1996), pp. 702–704.

[14] Territory is considered occupied when it is actually placed under the authority of the hostile army. The occupation extends to the territory where such authority has been established and exercised (The Hague Conventions of 1907, Convention Respecting The Laws and Customs of War On Land [Hague IV]; October 18, 1907, Section III Military Authority over the territory of the hostile State. Art. 42) http://avalon.law.yale.edu/20th_century/hague04.asp#art42. Retrieved 10 November 2012.

[15] Janis (2003), p. 193.

[16] Brownlie (2003), p. 125.

[17] Brownlie (2003), p. 71.

[18] Crawford (2006), pp. 50–53.

existence of the permanent population. Secondly, a political power may use referendums to legitimise itself by being the approved agent acting on behalf of this defined population.

Effective Government: The criteria of effective government refer to state competence. It is the capability of, and, the "legally circumscribed claim of right" to the exercise of sovereignty with respect to a certain territory and population. In addition, the question of effective government refers to the concept of internal and external sovereignty of the state.[19]

Thus, we may list the three dimensions that may be found within the subject matter of a sovereignty referendum as territorial, functional and human. Diverse experiences of sovereignty referendums that have been held within the process of resolution of international issues display a mixture of these three elements in varying degrees. For instance, when a referendum is held to resolve a territorial dispute, the territorial dimension is the first to be discerned, i.e., the question of which state should acquire the disputed territory. From a perspective of state competence, transfer of a territory from one state to another means a shift in the system of rules: a shift from one legal order to another. From this viewpoint, Scelle described the post-WWI referendums as the *acte-condition collectifs,* a process of decision by a people to confer the legal right of sovereignty on one of the states over the disputed territory.[20] Finally, regarding the population concerned, a change in the international status of a territory will have a direct effect on its inhabitants: a change in their nationality. Whereas referendums serve for the majority to decide on this issue, international law provides *droit d'option* for the minority. This enables the inhabitants, within a specified deadline after the cession, to choose the nationality of one of the party states of the treaty after cession. As a protective remedy for the minority, this tool has been included widely in the post-WWI treaties, along with the referendums.[21] In some cases, the functional element is the most visible, as is the case for the referendums on the transfer of sovereignty to the EU. Still, in this case, one may trace the hints of a prospect of creating European demos in an open-ending process.[22]

To summarise what has been said so far, within the framework of international law, the question of the making of the political unit, and the identification of the subject of constituent power, dissolves under the various headings of the broader subjects of state creation or state continuity.[23] In this vein, various "modes of creation states" may be reminded, each of which may appear as the legal substance of sovereignty referendums in different contexts: "devolution",[24]

[19] Crawford (2006), pp. 55–62.

[20] Scelle ([1932–1934] 1984), p. 281.

[21] Rousseau (1958), pp. 162–168.

[22] Rideau (1997), p. 84.

[23] Crawford (2006), pp. 667–723.

[24] Crawford (2006), pp. 329–373.

"secession",[25] "reunification of divided states"[26] and "union and federation of states".[27]

5.2.1 Devolution and Secession

The two most important methods of state formation are devolution and secession with their mutually exclusive features: the existence or absence of the consent of the former sovereign state. Namely, states may be created either through devolution, i.e. by the explicit granting of independence from the metropolitan state, or by secession, which is often the violent and conflict-strewn disintegration of the territory in question.

Devolution may take two distinct types with respect to the transfer of power to a local region. The first type involves an outright and straightforward act of immediate relinquishment of the sovereignty of the related territory. In this case, states choose to grant independence to their regions without considering any other form of dependency. In the second type, on the contrary, one may speak about gradual devolution, whereby the states choose to grant a certain degree of autonomy before or without granting complete independence to their local units. In the latter case, a state seeks to maintain certain ties with the territory where it is challenged by a legitimacy crisis by applying intermediate forms of constitutional status on a range between total dependence and total independence.[28]

Two sorts of gradual devolution may be distinguished: devolution within the context of decolonisation and "devolution within the unitary states".[29] In the first case, there is a process of gradual separation of a territory from the constitutional fabric of the parent state, whereas in the second a certain degree of autonomy is conferred by central authorities on local units, in an attempt to overcome ethnic and regional secessionist demands. The distinguishing feature of these two types lies in the legitimacy challenge against the possession of these territories. Decolonisation devolutions are undertaken by the states to meet the requirements of international law, with respect to their non-self-governing territories, as underlined by the right to external self-determination (Puerto Rico and New Caledonia). On the contrary, in terms of the devolution in the "previously unitary states", no challenges appear in international law concerning the legitimacy of the possession of the relevant territory. At most, a claim to the right of internal self-determination, i.e. the right to autonomy, may be raised, which merely results in a constitutional and internal reconstruction of the state such as in the UK and Spain.

[25] Crawford (2006), pp. 375–446; Oppenheim (1996), pp. 222–223.
[26] Crawford (2006), pp. 449–477.
[27] Crawford (2006), pp. 479–500.
[28] Crawford (2006), pp. 332–333.
[29] Crawford (2006), p. 500.

Despite their differences, two common traits of these two sorts of devolution may be identified: For one thing, both are considered as an open-ended process. The decolonisation devolution is "an ill defined and flexible process of transfer of power", which may or may not result in the total and formal independence of a territory. Likewise, the process of unitary-state devolutions may be identified to be "dynamic and to an extent unpredictable".[30] On the other hand, given the eventual acquisition of independence of non-self-governing territories in international law, the prospect for substantial and practical or formal independence is stronger when compared to unitary-state devolutions.[31]

The second common point is that almost the entire process of both types of devolution occurs within the municipal law of the metropolitan states and not within the remit of international law. While this trait may be deemed as justifiable with respect to unitary-state devolutions, decolonisation-related devolutions may create problems if the metropolitan state tends to impose the monopoly of its legal order instead of collaborating with the international community.[32] This problem lies at the heart of the question of fair administration of referendums that are held in the process of decolonisation.

The domination of the metropolitan states in the referendums of decolonisation-devolutions may create the "problem of grants of power in violation of self-determination". Two common problems may be distinguished: the first may be that the metropolitan states may attempt to outwit their international obligations, giving an illegitimate function to "unrepresentative" and "entrenched" people regarding the decision of the international status of the territory in question.[33] This is one of the most frequent legal problems of sovereignty referendums: the question of voter qualification, whereby a group of people politically or ethnically attached to the metropolitan state claim voting rights in the referendum.

5.2.2 Reunification of Divided States

The concept of "divided states" appeared after World War II, when certain territorial units were divided into two or more separate units of administration. These bodies had once been either one single state or at least "distinct territories" before

[30] Crawford (2006), pp. 350 and 500.

[31] In fact, unitary-state devolutions involve transfer of certain state powers upon a region where the outcome may be an extensive reconstruction of the constitutional structure of the state, until it transforms into a quasi-federal one. Different devolution experiences, such as those of Belgium, Spain, the United Kingdom, show us that, in contrast to the equality of the constituent units in a federal state, devolution creates a constitutional structure where different regions or communities have different constitutional competences (Crawford 2006, p. 500). See also Lijphart (1999), pp. 186–197.

[32] Crawford (2006), pp. 349–350.

[33] Crawford (2006), p. 333.

their division. In practice, the term "divided states" is used when two or more separate states or effective governments appear, dividing a single "people" or "nation", or a distinct geographical entity. Division of these states is considered as having a transitive or temporary status, either by the international community or by the relevant states themselves. The case of the two German states between 1945 and 1990 illustrates this concept. The Tripartite Convention on Relations of 26 May 1952 was the final document in the process of the establishment of the Federal Republic, by the part of Germany controlled by the Western Allies. Article 10 of this Convention said it was to remain in force only "until Germany is re-united".[34] In the same way, the constitution of South Korea stipulates, "The Republic of Korea seeks unification and formulates and carries out a policy of peaceful unification based on the principles of freedom and democracy" (Article 4).

This temporary character generates the question of the legal framework of the prospective reunification of divided states; referendums may be found in most of these legal frameworks. The South Korean Constitution provides for a facultative referendum on the initiative of the president, inter alia, on "unification" (Article 72).

5.2.3 *Unions and Federations of States*

Other groups of referendums occur in the case of the establishment of any relation of dependency between one state and another or a total or partial merger of the states so that they constitute a single new international body/person or the extinction of a state by the absorption of another, where the latter remains as the same international body/person. The widely held doctrinal distinction of such political unions is four-type: real and personal unions, federations and confederations. Among these, only the federation has actual existence.[35]

Creation of federations may be considered as the most common issue of referendums.[36] In terms of state creation, the creation of a federal state may involve two successive processes of extinction of the statehood of the component entities and creation of the federal state having exclusive international personality in terms of international law.[37]

---

[34] Crawford (2006), p. 455.

[35] "Personal unions are those where two states being wholly distinct and separate have the same ruling prince. Such unions became 'real' where certain state functions such as foreign affairs, defence or finance are delegated to joint institutions". Real and personal unions have a mere historical value. The last personal union, the Swedish-Norwegian union, ended on June 1905 with Norway's separation after a referendum (Crawford 2006, p. 482; Pavkovic and Radan 2007, pp. 68–73).

[36] Crawford (2006), p. 479; Oppenheim (1996), p. 210.

[37] Crawford (2006), p. 484.

In some cases, federal state formation may take the form of "remedial federations" where a legal instrument (constitution or treaty) of federal arrangements is introduced to overcome a political deadlock, often associated with secession and ethnic strife. Federation in Bosnia–Herzegovina is an example of this sort, and referendums have been commonly resorted to as a legitimating tool in such cases. The 2004 referendum on Cyprus unification may be considered under this heading. Similarly, the Comoros was reconstituted as a "Union of the Comoros" under a Framework Agreement signed on 17 February 2001. An ensuing *Loi Fondamentale de l'Union* was ratified by a referendum on 23 December 2001.[38]

Sometimes referendums are held on the formation of certain state-unions, which constitute "unusual formations", thus do not fit either category of unitary or federal states. Two referendums held in 1958 and 1971 in an attempt to establish the United Arab Republic by Egypt and Syria may be categorised as such.[39]

A further distinct category relates to "unions of states in international organizations". When states form an international organisation such as the UN, NATO, OAU or a supranational community like the EU, the process involves two distinct issues: the creation of separate international personality of the international organisation and transfer of "important sovereign rights" by the member states so that the organization may perform acts on behalf of member states. Among these, the EU is an outstanding example with its highly developed "centralizing organization" and an "unprecedented degree of functional unification".[40]

5.3 Legal Status of Sovereignty Referendums in Contemporary International Law

5.3.1 Legal Base: Hard Law and Soft Law

The main question in this section is: where do referendums stand in the procedural framework of state creation? With respect to the legal status of sovereignty referendums in international law, we should firstly distinguish between hard law and soft law. The former includes, *inter alia*, two traditional sources, treaties and customary law, whereas the latter implies the non-legally binding instruments used in contemporary international relations by states and international organisations. Soft law includes instruments such as state conference declarations, UN instruments (most notably the General Assembly resolutions in our case), codes of conduct, guidelines and recommendations of international organisations or supranational communities

[38] Crawford (2006), p. 490.

[39] The union of Senegal and Gambia (1982–1999), the union between Morocco (Referendum, 1984) and Libya (1984–1986).

[40] Crawford (2006), pp. 495–499.

(most notably in our case, the European Union).[41] Soft law is not law *per se*, but "it may be evidence of existing law or formative of the *opinio juris*, or State practice that generates new customary law". [42]

We should remember at this point the fundamental difference between international law and national law: the principle of sovereign equality of states excludes a superior lawmaking body above the states, as well as a centralised police enforcing power. This latter problem also blurs the line between hard and soft laws and encourages us to try not to stick to an excessive formalism and overlook the importance of the soft law instruments. Soft laws are the formal channels through which arguments of consent-based legitimacy flow backwards and forwards between national and international forums.

One may recall the incontestable moral authority of arguments of consent-based legitimacy in modern international relations. It may be argued that democratic norms in the exercise of political power have become prevailing maxims in international and national legal orders. Moreover, there is a process of merger of international and national legal orders in this respect. Lachmayer observes the interrelationships of domestic constitutional law, international law and European law: "[B]etween all three legal areas, direct and indirect legal influences exist, regulated by one or more of the different legal systems".[43] Wet argues that there is "an emerging international constitutional order consisting of an international community, an international value system and rudimentary structures for its enforcement". The democratic norms and basic tenets of human rights now constitute the fundamental elements of the "International Value System", including all other norms "with a strong ethical underpinning, which have been integrated by states into the norms of positive law and acquired a special hierarchical standing through State practice".[44] Franck stated at the beginning of the 1990s that the consent of the governed, i.e. "the democratic entitlement", has become "a new legal entitlement" for states in international law. This is "based in part on custom and in part on the collective interpretation of treaties" Moreover, he observed that the growing use of internationally organised and monitored sovereignty referendums were one of the elements of an "international rule system that defined the minimal requisites of a democratic process capable of validating the exercise of power".[45]

This shows that not only the legal status of rules concerning referendums but also their moral authority should be considered. In other words, the undeniably overwhelming authority of soft law instruments concerning self-determination and other democratic principles of state creation blur the line between hard law and soft law instruments. This is eloquently defined by Brownlie, who maintained that UN resolutions on decolonisation adopted by the quasi-totality of the member states

[41] Aust (2005), p. 12.

[42] Boyle (2006), p. 141; Thirlway (2006), p. 118.

[43] Lachmayer (2007), pp. 92–93.

[44] de Wet (2006), pp. 51 and 57.

[45] Franck (1992), pp. 47–49.

have "a quasi-constitutional status". Thus, for the rest of this study, soft law instruments, particularly the UN resolutions, will be referred to, without reservation, as legal bases having the same value as hard law instruments.

With respect to the particular question of hard law, a reflection should be made, firstly, with regard to the presence and status of sovereignty referendums in international treaties, and secondly, one may consider seeking the answer to the question as to whether referendums are now a rule of customary law.

5.3.2 Sovereignty Referendums in International Treaties

When a sovereignty referendum is treaty based, it typically appears as a complementary element in the cession treaties, i.e., the international treaties regulating the "peaceful transfer of a territory".[46] The legal nature of cession referendums may be described as an "additional condition" to the treaty of territorial adjustments, in that the international law stipulates only one requisite for the cession of territory: namely, the consent of the ceding state. This consent may be expressed through the competent body according to the domestic legislation of the state in question.[47] Furthermore, the legal nature of referendum clauses in cession treaties may be either suspensive or resolutory. When it is suspensive, a result in favour of the prospective acquiring state has to be obtained in the referendum for the cession to provide a legal effect. Almost all of the post-WWI referendums were suspensive, giving a veto right to the population concerned before the transfer of territory. When referendums are designed to have a resolutory effect on the transfer of territory, the acquiring state is conferred the sovereignty of the territory beforehand, and it is charged with the duty to organise a referendum within a specified period after the transfer of sovereignty. If the outcome of the referendum disfavours the newly acquiring state, it has the duty to retrocede the territory.

Treaties may be bilateral or multilateral. The first bilateral treaty, providing for a referendum in history, was between France and the Kingdom of Sardinia, predecessor of modern Italy: The Treaty of Turin (1860) concluded the cession of Savoy and Nice to France. Article 1 permitted the adhesion of the territories to France on the precondition of the consent of the inhabitants, albeit leaving the modality to the contracting parties.[48] Similar clauses could be found in the cession treaties between Greece and the United Kingdom on the cession of Ionian Islands (1863), Austria and Italy on the retrocession of Venetia and Lombardy to Italy (1866) and Denmark and the United States on the cession of the islands of St. Thomas and St. Jean (1867).

---

[46] Gawenda (1946), p. 101.

[47] Gawenda (1946), p. 103.

[48] Gawenda (1946), p. 55.

International law became acquainted with multilateral treaties as the legal base of the referendums after WWI. The Paris Peace Treaties were signed between the victorious allies of WWI on the one side and the defeated states on the other: namely, among others, the Treaty of Versailles with Germany and the Treaty of Saint-Germain with Austria. These treaties, which regulated the territorial adjustment of post-war Europe, provided for referendums to settle the territorial disputes between Germany and Poland on Upper Silesia, and Allenstein and Marienwerder (Treaty of Versailles, Articles 88, 94, 95, 96 and 97); between Germany and Denmark on Schleswig and Holstein (Treaty of Versailles, Articles 109 and 110); and between Austria and Yugoslavia on Klagenfurt (Treaty of Saint-Germain, Article 50).

Referendums may be found in treaties or agreements where the parties may appear to be not only the states but also other subjects of international law. In this context, it may be noted that only special types of international personalities/bodies are recognised and accepted under the doctrine of international law as agents of treaty making. Most particularly, non-self-governing peoples and "belligerent and insurgent communities" may be noted as two possible non-state parties to a treaty stipulating a referendum. In the case of New Caledonia, for instance, a future referendum is included in the Nouméa Accord concluded between France and the independence movement of the region, *Front de libération nationale kanak et socialiste* (FLNKS). Also, the representatives of the secessionist groups outside the decolonisation context may be a party to a treaty as the legal base for a referendum. This is the case in the Comprehensive Peace Agreement signed by the Government of Sudan and the Sudan People's Liberation Movement/Army.[49]

5.3.3 Sovereignty Referendums in Customary Law

5.3.3.1 State of Doctrine

The classical view is that referendums are not necessarily part of customary law. According to Oppenheim: "Several treaties of cession concluded during the nineteenth century stipulated that the cession should only be valid provided the inhabitants consented to it through a plebiscite. But it cannot be said that international law makes it a condition of every cession that it should be ratified by a plebiscite." In the same way, Cavaré notes that the plebiscite clauses in cession treaties were of

[49] In this context, Brownlie notes that "In practice, belligerent and insurgent communities within a state may enter into legal relations and conclude agreements valid on the international plane with states and other belligerents and insurgents. Belligerent community often represents a political movement aiming at independence and secession" (Brownlie 2003, p. 63; see also Aust 2005, p. 14).

a facultative nature and by no means an indispensable element for the legal validity of an act of cession.[50]

Rudrakumaran undertook to answer the question of whether the "requirement of plebiscite in territorial rapprochement" was a part of customary international law and arrived at a negative conclusion. With respect to state practice, he noted that the nineteenth century and post-WWI referendums "were not held consistently and were often influenced by historic and strategic considerations". He also assumed that *opinio juris* had always been absent in past practices: "plebiscites were employed primarily for reasons of political expediency, and not due to perceived legal obligations".[51]

Supporters of the "plebiscite" rest their view on natural law theories and the consent-based legitimacy arguments of self-determination and national and popular sovereignty. The normative assumption that people should be consulted when a territorial adjustment is at issue may be traced back to Erasmus, who opposed the right to conquest and asserted that any authority over people is only possible with their consent. This assumption has purportedly induced the consultations made (as generally mentioned) in the three bishoprics[52] of Verdun Metz and Toul.[53] Grotius wrote in 1625, "To render the alienation of the whole public dominion valid…and to confirm the transfer of any particular portion, the consent of the whole body as well as of that particular member will be necessary: for otherwise such alienation would be like the violent separation of a limb from the natural body".[54] Kant in his Perpetual Peace renounced the forceful annexation of the states or territories of states by other states. For him, such acts were against the idea of "the original contract".[55]

Induced by these moral arguments, the French and Italian writers of the late nineteenth and early twentieth centuries sought to sow the fundamentals of the "plebiscite" into the rhetoric of international law. For Fiore, the consent of the inhabitants for a valid cession had become an absolute principle in international law. Redslob asserted that despite its shortcomings, the referendum device was an

[50] Cavaré (1961), p. 355.

[51] Rudrakumaran (1990), pp. 29–31.

[52] The term "bishopric" refers to the "territorial jurisdiction of a bishop" (http://www.merriam-webster.com/dictionary/diocese; http://www.merriam-webster.com/dictionary/bishopric. Retrieved 23 June 2013).

[53] Scelle ([1932–1934] 1984), p. 263.

[54] Hugo Grotius, The Rights of War and Peace, including the Law of Nature and of Nations, translated from the Original Latin of Grotius, with Notes and Illustrations from Political and Legal Writers, by A.C. Campbell, A.M. with an Introduction by David J. Hill (New York: M. Walter Dunne, 1901). CHAPTER XX: On the Public Faith, by which War is Concluded; Comprising Treaties of Peace, and the Nature of Arbitration, Surrender Hostages, Pledges (http://oll.libertyfund.org/title/553/90825/2054090. Retrieved 2 February 2011).

[55] Kant ([1795] 2006), p. 68.

integral element of international law and had thus become a custom.[56] Scelle, on the other hand, was more specific regarding the question of the consistent use of referendum in international law, noting that "l'ancienneté de la pratique du plébiscite est un indice de sa tendance à s'imposer en droit coutumier".[57]

When we evaluate Scelle's estimation in the light of more recent experiences, including post-WWII and post-communist referendums, we may assume that historical experiences are not a bulk of dispersed consultations held randomly out of political expedience. Rather, they are the practices and elements evolved and improved through time, in the pattern of the historical transformation of international law, regarding the legitimacy of territorial possession. This assumption may be deduced from Franck's observation, which supposes an evidence of "pedigree" and "coherence" for the rule of self-determination in the historical evolution of the contemporary system of international organisation and monitoring of sovereignty referendums.[58] Thus, the question as to whether the referendum requirement on territorial issues is now a customary rule may be reconsidered in the light of contemporary international norms regarding self-determination and state creation.

5.3.3.2 Are Referendums Part of Customary Law? A Reassessment

We may consider the customary status of sovereignty referendums in terms of the following issues: decolonisation, recognition of states and occupation.

Decolonisation: It was mentioned in the fourth chapter that the UN Charter provided two separate procedures for decolonisation, namely, Trust Territories (Art. 73) and Non-Self-Governing Territories (Art. 76), the difference between which has gradually eroded over the course of time through a series of UN General Assembly resolutions. Two classes of trusteeship were established, "the ordinary trusteeships" under the authority of the General Assembly and the "strategic trusteeships" (or Trust Territories of the Pacific Islands) under the authority of the Security Council.

Referendums were held in several trust territories pursuant to General Assembly resolutions to ensure "the freely expressed wishes of the peoples concerned" (UN Charter, Art. 76). Furthermore, certain GA resolutions laid down the basis of decolonisation referendums in international law. By Resolution No. 742, the UN assumed the authority to declare any territory as non-self-governing ("a decision may be taken by the Assembly on the continuation or cessation of the transmission of information as required by Chapter XI of the Charter"). According to this, a territory may be assumed to have attained self-government if (1) "Independence is

[56] Fiore P, Nouveau Droit International Public t. II p.6] cited in: (Gonssollin, 1921, p. 14); [Robert Redslob, Les principles de droit de gens moderne, Paris 1937], cited in: Gawenda, (1946), p. 153 and Amiel, (1976), p. 436, footnote 4.

[57] Scelle ([1932–1934] 1984), p. 277.

[58] Franck (1992), pp. 52–55.

achieved"; (2) For other options, "There is a voluntary decision which is capable of revision, and which is arrived at by an adequately informed population in an open and democratic process". By this resolution, the UN expressly favoured independent statehood, while other forms of self-government "appeared *prima facie* suspect".[59]

According to Resolution No. 1541, three options were offered to non-self-governing territories as their right to self-determination: the territories could constitute themselves as a sovereign independent state, associate freely with an independent state or integrate with an independent state already in existence.[60]

These resolutions have two important implications: (1) there is a convincing argument that status other than independence should be put to referendum, in that the above-said *prima facie suspect* creates a burden of proof on the administering state; (2) when a territory opts for certain forms of dependency, either association, integration or colonial *status quo*, the issue is not perceived to be resolved once and for all, and the right to independence of this territory remains intact. The status is discussed and re-evaluated at different intervals either within the internal politics of the territory or by international agents. In particular, the choice of "association" has been endorsed by the US in its relationship with the former Trust Territories of the Pacific Islands. The model, "Freely Associated States", allows the territories to emerge as an independent state while bestowing certain state competences, including defence and security, to the United States of America. As and when status is different from a full-fledged independence, "associations may require ongoing appraisal by the international community and periodic readjustment".[61] This explains the occurrence of several sovereignty referendums within the same territory (most notably, New Caledonia and Puerto Rico). In this context, either the terms of the association are reconsidered or there is a procrastinated process of the resolution of the status of a non-self-governing territory (New Caledonia, Mayotte and, controversially, Puerto Rico). In both cases, there is, as Crawford put it, a "continued expression of the right to self-determination of the people". [62]

Considering the explanations above, it may be safely assumed that it is now a customary rule that when a decolonisation-related territory is a subject of conflict in international law, creating an international status other than independence may only be legitimised through a democratic decision process. The use of the referendum device is a common state practice to ensure this democratic decision. The ramifications of this concept in national law may be observed in the relationship of New Caledonia and Mayotte with France, and Puerto Rico, the Republic of the Marshall

[59] Fastrenrath (2002), p. 1093.

[60] A/RES/1541: The UN General Assembly Resolution of 15 December 1960, on "*Principles which should guide members in determining whether or nor an obligation exists to transmit the information called for under Article 73 e of the Charter*".

[61] Keitner and Reisman (2003), p. 62.

[62] Crawford (2006), p. 633.

Islands and the Federated States of Micronesia and Palau with the US. These cases will be discussed in details below.

Cession, Secession and Recognition of States: Whereas the substantial meaning of self-determination is very well established and clarified in the context of decolonisation, whether it confers the right of secession on the dissident ethnic groups and regions from nation states remains problematic. As argued in the previous chapter, this ambiguity constitutes the problem of the indeterminacy of the law of self-determination.

International lawyers need not be reminded of the common view that the formation or disappearance of a state is "a pure fact, a political matter remaining outside the realm of law".[63] Indeed, "the classical criteria for statehood were essentially based on effectiveness". Yet in the history of international relations, there have been effective entities that have not been recognised as states, as well as non-effective entities that have not ceased to be considered as states. Indeed, entities created in violation of *jus cogens* have always met with collective non-recognition by the international community, and the same is true for the extinction of states in an identical way. Therefore, "there is nothing incoherent about the legal regulation of statehood on a basis other than that of effectiveness".[64]

A mere referendum does not automatically confer on the breakaway communities the right of independence. This is the natural corollary of the indeterminacy of the law of self-determination regarding the right to secession. On the other hand, referendums fulfil a double function in the recognition of the seceding territories as a new state: (1) they serve as evidence to the international community that the secessionist actors have effective control of the disputed territory backed by the support of the relevant people; (2) they do not have this effective control against the wish of relevant people—that is, the new state is not born in violation of *jus cogens*. It is true that self-determination is unclear as a positive effect, i.e., whether self-determination means an outright secession of any ethnic group from a state. But its negative effect is clear: secession or other forms of state creation against the clear wish of the relevant population are deemed outrageous in international law and contrary to *jus cogens*. In other words, in the cases where the substantial content of self-determination is unclear (the question of "if"), the legality (or lawfulness) of state creation (the question of "how") comes into play as a secondary supportive norm, along with the effectiveness.[65]

Commenting on the requirement of the referendum in the Western Sahara case, Cassese stated[66]:

> Self-determination requires a free and genuine expression of the will of the peoples concerned: The principle lays down the method by which States must reach decisions concerning peoples: by heeding their freely expressed will. In contrast, the principle points

---

[63] Tancredi (2006), pp. 171–172.

[64] Crawford (2006), pp. 97–106; for the concept of collective recognition, see Grant (1999).

[65] Crawford (2006), pp. 128–131.

[66] Cassese (2001), p. 107.

neither to the various specific areas in which self-determination should apply, nor to the final goal of self-determination (internal self-government, independent statehood, association with or integration into another State, or the free choice of any other political status.)

The importance of procedural legitimacy was illustrated in the example of Southern Rhodesia. The referendum on the constitution by which the white minority government declared independence was declared as invalid by the UN, and a General Assembly resolution "Condemned the unilateral declaration of independence made by the racist minority Southern Rhodesia".[67] As Warbrick notes, the illegality of the Southern Rhodesian claim to independence stemmed from the fact that it "had been established without the consent of the people of the territory as a whole. . ."[68]

The international norms of fair popular consultation evolved significantly in the case of post-communist state creation: referendums were initially used, unilaterally by the actors for strategic reasons during the struggle of secession, as a sociological legitimating weapon. Then the international community endorsed it as an appropriate argument in the process of their recognition. The growing importance of legitimation via referendum was demonstrated by the international community's satisfaction in the case of the Baltic countries and by its request that a referendum be held, for example, in the case of the dissolution of Yugoslavia.

During the dissolution of Yugoslavia, the referendum was requested by the Badinter Commission, via its successive opinions, as a condition for the recognition of emerging states (Slovenia, Croatia, Bosnia–Herzegovina and Macedonia) by the European Community States.[69] The Commission had been initially established as an advisory body. When the process of dissolution proved to be irreversible, the Commission evolved to act as an arbitral committee to exert influence on the process of emergence of the new states.

With its Opinion No. 4, it recommended that a referendum be held under international supervision as a condition for the recognition of Bosnia–Herzegovina. Concerning Macedonia, Opinion 6 of the Commission noted the independence referendum "with approval". The independence referendum held in Slovenia was also mentioned in the Commission's Opinion regarding the recognition of the Republic of Slovenia by the European Community and its member states (Opinion No. 7).

The opinions of the Commission were consultative, and their soft law status goes without saying. The UN admitted Croatia, Slovenia, and Bosnia disregarding whether or not a referendum had been held. For this reason, "it is difficult to draw conclusions as to the extent of UN deference to the Badinter Commission holdings". Nevertheless, these documents constitute a significant breakthrough in

[67] A/RES/2024(XX): The UN General Assembly Resolution on the "*Question of Southern Rhodesia*" of 11 November 1965.

[68] Warbrick (2006), p. 235.

[69] For the text of Opinions 1–3, see Pellet (1992), pp. 182–185. For the text of Opinions 4–10, see Türk (1993), pp. 74–91.

international law, in that they transformed the moral arguments of consent on secession into a more formal format: to a "juridical form".[70] Referendums are acknowledged in this framework as the most convenient method for the ascertainment of the wishes of the people concerned in the process of secession and state creation. In this vein, Tancredi argues that there is a growing bulk of international norms, constituting a "normative course through which secessionist processes are channeled". Referendums are undoubtedly part of this "normative due process through which a secessionist act must happen".[71] Likewise, Eisner maintains that, in the face of the "weakness of using substantive criteria to judge current secessionist claims", referendums may be used, "in the heart of a procedural model", which may legitimately resolve the secessionist disputes.[72]

In the light of these explanations, the doctrine supporting the view that referendums for secession and cession is a customary rule deserves a reappraisal. Cassese argues that "self-determination renders null and void treaties providing for the transfer of territories, where such treaties do not include provision for any prior genuine consultation of the population involved".[73] We assume that this is not a mere restatement of the two century-old Grotiusian pro-referendum doctrine. It also rests on the developments of the contemporary international law of self-determination, particularly those on decolonisation and post-communist state creation. In other words, a requisite for the consent of the people is the corollary of the peremptory international legal duty on the states: a ban on foreign military occupation and the protection of territorial integrity. Therefore, in this case, referendums appear to be an indispensable part of international law: ensuring the negative right of self-determination by giving people the power of veto concerning dissolution, secession and cession of their state or territory.[74]

Occupation: Traditionally, occupation is considered as one of the ways of territorial acquisitions by states. Yet, today, almost every part of the world belongs to a state. Considering the *jus cogens* norms prohibiting the forceful annexation of a territory belonging to another state, occupation does not have any actual practical significance, in terms of legitimate acquisition of a territory by an occupying state. On the other hand, the concept of "belligerent occupation" is highly visible and present in contemporary international relations. This term indicates an effective establishment and exercise of authority by an army of one state upon the territory of another state.

The legality and/or legitimacy of such actions differ in the contemporary practice of military occupation of states and international organisations. There is a wide range of motives and methods of military occupations, ranging from UN peacekeeping operations for humanitarian intervention to illegal occupations by

[70] Grant (1999), pp. 161–165.
[71] Tancredi (2006), p. 189.
[72] Eisner (1992), p. 419.
[73] Cassese (2001), p. 108.
[74] Eisner (1992), p. 422.

individual states. Benvenisti discerns state-led occupations in four distinct categories[75]: the first group involves the occupations by states attempting to annex adjacent territories, as seen in the case of Kuwait (by Iraq-1990), Western Sahara (by Morocco in 1975) and East Timor (by Indonesia in 1975). The second category includes occupations where the occupants claim a voluntary invitation by the lawful government of the occupied country. The third category includes the armed interventions of a foreign state to implement the right to self-determination of a certain region at the expense of the territorial integrity of the occupied state. Examples include the emergence of Bangladesh after the Indian occupation and the Turkish Republic of Northern Cyprus after the Turkish occupation of the region in 1974.

Finally, in the fourth group, there are short-termed "limited-purpose occupations" such as the Coalition Occupation of Southern and Northern Iraq, concerning which the purported purpose was to deliver humanitarian assistance to the Kurdish refugees.

The legal appraisals and international reactions have varied from one incident to another, and a detailed analysis of this aspect is irrelevant to our study. On the other hand, these interventions have commonly created factual or legal conditions, resulting in territorial disputes in which referendums play a certain role for the post-occupation political settlement (East Timor, 1999; Cyprus, 2004; Western Sahara, to be implemented). There may be two conclusions considering these referendums: firstly, it is an established rule in customary international law that the occupying power is not deemed as sovereign and is precluded from annexing the territory or transforming its political structure.[76] Therefore, this rule excludes the choice of annexation to the occupant country in an eventual referendum. Secondly, a rightfully administered and internationally monitored referendum may play a legitimating role and correct the error, if there is any, caused by an act of occupation. Benvenisti notes that "infringements of the law of occupation, if such existed, (may be) healed by the institution of a democratic process through which the general public expresses its endorsement of the new political system".[77]

However, it is imperative to note that a referendum does not automatically legitimise an illegal occupation. Still, the legality of launching an occupation and its termination are two distinct problems. Notwithstanding the above-said diversity of the perceptions of legitimacy regarding the initiation of occupations, their termination rests solely on a settlement that enjoys the consent of the indigenous populations. It may be well argued that this is now an established rule of customary international law. As Benvenisti puts it: "The survey of contemporary occupations and of recent international instruments, has shown that the modern occupant is considered to be relieved of its duties as occupant once its forces have transferred control over an occupied territory…to an indigenous government that enjoys the support of the majority of the population".[78] Thus, referendums are resorted to in

[75] Benvenisti (1993), pp. 149–181.

[76] Benvenisti (1993), p. 3.

[77] Benvenisti (1993), p. 171.

[78] Benvenisti (1993), p. 215.

such cases to demonstrate that this is the case. In short, the termination of occupation, or any relevant interim administration, is the by-product of the outcome of referendums associated with the solution of the main territorial issue.

The explanations made so far offer substantial arguments deeming the requirement of referendums that the international law imposes as a condition for territorial alterations. However, the basis of the involvement of the international community in the implementation of these referendums remains unclear. One noteworthy observation is that states do not deny the principle of the right of people to be consulted about the status of their territory. Objection is made to the legal origin and the bases of this practice in international law. Amiel underlined this fact, through a comparison of the two basic conceptions of international law within the context of sovereignty referendums. The objectivist conception, which sees the existence of international law independent of the will of the States, assumes that "a plebiscite" is a rule binding on the states irrespective of their consent. On the contrary, the voluntarist conception claims that the sole legal source of the "plebiscite" is the consent of the state concerned. The advocates of the objectivist conception assert that referendums are part of customary law, as well as emanating from the resolutions of the General Assembly. The supporters of the voluntarist conception, on the contrary, claim that UN resolutions have no binding legal force on the states. The legal bases are provided by the consent of the states concerned, on an ad hoc basis, which should be taken neither as a consistent state practice nor as a formation of *opinio juris*.[79]

One of the most common consequences of the state-centred approach to sovereignty referendums in international law is the non-binding nature and indirect effect of the referendums that are held in the confines of international law. Indeed, the referendums of the nineteenth and early twentieth centuries were treaty based: i.e., state consent was the primary element of the legal base of the referendums. The referendums in these treaties were mere conditional elements of the cession of the territory. The cession treaties produced legal effects, not directly after the referendums but after municipal legal acts for the inclusion of the said treaties into domestic law.[80]

Thus, we may infer from these explanations that virtually no state denies, in principle, that the popular consultation is a requisite to legitimise the territorial changes. Most states consider it as a legal rule, but one that is at their discretion and can only be used under their national legal framework and control.[81] This is the natural corollary of one basic tenet of international law: consent of the states is one of the primary sources of international law. The extent of involvement of the international community is negatively linked to the existence of effective state power. Under revolutionary conditions where there is a lack of effective state

[79] Amiel (1976), pp. 436–444.

[80] Gawenda (1946), pp. 104–105.

[81] Amiel (1976), p. 429.

power, the international organisations are more visible, whereas in more stable conditions, states assume the implementation of the referendums. In the following section, we will deal with the nature and degree of involvement of the international community regarding the decision and implementation of sovereignty referendums from this perspective.

5.4 International Monitoring and Administration of Sovereignty Referendums

The international legal order, in which sovereignty referendums are decided and organised, pertains to a broader question of "international procedures relating to territorial dispositions". These procedures may involve "agreements between the states concerned", "joint decision of principal powers" and "Action by United Nation Organs".[82] Notwithstanding the principle of equality of states in international law, the pre-eminence of certain principal powers to bring about territorial changes and create new territorial units has been an indispensable element in international law.

In many cases, and this is as true of the nineteenth century as of the twentieth, international action has been decisive: international organisations or groups of states—especially the so-called Great Powers—have exercised a collective authority to supervise, regulate and condition such new creations. In some cases, the action takes the form of the direct establishment of the new state. . .whereas in others. . .it is rather a form of collective recognition.[83]

The experience of nineteenth-century state formation illustrates the preliminary pattern of the influence of "Great Powers" in territorial readjustments. Europe was the principal political power in these territorial settlements, taking a leading role in the negotiation and conciliation between parties, as well as providing opportunities and support for peace treaties and, as shown above, the several cession referendums that were held according to these treaties.[84] During this period, except for a couple of attempts, none of the referendums were administered by an international body. Among the embryonic international administrations was that of the referendum held in Moldavia and Wallachia (1857).[85]

In the post-WWI peace settlements, the role of the victors was decisive. Referendums, as part of the Paris Peace Treaties, were used tactically by the victors for the reformation of the Central European states at the expense of the defeated states. In this context, the most common criticism is that referendums were used

[82] Brownlie (2003), p. 168.

[83] Crawford (2006), p. 501.

[84] Crawford (2006), pp. 505–513.

[85] Eric Brahm, "Election Monitoring", (http://www.beyondintractability.org/essay/election-monitoring. Retrieved 12 August 2013).

selectively according to the wishes of the victors at the expense of defeated nations, namely, Germany and Austria. For instance, among the post-First World War sovereignty referendums, the referendum of Upper Silesia (1921) was the only one held as the concession to Germany.[86] Despite the lack of standard of application, post-WWI experience ascertained the ability of the referendums for the effective resolution of the territorial disputes. It is argued that "most neutral observers assert these referendums worked remarkably well", so that they resolved the disputes in the related areas decisively.[87] Besides, it may also be argued that these referendums constituted a significant breakthrough, by establishing a pattern for international involvement and tackling the many issues arising. Among these issues, the most notable included the neutralisation of the area, voter qualification, impartiality of referendum administration, international monitoring and effective and democratic campaigning.

From WWII onwards, the UN has been assumed to be the principal actor in the resolution of territorial disputes and creation of states. Before the UN, international intervention into sovereignty referendums was based on the explicit prescriptions on treaties. The UN has assumed this authority and responsibility in its intervention into referendums without any explicit rules in the UN Charter but rather by an interpretation of it.[88]

Broadly speaking, UN involvement into territorial issues may be examined under three categories: the first category of acts comprises those fulfilled by the UN as explicitly or implicitly authorised by the UN Charter. The competence of the General Assembly for the admission of new states and competences pertaining to the Trust Territories and Non-Self-Governing Territories fall into this category. The second category includes those acts that are not prohibited by the Charter and delegated to the United Nations by the related states. In this case, the UN may be present in the process of resolution of a territorial conflict by virtue of a request in the form of an agreement between the parties. An act fulfilled on the request of the states or other international actors is also considered as an act of the UN, to the extent that the purpose of that act falls under the purposes of the United Nations under Articles 1 and 2 and upon the condition that it is not forbidden by the Charter. Formally, such an act takes the form of an act of the UN, through authorisation by the appropriate organ or through its normal voting procedure. The third category includes acts that normally fall under state competence but where member states use the UN as a forum to perform these acts collectively. Collective recognition or non-recognition of states may be mentioned as a primary example in this category.[89]

The Security Council has a significant role within the international legal system of territorial disposition. The competences enumerated in Chapter VII provide the

[86] Beigbeder (1994), p. 82; Laghmani (1998), p. 203.

[87] Farley (1986), p. 34.

[88] Laghmani (1998), p. 205.

[89] Crawford (2006), p. 550.

way for the Council to be a decisive actor in the case of territorial disputes, either between two or more states or within a state between the government and secessionist groups. Article 33 says:

> The parties to any dispute, the continuance of which is likely to endanger the maintenance of international peace and security, shall, first of all, seek a solution by negotiation, enquiry, mediation, conciliation, arbitration, judicial settlement, resort to regional agencies or arrangements, or other peaceful means of their own choice. The Security Council shall, when it deems necessary, call upon the parties to settle their dispute by such means.

Under Article 39, the Security Council is authorised to take any "measures" it sees fit to prevent "the existence of any threat to the peace, breach of the peace, or act of aggression" and to "maintain or restore peace and security". One principle that should be underlined here is that, "even acting under Chapter VII of the Charter itself, the Security Council has no power to abrogate or alter territorial rights. . .or sovereignty".[90]

However, this limit does not obstruct the Security Council from being a fundamental actor in territorial disputes and taking its central role in the related referendums. As will be seen in detail in the cases of Western Sahara, East Timor, South Sudan and Cyprus, the Security Council, if not directly involved in the whole process of referendums, swings like a sword of Damocles over the parties to the conflict (i.e., central state authorities or occupant states, regional governments and national liberation movements).

Another important actor within the UN is the Secretary General. The Secretary General is an active and decisive element in the settlement of various territorial disputes between states or between central authorities and secessionist groups. The Secretary General becomes a part of the process of resolution of territorial conflicts under his "good offices" mission (particularly in Cyprus, East Timor, Western Sahara and South Sudan). The concept of good offices of the Secretary General may be defined as the "steps taken publicly and in private, drawing upon his independence, impartiality and integrity, to prevent international disputes from arising, escalating or spreading".[91] The good offices mission finds its legal basis in Articles 98 and 99 of the Charter. Article 98 gives the diverse UN organs—the General Assembly, the Security Council, the Economic and Social Council and the Trusteeship Council—the competence to assign and to act as a mediator wherever there is a territorial conflict. Article 99, on the other hand, gives the Secretary General the right to assume for himself the mediating role between the parties: "The Secretary-General may bring to the attention of the Security Council any matter which in his opinion may threaten the maintenance of international peace and security".

Finally, we should mention the central role of the General Assembly in sovereignty referendums, most notably, in those pertaining to decolonisation. The legal

[90] [Judge Fitzmaurice, ICJ Rep. 1971 p. 294], cited in Crawford (2006), p. 552.

[91] "The Role of the Secretary General" (http://www.un.org/News/ossg/sg/pages/sg_office.html, Retrieved 16 May 2012).

competence of the General Assembly to decide whether or not to hold a referendum in a trust or non-self-governing territory has been assumed to be one of the implied and derived powers of the UN under the Charter. In this context, the International Court of Justice held: "The right of self-determination leaves the General Assembly a measure of discretion with respect to the forms and procedures by which that right is to be realized".[92] Generally, the decision to hold and intervene in the referendums concerning decolonisation may be taken either on the initiative of the General Assembly or upon a request from the administrating state or from two states by virtue of a bilateral agreement or treaty. In any case, such a decision takes the form of a unilateral action of the UN, from a resolution of the General Assembly, the Security Council or the Trusteeship Council.[93]

The particular question of the place of referendums in the framework of the Trusteeship Agreements was discussed by Merle, who maintained that the competence of the General Assembly to hold a referendum was indisputable in view of Articles 76 and 85 of the UN Charter. In fact, these articles contain no specific provisions regarding the termination of trusteeship, nor do they provide an explicit competence to hold referendums. Article 76 (b) put the Objectives of the Trusteeship as the promotion of "the political, economic, social, and educational advancement of the inhabitants of the trust territories, and their progressive development towards self-government or independence" in compliance with the "the freely expressed wishes of the peoples concerned". Article 85 says: "The functions of the United Nations with regard to trusteeship agreements for all areas not designated as strategic, including the approval of the terms of the trusteeship agreements and of their alteration or amendment, shall be exercised by the General Assembly". The right of the General Assembly to terminate the agreements of trusteeship, albeit not explicitly specified, has been deemed as a competence a fortiori, according to the reading of Article 85. The decision to hold a referendum in this process might easily be considered as an inherent and implied competence. Thus, a cross-evaluation of Articles 76 and 85 of the Charter unequivocally provided the legal mandate of the UN: the General Assembly is entitled to (1) assess whether the degree of advancement reached by the territory justifies the termination of the trusteeship, (2) consult the peoples concerned in the process of such an assessment.[94]

The competence of the General Assembly to decide whether or not to hold a referendum is also very well established with respect to non-self-governing territories. As mentioned above, the category of non-self-governing territories presents no substantial difference compared to trust territories, in terms of decolonisation law. Respective General Assembly resolutions (Nos 742, 1514 and 1541) are the legal bases instituting the plenary power of the General Assembly to decide whether

[92] Western Sahara, Advisory Opinion of 16 October 1975, ICJ Reports (1975), p. 12, para. 71.

[93] Laghmani (1998), p. 205.

[94] Merle (1961), pp. 427–428.

a territory is self-governing, and the competence to apply popular consultation is deemed to exist a fortiori inherent in that power:

> The General Assembly, because of its competence to decide when territory has exercised self-determination, could take the initiative and determine that a plebiscite should be held in a particular territory as a condition for recognizing that it has exercised self-determination. Hence it could also uphold or dismiss a claim by a third state that a plebiscite should be held in non-self governing territory according to its own interpretation what self-determination means for the territory in question.[95]

Thus, bearing on its disposition to decide on the international status of the above-said territories, the General Assembly has used three methods in that respect: referendums, elections and commissions of inquiry. The General Assembly required referendums in three circumstances: for cases where there were other options than independence or where the local organ claiming independence had not been elected by universal suffrage or where an additional salient sovereignty issue accompanied the main question of the future international status of the territory.

In certain cases of independence, the General Assembly was concerned that a puppet government of the former colonial state would be in power after gaining independence. In such cases, it assumed that "a formal expression of will by the inhabitants of the colony is not necessary, and that the possible wish of the colony is to become independent" and opted for elections on the basis of universal suffrage, instead of referendums. Finally, Commissions of Inquiry were used when there was a need to resolve the issue with a "quieter method". This was the case for the ascertainment of the wishes of the people living in territories in dispute.[96]

5.4.1 The Evolution of the Function of the UN in the Sovereignty Referendums: From First-Generation to Second-Generation Operations

Having explained briefly the role of the UN in the decolonisation process, we may now turn to examine the historical evolution of its role in decolonisation referendums. During the first years of its existence, the UN did not act rigorously when approving the change of status of non-self-governing territories. Puerto Rico, Greenland, Surinam and Netherlands Antilles were all decided to be self-governing following processes where the UN had no supervising role. After 1965, when newly independent states entered the UN, a firm majority appeared that aimed at realising genuine consultations within the process of self-determination. Since then, the General Assembly has refused to approve those status changes in territories where the consultation has taken place without UN supervision. One of the reasons for refusing the referendum in French Somaliland was that France had not permitted the supervision of UN authorities. However, in the case of independence, there have

[95] Sureda (1973), p. 74.

[96] Sureda (1973), pp. 303–304.

been cases where the UN has accepted declarations of independence: the case of Fiji, for example, where the UN was not permitted to supervise the related consultation.[97] This may be explained by the UN's *prima facie* assumption that independence is a preferable option.

First-Generation Operations: As previously mentioned, the UN assumed a substantial function in ending Western colonialism. With the purpose of guaranteeing the genuine exercise of right to self-determination, it supervised or monitored the popular consultations or elections in trust and other non-self-governing territories.[98] The first generation monitoring missions included such operations carried out by the UN between 1952 and 1994 (the last one being that of Palau). These missions did not involve sovereign states and limited themselves to a single objective, i.e., a mere observation of the electoral process and subsequent reporting of the findings to the relevant body of the UN. They did not involve any further tasks such as nation building or the establishment of democratic institutions. Consequently, they were small in size and had a limited mandate.[99]

Resolutions adopted by the General Assembly, the Security Council and the Trusteeship Council provided the legal mandate for diverse missions. The resolutions were adopted upon a demand of the Administering Authority or by reference to the recommendation of a preliminary UN visiting mission. In this framework, resolutions provided for the UN's involvement, the appointment of a plebiscite commissioner and the overall legal mandate of the missions. As a rule, all stages of the organisation and conduct of popular consultations were specified within these missions. They included basic rules for the referendums such as the measures to be taken by legal and electoral authorities for guaranteeing the absolute independence and neutrality, the scheme for voter education, monitoring of the political campaign, regulations for penalties in case of electoral fraud, a detailed timetable, the system of voting, counting and tabulation of the votes and the announcement of the results and instruments of appeal and review.[100]

British Togoland was the first trust territory to emerge as an independent state in 1957. Togoland was a former German colony, which had been divided after World War I into two territories to be administered, by the UK and France respectively, under the framework of League of Nations mandates. Upon the demand of the General Assembly, the Trusteeship Committee dispatched a mission to Togolands to examine the tendency of the people concerning several options of self-determination, namely, separate independence, unification and/or integration with the Gold Coast.[101]

On 15 December 1955, the General Assembly adopted a resolution calling for a referendum in British Togoland, under the supervision of the UN and to be

---

[97] Sureda (1973), p. 314.

[98] Beigbeder (1994), p. 97.

[99] Beigbeder (1994), p. 97.

[100] Beigbeder (1994), p. 97.

[101] A/RES/860(IX): The UN General Assembly Resolution, of 14 December 1959, on "*The Togoland unification problem and the future of the Trust Territory of Togoland under British administration*".

organised by the UK as the Administering Power. The referendum would be held to decide upon a proposed unification with Gold Coast, another British-administered territory, which was also in the process of independence. France was also invited to fulfil the same task as regards the part of the territory under its administration.[102]

The referendum was held in British Togoland on 9 May 1956 under the supervision of the UN. The outcome was in favour of union with the Gold Coast. Following the report of the Plebiscite Commissioner, verifying the fairness of the vote, the UN General Assembly welcomed the result of the referendum and approved the formation of the new State of Ghana, created through the unification of this territory with the Gold Coast.[103] In a similar pattern, referendums were held in the territories such as British Cameroons,[104] French Togoland,[105] Ruanda-Urundi,[106] Western Samoa,[107] Niue,[108] and Trust Territory of the Pacific Islands.

Second-Generation Operations: In contrast to first-generation operations, second-generation operations claimed the more ambitious tasks in the overcoming of regional conflicts, including peacekeeping, the establishment of

[102] Beigbeder (1994), p. 131; A/RES/944(X): The UN General Assembly Resolution of 15 December 1955, on "*The Togoland unification problem and the future of the Trust Territory of Togoland under British administration*".

[103] Beigbeder (1994), p. 132; A/RES/1044 (XI): The UN General Assembly Resolution of 13 December 1956, on "*The future of* Togoland *under British administration*".

[104] A/RES/1352/(XIV): The UN General Assembly Resolution of 16 October 1959, on "The future of the Trust Territory of the Cameroons under United Kingdom administration: organization of the plebiscite in the southern part of the Territory"; A/RES/1350(XIII): The UN General Assembly Resolution of 13 March 1959 "The future of the Trust Territory of the Cameroons under United Kingdom administration" A/RES/1608(XV) The UN General Assembly Resolution of 21 April 1961, on "The future of the Trust Territory of the Cameroons under United Kingdom administration", and A/RES/1473 (XIV): The UN General Assembly Resolution of 12 December 1959, on "The future of the Trust Territory of the Cameroons under United Kingdom administration: organization of a further plebiscite in the northern part of the Territory".

[105] In fact, a referendum was held in French Togoland on 28 October 1956, which gave the inhabitants the options of either remaining a Trust Territory or remaining as a part of France with greater autonomy. The outcome was about 93 % in favour of remaining in France with around 77 % turnout. However, the United Nations General Assembly refused to endorse the referendum, since the option of independence had not been included in the ballot question, and thus decided to continue the trusteeship. Consequently, the issue was resolved through a UN-supervised election of an assembly, which then decided on the final status of the territory—namely, independence. A/RES/1046 (XI): The UN General Assembly Resolution of 23 January 1957 on "*The future of Togoland under French administration*" A/RES/1416 (XIV): The UN General Assembly Resolution of 5 December 1959 on the "*Date of the independence of the Trust Territory of Togoland under French administration*".

[106] In Ruanda, the divisive issue of the status of the "Mwami" was resolved through a referendum. (A/RES/1744(XVI): "*Question of Mwami of Ruanda*" The UN General Assembly Resolution of 23 February 1962).

[107] A/RES/1569(XV) The UN General Assembly Resolution of 18 December 1960, on "*The Future of Western Samoa*"; The UN "endorse(d)" the referendum held in Western Samoa on independence 1 January 1962 and consequently "resolved" that the trusteeship status would be (deemed) to end on the same day. (A/RES/1626 (XVI): The UN General Assembly Resolution of 6 November 1961, on "*The Future of Western Samoa*").

[108] Igarashi (2002), pp. 155–168.

democratic institutions and nation building. Territories like Namibia and Western Sahara were included in these second-generation operations. These required a new style of peacekeeping force involving both military and civilian elements. For instance, in Namibia, while organising, planning, observing and verifying the electoral processes, UN officials also executed the tasks of peacekeeping, disarming the conflicting parties, protecting human rights and constructing a democratic society. Not only non-self-governing territories but also sovereign countries have been subject to second-generation operations in their transition to democracy.[109]

The UN's operations in territories and countries such as Namibia, Angola, Cambodia and Western Sahara are known as UN "peace-keeping operations". Although their major objective was constructing the appropriate environment for free and fair elections or referendum, and then organising or observing the process, the UN management was required to hold classical peacekeeping responsibilities in several territories. These duties would include, for instance, monitoring a ceasefire or disarming the conflicting parties, which may have had both military and civilian elements. The peacekeeping missions are established through resolutions, by the Security Council in line with its competences under the Chapter VII of the UN Charter and, in rare cases, by the General Assembly. These missions are considered as "subsidiary organs" of the UN. The tasks of organising, conducting, and directing the operation are undertaken by the Secretary General, who reports to and keeps the Security Council up to date—it being the body that has the ultimate authority on the operation.[110]

To summarise: since its foundation, the operations of the UN have evolved over time, providing progressively effective remedies for resolving territorial conflicts. With the advent of second-generation operations, the UN started to assume ever more important tasks in terms of state creation. In the following sections, we will evaluate the most recent cases, where the UN has played the central role in the administration of the related referendums.

5.4.2 Western Sahara

The UN listed Western Sahara, which had been a colony of Spain since 1884, as a non-self-governing territory in 1963. On December 1965, the General Assembly called upon Spain to fulfil the necessary actions for the decolonisation of its colonies.[111] The following year, in line with the proposals of the Special Committee

---

[109] Beigbeder (1994), p. 120.

[110] Beigbeder (1994), p. 114.

[111] A/RES/2072(XX): The UN General Assembly Resolution of 16 December 1965, on the "*Question of Ifni and Spanish Sahara*".

on Decolonization, the General Assembly adopted Resolution 2229 (XXI). In this resolution, the General Assembly asked Spain to determine, in consultation with Mauritania and Morocco, the procedures for the holding of a referendum under the supervision of the UN.[112]

In the years that followed, the General Assembly decidedly restated its request that a referendum be held in the territory. Resolution 2983 (XXVII) of 1972 explicitly reaffirmed "the responsibility of the United Nations in all consultations intended to lead to the free expression of the wishes of the people".[113] Resolution 3162(XXVIII) in 1973 deplored the delay in visiting the territory by the United Nations mission, despite a recommendation for its active participation in the organisation and holding of a referendum since 1966. In the same document, the General Assembly reaffirmed its "…attachment to the principle of self-determination and its concern to see that principle applied with a framework that will guarantee the inhabitants of the Sahara under Spanish domination free and authentic expression of their wishes, in accordance with the relevant United Nations resolutions on the subject".[114]

In 1973, the "Popular Front for the Liberation of Saguia-el-Hamra and Rio de Oro" (POLISARIO) was established with the purpose of pursuing an armed struggle against Spain. This organisation was recognised and supported by the international community (i.e., the UN and the OAU) as the representative of the people of Western Sahara. In December, the General Assembly applied to the International Court of Justice for an advisory opinion on the legal status of the territory.[115]

The Court reiterated the right to self-determination of the people of Western Sahara. It held that the issue of the sovereignty ties of Western Sahara with Morocco and Mauritana "could (not) be limited to ties established directly with the territory and without reference to the people who may be found in it". Consequently, the Court found "no legal ties" of "territorial sovereignty" between Western Sahara and the Moroccan State and Mauritania.[116] However, Spain, Morocco

[112] A/RES/2229(XXI): The UN General Assembly Resolution of 20 December 1966 on the "*Question of Ifni and Spanish Sahara*".

[113] A/RES/2983 (XXVII): The UN General Assembly Resolution of 14 December 1972, on the "*Question of Spanish Sahara*".

[114] A/RES/3162(XXVIII): The UN General Assembly Resolution of 14 December 1973, on the "*Question of Spanish Sahara*".

[115] The Court was asked to answer two questions: (1) "Was Western Sahara at the time of Colonization by Spain a Territory Belonging to No-one (terra nullius)?" (2) "What Were the Legal ties of This Territory with the Kingdom of Morocco and the Mauritanian Entity?"

[116] Western Sahara, Advisory Opinion of 16 October 1975, ICJ Reports (1975), p. 12: Paras. 85 and 162.

and Mauritania ignored the judgment of the Court and decided to divide the territory between them.

The following events may be summarised as follows[117]: on October 1975, the King of Morocco, Hassan II, launched the Green March in which 350,000 unarmed Moroccans walked into Western Sahara. The Green March was followed by the following events: a violent conflict with the POLISARIO, Mauritania's relinquishment of its claim to Western Sahara and then its eventual occupation by Morocco. 26 February 1976 was the eventual date for the removal of Spain from Western Sahara as a colonial authority. The Saharawi Arab Democratic Republic (SADR) was declared promptly on 27 February, by the Provisional Saharawi National Council, supported and endorsed by the POLISARIO. On June 1981, King Hassan II announced his endorsement for a possible referendum in Western Sahara. On 2 December 1985, the UN General Assembly invited the Chairman of the OAU and the Secretary General "to exert every effort to persuade the two parties to the conflict (Morocco and Polisario) to negotiate the terms of a ceasefire and the modalities for the referendum".[118] On 11 August 1988, the then UN Secretary General, J. Perez de Cuellar, offered his peace plan, and it was accepted on 30 August 1988 by Morocco and the POLISARIO.

The Secretary General's implementation plan, approved by the Security Council, provided for a transitional period leading up to the referendum, in which the people of Western Sahara would choose between independence and integration with Morocco. The plan specified the basic framework of the future referendum[119]:

> The Special Representative of the Secretary-General would have sole and exclusive responsibility over all matters relating to the referendum, including its organization and conduct.
>
> He would be assisted by an integrated support group of UN civilian, military and civil police personnel, the UN Mission for the Referendum in Western Sahara, MINURSO;
>
> There would be a ceasefire monitored by UN military personnel, followed by an exchange of prisoners of war under the auspices of the International Committee of the Red Cross (ICRC);
>
> Morocco would undertake an appropriate, substantial and phased reduction of its troops in the Territory;
>
> Combatants on each side would be confined to locations specified by the Special Representative and monitored by UN military personnel.
>
> The UN would organize and conduct a referendum, and issue the necessary regulations, rules and instructions for that purpose (in particular, voting would be by secret ballot, with arrangements made for voters who could not read or write);

[117] Beigbeder (1994), pp. 191–195.

[118] A/RES/40/50: The UN General Assembly Resolution of 2 December 1985 on the "*Resolution of Question of Western Sahara*".

[119] Beigbeder (1994), p. 193.

The UN would monitor other aspects of the Territory's administration, especially the maintenance of law and order, to ensure the necessary conditions for the holding of a free and fair referendum;

After proclamation of an amnesty, political prisoners would be released and all laws or regulations which, in the view of the Special Representative, could impede the holding of a free and fair referendum, would be suspended to the extent deemed necessary;

All refugees and other Western Saharans resident outside the Territory and wishing to return would be enabled to do so by the UN, after the latter had established their right to vote;

Unless the Special Representative determined the circumstances dictated otherwise, the referendum would be held 24 weeks after the ceasefire came into effect and its results would be proclaimed within 72 hours; and

Neighbouring Algeria and Mauritania would cooperate with the Special Representative in ensuring that the transitional arrangements and the results of the referendum were respected.

In 1991, the Security Council adopted Resolution 690 to provide the mandate of a future referendum, in compliance with the report of the Secretary General. In this resolution, it was foreseen that the United Nations Mission for a Referendum in Western Sahara (MINURSO) would be established, and the referendum would be organised and conducted by the UN in cooperation with the Organization of African Unity (OAU).

Despite the demands of the UN Identification Commission to update the names of the voters, Morocco rejected a revision of the voter lists deriving from the 1974 Spanish census. The unresolved issue of voter identification has been the main obstruction in this process, and this conundrum has persisted until today.

5.4.3 *East Timor*

East Timor, a colony of Portugal, was first placed on the international agenda by the General Assembly declaring it as a non-self-governing territory in 1960. In 1974, Portugal sought to create a transitory government and a popular assembly, which would be in charge of the determination of the international status of East Timor. This attempt, however, failed when a civil war broke out between those who wanted independence and those who opted for union with Indonesia. Unable to cope with this situation, Portugal renounced sovereignty over it in 1975. Shortly after, the territory was occupied and annexed by Indonesia in an act that was roundly condemned and not recognised by the international community.[120] The Security Council and the General Assembly asked Indonesia to withdraw from the region, and it was kept in the list of non-self-governing territories. East Timor was continuously included in the list of non-self-governing territories, and the committee of 24 continued to revive the question.[121]

[120] A/RES/3485 (XXX): The UN General Assembly Resolution of 12 December 1975 on the "*Question of Timor*".

[121] S/RES/384(1975): The UN Security Council Resolution of 22 December 1975.

From 1982 and thereafter, regular negotiations took place between Indonesia and Portugal under the aegis of consecutive Secretaries General aimed at resolving the status of the territory. Following a regime change in the country, Indonesia proposed a new status for East Timor with a limited autonomy, whereas Portugal insisted on its complete independence. This step was followed by the New York Agreements signed between Portugal and Indonesia on May 1999. In these agreements, the party states authorised the Secretary General to organise and conduct a "popular consultation" on whether East Timorese people wanted independence or preferred to remain in Indonesia with a status of special autonomy.

In addition to the "Main Agreement", two other supplementary agreements provided the legal framework for the conduct of the referendum. In the "Modalities" agreement, the fundamental issues pertaining to the referendum were specified, such as the date for consultation, the question to be put before voters, voter qualification, the timetable of the pre-referendum period, voter education, political campaigning, voter registration and funding and security. In the "Securities" agreement, the need for "a secure environment devoid of violence or other forms of intimidation. . .for the holding of a free and fair ballot in East Timor" was emphasised. The Indonesian security authorities were given "the responsibility to ensure such an environment as well as for the general maintenance of law and order". The Secretary General, pursuant to his capacity under the New York Agreements, proposed the establishment of a United Nations Mission in East Timor to organise and conduct a popular consultation.[122] Consequently, the Security Council established the United Nations Mission in East Timor (UNAMET) on 11 June 1999, with the aim of organising the referendum and administering the region until the day of the vote.[123]

In the light of the foregoing explanations, we may summarise the legal framework of East Timor independence referendum as follows: the New York Agreements constituted the legal base of the referendum in East Timor. There were three agreements in this framework: the Main Agreement of 5 May 1999 between Indonesia and Portugal and two agreements between Indonesia, Portugal and the United Nations on Modalities and Security. During the referendum process, East Timor was considered by the United Nations to be an "occupied non-self-governing territory". Portugal was a party to these agreements under its capacity as the administering power and Indonesia as the occupying power. Portugal with *de jure* authority and Indonesia with *de facto* authority would exercise joint administration powers.[124]

The legal base of the competence of the UN in East Timor was twofold: on the one hand, East Timor was qualified as a Non-Self-Governing Territory; this status allowed the UN to "witness" the main framework agreement concluded between

[122] United Nations Security Council. "*Question of East Timor Report of the Secretary-General*". S/1999/595, 22 May 1999.

[123] S/RES/1246/(1999): The UN Security Council Resolution of 11 June 1999.

[124] Teles (2002), pp. 12–18 and 90–92.

Portugal and Indonesia. It also permitted the UN to be a party to the supplementary agreements. These supplementary agreements were the second sort of legal base for competence regarding the conduct of the referendum and were delegated by the contracting states via these supplementary agreements. In this framework, the mandate of the UNAMET was provided by the New York Agreements. Alternatively, the UN established the United Nations Transitional Administration in East Timor (UNTAET) on the direct legal basis of Chapter VII.

In the Main Agreement, the parties requested "the Secretary-General to establish, immediately after the signing of this Agreement, an appropriate United Nations mission in East Timor to enable him to effectively carry out the popular consultation" (Article 2). In addition, the Secretary General was entitled to "maintain an adequate United Nations presence in East Timor" "during the interim period between the conclusion of the popular consultation and the start of the implementation of either option" (Article 7).

The Modality Agreement gave the United Nations much of the competence and responsibility regarding information, registration and campaigning. When establishing UNAMET, the Security Council felt that it (UNAMET) should include political, electoral and informational components. The political component was supposed to monitor the fairness of the pre-referendum political environment. The electoral component would deal with technical issues such as registration, prevention of electoral fraud, and preparation of voters' lists. The informational component was there to tackle the issue of voter education. Leaving aside the responsibility for security, the UNAMET had the omnipotent authority to regulate, administer and review the referendum process by holding the executive, legislative and judicial powers.[125]

Soon after taking up its duty, the UNAMET realised that, due to the serious pro-Indonesian militia violence of recent months, the pro-independence villages had been destroyed and their inhabitants had been displaced. This ongoing disorder in the referendum zone and the attacks by militia groups upon the staff of UNAMET were the cause of many disruptions to the opening of registration. During this time, the Secretary General stated that he was unable "to ascertain, based on the objective evaluation of the UN mission, that the necessary security situation exists for the peaceful implementation of the consultation processes, as required by the agreements before the start of registration".[126] Despite this unsecured environment and ongoing intimidation, the East Timorese went on to be registered in large numbers. By the end of the registration period, around 450,000 people were registered, a number well beyond the UN's expectations.

The total delay of the ballot due to security issues was around 22 days, and by 30 August all the electoral measures were complete. These measures were assessed to be accurate and adequate, by both the independent Electoral Commission

---

[125] For the text of the agreement, see United Nations General Assembly-Security Council. "*Question of East Timor Report of the Secretary-General*". S/1999/513-A/53/951, 5 May 1999.

[126] Martin and Mayer-Rieckh (2005), p. 128.

appointed by the Secretary General and by the sizeable numbers of international observers present in East Timor. The security situation still remained uncertain though: with continuous displacement of voters because of militia violence and then a greater level of violence that became apparent following the referendum. However, the UN decided to continue with the procedure and accomplish the vote, in particular to correct its own historical error.

In 1969, it was manipulated on a much-disputed act of self-determination by Indonesia concerning West Irian. In this case, Indonesia annexed the territory through a farcical popular consultation called the "Act of Free Choice". This was provided for by the New York Agreements signed between the Netherlands and Indonesia, the two contesting states, both of which claimed title over the territory.[127] In this agreement, the word plebiscite or referendum was deliberately avoided as a concession to Indonesia.[128] Moreover, even the minimum requirements, as in the provisions of the above-said agreement, had not been implemented. Instead, the consultation was demoted to a vote, through the raising of hands by around 1,000 men (out of the approximate number of 800,000 West Irians) who were being subjected to "bribes" or "threats". All of this was done in the presence of the UN, which deemed the act sufficient to legitimise Indonesia's annexation of the territory.[129]

This historical background may prove insightful as to the determined but otherwise hasty manner of the UN in East Timor: the primary concern being to avoid a second manipulation by Indonesia. UNAMET) completed its duties regarding the referendum in less than 4 months from the date of the agreements, with only a 3-week delay. The referendum was then held on 30 August 1999, in which the East Timorese rejected the autonomy offer, opening the path to independence.

Immediately after the proclamation of the referendum result, a mass campaign of violence broke out, claiming many lives, committed by pro-integration militias, allegedly supported by Indonesian security forces. "The Indonesian authorities did not respond effectively to the violence, despite clear commitments made under the 5 May agreements".[130] The Secretary General and the Security Council actively intervened to stop the violence by requesting Indonesia to fulfil its duties of maintaining security and order. A Security Council mission visited the region, and the Secretary General went searching for support among the international community to help ease the region's violent state of affairs. Following the Security Council's mission, the Government of Indonesia agreed to receive military aid from the international community, and as a result the Security Council dispatched the International Force in East Timor (INTERFET).

---

[127] For the text of the New York Agreements, see http://www.freewestpapua.org/docs/nya.htm. Retrieved 12 June 2012.

[128] Saltford (2003), p. 19.

[129] Saltford (2003), p. 334.

[130] http://www.un.org/en/peacekeeping/missions/past/etimor/UntaetB.htm. Retrieved 10 October 2012.

This force under the command of Australia was tasked with restoring peace and order in East Timor and, additionally, to protect and support UNAMET in carrying out its tasks.

The outcome of the referendum was formally recognised by the Indonesian People's Consultative Assembly on 19 October 1999. In the following week, on 25 October, the Security Council established the United Nations Transitional Administration in East Timor (UNTAET) pursuant to Chapter VII of the UN Charter. The UNTAET was "endowed with overall responsibility for the administration of East Timor and (would) be empowered to exercise all legislative and executive authority, including the administration of justice". The establishment of UNTAET thus aimed at ending the post-referendum conflict, which had created widespread human rights violations, by maintaining the peace and providing an effective administration and security.[131]

Shortly after its establishment, the UNTAET created, in consultation with the leaders of East Timor, the National Consultative Council (NCC) comprising of 11 East Timorese and four UNTAET members. The NCC was entrusted with the supervision of the decision-taking process during the transition period leading to independence. The NCC was decisive in the creation and establishment of the basic components of state structure such as the creation of a legal system, restoration of the court system, the setting of an official currency and the establishment of border controls and taxation.

On October 2000, the National Consultative Council (NCC) was replaced by the National Council (NC). The NC was comprised of 36 members from East Timor's civil society, business and political parties and was to be a basis for the future legislature of the emerging state. On 30 August 2001, pursuant to a regulation by the NC, the East Timorese voted, this time, for the election of an 88-member Constituent Assembly, authorised to draft and adopt the first Constitution and transition to full independence. The entity became formally independent on 20 May 2002, and the UN formally admitted East Timor as a member on 27 September 2002.[132]

5.4.4 South Sudan

Except for a short 11-year period of peace, ethnic and regional strife has been persistent in Sudan since it became independent on 1 January 1956. The last internal war (north–south civil war) that started in 1983 lasted for more than 20 years,

---

[131] S/RES/1272 (1999): The UN Security Council Resolution of, 25 October 1999; Kondoch (2001), p. 260.

[132] A/RES/57/3: The UN General Assembly Resolution of 27 September 2002, on the "*Admission of the Democratic Republic of Timor-Leste to membership in the United Nations*"; see also "History", http://timor-leste.gov.tl/?p=29&lang=en (Official Website of the Government of East Timor) Retrieved 12 June 2012.

claimed the lives of over two million people and caused the internal displacement of almost two million persons and refugees. This civil war was fought between the Government of Sudan and the Sudanese People's Liberation Movement/Army (SPLM/A).

Over the years, there were several attempts by the international community to bring peace. One such development was the beginning of a peace process in 1993 under the aegis of the Inter-Governmental Authority on Development (IGAD).[133] This initiative was eagerly supported by the UN and then by the Security Council, setting up a special political mission: the United Nations Advance Mission in the Sudan (UNAMIS), whose tasks were to communicate with all the sides involved in the conflict and to arrange a possible UN peace operation.

A Comprehensive Peace Agreement (CPA) was signed in Kenya on 9 January 2005 between the Sudanese Government and the SPLM/A. The CPA included, among others, a power-sharing scheme between the central government and the region. This agreement envisaged a transition phase of six-and-a-half years, at the end of which an internationally monitored referendum would be held. It was foreseen that this referendum would be organised jointly by the Government of Sudan and the SPLM/A. Two options would be presented to voters in the eventual referendum: (1) confirmation of the unity of Sudan by voting to adopt the system of government established under the Peace Agreement, (2) secession (CPA Chapter I: The Machakos Protocol, Art. 2.5).

In the same year, on 6 July, both the legislature of the central government and the "National Liberation Council" of the SPLM simultaneously adopted "the Interim National Constitution of The Republic of Sudan". It included provisions in accordance with the CPA, and part 16 of the interim constitution was devoted to "Southern Sudan's Right to Self-Determination". The constitution stipulated an internationally monitored "referendum on self-determination" to be held 6 months before the end of the 6-year interim period (Art. 222). Also in the same document, it was stated that "A Southern Sudan Referendum Act (should) be promulgated by the National Legislature, and the presidency would be in charge of the establishment of the Southern Sudan Referendum Commission (Art. 220).

In 2009, the Sudan National Assembly enacted the Southern Sudan Referendum Act (SSRA)—"to provide the basic legal framework for conducting the Southern Sudan referendum". The referendum law was planned to be adopted in 2008, but it was subject to several interruptions over controversial issues, namely,

[133] IGAD is an intergovernmental organisation having six member states from East African region: Djibouti, Eritrea, Ethiopia, Kenya, Somalia, Sudan and Uganda. According to the Agreement Establishing the Inter-Governmental Authority on Development (IGAD), IGAD has "the capacity of a legal person to perform any legal act appropriate to its purpose, in accordance with the provisions of the present Agreement" (Art. 3). Its aims and objectives, among others, involve the following: "Promote peace and stability in the sub-region and create mechanisms within the sub-region for the prevention, management and resolution of inter and intra-State conflicts through dialogue" (Art. 7-(g)) (*Agreement Establishing the Inter-Governmental Authority on Development*) Retrieved on 7 February 2012, from http://igad.int/etc/agreement_establishing_igad.pdf.

turnout and voter eligibility criteria disputes between the central government and the SPLM/A. [134]

The Act regulated the following issues[135]:

Legal requirements for being included on the referendum register in Southern Sudan and other locations;
Who is eligible to vote in the referendum;
Conditions under which the referendum may be delayed or postponed, and actions to be taken to reschedule;
Corrupt and illegal practices and offences;
Appointment of an independent media committee to launch a media campaign to educate Sudanese people in general and Southern Sudanese in particular;
The referendum question;
The approval level by which the referendum will be binding;
The process for the counting of votes and declaring results.

On 8 January 2011, the Southern Sudan Referendum Commission released its final record of registration for the referendum: 3,755,512 were registered in Southern Sudan; 116,857 in the North; and 60,219 abroad. Voting took place from 9 to 15 January and continued without any significant occurrence of violence throughout Sudan and the eight countries selected for overseas voting: Australia, Canada, Egypt, Ethiopia, Kenya, Uganda, the United Kingdom of Great Britain and Northern Ireland and the United States of America.

The Southern Sudan Referendum Commission declared the preliminary results of the ballot on 2 February, followed by a three-day deadline for appeals. As there were no appeals, the Commission announced the final outcome on 7 February: a voter turnout of 97.58 % with a 98.83 % vote in favour of secession, as opposed to the pro-unity vote of only 1.17 %.

The observations of the international community on the referendum were positive. The three-member panel appointed by the Secretary General observed the referendum during polling, counting and aggregation, transmission (from 5 to 21 January) and during the statement of the outcome. "The panel found that the referendum reflected the free will of the people of Southern Sudan and that the process as a whole was free, fair and credible". Various international and national observers publicly expressed similar observations.[136]

The outcome was welcomed by the Secretary General, who felt that it represented the true will of the people of Sudan. He also greeted the parties to the conflict—the President of Sudan, Omar Hassan, and the President of Southern Sudan, Salva Kiir Mayardit—and thanked them for their sincere commitment to

---

[134] Curless (2011), p. 2.

[135] *The Southern Sudan Referendum Act: Frequently Asked Questions*, (2010).

[136] United Nations Security Council. "*Report of the Secretary-General on the Sudan*". S/2011/239, 12 April 2011, para. 5.

the peaceful and stable political pre-referendum atmosphere, which was crucial for a credible referendum.[137]

The Role of the International Community in the Implementation of the Referendum: In South Sudan, despite the primacy of the national authorities in the implementation, the referendum was highly internationalised. International organisations such as the African Union, the European Union and the League of Arab States and the International Authority on Development dispatched their observers to watch the referendum process.

The persistent presence of the United Nations throughout the process should also be noted. The Security Council established the United Nations Mission in the Sudan (UNMIS) on 24 March 2005. UNMIS was composed of military and civil elements, namely, 10,000 military personnel and 715 civilian police personnel. The mandate of UNMIS was specified by three consecutive resolutions of the Security Council: 1590 (2005), 1870 (2009) and 1919 (2010). According to this framework, UNMIS was entitled to "provide guidance and technical assistance to the parties to the Comprehensive Peace Agreement (CPA) in cooperation with other international actors" and "Support the preparations for elections and referendums including an advisory task related to security arrangements".[138]

UNMIS had been very active and decisive during the implementation process of the 2005 Comprehensive Peace Agreement. It performed its duties by supplying good offices and political support to the parties, monitoring and verifying their security arrangements and presenting technical support in several fields such as governance, recovery, development and any other aspect of the preparations for the referendum. The United Nations Integrated Referendum and Electoral Division (UNIRED) came into existence following the April 2010 elections in Sudan. It was formed after an act of merging the two former bodies, the UNMIS Electoral Assistance Division and the UN Development Programme. UNIRED then became the competent organ of the UN to support the Southern Sudan referendum.[139]

The activities of UNIRED during the referendum process may be listed as follows[140]:

Assisting the referendum authorities in the design of operational plans for conducting voter registration and polling;
Assisting in preparing the procedures and training for voters' registration, polling and counting;
Procurement and transportation of referendum related materials and equipment;
Security training for Southern Sudan and Sudan Police Forces Police Service officers;

---

[137] http://www.un.org/en/peacekeeping/missions/unmis/background.shtml. Retrieved 10 October 2012.

[138] *The United Nations Integrated Referendum and Electoral Division (UNIRED) Fact Sheet: Frequently Asked Questions,* (2010).

[139] The United Nations Integrated Referendum and Electoral Division (UNIRED) Fact Sheet: Frequently Asked Questions, (2010).

[140] *The United Nations Integrated Referendum and Electoral Division (UNIRED) Fact Sheet: Frequently Asked Questions,* (2010).

Advising in developing strategies for voter education, as well as public information materials;
Support to accredit international and domestic observers;
Coordination of international efforts in support of the referenda.

Thus, UNIRED contributed to the activities of the Sudanese authorities in areas such as building of the essential legal structure, scheduling of the timetable for the referendum, logistical arrangements, and security and education of the referendum personnel.

The six-and-a-half-year interim period, as provided by the CPA, was to end on 9 July 2011, and so in line with the result of the referendum, South Sudan formally became an independent state. The mandate of UNMIS would also end on the same day. However, on 17 May 2011, the Secretary General asked for an extension of the UNMIS mission since there were certain post-referendum issues in the region. In his report to the Security Council, the Secretary General said that this additional period, during which the mission would gradually downsize its existence in Khartoum, would provide the parties the necessary time and space to build an effective structure to resolve remaining post-referendum issues—particularly those concerning security and border control.[141]

Accordingly, the Security Council made its remarks about the "persistence of conflict and violence and its effect on civilians, including the killing and displacement of significant numbers of civilians..." Thus, having "determined that the situation faced by South Sudan continued to constitute a threat to international peace and security in the region, and acting under Chapter VII of the UN Charter", the Security Council established the United Nations Mission in the Republic of South Sudan (UNMISS), for an initial period of 1 year starting from 9 July 2011.[142]

According to Security Council Resolution 1996 (2011), UNMISS would be responsible for establishing peace and security and for stimulating the capacity of the Government of the newborn Republic of South Sudan to become an effective and democratic regime. In this perspective, the mandate of UNMISS includes the following:

Support for peace consolidation and thereby fostering longer-term state-building and economic development, through...Promoting popular participation in political processes, including through advising and supporting the Government of the Republic of South Sudan on an inclusive constitutional process.
Support the Government of the Republic of South Sudan in exercising its responsibilities for conflict prevention, mitigation, and resolution and protect civilians through: 1. Monitoring, investigating, verifying, and reporting regularly on human rights and potential threats against the civilian population as well as actual and potential violations of international humanitarian and human rights law, working as appropriate with the Office of the High Commissioner for Human Rights, bringing these to the attention of the authorities as necessary, and immediately reporting gross violations of human rights

[141] United Nations Security Council. "*Special report of the Secretary-General on the Sudan*". S/2011/314, 17 May 2011.

[142] S/RES/1996/2011: The UN Security Council Resolution of 8 July 2011, http://www.un.org/en/peacekeeping/missions/unmiss/mandate.shtml. Retrieved 12 July 2011.

> to the UN Security Council. 2. Deterring violence including through proactive deployment and patrols in areas at high risk of conflict, within its capabilities and in its areas of deployment, protecting civilians under imminent threat of physical violence, in particular when the Government of the Republic of South Sudan is not providing such security.[143]

At the time of writing, the region has not yet attained a sustainable state of security and stability. In its final report, of May 2012, the Security Council stated its concern about "the repeated incidents of cross-border violence between Sudan and South Sudan, including troop movements… and Sudanese Armed Forces aerial bombardments… and the continued fighting in the states of Southern Kordofan and Blue Nile, in Sudan…".[144] Therefore, UNMISS will be likely to remain in the region for an indeterminate period.

Popular Consultations in Blue Nile and Southern Kordofan: In addition to the referendum in South Sudan, the CPA mentioned "Popular Consultations" to be held in the states of Blue Nile and Southern Kordofan—these regions being situated on the northern and southern borders of South Sudan and Sudan, respectively. The CPA defined the popular consultation as "a democratic right and mechanism to ascertain the views of the people of Southern Kordofan/Nuba Mountains and Blue Nile States on the comprehensive agreement reached by the Government of Sudan and People's Liberation Movement" (Chapter V of the Resolution of the Conflict in Southern Kordofan and Blue Nile States, Art. 3.1). Furthermore, it says: "The comprehensive agreement shall be subjected to the will of the people of the two States through their respective democratically elected legislatures" (Art. 3.2). Thus, the expression "popular consultations" does not necessarily imply a referendum but rather implies an indirect consultation through the political elites of the people concerned. Indeed, in the period that followed the enactment of the CPA, the ruling National Congress Party (NCP) and SPLM agreed that the "consultations would not be a referendum and therefore not lead to separation, and that they would not address the concerns of one ethnic group only but those of the State at large, and put in place a Council of Elders to define their content".[145]

Question of Abyei: The CPA also included a separate chapter devoted to the resolution of the Abyei conflict (Chapter IV). This territory lies along the borderline of North and South Sudan and is thus one of the hubs of the sovereignty conflict between the two sides. There are two ethnic groups in the region: Ngok Dinka and Misseriya, the former being permanent residents of Abyei and the latter nomads that migrate seasonally across the region. Misseriya's concern had been the loss of their grazing rights in the case of South Sudan's secession. To alleviate such fears, the CPA stipulated a separate referendum in Abyei, to be held simultaneously with the referendum for South Sudan, to determine if the region would remain in the

[143] S/RES/1996/2011: The UN Security Council Resolution of 8 July 2011, para. 3.

[144] S/RES/2046 (2012): The UN Security Council Resolution of 2 May 2012.

[145] United Nations Security Council. "*Special report of the Secretary-General on the Sudan*". S/2011/314, 17 May 2011, para. 9.

North or become a part of the South. However, the referendum could not be held as scheduled on January 2011 due to a lack of agreement on voter qualification. The related chapter of the CPA specifying the referendum did not define either the territory or the eligible voters for this separate referendum. It was this outstanding question not being resolved in the period following the South Sudan referendum that became the main source of contention that thwarted the overall process. Consequently, fighting broke out in the region on March 2011, causing the displacement of 20,000 persons. The Security Council responded to this by its Resolution 1990 of 27 June 2011 establishing the United Nations Interim Security Force for Abyei (UNISFA).[146] The area is now controlled by the Sudanese Government, yet the dispute still remains unresolved up to this day.

5.4.5 *Cyprus*

Being on the crossroad between Europe, the Middle East and Africa, Cyprus is a fundamental geo-strategic point in the region. The island has been ruled by successive empires and civilisations such as the Assyrians, the Phoenicians, the Egyptians, the Romans, the Arabs, the Greeks, the Turks and, finally, the UK British under colonial rule before independence. All of this has led to Cyprus being a stage of conflict, internally, i.e. between the Greek and Turkish Cypriots, and internationally, i.e. between Turkey and Greece, to which the British colonial vestiges may be added as one of the sources of ethnic strife on the island.[147]

One noteworthy observation upon the Cyprus issue might be that the conflict, since the nineteenth century, has been revolving around the question of the Greek Cypriots' demand for Cyprus to be united with Greece (*enosis*). To this end, in 1950, the Greek Orthodox Church held a quasi-referendum on union with Greece, which showed that the overwhelming majority of Greek Cypriots were in favour of union with Greece.[148] In fact, the procedure involved a petition rather than a referendum. Large books were placed in various churches with the phrase "We demand the unification of Cyprus with Greece" on each page. The inhabitants of Cyprus could sign into these books, but the Turkish population did not participate in the vote. Reportedly, 215,000 out of the 224,000 Greek Cypriots expressed in favour of accession to Greece, but this move did not yield any reactions from the international community and Britain promptly refused to relinquish its sovereignty over the island. Greece requested, at the UN level, the implementation of the right of self-determination of the Cypriot people under UN auspices. However, the General Assembly unanimously decided that a decision on Cyprus would not be

[146] http://www.un.org/en/peacekeeping/missions/unisfa/. Retrieved: 12 May 2012; S/RES/1990 (2011): The UN Security Council Resolution of 27 June 2011.

[147] Ker-Lindsay (2009), p. 12.

[148] Ker-Lindsay (2009), p. 12.

appropriate "for the time being".[149] Eventually, a military movement against British colonial rule developed among the Greek Cypriots, leading to the bitter polarisation of the Greek and Turkish communities. Intense inter-communal fighting also caused increasing tensions between Greece and Turkey, the "motherlands" of the two respective communities. The crisis, with the increasing likelihood of a war between these two NATO allies, could be overcome by a compromise: the emergence of Cyprus as an independent state, an option that was not eagerly desired by the Greek Cypriots. Consequently, on February 1959, Greece and Turkey agreed to proceed along the path, giving Cyprus independence as concluded in the Zurich Agreement. Eight days later, the British Government and the leaders of the Greek and Turkish Cypriots were also present during the conclusion of the London Agreement, which then formed the basis of the Constitution of Cyprus. On 16 August 1960, British sovereignty over the island ended and Cyprus became an independent sovereign state.[150] The difficulty, however, with the procedure was soon to become apparent: the population of the island was not consulted during and at the end of the process either directly or indirectly. The consent of the Cypriot people was demoted to the presence of the representatives of the two communities only.[151]

There are three treaties that constitute the legal basis of the constitution and international status of Cyprus. Firstly, on 16 August 1960, Cyprus, Greece, Britain and Turkey concluded the Treaty of Guarantee.[152] In this treaty, Cyprus promised not to realise any sort of "union with any other State" or to proceed towards the separation of the two communities (Article I). Secondly, the three powers undertook to respect the "independence, territorial integrity and security" of the Republic, as well as the fundamental provisions of its Constitution (Article II). And finally, each guarantor state had the right to take action in the event of a breach of the treaty (Article IV). Two other relevant treaties include the Treaty of Alliance between Cyprus, Greece and Turkey and the Treaty of Establishment between Cyprus, Greece, the United Kingdom and Turkey. By these treaties, Greece and Turkey were allowed to station limited numbers of troops on the island, whereas Britain was permanently granted a piece of "sovereign" territory, to be used as a military base.[153]

The constitutional system incorporated the creation of a balance between the two communities. This new regime adopted a formula of partition of diverse posts of government such as the Council of Ministers, the civil service and the 50-seat parliament with a percentage ratio of 70 to 30 between Greek and Turkish Cypriots.

[149] Hoffmeister (2006), p. 45.

[150] Ker-Lindsay (2009), p. 13.

[151] Pericleous (2004), p. 277.

[152] The text of the treaty may be found at http://www.mfa.gov.cy/mfa/mfa2006.nsf/All/484B73E4F0736CFDC22571BF00394F11/$file/Treaty%20of%20Guarantee.pdf (Official Website or the Ministry of Foreign Affairs of the Republic of Cyprus), Retrieved 12 May 2012.

[153] Hoffmeister (2006), p. 6.

The system of government was modeled in a way that the president would always be Greek Cypriot and the vice president would be Turkish Cypriot, both having the right of veto on fundamental laws. The Republic of Cyprus became a member of the United Nations on 21 September 1960 and of the Council of Europe on May 1961. Yet within only a few years following independence, tensions between the two communities started to rise, most notably over several disputes, including taxation and the administration of separate municipalities. As regards the latter, Article 173 (1) of the Constitution states that "separate municipalities shall be created by the Turkish inhabitants of Nicosia, Limassol, Famagusta, Larnaca and Paphos". This provision related to an old disagreement on the issue. Since 1930, there had been demands on the part of Turkish Cypriots for the self-administration of the Turkish quarters in these towns, as the Greek mayors were thought to have been responsible for the underdevelopment of Turkish areas. Later after 1960, this provision became the target of Makarios's hostility, when it was largely used for the "self segregation" of the Turks in various districts.[154] Makarios then proposed 13 amendments to the constitution, which would erase the constitutional protection of the Turkish minority against the Greek Cypriots. The amendment project provided for the elimination of the veto rights of the President and Vice President, as well as the requirement of separate majorities of both communities in adopting legislation. The project also aimed at eliminating the possible creation of separate municipalities and the favoured status of the Turkish minority in the formation of civil service bodies.[155]

These events were followed by intense inter-communal violence on the island that started in 1963. The involvement of the UN under its peacekeeping capacity in Cyprus was initially based on Resolution 186 of the Security Council (4 March 1964). Following some failed initial attempts by the guarantor powers to restore peace and order, the UN deployed the United Nations Peace Keeping in Cyprus (UNFICYP). In its resolution, the Council noted "that the situation with regard to Cyprus (was) likely to threaten international peace and security", and the UN peacekeeping force would be mandated "to prevent a recurrence of fighting" and "to contribute to the maintenance and restoration of law and order and a return to normal conditions". The same document also recommended that a mediator should be appointed by the then Secretary General U Thant "to promote a peaceful solution and an agreed settlement of the problem confronting Cyprus in accordance with the UN Charter, having in mind the well-being of the people as a whole and the preservation of international peace and security".[156]

In 1965, Galo Plaza, the UN-appointed mediator, presented his report for the solution of the island's status problem, yet it was rejected by Turkey, which found it imbalanced, accusing the mediator of having transcended the limits of his authori-

[154] Hoffmeister (2006), p. 12.

[155] Hoffmeister (2006), p. 13.

[156] Pericleous (2009), p. 187; Hoffmeister (2006), p. 59.

sation.[157] In view of this experience, the UN subsequently confined its role to the Secretary General's good offices mission, which limited the role of the UN to the instigation and facilitation of negotiation between the two parties. Following this failure, several inter-communal talks were held between 1968 and 1974 on the basis of a UN Security Council resolution (No. 244, 22 December 1967). However, these talks remained ineffective in resolving the dispute, and serious inter-communal fighting continued.[158] These events eventually led to the occupation of the island by Turkey on 20 July 1974.

Following on from the Turkish occupation, there have been periodic inter-communal talks pursued under UN mediation, which have always remained inconclusive, failing to resolve the conflict. The deadlock has not been resolved so far over certain core issues such as the nature of power sharing between the communities, including both the nature of the central state and its powers *vis-à-vis* the communes and the portion of the territory to be left for the administration of respective communities, the freedom of movement, the freedom of settlement, compensation of property, repatriation of Turkish settlers and withdrawal of foreign troops.

The first meetings after the Turkish occupation were the five rounds of negotiations in Vienna between the two communities, which were then followed by two successive "High Level Agreements" between the two sides in 1977 and 1979. These agreements, among others, endorsed such principles as Cyprus should be an independent, non-aligned and bi-communal state and any form of union with another State or partition or secession should be banned.[159]

In 1983, the legislative assembly of Turkish Cyprus unilaterally declared independence and designated the new state as "The Turkish Republic of Northern Cyprus" (TRNC). Subsequently, the constitution that was drafted and published on May 1984 was approved in a referendum held in the Turkish zone on 5 May 1985. The only country that recognised this new entity as a state was Turkey, which declared that it stood as a guarantor power for its survival, whereas Britain and Greece promptly condemned this move.[160] On 18 November 1983, the UN Security Council adopted a resolution (UNSC Res. No. 541) stating that the proclamation of the TRNC should be considered "null and void" and that it was incompatible with the 1960 Treaties of Establishment and Guarantee. The Council also called upon all states not to recognise the TRNC.

From this declaration onwards, successive UN Secretaries General (Perez de Cuellar, Boutros Ghali and Kofi Annan) took up the mission to resolve the conflict under their good offices mission, on a possible bi-communal, bi-zonal federal state. None of them have succeeded, however. The 1980s saw many summits and talks at the instigation of the UN Secretary General, all of which ended in failure and for

[157] Pericleous (2009), pp. 169–170.

[158] Hoffmeister (2006), p. 60.

[159] Hoffmeister (2006), pp. 62–63.

[160] Hoffmeister (2006), p. 38.

which both parties blamed each other. There were also several failed attempts to reach accord on confidence-building measures in the period between 1992 and 1995. The years 1999–2000 also saw a series of proximity talks, under UN Secretary General Kofi Annan's mediation. He presented his settlement plan on 11 November 2002 in an attempt to resolve the Cyprus conflict before the island could join the EU. However, despite several intensive discussions, Cyprus, still a divided island, signed the Treaty of Accession to the European Union on 16 April 2003.

Following this, the UN-sponsored direct negotiations restarted on February 2004. On 10–13 February 2004, the leaders of the two communities Papadopoulos and Denktaş met in New York for another attempt to reach a consensus under Annan's mediation. These talks resulted in the New York Accords, which drew up the framework of the fifth Annan Plan and its eventual approval in the dual referendums of April 2004. The accord provided for a timetable starting with the reopening of the inter-communal talks on 19 February in Nicosia. In case of failure to reach an agreement by 22 March, Greece and Turkey were then empowered to intervene as guarantor powers for the resolution of the differences. The deadline by which agreement should be reached was set as 29 March, and in the absence of any consensus, the UN Secretary General would be entitled to use his discretion to create a final version of his settlement plan and to submit it to simultaneous referendums on 24 April 2004.

Inter-communal talks began in Nicosia on 19 February. The main long-standing issues that were discussed may be listed as follows: the organisation and competences of the central government; issues related to EU accession; the number of Greek Cypriot refugees to return to the north; matters related to territory; the number of Turkish troops allowed to be located in Cyprus; the status of the areas, including Varosha; and compensation for the loss of real estate properties. These talks being inconclusive, on March 19 Secretary General Annan invited the leaders of the Greek and Turkish Cypriot communities, as well as Greece and Turkey, to Lucerne in Switzerland. However, no agreement could be reached in the Lucerne conference, the issues of refugees and property rights being the major problems of controversy. As a response, Annan used his discretionary power under the New York Accord to produce a fifth and final version of his settlement plan, which was submitted to both sides on March 31. According to this latest version of the plan, a United Cyprus Republic was designed as a federal, consociational state. The new state of affairs would result in an indissoluble partnership between the federal government and two equal constituent states—called the Greek Cypriot Constituent State and the Turkish Cypriot Constituent State. Following consociational principles, the constitution specified the powers and functions vested in the federal government, devolving the bulk of powers (including the day-to-day functioning of the states) to the constituent states. Each constituent state was to exercise powers related to the administration of justice at state level, namely, law and order; criminal, company and family laws; public safety; industry and commerce; social security and labour; environmental protection; tourism; fisheries and agriculture; zoning and planning; sports; education; and health. Each constituent state would have also had corresponding executive, legislative and judicial offices to that outlined for the federal level.[161]

Eventually, simultaneous referendums took place, as agreed, on April 24, 2004. During the campaign in the run up to the referendum, President Papadopulos called for a rejection of the UN settlement plan by the Greek Cypriot community. On the Turkish side, the then TRNC President Denktaş was also against the plan, while Prime Minister Ali Talat and Turkish Prime Minister Recep Tayyip Erdoğan were in favour.

In fact, in the period before the referendum, the Greek Cypriot community had largely been opposed to the plan, particularly over issues such as the limitations set upon the return of the Greek Cypriot refugees to the north and the continued presence of Turkish troops on the island. In the face of these controversial issues, AKEL, the most popular political party in southern Cyprus, asked for a delay of the referendum. However, the proposed delay found no support, and accordingly the party advocated for the rejection of the plan. Consequently, the Greek Cypriot community overwhelmingly rejected the plan, with a 76 % "No" vote, whereas 65 % of the Turkish Cypriot community voted to accept the UN settlement plan. As a consequence, the Greek Cypriot-controlled south Cyprus joined the EU on the 1st of May, the status of the island remaining unresolved both in international law and within the EU.[162]

5.4.5.1 Legal Evaluation of Diverse Settlement Documents Related to the Cyprus Conflict

As may be inferred from above, the Cyprus question includes diverse and complex sets of political and legal issues both within and outside the island. For this reason, a concise evaluation of the legal nature of the settlement documents is useful to understand the principles behind the simultaneous referendums of 2004, as well as the ones that may be eventually held in a future resolution of the conflict.

In this context, we may discern four types of international law documents regarding the Cyprus question. Firstly, with respect to the agreements between the two communities, one may argue that they may not be categorised as treaties since the parties are not states. Instead, they may be defined as bi-communal agreements, the political guidelines to outline a future settlement that could take the form of a legal document at a later stage.[163] On the other hand, a counter-argument may be raised since non-state actors are to a certain extent accepted in the doctrine as the treaty-making agents in the process of state creation. In any case, when one refers to the content of these documents, this discussion remains pointless since the parties have always refrained from making strict and explicit

[161] Yakinthou (2009), p. 26.

[162] Pericleous (2004), p. 292.

[163] Hoffmeister (2006), p. 71.

commitments. Therefore, if not formally but materially, the so-called high-level agreements may merely be categorised as principles or *travaux préparatoires*, where the parties postpone giving their consent, pursuant to a possible settlement at a final stage.

Secondly, since the beginning of the Cyprus conflict, the Security Council has periodically laid down the principles for a prospective settlement. It has either referred to the high-level agreements of the parties or formulated its own detailed opinions on the issue.[164] As regards the legal nature of these resolutions, one may note that the resolutions pertaining to the Turkish occupation and the important human rights issues may be considered as legally binding. However, when it comes to the resolutions about a possible "political solution" of the overall Cyprus conflict, the Security Council has never referred, "explicitly" or "implicitly", to its competences under Chapter VII of the UN Charter. In addition to this, the discussions preceding these resolutions, as well as their wording, show that the Security Council resolutions were "mere recommendations". The same may be said for the legal value of the relevant UN General Assembly resolutions, which are the third sort of legal documents relating to the Cyprus issue. Pursuant to Article 10 of the UN Charter, the General Assembly has adopted several resolutions calling parties to resolve the conflict by peaceful means. However, these resolutions may not be taken as evidence of customary international law. Rather, they may be considered as the tools of political recommendation to the parties as regards the negotiations.[165]

Finally, one should recall the good offices mission of the Secretary General. The Cyprus case is particularly reputed for the successive interventions by UN Secretaries General: U Thant, Kurt Waldheim, Perez de Cuèllar, Boutros Ghali and Kofi Annan, under their good offices mission. From the beginning of the 1980s onwards, the Secretaries General have taken an increasingly active role in the dispute by formulating their own proposals. These proposals have been presented under diverse names such as "opening statements", "non-papers", "draft agreements" or "sets of ideas", which have served as the initial frameworks for the talks, the last one being the Annan Plan.[166]

In the Cyprus case, the explicit mandate of the good offices missions was provided by the Security Council.[167]Yet such authorisations do not give the

[164] Hoffmeister (2006), p. 71. See, for example, S/RES/716 (1991): The UN Security Council Resolution of 11 October 1991 S/RES/1179 (1998): The UN Security Council Resolution of 29 June 1998; S/RES/649: The UN Security Council Resolution of 12 March 1990; S/RES/1986 (2011): The UN Security Council Resolution of 13 June 2011.

[165] Hoffmeister (2006), s. 71–73.

[166] S/RES/367 (1975): The UN Security Council Resolution of 12 March 1975; Pericleous (2009), p. 185.

[167] S/RES/367 (1975): The UN Security Council Resolution of 12 March 1975; /RES/422 (1977): The UN Security Council Resolution of 15 December 1977; S/RES/649 (1990): The UN Security Council Resolution of 12 March 1990; S/RES/1250 (1999): The UN Security Council Resolution of 22 December 1999; S/RES/1475(2003) The UN Security Council Resolution of 14 April 2003.

Secretary General the competence to adopt a legally binding text. Good offices missions are viewed as the means of friendly resolution of international conflicts, and they are restricted to mere proposals. On the other hand, their political influence may not be denied since they are promoted as fair solutions by the highest UN administrative officer, who enjoys the confidence of a majority in the General Assembly and of the Permanent Five in the Security Council (Article 97 UN Charter). Furthermore, the Secretary General enjoys a *prima facie* image of objectivity and fairness, and proposals containing his signature may be legitimately said to express appropriate and balanced international opinion. Likewise, the good offices, other than those as requested explicitly by the Security Council, may also be decisive in the process (Article 99 of the UN Charter). In practice, this article has been interpreted in its broadest sense, permitting several Secretaries General to introduce peace building proposals on their initiatives; these activities do not have a direct legal effect, but their political authority is obvious.[168]

In short, the entire sets of legal documents relating to the Cyprus conflict are of a soft law nature, being devoid of genuine legal force. On the other hand, however, the UN documents are important because they offer a clear expression of the collective political will of the international community and the parties to the conflict. Consequently, they constitute the basic documents within the political framework for reaching a possible solution.[169]

5.4.5.2 Underlying Principles of the Separate Referendums

It is clear that "in a divided country like Cyprus, (the democratic principle of) popular assent requires a majority of the voters within each community". Any sort of settlement "should gain the support of the people of Cyprus through separate referendums. . .held simultaneously in both communities in the island".[170] This principle is supported by the political practice and legal sources relevant to the dispute.

Since the beginning, both sides have invoked their own versions of right to self-determination to suit their purposes. The Greek Cypriots, as well as the Government of Greece, used the concept in the 1950s for the justification of the island's union with Greece (*enosis*). The Turkish side, for its part, referred to self-determination for the purpose of partition (*taksim*). Nevertheless, neither of these interpretations was favoured in international law.[171]

This resulted in the rejection of the "dual" right to self-determination of Greek Cypriots and Turkish Cypriots. This was in line with the tendency of that era in international law regarding decolonisation, which refused to recognise the right to

[168] Pericleous (2009), p. 185.

[169] Hoffmeister (2006), p. 74.

[170] Auer (2009), p. 16.

[171] Hoffmeister (2006), p. 6.

external self-determination according to ethnicity, religion or language. Instead, a colonised territory as a whole (*uti possidetis*) was taken to be the unit for state creation, regardless of whether the people living in it were ethnically homogenous or not. The principle of *uti possidetis* in terms of decolonisation found its legal basis in the General Assembly's Resolution 1514 (XV) of 14 December 1960 on the granting of independence to colonial countries and peoples. According to this, former borders were taken as the legitimate units for independence and only the population of an integral former colony could invoke the right to independence. The independence of former African and Asian colonies during the 1960s and the 1970s was realised according to this framework.[172] Thus, the right to external self-determination for the communities was denied in the sense that adhesion to another state (*enosis*) or separation (*taksim*) was not considered as viable option, forcing the Greeks and Turks to be unified as part of an independent state.

On the other hand, the right to internal self-determination was recognised separately for the Greek and Turkish Cypriots. The existence of two constituents in the island had been acknowledged since the beginning. The 1959 Zurich/London Agreements and the 1960 Constitution used the term "communities" several times. The conception of bi-communalism was endorsed to imply the existence of two constituent units, the power-sharing arrangement between them and their intimate affiliation with their respective motherlands. From a legal perspective, "the two communities were political equals in the sense that each existed as a political entity".[173] This approach was consolidated following the Turkish occupation, after which the basic framework of a possible settlement became the creation of a bi-zonal and bi-communal federation. Bi-zonality meant in this context the territorial separation of Turkish and Greek Cypriots, whereas bi-communality referred to the constitutional power sharing on an ethnic basis. This model also created the principle that successive peace plans and formulas be presented to both sides.[174]

In this context, in the 1970s and 1980s, the UN endorsed a formula that emphasised a constitutional perspective instead of international mediation. This was initially expressed by General Assembly Resolution 3312 of 1 November 1974, which said that negotiations between the "representatives of the communities" should "take place on an equal footing".[175] Subsequently, this model of formal equality was sustained during successive peace talks between the two communities

---

172 Hoffmeister (2006), p. 6.

173 Hoffmeister (2006), pp. 10–11.

174 Ker-Lindsay (2009), p. 11; S/RES/649 (1990): The UN Security Council Resolution of 12 March 1990.

175 A/RES/3212(XXIX): The UN General Assembly Resolution of 1 November 1974 on, the "*Question of Cyprus*" The General Assembly reiterated this view in its subsequent resolutions: A/RES/3395(XXX): The UN General Assembly Resolution of 20 November 1975 on the "*Question of Cyprus*"; A/RES/32/15: The UN General Assembly Resolution of 9 November 1977 on the "*Question of Cyprus*"; A/RES/33/15: The UN General Assembly Resolution of 9 November 1978 on the "*Question of Cyprus*"; A/RES/37/253: The UN General Assembly Resolution of 13 May 1983 on the "*Question of Cyprus*".

in the following decades. Notably, the new formula of the "political equality of the two communities" was developed in the inter-communal negotiations between Vassiliou and Denktaş from September 1988 to March 1990. This concept was recalled and defined by Secretary General Pèrez de Cuèllar in his Opening Statement on 26 February 1990. The Security Council adopted a resolution in line with this approach on October 1991, "reaffirm(ing) that the Cyprus problem is based on one State of Cyprus comprising two politically equal communities".[176] This conception was later endorsed by subsequent Secretaries-General Boutrous-Ghali and Kofi Annan.[177] According to Ghali, political equality implied that "approval and amendment of the federal Constitution will require approval of both communities and that there are safeguards to ensure that the federal government will not be empowered to adopt any measures against the interest of one community".[178]

The explanations made so far inherently suggest that a possible settlement plan should be put to separate referendums in each community. A similar situation may be found in Western Sahara. In this case, the International Court of Justice has stated that the free and genuine expression of the will of the peoples constituted the core of the principle of self-determination.[179] For this purpose, the Court quoted Resolution 2625 of the General Assembly, which said:

> The establishment of a sovereign and independent State, the free association or integration with an independent State or the emergence into any other political status *freely determined by a people* constitute modes of implementing the right of self-determination by that people. (Emphasis added by the Court)

The Court also referred to Resolution No 1514. On the one hand, considering both English and French versions of the referred to resolutions, there may be more than one people existing either separately or as intermingled on a territory ("wishes of the territory's peoples"/"*la volonté des populations du territoire*"). On the other hand, the Court's emphasis on the consent of "a people" suggests that the collective will of each people should be democratically expressed. If this is so and in the case of more than one distinct ethnic group, the majority within each ethnic group is necessary to determine the international status of an entity.

In this vein, it may be argued that the difficulty with the 1950 petition on *enosis* was the absence of the Turkish Cypriots' participation even though the petition was open to them. "Accordingly, the will of the Greek Cypriot majority of 80 % of the Cypriot people as a whole, was not sufficient for joining Greece under the right to self-determination as it stood in 1950".[180] Thus, regardless of being in a minority,

[176] S/RES/716 (1991): The UN Security Council Resolution of 11 October 1991.

[177] Ker-Lindsay (2009), p. 11; Hoffmeister (2006), p. 75.

[178] Quoted in Hoffmeister (2006), p. 75.

[179] Western Sahara, Advisory Opinion of 16 October 1975, ICJ Reports (1975), p. 12: paras. 57–60.

[180] Hoffmeister (2006), p. 9.

the absence of a distinct ethnic group (either by a boycott or obstruction) seriously undermines the democratic credibility of a referendum. To conclude, the requirement of simultaneous and separate referendums in Cyprus comes not only from a mere political expedience but also from sound legal principles in international law.

5.4.6 Europe and the Independence Referendum of Montenegro

The European institutions, i.e. the Council of Europe, the European Union and the OSCE (formerly Conference of Security and Cooperation in Europe—CSCE), have always been active in assisting governments on electoral matters, undertaking a decisive role in the monitoring of national elections. Since its establishment in 1949, the Council of Europe has been considered as a "club of democratic nations", incorporating one of the most advanced regional protection systems on human rights. Additionally, it also played an important role in assisting the new democracies of Central and Eastern Europe in their building of a new democratic system based on the rule of law and human rights. An important institution, in this context, is the "European Commission for Democracy Through Law" (Venice Commission), which was created in 1990 under the auspices of the Council of Europe. It was initially established to serve as a consultative body for the advancement of democracy in Eastern and Central Europe. Today, the Commission claims to play "a unique and unrivalled role in crisis management and conflict prevention through constitution building and advice".[181]

Another key institution for electoral monitoring on a European level is the Office for Democratic Institutions and Human Rights (ODIHR) (formerly the Office for Free Elections) founded in Warsaw on July 1991. This office operates under the OSCE. It defines its task as "promoting democratic election processes through the in-depth observation of elections and conducting election assistance projects that enhance meaningful participatory democracy".[182] Part of the ODIHR's role is Electoral Assistance and Observation and, as with other European institutions, is based on the invitation or consent of the host government.

Montenegro gained its independence following a referendum on 21 May 2006. Prior to this, the State Union of Serbia and Montenegro was created in 2002 under the mediation of the EU by the "Belgrade Agreement", as the successor state to the Federal Republic of Yugoslavia. This Agreement specified a 3-year moratorium, after which each founding state of the Union would be entitled to hold a referendum to withdraw from the union. At the end of this 3-year phase, the Government of Montenegro declared its plan to hold an independence referendum. A need for a

[181] http://www.venice.coe.int/site/main/Presentation_E.asp. Retrieved 15 May 2012; Beigbeder (1994), p. 222.

[182] http://www.osce.org/odihr/elections/72781. Retrieved 15 May 2012.

neutral mediation party arose in view of the deep polarisation of the Montenegrin society on this divisive issue and the ensuing distrust between the two sides of the question. The political parties agreed that a decisive international figure be included in the process, and consequently on December 2005, Mr. Javier Solana, the European Union's High Representative for the Common Foreign and Security Policy, appointed Special Envoy, Ambassador Miroslav Lajcak (Slovakia), as a mediator. He was assigned to assist both parties in reaching a consensus on the basic terms and conditions of the referendum, succeeding on January to February 2006 when agreement was reached.

The legal framework of the Montenegrin referendum may be defined to be an eclectic mixture of various elements from international law, federal and local constitutional laws and several legal provisions on a statutory level. The legal documents that steered the referendum process may be listed as follows: the Constitutional Charter of the State Union of Serbia and Montenegro (2003), the Constitution of the Republic of Montenegro (1992), the Law on the Referendum on State Legal Status (LRSLS) (adopted by the Parliament of Montenegro on 1 March 2006), the Law on Referendums (2001), the Law on the Election of Councillors and Representatives ("the Election Law") (2000, as amended) and the Law on Voter Registers (2000).[183]

The Constitutional Charter was adopted on 4 February 2003 in line with the conclusions reached in the Belgrade Agreement. According to this Charter, Montenegro was a member state of the State Union of Serbia and Montenegro. However, it could withdraw from the Union following a referendum. Article 60 of the Charter said:

> Upon the expiry of a three-year period the member state shall have the right to initiate the procedure for a change of the state status, i.e. for withdrawal from the State Union of Serbia and Montenegro. A decision to withdraw from the State Union of Serbia and Montenegro shall be made after a referendum has been held. The Law on Referendum shall be passed by a member state, taking into account recognized democratic standards.

On 7 April 2005, an amendment to the Constitutional Charter was added, which required that the regulations for the independence referendum of each member state be in compliance with the "internationally recognized democratic standards". More explicitly, the amendment obliged the member states "to cooperate with the European Union on respecting international democratic standards, as envisaged by the Constitutional Charter".[184]

---

[183] OSCE/ODIHR. "*Republic of Montenegro (Serbia and Montenegro) Referendum 21 May 2006 Needs Assessment Mission Report*". Warsaw, 14 March 2006, p. 3; OSCE/ODIHR Referendum Observation Mission. "*Republic of Montenegro Referendum on State-Status: 21 May 2006 Final Report*". Warsaw, 4 August 2006, pp. 3–4; Cazala (2006), p. 165.

[184] European Commission For Democracy Through Law. "*Opinion on the Compatibility of the Existing Legislation in Montenegro Concerning The Organization of Referendums With Applicable International Standards*". Opinion No: 343/2005, Council of Europe, Strasbourg, 19 December 2005, para. 3 (Venice Commission, 19 December 2005, para. 3).

On the local constitutional level, the 1992 Constitution of Montenegro provided two different provisions (Articles 2 and 119) where there had been different interpretations: either the referendum would be binding or it would require an additional approval by the parliament. This contention was resolved by the Constitutional Court of Montenegro, which upheld the opinion that the referendum would be final and binding. Article 2 of the Constitution specifically stated that "any change in the status…shall be decided only by citizens in a referendum". Article 119 of the Constitution, however, required a two-thirds majority of the total members of the parliaments for constitutional amendments concerning provisions for regulating the "status of the country". Before it came to Court, the Movement for the Preservation of the State-Union alleged that Article 119 should be applied in the decision of the secession of Montenegro, and thus the referendum should be only of consultative nature. The Constitutional Court, to the contrary, held that Article 2 should prevail.[185]

On the statutory level, the basic framework was established by a special law (*lex specialis*) for that purpose: the Law on the Referendum on State Legal Status (LRSLS), which was adopted by the Parliament of Montenegro on 1 March 2006. The law regulated the most important issues regarding the implementation of the referendum such as the ballot question, voter qualification, the majority and turnout requirement, establishment of the bodies responsible for the referendum administration, financing of campaign expenses and media coverage and the rights of observer groups.[186] More generic issues in electoral law, where the LRSLS was silent, were covered by the law on voter registers (2000) and the Law on Election of Councillors and Representatives (as amended in 2002).

The influence of international actors, i.e. the EU and the OSCE, has been decisive in the making of the LRSLS. The presence of the EU was already specified by the above-mentioned amendment to the Constitutional Charter of State Union of Serbia and Montenegro. As regards the OSCE, it was the designated international observer of the electoral activities in Montenegro for the parliamentary elections of 2001 and 2002, and eventually the independence referendum of 2006. The observers from the OSCE were incontestably the best agents to enhance confidence in the conduct of the referendum process, and their presence was accepted in consensus by both sides in Montenegro.[187]

The LRSLS is the outcome of long and extensive negotiations between the opposing parties and the EU Special Envoy, who was acknowledged to have been

[185] OSCE/ODIHR. "*Republic of Montenegro (Serbia and Montenegro) Referendum 21 May 2006 Needs Assessment Mission Report*". Warsaw, 14 March 2006, p. 5.

[186] OSCE/ODIHR Referendum Observation Mission, 4 August 2006) (OSCE/ODIHR, 17 March 2006).

[187] OSCE/ODIHR. "*Republic of Montenegro (Serbia and Montenegro) Referendum 21 May 2006 Needs Assessment Mission Report*". Warsaw, 17 March 2006.

the leading mediating element during this process.[188] Moreover, it was observed that "the referendum conditions had to be essentially imposed by the EU Special Envoy".[189] Several reports by the OSCE also led the Montenegrin actors in their compliance with the internationally recognised standards: "Many of the measures adopted by the LRSLS had previously been identified as recommendations in the final reports of OSCE/ODIHR election observation missions in Montenegro".[190]

The referendum took place on 21 May 2006 with a high voter turnout of 86.4 and 55.50 % in favour of independence. The overall process was described by the OSCE/ODIHR to be "generally calm" and without any reported dispute. International endorsements of the results were also without any hesitation. The Government of Serbia, all five permanent members of the United Nations Security Council and the European Union accepted the results. The Assembly of Republic of Montenegro made its official declaration on independence on 3 June 2006.[191]

References

Amiel, H. (1976). La pratique française des plébiscites internationaux. *Revue générale de droit international public*, 425–501.

Auer, A. (2009). On the way to constitutional convention for Cyprus. In A. Auer & V. Triga (Eds.), *A constitutional convention for Cyprus* (pp. 13–26). Berlin: Wissenschaftlicher Verlag.

Aust, A. (2005). *Handbook of international law*. Cambridge: Cambridge University Press.

Beigbeder, Y. (1994). *International monitoring of plebiscites, referenda and national elections: Self-determination and transition to democracy*. Dordrecht/Boston: Martinus Nijhoff.

Benvenisti, E. (1993). *The international law of occupation*. Princeton, NJ: Princeton University Press.

Boyle, A. (2006). Soft law in international law making. In M. D. Evans (Ed.), *International law* (pp. 141–158). New York: Oxford University Press.

Brownlie, I. (2003). *Principles of public international law* (6th ed.). Oxford: Oxford University Press.

Cassese, A. (2001). *International law*. Oxford: Oxford University Press.

Cavaré, L. (1961). *Le droit international public positif* (2nd ed., Vol. I). Paris: Pedone.

Cazala, J. (2006). L'Accession du Monténégro à L'indépendance. *Annuaire Français de Droit International*, 160–177.

Crawford, J. (2006). *The creation of states in international law* (2nd ed.). Oxford: Clarendon Press.

Curless, G. (2011, February). Sudan's 2011 referendum on southern secession. *Ethnopolitics Papers*, *7*, 1–24.

[188] OSCE/ODIHR. "*Republic of Montenegro (Serbia and Montenegro) Referendum 21 May 2006 Needs Assessment Mission Report*". Warsaw, 14 March 2006.

[189] OSCE/ODIHR. "*Republic of Montenegro (Serbia and Montenegro) Referendum 21 May 2006 Needs Assessment Mission Report*". Warsaw, 17 March 2006.

[190] OSCE/ODIHR Referendum Observation Mission. "*Republic of Montenegro Referendum on State-Status: 21 May 2006 Final Report*". Warsaw, 4 August 2006.

[191] "Montenegro declares independence", http://news.bbc.co.uk/2/hi/europe/5043462.stm. Retrieved 21 June 2013.

de Visscher, P. (1986). Le plébiscite international. In F. Delpérée (Ed.), *La participation directe du citoyen la vie politique et administrative, Travaux des XXIIes Journées d'études juridiques Jean Dabin* (pp. 137–157). Bruxelles: Bruylant.

de Wet, E. (2006, January). The international constitutional order. *International and Comparative Law Quarterly, 55*, 51–76.

Eisner, M. (1992, Spring). A procedural model for the resolution of secessionist disputes. *Harvard International Law Journal, 33*(2), 407–425.

Farley, L. T. (1986). *Plebiscites and sovereignty: The crisis of political illegitimacy*. London: Westview Press.

Fastrenrath, U. (2002). Chapter XI. Declaration regarding non-self-governing territories. In B. Simma, H. Mosler, A. Randelzhofer, C. Tomuschat, & R. Wolfrum (Eds.), *The charter of the United Nations* (Vol. II, pp. 1089–1097). Oxford/New York: Oxford University Press.

Franck, T. M. (1992, January). The emerging right to democratic governance. *The American Journal of International Law, 86*(1), 46–91.

Gawenda, J. A. B. (1946). *Le plébiscite en droit international*. Fribourg: Imprimerie St. Paul.

Gonssollin, E. (1921). *Le plébiscite dans le droit international actuel*. Paris: Libr. Générale De Droit & De Jurisprudence.

Grant, T. D. (1999). *The recognition of states: Law and practice in debate and evolution*. Westport: Praeger Publishers.

Hoffmeister, F. (2006). *Legal aspects of the Cyprus problem: Annan plan and EU accession*. Leiden: Martinus Nijhoff.

Igarashi, M. (2002). *Associated statehood in international law*. Dordrecht: Martinus Nijhoff.

Janis, M. W. (2003). *An introduction to international law* (4th ed.). New York: Aspen Publishers.

Kant, I. (2006). *Toward perpetual peace and other writings on politics, peace, and history*. New Haven: Yale University Press [Edited and with an introduction by Pauline Kleingeld; translated by David L. Colclasure; with essays by Jeremy Waldron, Michael W. Doyle, Allen W. Wood].

Keitner, C. I., & Reisman, W. M. (2003). Free association: The United States experience. *Texas International Law Journal, 39*, 1–64.

Ker-Lindsay, J. (2009). A history of Cyprus peace proposals. In H. Faustmann & A. Varnava (Eds.), *Reunifying Cyprus: The Annan plan and beyond* (pp. 11–22). London: I.B. Tauris.

Kondoch, B. (2001). The United Nations Administration of East Timor. *Journal of Conflict and Security Law, 6*(2), 245–265.

Lachmayer, K. (2007). The International Constitutional law approach: An introduction to a new perspective on constitutional challenges in a globalizing world. *ICL-Journal, 1*(2), 92–99.

Laghmani, S. (1998). Référendum en droit international. In H. Roussillon (Ed.), *Référendum et dé mocratie* (pp. 195–218). Toulouse: Presses de l'Université des sciences sociales de Toulouse.

Lijphart, A. (1999). *Patterns of democracy: Government forms and performance in thirty-six countries*. New Haven/London: Yale University Press.

Luce, E.-P. (1958). *Le Referendum du Togo (28 Octobre 1956)*. Paris: Editions A.Pedone.

Martin, I., & Mayer-Rieckh, A. (2005, Spring). The United Nations and East Timor: From self-determination to state-building. *International Peacekeeping, 12*(1), 25–145.

Merle, M. (1961). Les plébiscites organisés par les Nations Unies. *Annuaire français de droit international, 7*, 425–445.

Oppenheim, L. F. L. (1996). In R. Jennings & A. Watts (Eds.), *Oppenheim's international law* (9th ed., Vol. 1, 2 vols.). London: Longman.

Pavkovic, A., & Radan, P. (2007). *Creating new states*. Aldershot: Ashgate.

Pellet, A. (1992). The opinions of the Badinter Arbitration Committee a second breath for the self-determination of peoples. *European Journal of International Law, 3*, 178–185.

Pericleous, C. (2004). The Cyprus question. In P. Calvert (Ed.), *Border and territorial disputes of the world* (pp. 275–292). London: John Harper Publishing.

Pericleous, C. (2009). *The Cyprus referendum: A divided island and the challenge of the Annan plan*. London: I.B. Tauris.

Rideau, J. (1997). Les référendums nationaux dans le contexte de l'intégration européenne. In A. Auer & J.-F. Flauss (Eds.), *Le référendum européen: actes du colloque international de Strasbourg, 21–22 février 1997* (pp. 81–113). Bruxelles: E. Bruylant.

Rousseau, C. E. (1958). *Droit international public approfondi*. Paris: Dalloz.

Rudrakumaran, V. (1990). The "Requirement" of plebiscite in territorial rapprochement. *Houston Journal of International Law, 12*, 23–54.

Saltford, J. (2003). *The United Nations and the Indonesian takeover of West Papua: The anatomy of betrayal, 1962–1969*. London: Routledge Curzon.

Scelle, G. ([1932–1934] 1984). *Précis du droit des gens. Principes et systématique* (Vol. 2). Paris: CNRS.

Sureda, A. R. (1973). *The evolution of the right of self-determination. A study of United Nations practice*. Leiden: Sijthoff.

Tancredi, A. (2006). A normative 'Due Process' in the creation of states through secession. In M. G. Kohen (Ed.), *Secession: International law perspectives* (pp. 171–207). Cambridge, e.t.c: Cambridge University Press.

Teles, P. G. (2002). *East Timor and international law: A contribution to the study of how the international legal order deals with the violations infringed upon it* (Non-Published Ph.D. thesis presented to the University of Geneva, Geneva).

Thirlway, H. (2006). The sources of international law. In M. D. Evans (Ed.), *International law* (pp. 115–140). New York: Oxford University Press.

Türk, D. (1993). Recognition of states: A comment. *European Journal of International Law, 4*, 66–71.

Warbrick, C. (2006). States and recognition in international law. In M. D. Evans (Ed.), *International law* (pp. 217–274). New York: Oxford University Press.

Yakinthou, C. (2009). Consociational democracy and Cyprus: The house that Annan built? In H. Faustmann & A. Varnava (Eds.), *Reunifying Cyprus: The Annan plan and beyond* (pp. 25–39). London: I.B. Tauris.

Chapter 6
Sovereignty Referendums in Constitutional Law

Abstract In this chapter, there will be an analysis of the sovereignty referendums from the perspective of constitutional law. In constitutional law (as is the case with international law), sovereignty referendums have both a formal and material aspect. In its material context, the concept of sovereignty is the central theme of constitutions and constitution making. In other words, if we refer to the final authority to make and execute laws in an organisation when we use the term "sovereignty", then the sovereignty becomes the basic condition, which should be secured before any constitution may be established. Formally, the question of the legal status of sovereignty referendums may be considered within the larger framework of constitutional change, boiling down to two questions: (1) the legal evaluation of the constitution-making activity (constituent power) in a state and (2) the overall picture of sovereignty referendums in comparative constitutional law. Having dealt with these two questions, we will go on to tackle the in-depth cases: France, the United Kingdom, Canada (Quebec) and the United States of America.

6.1 Subject Matter

This section argues that the common subject matter of all sovereignty referendums—the problem of creation of a political body and the determination of its boundaries and members—is already immanent within the concept of constituent power. It follows that, as Auer notes, from a standpoint of municipal law, sovereignty referendums are "undoubtedly" constitutional referendums.[1] This basis is underpinned by the idea that there should first exist a political unit before the political organisation of it. In this context, Dahl offers us one helpful initial insight. For him, the legitimate entitlement of a group of persons to self-government rests on their capacity to constitute themselves as an entity, "a political order" as well as its permanence in a political system within legitimate and stable boundaries.[2]

[1] Auer (1996), p. 82.

[2] Dahl (1989), p. 106.

İ.G. Şen, *Sovereignty Referendums in International and Constitutional Law*,
DOI 10.1007/978-3-319-11647-1_6

Likewise, Linz and Stepan coin the notion of "stateness problem". According to them, the stateness problem arises when there are severe disagreements in a political community regarding its territorial boundaries and "who has the right of citizenship in that political community". Commenting on post-communist transitions, they note that as far as the democratic transition is concerned, there is a widely held assumption that the only aim that is pursued is the transformation of the non-democratic character of the political regime to a democratic one. However, typically when a "non democratic polity" is confronted with a crisis of legitimacy, there are also "profound differences about what should actually constitute the polity (or political community) and which *demos* or *demoi* (population or populations) should be the members of that political community".[3] In the same vein, Offe notes that the "'decision'. . .as to who 'we' are; that is, a decision on identity, citizenship and the territorial. . .boundaries of the nation state", is situated at the most fundamental level of the "three hierarchical levels of decision-making" on which the other two are founded: constitutions and daily political decisions.[4] According to Preuss[5]:

> . . .the generation of a constitution for a group presupposes the very existence of the group. Hence, before the group gives itself a constitution (e.g. by establishing a kingdom), it must clarify who is subject to this constitutional determination, and who is entitled to participate in this decision; in other words, who is the member of the group. . .More important for our contemporary problems is the constitutional state presupposes some minimum degree of pre-political sameness and homogeneity of the constituent power.

In short, it might be a priori assumed that there should first exist a stable political unit before the determination of its constitution, this stability involving both the territorial and demographical elements of the political unit (i.e., generally but not exclusively the state). In this context, we may consider the concept of constituent power on empirical and philosophical levels where the issue represents two distinct but interacting dimensions: the formation of the body politic and the identification of the constituent power.

---

[3] Linz and Stepan (1996), p. 16.

[4] Offe (2004), p. 505.

[5] Preuss (1994), pp. 161–163; we may observe the seminal assumption in Schmitt: "The theory of the people's constitution-making power presupposes the conscious willing of political existence, therefore, a nation" Schmitt ([1928] 2008), p. 127; see also Beaud (1997), p. 147: "*Pour être capable de s'exercer, le pouvoir constituant présuppose un peuple capable d'agir et doté d'un minimum d'unité*"; Rosenfeld (1994), p. 4 reminds us that "without some predominant identity, such as that of a sovereign nation or of the constitutional self, it is difficult to imagine how one could justify the imposition of a constitutional order".

6.1.1 Agreement of the People on the Creation of the Political Unit

From an empirical point of view, historical evidence shows that state creation has in most instances been associated with the constitution-making process. According to Poggi, state formation of the eighteenth and nineteenth centuries owed much "to an act of (collective) will and deliberation, sometimes embodied in explicit constitutional enactments".[6] We may argue that the notion of constituent power was born out of the historical process of creation of the modern nation state with its two mutually complementing elements: the creation of a political community and the institutional (or political) organisation of it.

In this vein, and commenting on the earliest community formations in America, Wyse concluded that, for "a multitude of man" to be transformed into a new political community (commonwealth), they should enter two separate but sequential covenants: the first one is for the foundation or creation of the political community—every man should interchangeably "covenant to join in one lasting society". The second covenant, provided that the first covenant is agreed upon, is on the "particular species of government" that will reign in that society.[7]

Thus, the concept of constituent power encompasses both the creation of a political unit and the choice of the ground rules of its government. In other words, the constitution-making power, a fortiori, fulfils the function of the creation (or definition) of the political unit. This assumption is eloquently conceptualised in constitutional law theory. Malberg, for example, distinguishes two succeeding functions of the constituent power: "the initial formation of state" and "its first organization". For him, the first constitution of a state is the act from which the state is born.[8]

The constituent power may therefore emerge either during the formation of a new state or during a regime change in an existing state. Similarly, authors such as Cadoux, Chantebout and Gözler underline the state-creating function of the constituent power. What we may presume from them is that a constitution creates the state—or in more general terms, the political community. The political community may be already existent during the constitution-making process, or the constitution may simultaneously create it where it does not yet exist. The revolutionary circumstances in which the incumbent constituent power has to create states may be a decolonisation process, an independence movement, a federation of independent states or the dismemberment of a state.[9]

---

[6] Poggi (1978), p. 95.

[7] Borgeaud ([1895] 1989), pp. 6–14.

[8] Malberg (1920), pp. 489–491.

[9] Gözler (1999), p. 17; Beaud (1997), p. 155 distinguishes two basic functions of constitutions: limitation of political power and creation and organisation of a political community; Cadoux (1980), p. 174 refers to the provisional constitutions during transition of states to independence and asserts that those constitutions provide the legality and legitimacy of the transitory regime. For

6.1.2 Agreement of the People on the Subject of Constituent Power

On a philosophical level, the primacy and precedence of the existence of the political unit may be sensed in the theorisation of the identity of the constituent power. While one aspect of sovereignty referendums is the creation of the political unit, it may also refer to a change of the subject of constituent power. The notion of the constituent power of the people, as a nation, is an outgrowth of the historical process of the shift of the source of legitimation of political power from above (God or monarch) to below (people). With the advent of the modern age, the nation, while creating its constitution, simultaneously found itself in a course of self-legitimation as the new agent of constituent power. Since then, the "collective selfhood"—taking the names of the nation or the sovereign people depending on the context within which it is referred to—is invoked by the author as well as the addressee ("by" and "for") of the constitution. Identity comes into play when the act of constituent power takes the form of the "self-constitution" of a polity.[10]

We may sense this effort in the emotional expressions in the preambles such as "we the people". These proclamations, as Rosenfeld comments, "rest on the normative assumption that" the people "on their free consent wish to *live together* under this constitution".[11] Therefore, constitutions, besides being the political self-organisations, are the tools for the materialisation of national identity and unity.[12]

Schmitt discerns two patterns of constitutional revolutions.[13] Firstly, "constitutional annihilation" is the "simultaneous abolition of the existing constitution as a whole and the constituent power that supports it". Contrarily, "constitutional elimination" is a simple eradication of the extant constitution, but by retaining the concurrent constituent power. In the former case, the constituent agent obliterates "the very foundation of the prior constitution" with the aim of "a conscious break with the past"—through this process, a new subject of constituent power emerges along with a newly established constitution. Yet in the case of constitutional elimination and despite the entire abolition of the constitution, the existing constituent power remains intact. In this case, for example, in a nation state, when the people engage in a revolutionary constitution-making act, neither the boundaries of the state nor the membership of it is put into question. Consequently, "the intention of the people to achieve political unity on a national basis remains". Thus, Schmitt discerns two types of legal and constitutional discontinuity, one that results in a simultaneous "elimination of the identity of the political unity" and one that

constitutional aspects of decolonisation and foundation of federation, see Chantebout (1991), pp. 38–39.

[10] Lindahl (2007), p. 9.

[11] Rosenfeld (1994), p. 7. Emphasis added.

[12] Preuss (1994), p. 148.

[13] Schmitt ([1928] 2008), pp. 140–148.

does not.[14] Preuss offers a similar dichotomy from the perspective of the political unit. For him, there are two types of constitutional revolutions: "Transformative" revolutions, which result in a mere institutional reconstruction and a change in the political regime, and "systemic" revolutions, which involve the very existence of the political unit: "The agents of systemic revolution not only dismantle an old regime, but also find themselves where a new society, its interest structure and actors remain to be established".[15] These accounts serve to illustrate that the issues of the subject of the constituent power and the continuity of states (or the boundaries of the political unit) are intimately related.

Moreover, the legitimacy of a constitution rests not only on the approval by a mass of people but also on the fact that those people have acted in concert by expressing the "conscious willing of political existence" as a nation.[16] In this vein, Lindhal highlights the nuance between "sameness" and "selfhood". The former refers to the togetherness of the people in the making of the constitution, with a reference to ethnicity, historical and cultural bonds and common fate. Sameness implies the unity and "collective intentionality" of individuals: where they act as the constituent power in a "shared activity". On the other hand, selfhood is all about denouncing any foreign elements from outside the community. In this context, "we" is invoked in contradistinction to "other" or "alien". These two senses of collective identity reciprocally interact in the creation of the people's "own" constitution, in contradistinction to an "alien" constitution.[17] Here, as Tierney notes, "the people as collective political agent is considered to have been formed in the very act of self-conscious state creation, i.e. where the concept of the people only becomes meaningful through its political mobilization as a collective force which created the polity, and in the process was itself created".[18]

6.1.3 *Synthesis*

Thus, there is always a preliminary authentication of the legitimacy of existence of a political unit and its constituent power, inherent in all acts of constitution making. This way of thought refers to the constituent power as an ideological amalgam in the state-creation or nation-building process. According to Preuss, "[a] constitution not only constitutes a structure of power and authority, it constitutes a people in a certain way".[19] Beaud indicates the mutual correlation between constituent power and the nation in the fabrication of the nature and source of a political

[14] Schmitt ([1928] 2008), p. 140.
[15] Preuss (2007), pp. 223–224.
[16] Beaud (1997), p. 146.
[17] Lindahl (2007), pp. 14–17.
[18] Tierney (2007), p. 231.
[19] Preuss (1994), p. 148.

community.[20] In this sense, the constitution-making process fulfils two functions with reference to the self-determination of the people: self-construction and self-organisation. In the first sense, the people constitute themselves as a nation by giving themselves a constitution, whereas in the second, the nation decides on "the particular form of its political existence".[21] In short, it is arguable that in a general sense, all constitutional referendums contain, to a certain extent, a decision on sovereignty: constitutions, besides their content about the organisation of the state and definition of basic rights, are the documents that (re)affirm the community's will to live together within its defined borders as a nation.

To summarise, recalling the above theoretical survey and chiefly Wyse's division of foundation and organisation of the political community, we may assume that the question of founding a political unit (including the decisions on membership to it) and its constitutional organisation are two distinctly separate (or separable) decisions. And either chronologically or conceptually, the formation of a political unit should precede its constitution. In other words, in the totality of constitution-making processes, including the cases where ethno-nationalist or territorial questions are not the most salient issues, these two questions are always "analytically distinct".[22] We may presume that in every referendum by which a constitution is approved, there is at least a hypothetical separation of these two questions while approving an overall constitutional project.

After having shown the presence of the issue of sovereignty in various degrees in all actions of constitution making, we may now focus on the area under discussion, i.e. sovereignty referendums, and where this issue appears in its most crystallised and distinct form. In this context, it is useful to recall the metaphorical definition of constituent power with reference to the biblical notion of *potestas constituens* of God.[23] Indeed, since Sieyes, the theory of the constituent power of the people may be characterised as the "secularized version" of God's power to create *ex nihilio*.[24] In Kelsenian terms, the issue of the existence of a polity is no doubt inherent in the *Grundnorm*, i.e., "the starting point of any organized political entity".[25] In this vein, on a continuum between two extremes of nothingness and a perfectly established constitutional system, one may argue that the decision on the existence of the political unit and the subject of constituent power, i.e. formation of the sovereign self, is located in the very initial phases. It follows from this, and considering the historical evidence, that sovereignty referendums occur in such critical moments of the most fundamental decisions. In this perspective, we may broadly divide sovereignty referendums into two groups.

[20] Beaud (1997) pp. 144–151.

[21] Schmitt ([1928] 2008), p. 127.

[22] Preuss (1994), p. 161.

[23] Schmitt ([1928] 2008), p. 126.

[24] Klein (1996), p. 4; Preuss (1994), p. 144.

[25] McWhinney (2007), p. 61.

In the first group, the question of sovereignty may precede the decision on the constitution. In the second group, an intermediate or a final document—a constitution, a treaty or a charter resolving the fundamental questions of the related sovereignty conflict—may be voted for at the end of a process (international and/or intergovernmental negotiations, negotiations between the states and dissident groups/regions) with the aim of resolving a sovereignty problem. In other words, the sole question of sovereignty may either be separately the subject of referendum or be accompanied by a reworked constitutional document. This document may be put forward for the approval of the people of a certain territory, ratification of which, simultaneously, results in secession from, adhesion to, merger into or remaining within a state.

In the case of the first group above, voting affirmatively on the referendum would imply a simple acceptation of inclusion within a new political unit, as well as the new constituent power that will create the future constitution. This is the case, for example, of the post-communist independence referendums as well as post-WWI border referendums, where the basic constitutional decisions remained to be taken.

The second case adds to the act of entering a political unit: a new constitution, a jointly determined compact of the fundamental terms of future coexistence. The new constitution, an interim charter or a status treaty simultaneously creates the new political unit. In this case, the founding units agree to annihilate their own constitution to replace them with a new one. The referendum on the reunification of Cyprus (2004) may be considered an example in this context.[26]

Moreover, in the case of accession of a territory to a sovereign state, the population of the territory in question agrees to enter into an already constituted legal order that a fortiori involves an implicit approval of the constitution of the host country. Italian, Swiss, Australian and American unifications have all been realised through the ratification of the constitutions by the relevant local units. Italian unification was accomplished by a series of referendums upon the royal charter of Sardinia. Likewise, during the unification of Switzerland, the 1848 Federal Constitution was put to the popular approval in each canton.[27]

To compare sovereignty referendums, we can state that they fall into either of two types of pattern that leads to the creation of a state. In the first type, a single referendum can bring about the formation of a state. The second type of referendum will involve a step-by-step approach, each new referendum building on and progressing the results of the previous referendum. Cumulatively, the referendums build to the creation of a new political unit.

This assumption also presumes a dynamic and flexible character of the formation of the constituent power or the political unit. In this way, Tierney opposes the traditional unitary conception of constituent power that rests on the presumption of

[26] From a perspective of Federation, see Schmitt ([1928] 2008), p. 384.

[27] For Italy, see Wambaugh (1920), pp. 14 and 61–65; for Swiss and American unification, see Borgeaud ([1895] 1989), pp. 131–191 and 296–297.

the uniformity of the state and its nation. He challenges the perception by which a unique and unchangeable *demos* is taken to be the constituent power covering the totality of the populace. According to this classical conception, "Inside every political unity, there can only be one bearer of the constitution-making power".[28] The constituent power is "assumed to map neatly onto the boundaries of the state".[29] Tierney highlights the dynamic nature of the formation of new locations of constituent power in both directions, from above and below—from the point of the nation state. Concerning the particular case of European Integration, the debates on constituent power revolve around the question of the creation of a "supra-state demos" and thus "a new site of constituent power at the level of the European Union".[30] On the lower level, regional and ethnic challenges to the unity of nation states, such as in Canada, Spain and the United Kingdom, are explained by the assumption that sub-state territories are the political spaces where the new agents of constituent power are mobilising. Referendums are held unilaterally in these territories, as in the case of the Quebec referendum (1995), as the tools for constitutional justification to legitimise the creation of a new sub-state constituent power.

This so-called dynamism and flexibility in most cases generate chaotic and anarchic scenes of political transformations—examples of which are dramatically illustrated in the case of post-communist constitutional revolutions. As mentioned above, this era witnessed a momentous challenge not only to the political and economic fabric of the states but also to the very existence of them. This was particularly the case for states such as Yugoslavia and the Union of Soviet Socialist Republics (USSR), which had "no pre-constitutional cohesive forces" before communism. Thus, the collapse of communism "not only destroyed the political regime but the polity itself". Marked by the "ethnification of politics", post-communist constitutional revolutions may be said to have displayed the most dramatic historical examples of simultaneity of constitution making, the naissance of a new constituent power and the formation of the political unit.[31]

6.2 Legal Base: Sovereignty Referendums in Comparative Constitutional Law

6.2.1 Constituent Power and Legality

Having shown that decisions on sovereignty are inherent in the constituent power, we may now turn to consider the legal status of these decisions in constitutional

[28] Schmitt ([1928] 2008), p. 105.

[29] Tierney (2007), p. 231.

[30] Tierney (2007), p. 230; for instance, Rideau (1997), p. 84 paraphrases in this respect Monnet's dictum: "Nous unissions des peuples et non des Etats".

[31] Preuss (2007), pp. 212–224.

law. The question of the legal evaluation of constituent power, the constitution-making activity, is problematic and the subject of an everlasting debate. As one commentator observed: "In fact, constituent power resists being constitutionalized: studying constituent power from the juridical perspective presents an exceptional difficulty. . .constituent power always remains alien to the law".[32] The same is true for the role of referendums in such circumstances. As Borgeaud wrote more than a century ago: "Whenever the question of a particularly grave change shall be raised, it may become difficult to agree upon the nature of the constitutional principles which establish approval by the people".[33] These comments underline the tension between the actual practice of constituent power and constitutional form.

In terms of the legal typology of the concept of constituent power, formalist French conceptions of "original constituent power" (*pouvoir constituant originaire*) (OCP) and "derived constituent power" (*pouvoir constituant derivé*) (DCP) may be useful. The former entails the process of foundational constitutional transformations in times of radical change, such as revolutions, *coup d'états* and wars. The latter refers to constitutional amendments made according to and in compliance with the procedural rules laid down by the prevailing constitution.[34] In this context, there may be two interrelated questions regarding the legal appraisal of sovereignty referendums: (1) from a formal point of view, may we evaluate *de facto* sovereignty referendums held in the context of OCP in legal terms? (2) Materially, are the sovereignty issues subject to a special form of amending procedure other than that prescribed by the relevant constitution?

The debates about the first question are structured around antithetical views of naturalist and positivist law theories. From a perspective of natural law, the people should have the final word regarding the most fundamental political decisions (i.e., a fortiori the creation and determination of the political unit). Naturalists attribute a legal value to the philosophical conception of the normative consent-based legitimacy. Following this train of thought, certain jurists maintain the view that the final constitutional text, which is the product of a process within the framework of OCP, should be put to referendum in order to be valid.[35] In their view, the popular ratification of a constitution is a supra-constitutional fundamental rule, which confers the legal validity of a constitution.

Positivists, on the contrary, stick to the formal view. According to them, and with respect to constitutional changes during revolutions and similar states of affairs, the force is decisive. Therefore, the process of constitution making is unlimited in terms of law. It is a meta-legal concept and has a non-legal nature.

[32] Negri (1999), p. Xi.

[33] Borgeaud ([1895] 1989), p. 69.

[34] Gözler (1997), pp. 12–15.

[35] *La constitution. . . ne sera juridiquement parfaite qu'après avoir été soumise* à *la ratification du peuple et adopte par lui.* Burdeau (1943), p. 40. For the relevant discussion, see Gözler (1997), pp. 7–112; also from the same author: *le fait qu'une constitution est faite par voie de référendum, au lieu de celle de l'octroi, ne rend pas cette constitution plus juridique*, Gözler (1992).

According to this view, during the process of constitution making, there is no existing constitution and no valid legal order and OCP operates in a legal vacuum. In brief, for positivists, people may approve any fundamental decision, including sovereignty issues by referendum, as well as constitutions may be enacted by any power, not only by the people. However, since the whole process of OCP is out of the scope of law, this referendum falls out of the scope of any legal evaluation, thereby leaving it as a legitimating tool in a mere sociological sense.[36]

As to the second question, two opposing views appear as to whether sovereignty issues are subject to referendum. The positivist view retains that a question should be put to referendum, if and only if it is prescribed by the constitution. Therefore, notwithstanding the fundamental importance of the subject matter of the constitutional change, a referendum may be initiated on the sole condition that it is included in the amendment procedure as stipulated by the constitution.

Alternatively, according to the non-positivist material approach, the validity of the constitutional changes regarding sovereignty issues rests on the indispensable condition of approbation by referendum.[37]

The material conception discerns constituent power according to the subject matter of constitutional change. Schmitt coins the phrase "absolute concept of the constitution". For him, constitution is a "complete, concrete collective condition of political unity and order": "the equivalent of state form" and, additionally, a unified and total act of normative "command" that constitutes the whole legal order. In this way, Schmitt distinguishes "constitution" and "constitutional laws". The former denotes "fundamental political decisions" and "overall preferences concerning the nature and form of a political community". He equates the constitution to "the state in its concrete political existence". In this sense, the preferences about the democratic or non-democratic nature, unitary or federal structure of a state and its international status are all included in the concept of the absolute constitution. On the contrary, constitutional laws, notwithstanding their inclusion in the text of the constitution, are "secondary" and mundane regulations. [38] They are the "constitutional details" and are by no means equal to the fundamental provisions, such as the clause on the republican form of government. [39] This distinction is the corollary of the discussion as to whether there are hierarchical differences in the different norms of the same constitution. The positivist view and the majority of French doctrine maintain that there is no hierarchical difference among the different norms of the constitution. On the contrary, the material view asserts that there are constitutional norms that are more important for the political community and occupy a higher rank in a constitution. Consequently, it is this nature of the constitutional norm, not the legal framework, that determines the legal nature of constitution making.[40]

[36] Gözler (1997), pp. 21–29; Gözler (1999), pp. 21–29.

[37] Gözler (1997), p. 34.

[38] Schmitt ([1928] 2008), p. 79.

[39] Schmitt ([1928] 2008), p. 67.

[40] Gözler (1997), pp. 29–35.

Following this train of thought, the material view rejects the formalist distinction of OCP and DCP. Instead, there is a distinction between constituent power in its proper sense and amending power. Within this perspective, Schmitt supports a single constituent power: the power to make the "constitution", which belongs, either to the people in a democracy or in the contrary case, to the monarch. For Schmitt, the power to make the constitution and to change it are two different areas of competence, and the holder of the constitution-changing power may not make, change or eliminate the "fundamental political decisions that constitute the substance of the constitution". [41]

On the other hand, the power to change the constitution, i.e. the amending power, is the power to make constitutional changes according to the procedure as stipulated by the relevant constitution. This procedure may or may not include referendums. Whatever the procedural fabric is, the amending power is solely competent to change "constitutional laws" but not the "constitution". In other words, according to the material approach, the scope of the amending power is limited.[42] In the Schmittian conception of the absolute constitution, changing or eliminating a single article regulating the sovereignty issues means changing or eliminating the whole constitution. Then such a constitutional article may be changed or eliminated exclusively by the constituent power, that is, in a democratic society, by the direct intervention of the people. Thus, whenever sovereignty is in question, "only the direct, conscious will of the entire. . .people, not some parliamentary majority, would be able to institute such fundamental changes".[43]

In support of Schmitt, Beaud highlights that clauses on sovereignty are the fundamental dispositions of the constitution, whereas the rest are considered to be secondary objects. In this way, the former may be amended by a constituent act (*l'acte constituant*) and the latter by an amendment act (*l'acte de révision*).[44] For him, there is a hierarchical relationship between these two acts of constitutional change. Given that the only subject of constituent power is the "people", constitutional changes involving sovereignty issues should be made only by means of referendum such that only the people with their capacity as sovereign may "alienate" or "exchange" their sovereignty. Such a rule does not necessarily have to be explicitly written in legal texts. This is an *autonome* and a *tacite* limitation emanating from a reasonable and systematic reading of the French Constitution.[45]

So far, a review on the formalist and materialist conceptions of constitutional change has been developed, and the question remains as to how these conceptions may provide insights for a conceptual framework of this study. From a formalist

---

[41] Schmitt ([1928] 2008), p. 79.

[42] Gözler (1999), p. 30.

[43] Schmitt ([1928] 2008), p. 80.

[44] Beaud (1994), pp. 307–320.

[45] Beaud (1994), pp. 480–491; see also Gözler (1999), pp. 27–28.

point of view, sovereignty referendums, like other types of constitutional referendums, may be either *de jure* or *de facto*.[46] Referendums may be held as authorised by the relevant constitution, or they are held either under revolutionary conditions or in cases for which a referendum is not stipulated by the relevant constitution. Also according to this distinction, referendums held during the process of OCP may be classified as *de facto*, whereas those held as authorised by PCD are *de jure*. Thus, whereas the formalist conception will be the guideline for the comparative study of the constitutional provisions, the materialist conception will be useful to explain the interaction of the political demands and the saliency of the sovereignty issues in diverse contexts. In this perspective, in the following sections, we will first search for an answer to the question whether the high importance of sovereignty issues renders the holding of a referendum as *de facto* obligatory, even if they are not specified by the relevant constitution. Second, a survey of some of the constitutions of the world will be presented. This survey aims to develop a report on sovereignty referendums from a comparative perspective and an in-depth analysis of three cases: France, the UK and the US. These three countries are chosen as models since they offer abundant data in terms of practice, legal provisions and doctrinal accounts.

6.2.2 Unwritten Rules of Constitution and the Sovereignty Referendums

The unwritten rules of a constitution are accepted in the doctrine, albeit with a certain caution concerning their status *vis-à-vis* the written constitutions. Two sorts of unwritten rules may be distinguished, "customs in the strict sense" and constitutional conventions. Customs may be defined as consistently repeated practices over a "fairly long duration" and are thus believed to be obligatory (*opinio juris*). Customs are recognised as having certain limitations as a legal source within legal theory. In this way, we may distinguish three groups of customs. *Praeter legem* customs are those that are resorted to complete or fill legal voids in written legal instruments. *Secundum legem* customs are the ones used to interpret indeterminate legal rules. Finally, *contra legem* customs are said to abrogate or amend the explicit provisions of the written rules.

The French doctrine generally recognises the first two types while unquestionably denying the *contra legem* customs.[47] Still, the concept of convention in a positivist constitutional system, in particular France, remains problematic. Hamon and Troper, for example, oppose the *praeter legem* customs, indicating that a constitutional provision may only be established through constitutionally

[46] Auer (1996), pp. 80–82.

[47] (Jean Gicquel, Droit constitutionnel et institutions politiques Paris: Montchrestien, 1993 p. 191; Charles Cadoux, Droit constitutionnel et institutions politiques Paris: Cujas, 1988, Vol. I p. 133 ; Bernard Chantebout, Droit constitutionnel et science politique, Paris : Armand Colling, 1994 p.29.) Cited in Gözler (2011), p. 201.

prescribed formal rules.[48] Maybe for this reason, the judiciary is reluctant to use it. Ardant notes that the courts and the Constitutional Council have never resorted to the concept of constitutional custom to settle a dispute. [49]

Constitutional conventions differ from customs in two ways. Firstly, in contrast to customs, conventions are not considered to be legal rules, i.e. they are not recognised and reinforced by the courts. Secondly, the element of precedent is not as strictly required as it is for customs. While only one precedent may create a convention, numerous precedents may not.[50]

Conventions have an "indirect" force in a constitutional system, that is, they are not legally binding in the strictest sense, but serious consequences of non-compliance render them psychologically obligatory. Politically, conventions have a *grande force obligatoire*, which distinguishes conventions from mere political practices. In this way, they may be seen as an "intermediary category of norms" between customs and simple practices.[51]

Conventions are found both in written and unwritten constitutional systems, albeit with differing status. In France, for example, conventions are seen as "indispensable complementary" elements of a written constitution. On the other hand, the British conception is more inclusive, in that they are seen as one of the essential elements of the Constitution. In other words, the conventions are considered to be the non-legal rules of the constitution.[52]

Conventions may be defined as the "rules of political practice which are regarded as binding by those whom they concern, especially statesmen – but which could not be enforced by the courts if the matter came before them".[53] Jennings asked three questions that he believed to distinguish a convention from a habit of political practice: what are the precedents? Do the actors believe they are bound by the rule? Is there a reason for the rule?[54] The precedents here refer to the certain political practices of the political actors. The element of political precedent as discussed above is not required as strictly as for custom. The "belief" is akin to the *opinio juris* of customs that should be shared by all the authors (i.e., statesmen, central government and other political authorities) and addressees (i.e., people, regions, opposition, civil society and other political actors) of the political practice. Finally, "reason" refers to the saliency of the related issue, with respect to the underlying tenets of the constitutional government. Convincing arguments in support of a convention are found in the essentials of the "prevailing political philosophy".[55]

---

[48] Hamon and Troper (2005), p. 54.

[49] Ardant (2005), p. 62.

[50] Phillips et al. (2001), p. 143.

[51] Ardant (2005), p. 62.

[52] Ardant (2005), p. 62.

[53] Phillips et al. (2001), p. 24.

[54] Jennings (1959) cited in Chander (1991), p. 479.

[55] Jennings (1963), p. 136.

Why are conventions observed? Jennings argued that conventions may claim authority with reference to legality. For him, the breach of a convention may have long-term detrimental effects on the overall constitutional system, and "sooner or later" it may result in a breach of law.[56] Yet "the consequence of violating a conventional rule is political rather than legal".[57] However, it should be noted that the consequences would be more serious than a simple loss of political popularity. A political actor violating a convention will receive legitimate criticisms of "unconstitutional conduct" from all parts of the political spectrum.[58] While a mere political blunder would prejudice the actor's political popularity, a breach of a convention may undermine the "stability of constitution".[59] This illustrates the strong moral authority of the conventions. Jennings' "reason" provides this moral force, in that breach of a convention would generate a "moral opprobrium": "One of the main objectives of conventions is to ensure that power is used in accordance with the ideological principles on which the constitution is based".[60] Therefore, arguments of consent-based legitimacy may be vigorously invoked to ensure the authority of conventions.

There are convincing arguments with respect to the conventional status of sovereignty referendums in diverse contexts. In this vein, Morel coins the term "politically obligatory" or "*de facto* obligatory" referendums. She notes that representative institutions are "compelled to organize a referendum as a result of an inescapable pressure—either normative or by external actors"—even though they are not constitutionally obliged.[61] Auer underlines the irreversible nature of these *de facto* obligatory referendums, that is, when such issues requiring a "high degree of legitimacy" become a subject of referendum, they can only be changed or overruled by another referendum. Commenting on the referendums on European Integration, he notes that no parliament could dare to overrule the verdict of the people. In this way, for example, "there is no possibility" that Norway could enter the European Union, in the face of the negative result of the referendum in 1972. Accordingly, no mere parliamentary Act would suffice politically for the UK to withdraw from the Union.[62]

---

[56] Johari (2006), p. 191.

[57] Barnett (2006), p. 31.

[58] Barnett (2006), p. 30.

[59] Carroll (2003), p. 57.

[60] Carroll (2003), p. 57.

[61] Morel (2007), p. 1056; he noted earlier: "With regard to the 1997 devolution referendums in Scotland and Wales, it is clear that it was impossible, after having consulted the population on the same issue in 1979, not to consult it a second time-a fortiori since this would have implied defying the will expressed at previous referendums", Morel (2001), p. 62.

[62] Auer (2007), p. 63.

6.2.3 *A General Overview on the Sovereignty Referendums in the Constitutions of the World*

The referendum element, either obligatory or facultative, is a widespread procedure for constitutional amendments in diverse constitutions. In the case of the presence of a referendum requirement for the constitutional amendment of a constitution, the articles involving sovereignty will be subject to referendum by design. The aim of this section, however, is to explore specific referendum regulations on the particular question of sovereignty.

6.2.3.1 Specific Referendum Requirements for Particular Sections Regulating Sovereignty

Typically, general provisions establish the legal basis of the states, their independence, their unitary or federal character and include fundamental provisions regarding sovereignty, territory and nationhood. The Estonian Constitution creates an obligatory referendum (Art. 162) for the amendment of "Chapter I General Provisions". This chapter includes the articles on "sovereignty" and "territory". The sovereignty article says, "Estonia is an independent and sovereign democratic republic", and "Estonian independence and sovereignty is interminable and inalienable" (Art. 1). According to the article on territory, "the land area, territorial waters and airspace of Estonia are an inseparable and indivisible whole" (Art. 2). These articles together constitute the general provisions, which "establish the legal basis of Estonia as a democratic independent state".[63] Similarly, the Latvian Constitution requires an obligatory referendum for any constitutional amendments involving, among others, territory and sovereignty issues (Art. 77).[64] According to the Lithuanian Constitution, "The provision of Article 1, that the State of Lithuania is an independent democratic republic, may only be amended by a referendum..." Similar provisions are found in the Constitutions of Poland (Art. 235), Belarus (Art. 140), Madagascar (Art. 141) and Moldavia (Art. 142).

6.2.3.2 Specific Constitutional Regulations on the Territory: Secession, Border, Cession

Differing from the above-mentioned specific referendum provisions for one or more articles regulating territory and sovereignty, the referendums in this section are stipulated within the framework for resolution of potential territorial disputes emerging from secessionist movements or from foreign states. These referendums

[63] Ruus (2001), p. 49; Ruus (2004), p. 56.

[64] Usacka (2001), p. 94; Feldhune (2004), p. 79.

are provided as a prerequisite for any sort of territorial alteration and thus bestow the relevant people or nation the veto right in that respect.

Referendums as a part of the procedures of the unilateral right to secession are available, but they are very rare. Christakis reports that among 108 constitutions, only two include the unilateral right to secession: Saint Christopher and Nevis, and Ethiopia. We should also add to these two examples the Constitution of Uzbekistan, which confers the Republic of Karakalpakstan the right to secede from the Republic of Uzbekistan "on the basis of a nationwide referendum held by the people of Karakalpakstan" (Art. 74).

According to Article 39 of the Ethiopian Constitution, "every nation, nationality or people in Ethiopia shall have the unrestricted right to self determination up to secession". For any of these constituent units of the Ethiopian Federation to secede, there should first be a demand for secession as adopted by a two-thirds majority of the local legislature. Upon the receipt of a decision by the legislature of the nation, nationality or people demanding secession, the federal government must organise a referendum within 3 years for the relevant unit—the people of which will then decide by a simple majority. This referendum is then binding on the federal government, which should subsequently tackle the succession issues of the emerging state.

With the exception of these rare cases, unilateral secession is forbidden by the quasi-totality of the World Constitutions. This does not exclude, however, the constitutional regulation of the territorial modification of a state. It is not illogical to assume that the constituent power anticipate a future threat to the territorial integrity and prefer to frame a procedure to regulate against such an occurrence. Consequently, numerous constitutions include the referendum device as a condition for secession or other forms of territorial alteration that may prove inevitable and irreversible. The conservative effect of referendums comes into mind at this point. As mentioned in the third chapter, referendums may fulfil an effective veto function whenever there is a threat to territorial integrity. Thus, a constitutional requirement for the consent of the majority as a condition for a territorial modification may be portrayed as a wise safeguard in the face of political realities.[65] A considerable number of constitutions provide for compulsory referendums to this end, whenever there is an inevitable and irreversible act of secession. One typical example of such a constitutional provision is Article 53/3 of the French Constitution: "No ceding exchanging or acquiring of territory shall be valid without the consent of the population concerned". The constitutions of Guinea (Art. 77), Senegal (Art. 77), Togo (Art. 138) and Mali (Art. 115) copied this provision with the exact same phrasing. Mauritania (Art. 78) and the Republic of Congo (Art. 172) prefer to use the explicit term "referendum", whereas the Gabonese Constitution specifies the timing—that the referendum takes place "before" any constitutional change regulating the secession (Art. 114).

---

[65] Christakis (1999), p. 286.

Referendums have been a significant device during the transition of Eastern European countries to democracy and independence. We may see the implications of this historical record in the constitutions of the post-communist countries. Obligatory referendums for border and territorial reconfiguration are a common trait in post-communist constitutions. In addition to the above-mentioned obligatory referendums for general provision chapters, some constitutions include a specific referendum requirement for border and territorial alterations. According to the Serbian Constitution, "any change in the boundaries of the Republic of Serbia shall be decided upon by the citizens in a referendum" (Art. 4). The former Montenegrin Constitution (1992) required that any change in the status of the country, change of the form of government and "any change of frontiers shall be decided upon only by citizens in a referendum" (Art. 2). It was one of the basic legal bases of the independence referendum of Montenegro. The Constitution of Ukraine says that "issues of altering the territory of Ukraine are resolved exclusively by an All-Ukrainian referendum" (Art. 73). Similar provisions may be found in the constitutions of Macedonia (Art. 74)[66] and Azerbaijan (Art. 11)".[67]

6.2.3.3 Transitory Provisions on Territorial Disputes

Certain states contain referendums for the peaceful resolution of pending territorial disputes to which they are a party within their constitutions. The Constitution of Guatemala says, "the Executive is empowered to make efforts aimed to resolve the situation regarding the rights of Guatemala to Belize, in accordance with national interests. Any final agreement must be submitted by the Guatemalan Congress to the popular consultation procedure laid down in Article 173 of the Constitution" (Art. 19).[68] In Panama, every treaty or international convention on the Panama Canal must be submitted to a referendum (Constitution of Panama, Art. 319).

In certain cases, an agreement between the state authorities and a secessionist movement is inserted into the constitution. Article 77, regulating the status of New Caledonia of French Constitution, was amended to comply with the Nouméa Accord. This model was endorsed in the Constitution of Papua New Guinea, which provides for a referendum for the solution of the Bougainville conflict.

---

[66] The Constitution of Macedonia goes as follows: "The decision on any change in the borders of the Republic is adopted by referendum, in so far as it is accepted by the majority of the total number of voters" (Art. 74, Para. 2).

[67] "[S]tate borders of the Azerbaijan Republic might be changed only by free decision of its peoples made by way of referendum declared by Milli Majlis of the Azerbaijan Republic."

[68] Article 173 entitled as "Consultative Procedure" goes as follows: "Political decisions of special significance should be subject to consultation procedure for all citizens. The consultation will be convened by the Supreme Electoral Tribunal on the initiative of the President of the Republic or the Congress, which set a precise or questions to be undergo the people. The Constitutional Law on Elections regulate what this institution".

According to the Constitution, the referendum on the future status of Bougainville "shall be held on a date agreed after consultation by the Bougainville Government with the National Government, which date shall be not earlier than 10 years and, notwithstanding any other provision, not more than 15 years after the election of the first Bougainville Government" (Art. 338-1). "The Referendum shall not be held where the Bougainville Government decides, in accordance with the Bougainville Constitution, after consultation with the National Government, that the Referendum shall not be held" (Art. 338-7).[69]

6.2.3.4 International Relations (Transfer of Sovereignty)

Referendums may be found as a part of the procedures and provisions that govern the international relations of the states. Transfer of sovereignty and the issues of union and federation of states may appear as the subject matter of referendums in different constitutions. The most common example of this is the referendum on European Integration. In this vein, the fundamental constitutional question in a country regarding its membership to the EU is the transfer of state competences to the institutions of the Union. The majority of these countries include specific constitutional provisions in this respect.[70] EU-related referendums may be classified into three categories with respect to their rapport with the European Union: accession, integration and enlargement.[71]

Firstly, accession referendums are held in a European country to decide whether or not to join the EEC, EEA, EU and/or Euro. Secondly, by means of integration referendums, "the voters decide on the continuation and intensification of the integration process". These are the national referendums held in EU countries on amendments of the founding treaties, such as the Single European Act (SEA) of 1986, the Maastricht Treaty of 1992, the Amsterdam Treaty of 1998, the Nice Treaty of 2001 and the Constitutional Treaty of 2004. Finally, enlargement referendums are held in a member state to decide the accession of a candidate state. It is an invention of France and will be discussed in greater detail under the following section examining France. In the following paragraphs, examples are given for accession and integration referendums.

[69] Bougainville is a region in Papua New Guinea where the secessionist movement arose in 1988 and conflict between Bougainville Revolutionary Army (BRA) and the government of Papua New Guinea continued until 1997 after the negotiations sponsored by New Zealand. A peace agreement was concluded in this process in 2000, which provided for the institution of an Autonomous Bougainville Government and for a constitutionally guaranteed referendum for the final decision on the international status of the region. Alley (2003), p. 249.

[70] Schwarze (2001), p. 489.

[71] Auer (2007), p. 264.

The first series of accession referendums were held by Ireland, Denmark and Norway in 1972.[72] In Ireland, the Constitution conferred the exclusive right to make the laws of state to the national parliament. Accession to the European Community contradicted this provision, which required a constitutional change. The referendum on accession was held pursuant to the obligatory referendum clause for constitutional amendments (The Constitution of Ireland, Art. 46). In the Danish case, the referendum was held according to the referendum obligation stipulated as an alternative to the enhanced majority of the *Folketing* (i.e., five-sixths of the members of the parliament) (Constitution of Denmark, Art. 20). This article stipulates a referendum for the transfer of state powers to the international authorities. In Norway, there was no constitutional base at all. This country does not have any constitutional provision regarding referendum. The referendum was held ad hoc on the initiative of the government.

Three other countries joined the EU after referendums: Austria, Finland and Sweden. Austria did this pursuant to the obligatory referendum clause in its Constitution (Art. 44/3), which requires a referendum for a total or fundamental change in the constitution. The coalition government of the day decided to hold a referendum on their accession to the EU based on this article and a past decision of the Austrian Constitutional Court concerning the jurisdiction of the European Court of Human Rights.[73] The 1919 Constitution of Finland created a consultative referendum, without specifying any subject matter, and the parliament was granted the right to hold that referendum by an Act. The accession referendum was held according to this provision.[74] In Sweden, the Constitution says: "provisions concerning consultative referendums throughout the whole country and concerning procedure for holding referendums on matters concerning the fundamental laws shall be laid down by an act of law" (Chapter 8, Article 4). This article also says, "a simple majority of the Parliament can call for a popular vote on any issue", and the referendum on the accession of Sweden to the EU was held according to this provision.[75]

A third wave of accession referendums began during the accession of Eastern European countries to the EU. With the exceptions of Romania and Bulgaria, all of

---

[72] For Ireland, see Gallagher (1996), p. 91; Rideau (1997), p. 105. Taaffe (2004), pp. 70–73. For Denmark see: Svensson (1996), p. 41; Kjaerulff-Schmidt (2004), p. 53; Rideau (1997), p. 104. For Norway, see Wyller (1996), p. 139; Björklund (2004), p. 99.

[73] Rideau (1997), p. 109.

[74] Anckar (2004), p. 59; Suksi (1996), p. 56. For the 1919 Constitution: http://www.servat.unibe.ch/icl/fi01000_.html. Retrieved 15 December 2010. A similar sort of referendum is found in Finland's new Constitution of 2000 Art. 53: "The decision to organize a consultative referendum is made by an Act, which shall contain provisions on the time of the referendum and on the choices to be presented to the voters. Provisions concerning the conduct of a referendum are laid down by an Act". http://www.finlex.fi/fi/laki/kaannokset/1999/en19990731.pdf. Retrieved 15 December 2010 Available at the official site of ministry of justice: http://www.om.fi/21910.htm. Retrieved 15 December 2010.

[75] Goldmann (2004), p. 115; Ruin (1996), p. 171.

the Eastern European countries held referendums before accession to the EU. In Poland, the referendum was held according to the Polish Constitution, which requires a referendum for the transfer of powers to international organisations as an alternative procedure to the enhanced majority of the Polish parliament (*Sejm*). According to Art. 90, a referendum is required if the parliament (*Sejm*) cannot secure a two-thirds majority.[76] The Slovak Constitution contains two types of referendums. There is an obligatory referendum for the international treaties that provide accession to "alliances with other states" (Art. 7 and 93/1) and a facultative-consultative referendum on "other important questions of public interest" (Art. 93/2). According to Barany, Brhlikova and Colotka, the question of EU accession did not require a referendum under Article 93/1, considering that the EU did not have the character of a "state".[77] The practice affirmed this interpretation: for accession, a consultative referendum was held pursuant to a parliamentary decision according to Article 93/2 of the Constitution.[78] The accession of Slovenia to the EU as well as to NATO was put to referendum, according to Article 3a on "European Union", which provides a facultative but binding referendum following the initiation of the parliament. In Hungary, a constitutional amendment was made by an inter-party consensus in the parliament. The amendment to the constitution provided an obligatory and binding referendum for Hungary's accession to the EU, and the vote was held according to this provision.[79] In the case of Latvia, its membership required a constitutional amendment in the sovereignty clause (the Constitution of Latvia, Art. 2), which was subject to a compulsory referendum (Art. 77). To circumvent the condition of the support of one-half of the electorate as required by this article, the Latvian parliament (the Saeima) chose to amend the constitution to add a specific obligatory referendum clause for accession to the EU. The referendum was then held according to this provision (Art. 68. par. 2 and Art. 79).[80] The Estonian accession was made in the form of a constitutional change, and the question was put to referendum under the articles governing the amendments to the constitution (Constitution of Estonia, Art. 105, 162, 163, 164 and 167). In the Czech Republic, the 1993 Constitution does not have any explicit reference to referendum. The only constitutional provision is that "a constitutional act may designate the conditions under which the people may exercise the state authority directly".[81] The accession referendum was held on an *ad hoc* basis pursuant to a law

[76] Gebethner (2001), p. 132.

[77] Barany et al. (2001), p. 172.

[78] http://www.c2d.ch/detailed_display.php?lname=votes&table=votes&page=1&parent_id=&sublinkname=results&id=39083. Retrieved 15 January 2011.

[79] Reti (2004), p. 69

[80] Feldhune (2004), p. 82.

[81] Gillis (2001), p. 42.

enacted by the parliament.[82] In Croatia, referendum was held on 22 January 2012, which was held pursuant to Article 135 of the Croatian Constitution regulating the "alliances with other states".

As to the integration referendum, it was originally applied in Denmark when, in 1986, the treaty on the Single European Act was voted for by the electorate. Contrary to other integration referendums, the referendum was not held according to Article 20 Par. 2. It was an ad hoc consultative referendum after a parliamentary Act, which did not have any self-executing effect as provided in Article 20. In Ireland, the integration referendum has been the standard procedure since the ratification of the Single European Act (SEA). In 1987, the Irish Supreme Court decided that the ratification of the SEA could not be made by a mere parliamentary majority, which is the normal mode for the ratification of international treaties. It required a change in the constitution. Since the Irish Constitution provides an obligatory referendum for constitutional amendments, this decision made the referendum an indispensable element for the adoption of any treaty related to the EU within an Irish context.[83]

Although not as successful as the European Union, we may observe similar aspirations of regional integration elsewhere in the world and referendums are found as a common element of an eventual integration procedure in the constitutions concerned. Following this pattern, the constitutions of certain African states have created referendums on future African Unity.[84] According to the Constitution of Burkina Faso, the treaties pertaining to the entry into confederation, federation or Union of African states will be submitted to the people's approval via referendum (Constitution of Burkina Faso, Art. 147). In the same way, the Constitution of the Central African Republic says: "the Republic may, after referendum, conclude with any African state accords of association or of fusion including partial or total abandonment of sovereignty in view of realizing African unity" (Art. 67).

The same goal for interstate unification is found in Latin America. El Salvador gives herself the duty to promote "total or partial re-establishment of Central America, and if this is realized, the project and the bases of the union shall be submitted to popular consultation".[85]

[82] The referendum of Czech Republic represents a convincing example for the entrenchment of referendum obligation in the political practice on important sovereignty issues: "In the referendum on the country's accession to the EU, pressure from abroad played an important role. It no longer seems possible for any country to join the EU without its being sanctioned by the citizens in a referendum" Valach (2004), p. 50.

[83] Gallagher (1996), p. 91.

[84] Official Site of the African Union: http://www.au.int. Retrieved 15 July 2012.

[85] Suksi (1993), p. 145. Other examples of referendums for regional integration may be listed as follows: the Croatian Constitution contains a procedure for the association (and disassociation) of the Republic of Croatia into (and from) alliances with other states. This procedure contains an obligatory referendum (The Constitution of Croatia, Art. 135). A similar procedure with a referendum is also found in the Constitution of Slovakia [Art. 7 and (93/1)]. In Rwanda, "The federation of the Republic of Rwanda with one or several other democratic states must be approved by means of a referendum" (The Constitution of Rwanda, Art. 44). The Tunisian

6.2.4 Sovereignty Referendums in France

The French are sceptical about the referendum device. It is a common doctrinal assumption that French political thought and tradition are categorically hostile to referendum, and one of the chief reasons is that it was shrewdly distorted by Napoleon to legitimise his authoritarian rule.[86] Nevertheless, referendums have played a major role in the turning points of the constitutional history of France, that is, all French constitutions have been approved by a referendum. Commenting on this, Auer highlights that the use of referendum in the adoption of the constitutions is a genuine tradition dating back to the early years of French Revolution.[87] There was a marked increase in the use of referendums in the Fifth Republic during the presidency of De Gaulle, who resorted to referendum to overcome legal and political problems created by domestic and foreign policy issues—particularly those of decolonisation. The early years of the Fifth Republic, like any other transitory period, were marked with instability and referendum proved to be an effective tool in overcoming the political deadlock during the settlement of the constitutional structure of the Republic and post-WWII territorial readjustments.[88]

France is the first country in Europe that renounced the war of conquest. The Constitution of 1791 said: "*la nation française renonce à entreprendre aucune guerre dans la vue de faire des conquêtes et qu'elle n'emploiera jamais ses forces contre la liberté d'aucun peuple*". It was following this principle that post-revolutionary territorial acquisitions were always effectuated through referendums. It may also be said that France was an avid defender of the principle of nationalities, which in this context meant that each nationality has the right to constitute its own state.[89]

These historical facts made France a pioneer of sovereignty referendums in Europe. Needless to say, it was also the inventor of constitutional referendums in general. Moreover, the Fifth Republic saw a boost in sovereignty referendums. Dobelle argues that the biggest number of "self-determination referendums" of the

---

Constitution has the following provisions: "Article 2 [Arab Nation, Treaties] (1) The Tunisian Republic constitutes part of the Great Arab Maghreb, towards whose unity it works within the framework of common interests. (2) Treaties concluded to this effect and being of such nature as to bring about any modification whatsoever to the present Constitution have to be submitted to a referendum by the President of the Republic after having been adopted by the National Parliament in the forms and conditions established by the Constitution".

[86] Ardant (2005), p. 148; Hamon (1995), p. 57; Roussillon (1996), pp. 181–186.

[87] Auer (1996), p. 91.

[88] Hamon (1995), pp. 88–89; Morel (2001), p. 57.

[89] Amiel (1976), pp. 445–447 notes that this should not be confused with self-determination of the people. While the principle of nationalities means a set of facts, conditions and historical determinism, the self-determination of people emphasised the free will of the people to choose which state to belong.

world belongs to those of France: held in the context of its policy of decolonisation since 1958.[90] On the other hand, sticking to a voluntarist conception of international law, France has consistently rejected the objectivist conception of sovereignty referendums. As noted before, objectivists hold the view that the legal base of sovereignty referendums are provided either by custom or by several resolutions of the UN General Assembly. France, on the contrary, considers that sovereignty referendums are not part of international customary law and that the United Nations resolutions are only of a facultative nature. Assuming that sovereignty referendums are acts of internal law emanating from its own will, France has often shown a certain degree of mistrust and reluctance with regard to international interference. According to French state practice, referendums in international law may only find their legal foundations when France gives its consent by means of bilateral or multilateral treaties. Nevertheless, neither of these treaties may be taken to constitute a precedent, nor do they imply any sort of *opinio juris* of France on the issue. The consent given by France is, by definition, ad hoc and has to be obtained for each separate incidence of referendum. The international aspect of referendum, in most cases, is confined to the outcome of the proceedings: building a new state and recognition of it by France. With certain exceptions where limited international involvement is allowed *à titre gracieux*, the whole process has been presumed to be under the exclusive control of France and French laws. [91]

In short, the French conception of sovereignty referendums results in the rejection of any international interference with regard to initiation, procedures, implementation and judicial review of referendums. Then the legal source is provided by the Constitution. This puts France in a unique position: while being the inventor of sovereignty referendums, France shows a strong tendency to domesticate this very international question under its own constitutional system. Consequently, France offers a rich source of constitutional-legal rules and practices for a student of comparative constitutional law within the context of sovereignty referendums.[92]

6.2.4.1 Constitutional Provisions

The Constitution of the Fifth Republic[93] recognises the right of people to exercise their sovereignty by means of referendum (Art. 3). Article 11 stipulates a legislative referendum: the possibility to hold a referendum on any government bill concerning, among others, "the organization of the public authorities", (*pouvoirs publics*) and "authorization to ratify a treaty which, although not contrary to the

[90] Dobelle (1996), p. 54.

[91] Dobelle (1996), p. 55; Amiel (1976), p. 436.

[92] Amiel (1976), p. 436.

[93] An official English translation of the Constitution may be found at http://www.conseil-constitutionnel.fr/conseil-constitutionnel/root/bank_mm/anglais/constiution_anglais_oct2009.pdf. Retrieved 10 September 2011. This text will be used in this and other relevant sections.

Constitution, would affect the functioning of the institutions". The Constitution reserves the power to initiate the referendum to the president, and this is one of the presidential powers that is not subject to a countersignature (Arts. 19 and 11). The president, being the decisional authority on the referendum, is not alone in the process: he may act only "on a recommendation from the Government when Parliament is in session, or upon a joint motion of the two Houses". However, this restriction imposes very little difficulty on the president. Considering the political and constitutional nature of French semi-presidential system, particularly when the president and parliamentary majority are from the same political party, the prime minister who is appointed by the president would have no disagreement with the president concerning the "proposing" of the referendum. Therefore, it may be safely said that referendum is a "presidential prerogative" in terms of this article.[94] In fact, on 23 July 2008, the constitutional monopoly of the president to decide on a referendum was ended by a constitutional amendment. The new system creates a double initiative: the proposal to hold a referendum should emanate from one-fifth of the members of the Parliament and should then receive the signature of one-tenth of all registered voters. However, there is no legal obstacle requiring voter support to be submitted beforehand, which allows us to define this new device (also) as "a popular initiative". Yet at the time of writing, the executing organic law has not been enacted, obstructing the actual working of this new procedure.[95]

Article 89 stipulates two types of constitutional revisions: those initiated by the Parliament (proposal) and those initiated by the President on the recommendation of the government (project). The referendum is obligatory for parliamentary proposals, whereas for the projects initiated by the President, it is facultative. The President, in the latter case, may either submit the project to referendum or send it back to the Parliament to obtain an enhanced majority of 3/5 of the votes cast. Also according to this article, the President is the main actor in the decision of holding a referendum, with just one exception: in contrast to Article 11, Article 89 holds that constitutional revisions should be first approved by the Parliament before the referendum.

There is another category of referendum on the accession of new states to the European Union (Art. 88-5). This sort of referendum may be termed as "enlargement referendums", where the voters of one state decide on the accession of a candidate state. This relatively recent article has been vehemently criticised by certain authors, in that it was introduced during Jacques Chirac's presidential term to defer the discussions on Turkey's accession, thus staying cynically neutral on the issue and avoiding any political responsibility. This political manoeuvre on the very divisive issue of the adhesion of Turkey to the EU has created an awkward sort of referendum that has defects in many aspects. Auer, for instance, criticises it on moral grounds as a simple parody of democracy and a distortion of the referendum device. For him:

[94] Conac (1987), p. 420.

[95] Formery (2011), pp. 39–40.

> *Il n'y a rien de moins démocratique que de demander aux citoyens d'un pays de décider de l'adhésion d'un pays, parce que le résultat affecte principalement le gouvernement et le peuple de l'Etat candidat, sans même que la volonté de ce peuple ne soit prise en considé ration. Faisant implicitement appel aux instincts les plus bas, comme un sentiment de supé riorité, un nationalisme exagéré, voire la xénophobie, le procédé manque singulièrement de cette qualité qui est le propre des instruments de démocratie directe: la légitimité.*[96]

For Carcassone, this provision is "*vain*", "*inadequat*", "*inepte*" and "*trompeuse*".[97] Foremost, the issue of Turkey will probably no longer exist in ten or more years: either the adhesion process will fail or the negotiation will take a positive course and public opinion in France will be less sceptical on the issue. In both cases, a referendum will be irrelevant. Even if the question remains divisive, rendering such a *de facto* obligatory referendum as *de jure* obligatory is superfluous and unnecessary. Article 11 might have well served as the legal basis for such a referendum, as had been the case for the referendum on the adhesion of the UK, Denmark, Ireland and Norway in 1972. This rigidity means, whatever the political circumstances surrounding the adhesion of a country may be, the statesmen will have no way of escaping from a referendum putting France in a ridiculous position regarding its international relations in the case of an unexpected result.

This provision is also deceptive. The article speaks only of "governmental bills" (*projet de loi*), which may imply that if the adhesion of a new state to the EU is made by virtue of a parliamentary initiative (i.e., proposal), it may be exempted from a referendum. There is no constitutional obstacle for a parliamentary majority to prefer this method of proposal instead of governmental bills. The president, providing he controls the parliamentary majority, may use this tactic if he wants to avoid a referendum. Yet, in such a case, he may possibly meet legitimate criticisms of constitutional fraud.

Finally, the third paragraph of the Article 53 stipulates: "No ceding, exchanging or acquiring of territory shall be valid without the consent of the population concerned". This article was the constitutional foundation for referendums held in the framework of decolonisation in overseas regions. In the face of the explicit articulation of "referendum" in Articles 11 and 89, the "consent" may not readily be associated with referendum: considering there may be other forms of acquisition of consent. The Constitutional Council, for example, refused to interpret this wording as a genuine referendum, which led to a self-restraint of competence in the referendums held in the overseas territories. Commenting on this, Favoreu notes that the popular consultation specified by Article 53/3 may not be construed as a referendum, as it is under Articles 11 and 89.[98] According to Amiel, this article does not exclusively indicate a *plébiscite* but also indicates any other method to ascertain the consent of the population concerned. Nevertheless, the interpretation known as the Capitant's doctrine served to overcome this ambiguity. Officially endorsed, this

[96] Auer (2007), p. 68.

[97] Carcassonne (2007), pp. 376–378.

[98] Favoreau (1976), p. 568.

doctrine maintains that this article may serve as the constitutional basis for sovereignty referendums.[99] Capitant's doctrine and its counter-arguments will be discussed in detail below.

6.2.4.2 Practices: Overseas Territories of France

Approval of the 1958 Constitution The 1958 Constitution provided for two distinct constitutional statuses for its insular regions. They are Overseas Departments (Département d'Outre Mer: DOM) and Overseas Territories (Territoire d'Outre Mer: TOM). The former category included the regions that had closer links to Metropolitan France in comparison to the latter. In 1958, the Constitution offered the possibility for the Overseas Territories to choose their political future. By means of the referendum of 28 September 1958, they could stay within the French Republic or become immediately independent. To do so, they had to reject the draft Constitution. The only support for the "no" was in Guinea, which became independent on the 30th of September 1958. Furthermore, the Overseas Territories were given the option to become a member of the French Community, which meant a loose association with France while gaining independence within a 4-month period after the promulgation of the Constitution. Five small overseas territories decided to remain in their existing status, whereas other large overseas territories in Africa decided to be independent and become a part of the Community.

At the end of this process, the Republic of France was declared to be "indivisible", comprising Metropolitan France, its Overseas Departments and Overseas Territories. Article 86 provided the procedure for the withdrawal of a member state from the Community. The article specified two alternative ways a member state could withdraw, either by virtue of a Parliamentary decision or by a decision of the local parliament ensuing a local referendum. However, this and other provisions in the Constitution about the Community remained obsolete, when within 2 years all the Communities became (entirely) independent without any referendum.[100]

The Independence of Algeria During the process of accession of Algeria to independence, there were two referendums in Metropolitan France (1961–1962) and one in Algeria (1962). The constitutional base was Article 11 for the Metropolitan referendums and Article 53/3 for the one in Algeria. In the face of a war that had continued for almost 4 years, the President declared the possibility of holding a referendum on the future status of Algeria on 16 September 1959. This first referendum (8 January 1961) was to decide on the new political orientation concerning Algeria and to recognise, in principle, the right to self-determination of the Algerian people. The governmental bill put to referendum laid the legal base of the interim regime, that is, "the organization of the public powers until (deciding

[99] Amiel (1976), pp. 447–449.

[100] Maestre (1976), pp. 434–435; Amiel (1976), pp. 448–449.

on) self-determination". The second referendum (8th of April 1962) was on the government bill, legalising the Evian Agreements, which officially recognised Algerian independence. The final referendum was held in Algeria on the 1st of July 1962, and on the 3rd of July 1962, President de Gaulle officially declared its independence.[101]

New Caledonia New Caledonia is a French overseas territory located in the Pacific Ocean with a population of around 250,000. It is classified as a *sui generis* community according to the Constitution of France (Articles 76 and 77) and considered as a Non-Self-Governing Territory by the U.N.[102]

The region is troubled by the Kanak independence movement that started in the 1970s, being induced by the decolonisation process in Africa and ensuing mass immigration of French descendants. In 1984, this movement had transformed into the *Front de libération nationale kanak et socialiste* (*FLNKS*), an umbrella organisation established for the pro-independence parties. The FLNKS established a transitory independent government later in 1984, and this was immediately followed by a violent strife between the pro-independence and loyalist groups, which continued until 1988. The violence was brought to an end with the conclusion of the Matignon Accords on 26 June 1988 between FLNKS, the loyalists *Rassemblement pour la Calédonie dans la République* (*RPCR*) and the French government. The Matignon Accords endowed the region with a greater local autonomy and specified a 10-year transitory status, after which a self-determination referendum would be held. However, in 1998 in the run up to the referendum, the Matignon Agreements were replaced by the Nouméa Accord. This Accord defined the devolution process as "irreversible". It provided for a practically sovereign status, including the Caledonian citizenship, which left only basic state powers such as security, justice and international relations to the mainland. The agreement sought a "middle course between the respective political aspirations of RPCR and FLNKS and avoided the need for a divisive referendum on independence".[103] The Accord was signed on 5 May 1998 and approved in a referendum held in New Caledonia on 8 November 1998 with 72 % support. The Accord was then ratified by the National Assembly and the Senate of France. A subsequent French law legalised the rules that would govern the said referendum. This organic law (*Loi organique n°99-209 du 19 mars 1999 relative à la Nouvelle-Calédonia*) and an ordinary law were presented in the French Parliament. The organic law codified the matters addressed in Article 77 of the French Constitution as amended by the reform, namely, the powers that would be transferred to the newly created institutions in New Caledonia, the organisation of those institutions, rules concerning New

[101] Maestre (1976), p. 438.

[102] The UN General Assembly Document: "New Caledonia: Working paper prepared by the Secretariat" of 21 March 2011, A/AC.109/2011/16, Paras. 1–4.

[103] The UN General Assembly Document: "New Caledonia: Working paper prepared by the Secretariat" of 21 March 2011, A/AC.109/2011/16, Para 6.

Caledonian citizenship, and the electoral regime and conditions and deadlines by which New Caledonians would determine their accession to full sovereignty. [104]

The Nouméa Accord provided for a transitional phase. It commends France to transfer certain state competences, excepting sovereign powers, to the government of New Caledonia between 1998 and 2018. At a certain date between 2013 and 2018, a referendum will be held for a final resolution of the territory's sovereignty status. The fundamental issues to be the subject of the future referendum are transfer of sovereign powers, access to an international status of full responsibility and the regulation of New Caledonian citizenship.

The determination of the exact date of this referendum is left to the territorial Congress, that will be decided by three-fifths of its members. If the outcome of the referendum is negative, one-third of the members of the Congress are entitled to call two more referendums on the same subjects. If the outcome of these referendums is positive, the parties of the Nouméa Accord will meet to consider the situation. In any case, "the political organization set up by the 1998 Agreement will remain in force in its latest stage of evolution, without there being any possibility of reversal; such 'irreversibility' being constitutionally guaranteed".[105]

Comoros and the Question of Mayotte The Comoros Archipelago, consisting of four islands (Mayotte, Grande Comoros, Mohéli and Anjouan), became a TOM in 1957, and following the referendum on the French Constitution of 1958 the same status remained. In the period that followed, the autonomy of Comoros has gradually increased. In 1961, for example, a law established a specific organisation as an autonomous administration and created a Local Executive and a Local Assembly. A new law of January 1968 has reinforced the internal autonomy of the territory by extending the powers of the legislature against the executive.[106]

In 1973, a joint declaration of French and Comorian authorities was made on the future of the territory. This declaration provided a 5-year transitory period of gradual devolution, at the end of which a popular consultation would be held. A dispute arose concerning the demarcation of the voting districts of a future referendum, in other words, whether the referendum would be held on an island-by-island basis or the four islands would be consulted collectively.

The demand for independence came earlier: on the eve of the presidential elections in Comoros, President Abdallah decided to resolve the issue prematurely with a prospect of boosting his political popularity. Pursuant to this, the French parliament adopted the law of 22 November 1974 and the referendum was held on

[104] Marrani (2006), p. 20; we prefer to use the term "Organic Law" rather than the term "Institutional Act", as appears in the official English translation of the 1958 French Constitution.

[105] *"Nouméa Accord – Digest" (2002) 7 Australian Indigenous Law Reporter 88*, Retrieved on 12 August 2011 from http://www.austlii.edu.au/au/journals/AILR/2002/17.html.

[106] Freedman (2004), pp. 12–13.

22 December 1974. The result was for independence with a 94.57 % vote.[107] Yet Mayotte's vote, when counted separately, was for remaining a part of France. On this occasion, France adopted a "Comoro Islands Independence Bill", which provided for a preparation of a constitutional draft to be put to referendum on an island-by-island basis. Comoro's reaction was an outright unilateral declaration of independence. This declaration was followed by a French Law of 31 December 1975, which recognised the independence of three other islands apart from Mayotte. A referendum was then to be held on the future of the island within 2 months from the promulgation of that law. The referendum was held on 8 February 1976, asking the electorate of Mayotte whether they wanted to "remain with France" or join Comoros. The result was overwhelmingly for retaining links with France (99.4 %). In a second referendum held on 11 April 1976, the voters of Mayotte were asked whether they wished the island "to retain its status as an overseas territory". The result was 97.46 % for abandoning that status, which was construed by France as Mayotte wishing to gain a constitutional status for closer ties with Metropolitan France. Consequently, a French law gave Mayotte a special status as a *collectivité territoriale*. Mayotte's status was consolidated by a French Law of 1979, which said Mayotte would not "cease to belong to France without the consent of its population". In the following years, this *status quo* remained with continuing disputes.

Mayotte remained a subject of controversy in international law: its adherence to France was strongly contested and condemned by a majority of the UN and by the Organization of African Unity (OAU). The General Assembly adopted a resolution by 102 votes asking France to withdraw from Mayotte while accusing the previously mentioned referendums as "null and void". Furthermore, in the same resolution it is said: "Considering that the referendums imposed on the inhabitants of the Comorian island of Mayotte constitute a violation of the sovereignty of the Comorian State and of its territorial integrity". Finally, the General Assembly "Condemned and considered null and void the referendums of 8 February and 11 April 1976 organized in the Comorian island of Mayotte by the Government of France. It also reject(ed) any form of referendum or consultation which may (thereafter) be organized on Comorian territory in Mayotte by France".[108] On 28 November 1980, the UN reaffirmed its position by another resolution recognising "the sovereignty of the Islamic Federal Republic of Comoros over the island of Mayotte".[109]

---

[107] http://www.c2d.ch/detailed_display.php?lname=votes&table=votes&page=1&parent_id=&sublinkname=results&id=38240. Retrieved 12 November 2012.

[108] A/RES/31/4: The UN General Assembly Resolution of 21 October 1976, on the "*Question of the Comorian island of Mayotte*".

[109] A/RES/35/42: The UN General Assembly Resolution of 28 November 1980, on the "*Question of the Comorian island of Mayotte*". This view is reiterated in further resolutions: A/RES/36/105: The UN General Assembly Resolution of 10 December 1981 on the "*Question of the Comorian island of Mayotte*", A/RES/41/30: The UN General Assembly Resolution of 3 November 1986, on the "*Question of the Comorian island of Mayotte*". In the meantime, the secessionist demands spread out to the other islands, Anjouan and Moheli. In Anjouan, for example, there were two

On 27 January 2000, an agreement was signed between the French government and the major political parties in Mayotte. A referendum was held on 2 July 2000 by which the Mahorais approved this agreement by 72.94 %. On July, 2001, France adopted a law giving Mayotte the status of a Departmental Collectivity. This law said that Mayotte was a part of the French Republic and could not cease to be so without the consent of its population.[110] Finally, in 2009, Mayotte had another referendum pursuant to the aforementioned agreement and Article 72-4 of the French Constitution. In this referendum, the Mahorais gave their approval to becoming an Overseas French Department governed by Article 73 of the Constitution[111].

6.2.4.3 Review of Doctrine and Debates on Articles 11 and 53/3

Several sovereignty referendums, including two Algerian referendums, the referendum on New Caledonia and the referendum on the accession of new countries to the EU, were held pursuant to Article 11. This raised criticisms in the doctrine. The question within this context was a "delicate problem of interpretation" of the scope of Article 11: should the phrase "any…bill concerning the organization of the public authorities" be understood in a narrow sense, covering the secondary administrative institutions, or in a broad sense, which could also imply constitutional matters? The narrow interpretation is supported by the majority of the doctrine, whereas the political practice proved contrary. [112]

The discussions were both from a material and a formal point of view. Materially, it was questioned, by Pavia for example, as to whether the issues of self-determination and the legal provisions for the interim constitutional regime until the decision of self-determination could be simply demoted to the "organization of the public authorities". Commenting on the metropolitan referendums on Algeria and New Caledonia, he noted that *"l'organization des pouvoirs publics veut dire "autodétermination et l'on ne peut que constater le ralliement a une interprétation très extensive du domaine de l'article 11"*.[113] The referendum on the accession of new countries to the European Community in 1972 was criticised in a similar manner. In this context, it was questioned whether the treaty of accession of new countries affected "the functioning of the French Institutions".[114]

Formally, the question was raised as to whether the *tout projet de loi* would entail, with a large interpretation, the constitutional revisions or only ordinary laws

respective independence referendums (1997 and 2000) held unilaterally by the Anjouan separatist movement (Freedman 2004, p. 16).

[110] Freedman (2004), p. 18.

[111] http://www.c2d.ch/detailed_display.php?lname=votes&table=votes&page=1&parent_id=&sublinkname=results&id=57807. Retrieved 11 October 2012.

[112] Hamon (1995), pp. 83–84.

[113] Pavia (1989), p. 1708.

[114] Rideau (1997), p. 107.

as defended by the narrow interpretations. The doubt was raised about the constitutionality of the use of Article 11 for constitutional revisions, in the face of Article 89, which specifically laid down the procedure for that purpose.

This controversy arose during the referendums concerning the direct election of the president and the senate reform. On the other hand, ramifications of this debate may be sensed in the context of sovereignty referendums. Capitant, for instance, argued that the two Algerian referendums, by the secession of two departments of France, resulted in a constitutional revision, and it was legitimate for the president to hold a referendum according to Article 11, which according to him "autorise le Président de la République a soumettre au peuple Français directement tout projet de loi de révision constitutionnelle, car toute la constitution est consacrée a l'organization des pouvoirs publics".[115]

On the opposite side, arguments were for the defence of the formality of the constitutional change and *parallélisme des formes*. Pavia refers to the different types of legislative acts in the French Constitution, which are in an up-down row in the hierarchy of norms: constitution, organic laws and ordinary laws (the Constitution of France Art. 38). Each of these legislative acts has its own adoption procedure. The use of Article 11 renders this normative order futile, by making the president the only authority to decide the content of the law to be put to referendum by circumventing the parliament.

Article 53/3: Whereas Article 11 was preferred for the referendums in mainland France, Article 53/3 was cited as the constitutional basis of the referendums held in the overseas territories such as Algeria, the Comoros, the Republic of Djbouti (Territory of the Afars and Issas) and New Caledonia.[116] The interpretation of this article has also given rise to controversy on a doctrinal and political level.

The question arose as to whether Article 53/3 could be applicable not only for the cases of "cession" (i.e., ceding of a territory by France on its own consent) but also in the cases of "secession" of territories belonging to France. Discussions revolved for the most part from a material point of view around the right to external self-determination of those overseas territories and departments (TOMs and DOMs) that had already accepted the 1958 Constitution and had become an integral part of France. In the face of the "indivisibility" of the republic, it became contentious whether Article 53/3 gave the overseas territories the right to outright secession or there should be a constitutional revision before it.[117] René Capitant answered this question, whose interpretation afterwards was widely endorsed by statesmen and the Constitutional Council. He was asked whether the referendum in the Territory of the Afars and Issas (Djibouti) was constitutional. He concluded that Article 53/3 could be used as the legal basis for the referendum in question. Capitant made a distinction between TOM and DOM. For Capitant, the territories falling under the former category have not lost their right to leave the Republic even

[115] Maestre (1976), p. 446.
[116] Debbasch et al. (1986), p. 468.
[117] Christakis (1999), p. 292.

after the expiration of the 4-month deadline as specified by the 1958 Constitution. Thus, the right to external self-determination of these territories was said to have a permanent status under Article 53/3 and thus could be used not only in case of transfer of territory to a foreign state (cession) but also for the secession.

The difficulty arising from the fact that this article governs "international treaties" but not the creation of states could be overcome by the supposition that the so-called international treaty took "*par la force des choses*", "*une forme spé ciale*", in which the recognition of independence by France was a "*l'acte international*". For Capitant, in order to effectuate a secession of a territory under this article, two conditions should be fulfilled: (1) prior consent of the population concerned, (2) the approval of the parliament by a subsequent law authorising the secession.[118] Certain other scholars, such as Duverger, went one step further by believing that Article 53/3 could be used for any incidence of secession, provided that the consent of the relevant people and an ensuing approval by the parliament are secured. [119] Pellet argued in a similar manner that "*Le dernier alinéa de l'article 53 constitue bien la base juridique du droit a la sécession des territoires, intègres dans la République, qui désirent accéder a l'indépendance*".[120]

Capitant's doctrine was endorsed by the parliament of the era, and the interpretation of the Constitutional Council supported even the wider application. In its decision on 30 December 1975 on the self-determination of Comoros islands, the Council asserted in this way that[121]:

> *Les dispositions de cet article doivent être interprétées comme étant applicables, non seulement dans l'hypothèse où la France céderait à un État étranger ou bien acquerrait de celui-ci un territoire, mais aussi dans l'hypothèse où un territoire cesserait d'appartenir à la République pour constituer un État indépendant ou y être rattaché.*

On the other hand, the counter-argument against Capitant's doctrine was raised, notably by Maestre. For him, the decision of the Constitutional Council was *à la limite du contra constitutionem.* A literal and narrow interpretation of Article 53/3 plainly excluded the possibility of secession, in that the constituent power would have simply added the word "secession" if it had been so desired.[122] While the wording includes only "ceding", "exchanging" and "acquiring", each having distinct meaning in international law, the non-inclusion of "secession" should be construed in this manner. He also indicates that Article 53 speaks of genuine international treaties that presuppose two or more sovereign states. This does not fit the relationship between Metropolitan France and its territories.

---

[118] Maestre (1976), p. 136.

[119] Maestre (1976), p. 136.

[120] Pellet (1987), p. 1056.

[121] *Décision n° 75–59 DC du 30 décembre 1975 "Loi relative aux conséquences de l'autodé termination des îles des Comores"* (http://www.conseil-constitutionnel.fr/conseil-constitutionnel/francais/les-decisions/depuis-1958/decisions-par-date/1975/75-59-dc/decision-n-75-59-dc-du-30-decembre-1975.7429.html. Retrieved 11 November 2009).

[122] Christakis (1999), p. 292; Amiel (1976), p. 449.

These arguments were mainly from a material point of view. On the formal side, Maestre noted that no law organising the referendums or putting into effect their outcomes had made explicit reference to Article 53/3. This, he assumed, stemmed from the intention of the government to deter any possible "institutionalization" of Article 53/3 for the "hypotheses" that are not provided by the Constitution. His conclusion was that recourse to Article 53/3 for these referendums was no more than a *coloration juridique à des opérations inconstitutionnels.*[123] On the other hand, further practices refuted this argument. For example, the law stipulating the referendum in New Caledonia in 1998 explicitly mentioned Article 53/3 as the constitutional base.[124] In any case, it is evident that this legal problem of "internal order" stemmed from the intensive effort to find a legal basis for the irreversible process of decolonisation being vigorously imposed by the "international order".[125] France had no possibility of escaping from the pressures of the international community concerning its overseas territories, as they undoubtedly fell under Article 73 of the UN Charter and Resolutions 1514 and 1541, and consequently from which the international community recognised the explicit right to independence. The Capitant doctrine may be taken in this way: as a mere *ex post facto* constitutional explanation to internally legitimise the unyielding decolonisation movement. Commenting on the decision of the Constitutional Council, Favoreu observed that "*En 'recréant le droit', le juge constitutionnel adapte la Constitution aux exigences nouvelles et évite ainsi soit un blocage du processus de décolonisation, soit une révision de la Constitution*".[126] France, thus, has attempted to tame the harsh issues of decolonisation within the safe confines of its national constitutional system.

Notwithstanding the arguable legitimacy of this application of Article 53/3 to sovereignty referendums, and considering the exigencies of the decolonisation, the debate remained inconclusive. Capitant's "*curieux raisonnement juridique*",[127] while functioning as a rubber life raft for the internal actors, still left certain questions unsettled. The ambiguous wording of Article 53/3, in particular, generates certain legal voids that may undermine the legitimacy of any referendum held according to it. Firstly, it is open to contention as to whether the term "consent of the population" automatically means a referendum. Even if this is the case, further questions arise: who may be included within the concept of the population concerned? Who should be competent to initiate the referendum? Should the referendum be binding or non-binding? Does it provide for a referendum on an

[123] Maestre (1976), p. 456.

[124] ***LOI no 88–1028 du 9 novembre 1988*** *portant dispositions statutaires et préparatoires à l'autodé termination de la Nouvelle-Calédonie en 1998* (***JOURNAL OFFICIEL DE LA RÉPUBLIQUE FRANÇAISE du 10 novembre 1988***) The text of this law may be found at http://www.assemblee-nationale.fr/11/dossiers/Nouvelle-caledonie/881028.asp. Retrieved 11 July 2011.

[125] Pavia (1989), p. 1710.

[126] Favoreau (1976), p. 568.

[127] Pavia (1989), p. 1709.

explicit legal text or a mere policy vote? If it is on a legal text (i.e., legislative or constitutional), should the referendum be held before or after the adoption of the relevant legislation by the parliament? These constitutional voids, allowing a simple majority in the parliament to mould the referendum process, hinder Article 53/3 from becoming an effective constitutional tool for a legitimate referendum.

6.2.4.4 Constitutional Reforms of 2003

A significant attempt to overcome this conundrum was the introduction of a comprehensive constitutional revision package within the framework of the decentralisation reforms of 2003. The early distinction of DOM and TOM was replaced by "Overseas Departments and Regions" (Art. 73) on the one side and a residual category of "Overseas Territorial Communities" on the other (Art. 74). The status of New Caledonia had already been subsumed under a separate title (Title XIII) following the Nouméa Accord and the unique article as "transitional provisions" pertaining to New Caledonia.

In this framework, "assimilation" of the Overseas Departments and Regions to mainland France became a prospect. The latter category regulated by Article 74 was developed to be a "status directed towards a future independence".[128] Assimilation applies to the Overseas Departments and Regions, and following Captitant's doctrine, no right to secession is conferred. In addition, these regions have a relatively weak autonomy in comparison with the other overseas territories and New Caledonia. As a rule, the metropolitan laws and other regulatory acts automatically apply to the Overseas Departments and Regions, which was already the case for the DOMs in the previous regime. On the other hand, the 2003 reform brought the possibility of a limited derogation by virtue of an ordinary law (i.e., consent of metropolitan France expressed through a simple parliamentary majority) (Art. 73).

As regards the Overseas Territorial Communities, the principle of assimilation does not apply and they have a wider legislative autonomy. The procedural rules for a change of their constitutional status are more rigid: the legislative competences and institutional structure of territory should be specified by an organic law following a consultative opinion of the local assembly. Furthermore, Article 74 confers on the territories under its jurisdiction a limited competence to enter international relations.

Currently, Guadeloupe, Guyane, Martinique, Réunion and Mayotte (after 2009) are overseas departments of France under Article 73 of the French Constitution. Overseas Territorial Communities governed by Article 74 consist of Saint Barthélemy, St. Martin, Wallis and Futuna, Saint-Pierre and Miquelon and French Polynesia.

The 2003 reforms also introduced the institution of referendum within the procedure for a change of status of the aforementioned territories. Yet this

[128] Palayret (2003), p. 229.

procedure is "very restrictive", as it is the government and/or the president who decides when and if to hold a referendum.[129] There are two provisions that may serve as the legal basis for the new regime:

> No change of status as provided for by articles 73 and 74 with respect to the whole or part of any one of the communities to which the second paragraph of article 72-3 applies, shall take place without the prior consent of voters in the relevant community or part of a community being sought in the manner provided for by the paragraph below. Such change of status shall be made by an Institutional Act.
>
> The President of the Republic may, on a recommendation from the Government when Parliament is in session or on a joint motion of the two Houses, published in either case in the *Journal Officiel*, decide to consult voters in an overseas territorial community on a question relating to its organization, its powers or its legislative system. Where the referendum concerns a change of status as provided for by the foregoing paragraph and is held in response to a recommendation by the Government, the Government shall make a statement before each House which shall be followed by debate. (Article 72-4; Constitution of France)

With the introduction of this article, a change of status is made possible between the two regimes of Articles 73 and 74. The procedure includes a preliminary referendum in the relevant territory and an ensuing organic law. In this case, the referendum preceding the organic law is obligatory. However, its binding effect is only negative, that is, the residents of the relevant territory have a "right to veto" any prospective change, but if their decision is positive, the parliament, at least in the strict legal sense, is not bound.[130] The second paragraph also provides for a consultative referendum on the organisation, competence and legislative system of an overseas territorial community. This device is a replication of Article 11, and the same procedure applies since it is the president who decides whether to consult the population concerned.

6.2.5 Sovereignty Referendums in the United Kingdom

The importance of the United Kingdom (UK) with respect to our study lies in the fact that, with the exception of the referendum on the alternative vote system held in 2011, the totality of the country's record has been comprised of sovereignty referendums. The referendums held throughout British constitutional history "have all been concerned with the legitimacy of transferring the powers of Parliament, either by excluding an area from Parliament's jurisdiction as in the Northern Ireland border poll—or for transferring powers to separate authorities such as the European Community or directly elected bodies in Scotland, Wales, Northern Ireland or London".[131] McCorquodale noted that the referendums held on the

[129] Palayret (2003), p. 250.

[130] Formery (2011), p. 151.

[131] Bogdanor (2003b), p. 697.

Scottish and Welsh devolution, as well as the referendum requirement on the future of Northern Ireland, show that "there is a definite assumption by the United Kingdom that there exist different peoples within its territory".[132] Thus, the British experience of sovereignty referendums illustrates manifestly the concept of the permeation of law of self-determination between the spheres of international and national laws.

The basis of the use of referendum in the UK may be sought in the assertions of Dicey, who defended the introduction of this instrument to the British Constitution. He was most concerned that Parliament might make "a fundamental change passing into Law which the mass of the nation do not desire". Therefore, he saw a "people's veto" in the referendum, which could prevent Parliament from enforcing "any important Act which does not command the sanction of the electors".[133] Bogdanor sees a consent-based explanation in the British use of referendums: "validation from the people. . .for a transfer of the powers of the Parliament has a clear rationale in liberal thought; and the referendum has become in part an instrument of entrenchment since it prevents the power of Parliament from being transferred without the approval of the people".[134]

To conclude, a debate on sovereignty referendums in a British context may provide useful insights with respect to legal theory in terms of both international and constitutional laws.

6.2.5.1 Practices

There have been "eleven national, regional and/or UK-wide referendums" in the UK since the first one took place in 1973.[135] The first referendum was the Northern Ireland sovereignty referendum of 1973, also known as the border poll. The purpose of the referendum was to determine whether the people of Northern Ireland wanted to remain with the UK or create a United Ireland with the Republic of Ireland. Of those eligible to vote, 58.7 % turned out and 98.9 % unanimously voted in favour of staying a part of the UK, with only 1.1 % voting for a United Ireland. This resulted in Northern Ireland remaining within the UK. The second major referendum was the United Kingdom European Communities membership referendum of 1975. The question put forward to the electorate was whether or not they wished the UK to remain a part of the E.E.C. (European Economic Community). There was a turnout

[132] McCorquodale (1995), pp. 294–295.

[133] A. V. Dicey, *Introduction to the Study of the Law of the Constitution* 8th Edition Retrieved from http://www.constitution.org/cmt/avd/law_con.htm on 10 November 2012.

[134] Bogdanor (2003b), p. 697.

[135] http://www.electoralcommission.org.uk/elections/referendums. Retrieved 12 November 2012.

of 64 %, and a majority of 67.2 % voted in favour of the U.K. remaining in the E.E.C. As a result, the decision committed the U.K. to Europe.[136]

The third referendum was in 1978 and was only open to the Scottish electorate. It asked them to vote either in favour of or against a piece of legislation that had just been introduced: the Scotland Act of 1978, which created a deliberative assembly for Scotland. The stipulation in the referendum was that if less than 40 % voted in favour of the Act, it would be repealed. There was a turnout of 63.6 %, of which 51.6 % voted in favour of the Act being put into effect. However, the Act was repealed because the full electorate did not turn out, and as a result, the required 40 % of the whole electorate was not achieved; thus, devolution was not put into effect. In the same year, Wales also had a referendum on devolution. The Welsh devolution referendum of 1979 asked the Welsh electorate if they would like the provisions of the Wales Act of 1978 to be put into effect, which would have given further budget control and powers to the Welsh Secretary of State. There was a turnout of 58.8 %, of which only 20.3 % voted in favour of the Act being put into effect. As with the Scottish referendum, there had to have been at least 40 % of the electorate in favour of the Act to be put into practice, and as a result, the UK repealed the Act.[137]

Devolution was the main point of the next UK referendum, taking place 18 years after the previous referendum. The Scottish devolution referendum of 1997 asked the Scottish electorate a two-part question: namely, whether they wanted the creation of a Scottish Parliament and, if so, whether they wanted it to have tax-varying powers. There was a turnout of 60.2 % of the electorate, and 74.3 % voted in favour of the creation of a Scottish Parliament, with 63.5 % believing it should have tax-varying powers. As a result, the government enacted the Scotland Act of 1998 and created a Scottish Parliament and Executive. Wales would also have a referendum on its own devolution in the same year. The Welsh devolution referendum of 1997 asked the Welsh electorate if they would like to have a Welsh Assembly. There was a 50.1 % turnout, and 50.3 % voted in favour of a Welsh Assembly. Although it was an extremely close decision, the majority had voted in favour of the Assembly, and as a result the Welsh Assembly was created.[138]

In 1998, there were two further referendums concerning devolution. The first was the Greater London Authority referendum of 1998, which asked only the London electorate whether they felt there was a need for a separate London Assembly and an elected Mayor of London. The turnout was only 34.1 %, of

[136] http://www.publications.parliament.uk/pa/ld200910/ldselect/ldconst/99/9903.htm. Retrieved 12 October 2012.

[137] http://www.publications.parliament.uk/pa/ld200910/ldselect/ldconst/99/9903.htm. Retrieved 12 October 2012.

[138] http://www.publications.parliament.uk/pa/ld200910/ldselect/ldconst/99/9903.htm. Retrieved 12 October 2012.

which a majority of 72 % voted in favour of the London Assembly and appointment of a Mayor. As a result, the Greater London Authority Act of 1999 was passed.[139]

In 1998, there was also the Northern Ireland Belfast Agreement referendum, which asked the Northern Irish electorate if they were in favour of passing the Northern Ireland Act of 1998, which would give the state devolved power and create a Northern Irish Assembly. There was a turnout of 81 % and a majority of 71.1 % in favour of enforcing the Act; thus, as a result, the U.K. gave devolved legislation to Northern Ireland. Another referendum in the U.K. was the Northern Eastern England devolution referendum in 2004, which asked the electorate in Northern Eastern England if they too felt that they should have a separate Assembly representing them. There was a turnout of 47.7 %, but the majority was against this, with around 78 %, and therefore the government did not create this Northern Eastern England Assembly.[140] The last sovereignty referendum that took place was in Wales, on the extended powers of the regional assembly. This referendum produced an affirmative result by a 35.63 % turnout and 63.49 % yes vote. [141]

6.2.5.2 Constitutional Status of Referendums in the UK

The Meaning of "Constitution" in the UK Context Two distinctive features of the Constitution of the United Kingdom may be distinguished: it is unwritten and flexible. It is a combination of legal (binding international treaties, court judgments and statutes) and non-legal (or conventional) rules. This combination organises the behaviour of the political actors, i.e., Members of Parliament, the Crown and the Government. The difference with the written constitutions of most other states is that the UK has no "single instrument" or "one formal document specifically enacted"[142] to set out and define the constitution.[143] The unwritten nature of the constitution is inevitably followed by its flexible character. In contrast to rigid constitutions, the flexible UK Constitution entails no special amending procedure such as special quorum, enhanced decisional majority, establishment of a separate constitutional convention or referendum.[144] It may well be argued that it is mainly with regard to the UK Constitution that the doctrinal accounts involve a balanced interaction of positive legal rules and political facts. In this context, the Constitution

[139] For the referendum results, see http://www.election.demon.co.uk/london.html. Retrieved 12 October 2012.

For the text of the Greater London Authority Act, see http://www.legislation.gov.uk/ukpga/1999/29/contents. Retrieved 12 October 2012.

[140] http://www.publications.parliament.uk/pa/ld200910/ldselect/ldconst/99/9903.htm. Retrieved 12 October 2012.

[141] http://www.c2d.ch/detailed_display.php?lname=votes&table=votes&page=1&parent_id=&sublinkname=results&id=130926. Retrieved 12 October 2012.

[142] Phillips et al. (2001), p. 5.

[143] Marshall (2003), p. 31.

[144] Phillips et al. (2001), p. 6.

is assumed to be a combination of written legal documents, conventions and political practices, each of which may govern the political situations, either single handedly or interactively.

Parliamentary Sovereignty, "The dominant characteristic" of the Constitution: the rule of parliamentary sovereignty has been seen as the "one fundamental law of the British Constitution" that cannot be altered even by Parliament itself. [145] Dicey defined it as "the dominant characteristic" of the UK's political institutions and an "undoubted legal fact".[146] The doctrine is very well established as one of the fundamentals of common law so that it is said to "have never been contested in courts".[147] This principle boils down to three basic legal rules. Firstly, Parliament can pass any rule or law that it sees fit. The legislative powers of parliament are unlimited, and Parliament may enact laws on any subject matter.[148] In other words, the parliamentary Act is the ultimate source of the Constitution. This blurs the line between the ordinary and fundamental laws and gives the Constitution its flexible nature.[149]

Secondly, on the negative side, there is no legal body that may overrule the acts of parliament, that is, an act of parliament cannot be repealed or changed by a court. Courts may not review parliamentary acts, nor may they declare them unconstitutional or *ultra vires*. Parliament is the "supreme law-making authority".[150]

Finally, Parliament may change or repeal any laws as it so wishes: "no act is irreversible".[151] This feature leads to the paradoxical nature of parliamentary sovereignty as being unable to limit itself. Parliament may not enact unchangeable laws. In other words, "no parliament may be bound by a predecessor or bind a successor".[152]

Referendums as a New Challenge to Parliamentary Sovereignty Borthwick identifies the rising practice of and demand for referendums in the deciding of sovereignty issues as one of the most serious challenges directed against the sovereignty of the parliament.[153] Since the initial practices, referendums in the U.K. have been seen as "a remarkable innovation, insofar as they have represented an obvious political challenge to the sovereignty of parliament".[154] Most observers argue that the initial practices in the 1970s were random, ad hoc and resorted to with mere concerns of political expediency, either to avoid an internal party split or to

[145] Phillips et al. (2001), p. 22.

[146] Dicey ([1902] 2010), pp. 37 and 66.

[147] Phillips et al. (2001), p. 54.

[148] Barnett (2006), p. 164; Allen and Thompson (2005), p. 55.

[149] Phillips et al. (2001), pp. 21–22.

[150] Phillips et al. (2001), p. 22; Barnett (2006), p. 164.

[151] Phillips et al. (2001), p. 64.

[152] Barnett (2006), p. 164.

[153] Bortwick (1997), p. 39.

[154] Loveland (2003), p. 672.

evade the political consequences of taking certain hard decisions.[155] On the other hand, these political precedents created a relatively consistent practice and legitimate expectations in British society for the use of referendums in European and devolution issues. This situation corresponds to the above-mentioned "politically obligatory" or "*de facto* obligatory" referendums. Politically, it is highly unlikely that the UK Parliament would take any decision on Europe or devolution without holding a referendum. Parliament in these matters may be said to undergo a "declining"[156] or, in a more euphemistic term, a "highly attenuated" status.[157] Despite this undeniable political reality, "the status of referendum in constitutional theory is (still) unclear".[158] Thus, a legal appraisal of the constitutional status of the referendum remains to be tackled. We may try to handle this problem by examining the constitutional status of a referendum statute and if the requirement of referendum has become a convention.

The status of a law providing a referendum with regard to parliamentary sovereignty may be subsumed under the question as to whether a parliament is bound by its predecessors. Particularly in our case, the question is whether a parliament may bind a future parliament with an Act that simplifies or complicates lawmaking on a specific subject matter, namely, whether a parliament may repeal an Act stipulating and requiring referendum for a particular piece of legislation.

This question may be tackled by considering the particular example of the Northern Ireland Act (NIA) of 1998, the only statute that provides an obligatory referendum for a pre-defined subject matter. The Act says: "Northern Ireland remains part of the United Kingdom and shall not cease to be so without the consent of a majority of the people of Northern Ireland voting in a poll" [NIA Art. 1 (1)]. Then the question arises as to whether a future parliament has the legitimate authority to repeal this Act and arrogate the aforementioned right of the residents of Northern Ireland to itself.

From a formal point of view, a change in the procedure of lawmaking may either involve a requirement for referendum or an enhanced majority in the Parliament. Two opposing views appeared as to whether such "entrenchment" has a binding effect on future parliaments. The traditional view of parliamentary sovereignty holds that the concept of parliamentary sovereignty is incompatible with any sort of legal restraint on the exercise of lawmaking power, either in the material or formal sense. In other words, the unlimited sovereignty of Parliament knows no limits with regard to changing any substantial content of law, along with any specific procedural rules. Particularly, from a formal point of view, Parliament is the master of its own procedure, yet "it cannot bind itself as to the form of subsequent

[155] Bogdanor (2003b), p. 696.
[156] Bortwick (1997), p. 39.
[157] Bogdanor (1998), p. 13.
[158] Bortwick (1997), p. 39.

legislation".[159] With respect to the referendum requirement in the Northern Ireland Act, Phillips et al. (2001) argue:

> Steps taken to hold national referendum or plebiscite in Northern Ireland would be lawful. What we are saying is that the same parliament or a subsequent parliament (probably of a different political complexion), could repeal these provisions or simply ignore them. There is no reason why a later Act should be accorded less authority than an earlier one.[160]

According to this view, the statutes that require referendum have no special or higher constitutional status in comparison with any other. Parliament may, as for any other statute, repeal or ignore them with a simple majority.

On the opposite side, there is the new doctrine of "manner and form". According to this view, if a statute stipulates a particular method for its repeal or amendment, any alteration "except by that method would be ineffective".[161] This doctrine distinguishes the material sense and the formal sense of the law. While retaining full legislative supremacy of the Parliament for the content of the laws, the new view holds that "the manner and form in which Parliament may legislate may be circumscribed".[162]

Among supporters, Marshall argued that it was time to recognise the referendum as one of the necessary constitutional fundamentals to reduce the "dangerous absolutism" of Parliament. Heuston claimed that sovereignty is a legal concept and the rules that identify the composition and functions of it are beyond the limits of the parliament. Therefore, courts should be competent to decide on the validity of acts on the grounds of procedural rules.[163]

Two cases may be cited in support of this view. In *Attorney-General of New South Wales v Trethowan*, the High Court of Australia and Privy Council upheld a New South Wales law, stipulating a referendum requirement for any future changes of the constitution of the Upper House before they could acquire royal assent and be passed as legislation. This case may be described to include the most explicit statement concerning a referendum entrenchment against the unlimited lawmaking power of a parliament. However, this was a case concerning Australia, and the difficulty with applying it to the British Constitution is that there is no clear "constitutional grundnorm" that authorises any changes to parliament's lawmaking abilities. Indeed, the referendum entrenchment was pursuant to the Colonial Laws Validity Act, which authorised New South Wales to pass legislation concerning its own powers and lawmaking procedures.[164] Considering the fact that the Validity

---

[159] [Maugham LJ's statement in *Ellen Street Estates Ltd. v. Minister of Health* (1934)], cited in Parpworth and Padfield (2002), p. 69.

[160] Phillips et al. (2001), p. 75.

[161] For the definition of the concept, see Carroll (2003), p. 88.

[162] Parpworth and Padfield (2002), p. 70.

[163] (R.F.V.Heuston, Essays in Constitutional Law (2nd.edn, 1964), Ch1, pp.6-8; G.Marshall, Constitutional Theory, (1971), pp.42-43) Cited in Allen & Thompson, (2005), pp. 68-69.

[164] (*Attorney-General of New South Wales v Trethowan and Others* (*1932*) AC 526, PC). Cited in Allen and Thompson (2005), pp. 69–73; Marshall (2003), p. 45.

Act remained intact, this case does not provide necessary argument supporting the view that Westminster Parliament may impose procedural restraint on itself.

In *Manuel v. Attorney General*, Canadian aboriginal people challenged the validity of the Canada Act by claiming that their consent was not obtained in the making of this Act; thus, it was a breach of the fourth article of the Statute of Westminster 1931. The Court of the case (Court of Appeal of England and Wales) admitted the argument that parliament "can effectively tie the hands of its successors" if it passes a statue that requires a "certain specified consent" for a certain type of legislation.[165] The Court, on the other hand, restrained from deciding on this issue and upheld the Canada Act.

These cases fall short of providing explicit judicial precedent in favour of the referendum entrenchment. At best, they may be said to provide some "tiny judicial hint" that English courts may one day consider a referendum requirement as binding on the parliament.[166]

Nevertheless, British courts consistently refuse to review the compliance of Parliament to procedural rules. In other words, when a parliamentary Act appears before a court, it accepts its validity as law, without further investigating whether certain parliamentary procedural rules are observed. This non-involvement has one exception: the courts control whether the alleged Act has the approval of the majority of the House of Commons and the Royal Assent. However, the legal rationale of this control is not the procedural accuracy but "the rule of recognition". [167]

This common law rule generates a third argument in defence of special procedures, namely Jenning's theory of "redefinition of parliament" or "self embracing" sovereignty. According to this approach, the concept of parliament is currently a combination of House of Commons, House of Lords, and the Monarch. When Parliament establishes a new procedural requirement, it will create a new element in the definition of Parliament, and that will mean a new rule of recognition.[168]

Therefore, if the Parliament adopts a referendum requirement for certain types of legislation, it will have to include the referendum as an inseparable component of the Parliament. In this way, Carroll argues that the referendum provision in the Northern Ireland Act could be "understood as redefining the parliament to include the Northern Ireland electorate for any relevant legislation".[169] On the other hand, this "purely academic" support was criticised for being "a fiction or formula designed to avoid classifying the matter as procedural". [170] Considering what has

[165] [*Manuel v Attorney-General* (1983) 1 Ch 77], cited in Allen and Thompson (2005), p. 243, and Ellis (2004), p. 147. The full text of the decision may be found at http://www.bailii.org/ew/cases/EWCA/Civ/1982/4.html. Retrieved 15 September 2013.

[166] Ellis (2004), p. 147.

[167] Phillips et al. (2001), p. 74; Ellis (2004), p. 146.

[168] Carroll (2003), p. 89.

[169] Carroll (2003), p. 85.

[170] Phillips et al. (2001), p. 76.

been said so far, from a strictly legal point of view, there are no sufficient grounds for asserting that a referendum has precedence over parliamentary sovereignty. Westminster would meet no legal challenge in the courts if it wished to repeal or ignore a referendum statute or even if it disregarded the result of a referendum whenever it was held.

On the other hand, one should consider that in the case of a possible parliamentary Act, repealing or ignoring a referendum statute, "serious controversy" would ensue from the clash of this established judicial restraint and sociological-political expectations.[171] If the courts are haunted by the possibility of very strong public pressure, they may legitimately resort to the redefinition doctrine to impose the rule of referendum on Parliament. Following this line of thought, Ellis notes: "If parliament ever sought to detach Northern Ireland from the United Kingdom without securing the consent of the majority of its people, the event would undoubtedly provide the most appropriate test yet seen for the redefinition theory".[172] Any comment as to whether this may happen is irrelevant to the legal theory but rather a prediction on the future conduct of the judges.

This leads us to consider the sociological authority of the referendum. Indeed, while in its strict legal sense the question remains problematic, we may seek to answer it from a sociological viewpoint: whether the referendum has now become a convention. We may gauge this question by applying Jennings's three-criterion test.

Referendum as a Constitutional Convention ***Precedent*** It is mentioned above that to constitute sufficient practice in order to establish a convention, political precedents need not be numerous nor need to have been in use for a long time. In the case of sovereignty issues requiring a "high degree of legitimacy", a single practice may suffice as a precedent.[173] This rests on the undeniable moral and sociological authority of the popular will, which can be straightforwardly invoked against a possible parliamentary majority disregarding the use of referendum. According to Morel, "it was impossible, after having consulted the population on the same issue in 1979, not to consult it a second time *a-fortiori*, since this would have implied defying the will expressed at previous referendums".[174] Therefore, in the face of the saliency of sovereignty issues, even a single referendum may be sufficient to support the argument of precedent.

Belief Belief is not readily discernible, though we may track it down in the conduct and statements of the political actors. The UK experience offers persuasive evidence that there is a "growing demand for referendums" on the EU and devolution.[175] Hadfield observes that "there is an increasing, and possibly irreversible acceptance on the part of British governments of seeking popular support for

[171] Ellis (2004), p. 147.

[172] Ellis (2004), p. 153.

[173] Auer (2007), p. 63.

[174] Morel (2001), p. 62.

[175] Bortwick (1997), p. 28.

developments of constitutional significance".[176] This assumption is fairly well founded when considering, for example, that the Labour Government had promised to hold a binding referendum on an eventual accession of Britain to the European single currency.[177] It may be that civil society, opposition and general public opinion share the belief on the requirement of referendum. From these explanations, we may safely suppose that sufficient belief is established within British society concerning the requirement of referendum.

Reason As noted above, reason refers to the moral underpinning of a certain conduct that is grounded in the philosophical fundamentals of a constitutional system. Therefore, while belief corresponds to the sociological aspect of political legitimacy, reason may be discussed in terms of moral authority. In this perspective, the premise "referendum is a constitutional convention" is self-referential, considering the fact that "the ultimate object of most conventions is that public affairs should be conducted in accordance with the wishes of the majority of the electors".[178] Thus, the referendum might have the strongest authority with respect to Jennings' criterion of "reason".

On the other hand, one question remains to be answered: whether there is a philosophical shift in the legitimating of political power in the UK, namely, whether the conception of parliamentary sovereignty faces a decline in the advantage of a new legitimating argument: "popular sovereignty". Seaward and Silk assert that in British politics there is a significant change of political conception "from representational democracy to direct democracy in which there is a need to win a daily mandate".[179] Similarly, Hadfield notes: "the legal doctrine of Westminster's sovereignty meets its limits in the assertion of popular sovereignty". Crucially, "the source of the Scottish constitution becomes rooted in the people as well as in the Westminster Parliament".[180] These accounts show that the absolutist nature of parliamentary sovereignty is now under question in British political thought and that the conception of popular sovereignty as a legitimating argument is in an evolving process.

This brief analysis of the threefold criteria of convention (i.e., "precedents, supporting reasons and feelings of obligation among political actors") allows us to infer that there are now "sufficient grounds" for the referendum to be considered as a constitutional convention.[181]

---

176 Hadfield (2003), p. 621.

177 Qvortrup (2005), p. 109.

178 Philips (1962), p. 79.

179 Seaward and Silk (2003), p. 185.

180 Hadfield (2003), p. 623.

181 Marshall (2003), p. 63.

6.2.6 Canada and the Quebec Question

The history of federalism in Canada offers noteworthy examples of sovereignty referendums, including the subject matters of adhesion, sub-national territorial modification and secession. The entrance of New Foundland to the Confederation in 1949 involved a two-stage referendum. The first referendum was held on June 1948, where the voters were given three options: (1) responsible self-government, (2) confederation with Canada and (3) continuation of the Commission government. This referendum remained inconclusive since there was no clear majority in favour of any of the choices. Another vote was scheduled for the following month, asking the voters to choose between the first two options. Subsequently, 52 % opted for Confederation with Canada over the choice of "responsible self-government".

The province of Nunavut was created out of the North West Territories in a process including three referendums taking place over a period of 10 years. The first referendum took place on April 14, 1982, in which the voters were asked whether they were in favour of a division of the territory into two parts. Following the positive outcome of this first referendum, a second was held on May 1992 to fix the final boundary line between these two territories. Lastly, in the third referendum of November 3–5, 1992, the residents of the eastern Arctic approved the creation of Nunavut when 69 % of the voters voted in favour of the project.[182]

Despite these preliminary examples, Canada is particularly known for the Quebec issue and the two referendums held as part of this process. Quebec is one of the ten federal entities (province) of Canada having roughly 7.5 million inhabitants. Among the population, the vast majority (six million) is French speaking, typically descendants of the first French settlers of Canada. The rest of the population comprises the English-speaking residents, aboriginal peoples and immigrants whose native language is neither English nor French.

The territory that forms the southern part of contemporary Quebec belonged to France in the seventeenth century. This region was then handed over to Britain after the defeat of the French royal army pursuant to the Treaty of Paris (1763). Since then the legitimacy of British rule and the succeeding union with Canada have been under question in public opinion: it has come to be called as "the British Conquest". [183]

The origins of today's Canadian Constitution may be found in the British North America Act adopted in 1867 by the Imperial Parliament in London. Under this Act, the Dominion of Canada was established as a "Confederation" comprising the provinces of Ontario, New Brunswick, Nova Scotia and Quebec. This legislation provided substantial autonomy to Quebec, including the permission to the use of the French civil code, the preservation of separate religious schools in the province and the recognition of French as the second official language both on a local and federal level. This constitutional regime created a fairly congenial atmosphere for the

[182] LeDuc (2003), pp. 102 and 122; Rourke et al. (1992), pp. 40–42.

[183] Pavkovic and Radan (2007), p. 79.

development of a distinct nationalist sentiment. This sentiment turned into a political movement in the late 1960s, the main political goal of which was the secession of Quebec from Canada. The course of events that formed this new modern nationalist thinking may be dated back to the late 1950s, when a high level of urbanisation created what was called the “Quiet Revolution” in Quebec. This revolution, among others, transformed the traditional and rural Catholic Quebec to a more urbanised and modernised society, where a new neo-nationalist ideology emerged endorsing the values of self-determination and national sovereignty.[184] In 1968, a neo-nationalist party, Parti Québécois (PQ), was formed that promised to declare the independence or sovereignty of Quebec once it came into power. [185]

6.2.6.1 Referendum of 1980

The events leading up to Quebec’s first referendum may be dated back to the victory of the PQ in the 1976 provincial election. The PQ promised a referendum on sovereignty during the election campaign to decouple this issue from other election issues, thereby alleviating the fears of the anti-secessionist voters, which had been the main reason for the party’s defeat in previous elections.[186] The referendum was held in 1980, when the PQ government asked the Quebecers for a mandate to negotiate “a new arrangement with the rest of Canada based on the equality of nations”. This new arrangement, as articulated by the referendum question, would involve Quebec’s “exclusive power to make its laws, administer its taxes and establish relations abroad – in other words, sovereignty – and . . . to maintain with Canada an economic association. . .”

Two observations may be made regarding the wording of this referendum: the first, where the explicit articulation of independence or secession was avoided and, the second, where there was a visible emphasis on an economic association with Canada in the referendum question. By this long and imprecise wording, the PQ government sought to reassure voters that a possible gaining of sovereignty for Quebec would not mean a sudden separation from Canada. This first sovereignty referendum in Quebec, however, produced a negative outcome: 59.6 % of voters said No, and 40.4 % of the vote was for Yes, with a turnout of 84 % of the electorate.

The electoral defeat of the PQ in the 1985 provincial elections caused a momentary suspension of the debate on sovereignty. This occasion opened the way for a new initiative to resolve the sovereignty problem: through a new constitutional project. The executives of the ten provinces and the federal government negotiated a new constitutional reform package to “bring Quebec in”. These negotiations

[184] Pavkovic and Radan (2007), pp. 80–81.

[185] Pavkovic and Radan (2007), p. 82.

[186] LeDuc (2003), p. 102.

produced the Meech Lake Accord, a package of constitutional proposals recognising Quebec as a "distinct society", bestowing a greater autonomy to the province and building a more decentralised type of federalism. However, this attempt failed. The ratification procedure included the approval of the constitutional proposal by the federal Parliament and a subsequent ratification of it by the provincial legislatures within a deadline of 3 years. The Accord expired in 1990, by which deadline two provinces, Manitoba and Newfoundland, had still not ratified the project. [187]

This failure was followed by a second attempt: the Charlottetown Accord. The Accord was concluded between the federal government and the provinces on August 1992. The Charlottetown Accord included an extensive power-sharing arrangement, as compared to the previous constitutional proposals. It provided a renewed Senate where the equal representation of all provinces would be guaranteed. Quebec was once again recognised as a distinct society, and it was further guaranteed a 25 % quota of the representatives in an enlarged House of Commons.[188]

Initially, the ratification procedure of this project was planned to exclude the referendum device, as was the case in the Meech Lake Accord where the Parliament and the provincial legislatures would be the sole competencies for debate and ratification. Yet this time, a strong demand for the ratification of this project in a referendum came from the provinces, firstly from Quebec and then from Alberta and British Columbia. Quebec declared that it would hold a referendum on the proposed constitutional reform package no later than 16 October 1992, following its own procedural rules and under its own control. The federal and provincial governments that had negotiated the agreement saw the evident difficulties of separate referendums in Quebec and other provinces: they would be held at different times and according to different rules. Consequently, the federal government moved to schedule a referendum on a federal level on the same day as specified by Quebec. The outcome of the referendum was against the proposal by a roughly 55 % "No" vote, with a 75 % turnout. Thus, this attempt to resolve the Quebec issue failed following this vote.[189]

6.2.6.2 Referendum of 1995

Following these two failed attempts, the Parti Québécois regained power in 1994 and moved immediately to hold another referendum in 1995.[190] The following question was put to referendum: "Do you agree that Quebec should become sovereign after having made a formal offer to Canada for a new economic and

[187] LeDuc (2003), p. 53.

[188] LeDuc (2003), pp. 53–54.

[189] LeDuc (2003), p. 53.

[190] LeDuc (2003), p. 105.

political partnership within the scope of the bill respecting the future of Quebec and of the agreement signed on June 12, 1995?"

The turnout was considerably higher at 94 %, and among those who voted, 50.6 % said No, whereas 49.4 % of the votes cast were for Yes. Notwithstanding, once again, the avoidance of the words "independence" or "separation", this second referendum was defeated by a slight difference in votes.[191]

The federal government, on the other hand, moved to accommodate Quebec's neo-nationalist demands: a resolution was adopted in the federal parliament, recognising (once again) Quebec as a distinct society, and a law was passed granting all provinces, including Quebec, a veto on constitutional matters. The federal government also asked the Supreme Court of Canada to decide on the legality or constitutionality of a unilateral secession of Quebec. This was due to a concern for specifying a legal or constitutional framework that could be used for any possible future attempts of secession in Quebec.[192] On 20 August 1998, the Supreme Court gave its decision, which was thereafter known as the "Secession Reference".[193]

The Supreme Court of Canada and Secession Reference The particular importance of the Secession Reference of the Supreme Court of Canada lies in the fact that it offers a very comprehensive judicial analysis of the right of secession from the perspective of a state's constitutional law.[194]

The Supreme Court was asked three questions:

1. Under the Constitution of Canada, can the National Assembly, legislature or government of Quebec effect the secession of Quebec from Canada unilaterally?
2. Does international law give the National Assembly, legislature or government of Quebec the right to effect the secession of Quebec from Canada unilaterally? In this regard, is there a right to self-determination under international law that would give the National Assembly, legislature or government of Quebec the right to effect the secession of Quebec from Canada unilaterally?
3. In the event of a conflict between domestic and international law on the right of the National Assembly, legislature or government of Quebec to effect the secession of Quebec from Canada unilaterally, which would take precedence in Canada?

Unwritten Rules of Canadian Constitution and the Referendums Maybe the most important aspect of this decision is that it recognises the existence of unwritten rules of the constitution that should govern the possible secession of Quebec. The Court first remarked on the linkage between "legality" and "legitimacy" within the Canadian constitutional tradition, the former referring to written rules, the latter involving moral principles.[195] According to the Court, a political system may not

---

[191] Pavkovic and Radan (2007), p. 83.

[192] Pavkovic and Radan (2007), p. 83.

[193] *Reference re Secession of Quebec*, *[1998] 2 S.C.R. 217.*

[194] Pavkovic and Radan (2007), p. 226.

[195] *Reference re Secession of Quebec, Para. 33.*

survive through a simple "adherence to the law". It should also possess legitimacy, which in the Canadian political culture requires an interaction of the principles of the rule of law and democracy. "A (sole) review of the written provisions of the Constitution does not provide the entire picture", and there are certain "underlying constitutional principles" "behind the written words" of the Constitution.[196] In this regard, the Court mentioned "four foundational constitutional principles that are most germane for resolution" of the question of Quebec's secession: federalism, democracy, constitutionalism and the rule of law, and respect for minority rights. "These defining principles function in symbiosis. No single principle can be defined in isolation from the others, nor does any one principle trump or exclude the operation of any other".[197] These principles need not exist in a written form since they are indispensable elements of the Canadian Constitution and were assumed to exist a priori by the framers of the Constitution. The principle of democracy itself, for example, "was not explicitly identified in the text of the Constitution Act, 1867. To have done so might have appeared redundant or even silly to the framers". Therefore, for the Court, not only the written text of the Constitution but also the constitutional conventions, which are "nowhere explicitly described", should be taken into account in any possible secession of a territory from Canada. [198]

Thus, the Court recognised four principles that should be considered in concert in a case of possible secession. In this perspective, "federalism" was defined to be "a political and legal response to the underlying social and political realities" of Canada. The ethnic particularity of Quebec was one of the chief reasons for the creation of the Canadian union as a federal entity in 1867. Moreover, the principle of federalism recognised the diversity of the constituent units of Canada and the self-rule of provincial governments in the development of their societies in line with their regional, cultural and ethnic particularities.

As to democracy, it was viewed as a "fundamental value in (Canadian) constitutional law and political culture". The Court recalled the two interacting aspects of democracy, which involves not only the government by consent but also the accommodation of cultural and group identities. Consequently, if in a future referendum the voters in Quebec express a desire for a unilateral secession, it could well be qualified as an articulation of the "sovereign will of a people".[199] However, the Court held that, at this point, such an expression of sovereignty will and should be considered in the light of the other mentioned underlying principles. Federalism, for example, comes into play to put a restraint upon the capacity of the unilateral secession of Quebec. Indeed, federalism meant that "in Canada there may be different and equally legitimate majorities in different provinces and territories and at the federal level. No one majority is more or less 'legitimate' than the others

[196] *Reference re Secession of Quebec, Paras. 49 and 55.*

[197] *Reference re Secession of Quebec, Para. 49.*

[198] *Reference re Secession of Quebec, Para. 62.*

[199] *Reference re Secession of Quebec, Paras. 61 and 64.*

as an expression of democracy". Furthermore, when Canada was considered in its entirety as a democratic community, the question of secession of a province thereof required a "continuous process of discussion", where both on a federal and provincial level compromise, negotiation and deliberation were essential.[200] On the other hand, the Court underlined the "corresponding duty" of every province in Canada to engage in negotiations in response to the democratic aspirations for constitutional change in other provinces. In short, the interaction of democracy and federalism imposes reciprocal duties on both parts, including, most importantly, negotiating the question.

Moreover, constitutionalism in its simplest sense meant limited government. More particularly, for the Court, the entrenched procedure for constitutional amendment (rigidity of the constitution) lay at the heart of constitutionalism, in the sense that it protected fundamental rights and freedoms, as well as democratic forms of government, from the reach of simple majority rule.[201]

Finally, the Court defined the protection of linguistic, ethnic and religious minorities as an independent value that constitutes the basic structure of the Canadian Constitution. The basis of protecting minority rights therefore should exercise influence in the operation and interpretation of the Canadian Constitution. [202]

After having defined the Constitutional Principles that are dominant in the Canadian Constitution, the Court moved to elucidate "the operation of these principles in the Secession Context". Firstly, the Court made it clear that a possible secession of any province from Canada required a constitutional amendment "because an act of secession would purport to alter the governance of Canadian territory in a manner which undoubtedly is inconsistent with … current constitutional arrangements".[203] As to the amendment procedure, however, it refrained from offering an explicit procedural pattern. Part V of the Constitution Act, 1982, specifies two different ways for amending the Canadian Constitution, and neither of them mentions the referendum. According to the general procedure, an amendment project should receive the consent of both houses of the federal parliament first, then the consent of at least seven provincial legislatures representing at least 50 % of Canada's population. The unanimity procedure requires an approval of both houses of federal parliament and of the legislative assembly of each province. According to the Constitution, these procedures apply according to the subject matter as envisaged for each procedure, yet there remains a void as regards the secession of a province. Consequently, the Supreme Court refused to pronounce on "the applicability of any particular constitutional procedure to effect secession unless and until sufficiently clear facts exist to squarely raise the issue for judicial determination".

---

[200] *Reference re Secession of Quebec, Para. 65.*

[201] *Reference re Secession of Quebec, Para. 75.*

[202] *Reference re Secession of Quebec, Para. 81.*

[203] *Reference re Secession of Quebec, Para. 84.*

Refraining from offering a fixed constitutional procedure, the Court reinforced the notion of the role of referendum in the light of the underlying constitutional principles. It asserted that the referendum has no direct legal effect in Canadian Constitutional Law and thus "a referendum, in itself, has no direct legal effect, and could not in itself bring about unilateral secession". On the other hand, considering the principle of democracy, "expression of the democratic will of the people of a province carries weight, in that it would confer legitimacy on the efforts of the government of Quebec to initiate the Constitution's amendment process in order to secede by constitutional means".[204]

Secondly, the Court held that the competence to amend the constitution belonged to the "democratically elected representatives of the participants in Confederation". Referendums, in this context, might merely serve as "cues" for these representatives as to the people's preferences. On the other hand, for the Court, a clear expression of the wish to secede by a province may not simply be ignored:

> The clear repudiation by the people of Quebec of the existing constitutional order would confer legitimacy on demands for secession, and place an obligation on the other provinces and the federal government to acknowledge and respect that expression of democratic will by entering into negotiations and conducting them in accordance with the underlying constitutional principles.[205]

According to the Court, therefore, in the light of the underlying constitutional principles, an expressed desire for secession via a referendum including a clear question and a clear majority should be taken as the first step in the procedure of a negotiated agreement between Quebec and the rest of Canada. It may be argued that the Court considered this negotiated agreement as a legal condition for the secession of Quebec.[206]

However, the questions of the contours of the procedure and the content of these negotiations, including the legal framework of a possible referendum, were left unanswered by the Court. It was explicitly stated that these were to be decided through a political process, and the same may be said for the legal enforcement of these requirements. Consequently, three issues may be listed as unresolved by the Court. First, there is no legal remedy in case of failure of the federal government to negotiate the secession in good faith. Likewise, it is not explicitly specified whether a unilateral right to secession may be invoked for Quebec in the case of such a failure. Second, the question remains as to whether the federal government has the legitimate authority to use force if Quebec for its part fails to negotiate in good faith and declare secession unilaterally. Third, if Quebec purports to realise a unilateral secession, it is not clear whether there is a right for the non-secessionist groups (particularly Aboriginal people) to resist this attempt by force.

---

[204] *Reference re Secession of Quebec, Para. 87.*

[205] *Reference re Secession of Quebec, Para. 88.*

[206] Pavkovic and Radan (2007), p. 83.

Following this decision, both the Quebec and federal governments moved to enact legislation that would control a future referendum. In 2000, the federal parliament adopted the Clarity Act, conferring on the federal House of Commons the competence to decide whether the wording of the referendum was clear and whether the referendum result showed the clear expression of the will of Quebecois to secede. An absolute majority (50 % plus one) of all eligible voters was required in this legislation for secession to take effect.

The Clarity Act permitted the majority of members of the federal parliament to decide whether the referendum held in Quebec was legitimate. This provision is clearly at odds with the Supreme Court's holding on the compromise and negotiation of both parts, as well as the requirement for inclusion of all parties—other Canadian institutions and Aboriginal peoples as specified in the same document. The Quebec government reacted rapidly to this legislation when in 2000 it enacted Bill 99. This law gave the exclusive competence to the Quebec National Assembly to resolve all the questions arising from a referendum. In the same legislation, the required majority in future referendums was set at 50 % of votes cast plus one, and an alteration of Quebec's boundaries without the consent of the provincial legislature was prohibited. These events show that the resolution of the Quebec question will face considerable difficulties and produce a probable stalemate between federal and Quebec governments in the future.[207] Notwithstanding this conundrum, one thing is certain: "The experience of Quebec has clearly established the precedent that any future changes in its political status can come about only through the consent of its citizens in a referendum. . .the principle that a referendum must be a key part of any process leading to the independence of Quebec now seems well established".[208]

6.2.7 *The USA and Its Overseas Territories*

"Consent of the governed" has been the prevailing ethos throughout the constitutional history of the United States. Referendum, though, has not been an indispensable element in the American unification process. Observers of the early twentieth century noted that the majority of American doctrine had been against the use of "plebiscite".[209] Gawenda noted that this doctrine was also visible in the nineteenth-century American state practice: Louisiana,[210] Florida, Alaska, Puerto Rico and Hawaii had been acquired without any prior consultation of the populations concerned. The only exception in that era was the acquisition of the Islands of St

[207] Pavkovic and Radan (2007), p. 84.

[208] LeDuc (2003), p. 102.

[209] Gawenda (1946), p. 155; Wambaugh (1920), p. 26.

[210] Sparrow (2006), p. 22 notes: "With the Louisiana purchase, the United States for the first time absorbed other peoples involuntarily into the political system".

Thomas and St Jean (today's American Virgin Islands) from Denmark; the consultation was held following a demand from Denmark.[211]

The Federal Constitution was not submitted for popular ratification. In fact, the initial unification had been based on the separate ratification of the Federal Constitution by the original 13 states, that is, each founding state entered into the Union after having adopted the Constitution. There was, however, no referendum in this process: "no proposition seem(ed) to have been made in the Federal Convention to submit the plan to the direct vote of the people". Instead, special conventions were in charge of accepting the Federal Constitution—specially chosen by the people for that purpose. This system was viewed "as a normal mode of appeal to the people".[212]

On the other hand, the referendum has been gradually introduced and used by the states in the making of their constitutions. The practice in Massachusetts provided the template: it created a three-stage process for the establishment and/or total revision of the state constitution. In the first stage, there is a first vote where the voters are asked in a referendum whether they want to elect a constitutional convention (assembly) to create a new constitution. In the second stage, there is a second vote to create the new constitutional convention, which then prepares and approves the new convention. Finally, in the third stage, there is a third vote, whereby the draft text that is prepared by the new assembly is put to popular approval.

This system was endorsed by the federal government, and it has been imposed by the Congress upon "territories" that were aspiring to become members of the Union.[213] The question of referendum was debated in Congress during the accession of Kansas to the Union. It was discussed at a certain stage in the preparation of a state constitution to be submitted to Congress, during the process of requesting the title and rights of a state. The inhabitants of the territory of Kansas were divided over the question of adopting an anti-slavery or pro-slavery constitution. While the anti-slavery party prepared its own constitution, which was ratified in a referendum, the Congress rejected this unilateral attempt. The pro-slavery group, in turn, submitted its own project to another referendum, where it was overwhelmingly adopted. This referendum raised serious doubts concerning the fairness of the vote, and being condemned by Congress, it was decided that "the new state should be admitted if the people themselves" would decide on their new sovereignty status. To ensure the fairness of the vote, the Congress also determined the procedure to be applied for election of a constitutional convention and subsequent referendum in

[211] Gawenda (1946), p. 155.

[212] Borgeaud ([1895] 1989), p. 133. The exception to the referendum-free process of the ratification of the US Constitution was Rhode Island, which rejected the Constitution on March 1788 by a referendum. Yet 2 years later, "faced with threatened treatment as a foreign government", Rhode Island called a ratifying convention in 1790 as prescribed by the Constitutional Convention, which subsequently ratified the Constitution on May 29, 1790. (http://www.archives.gov/education/lessons/constitution-day/ratification.html. Retrieved 12 June 2013).

[213] Borgeaud ([1895] 1989), p. 136.

which the constitutional project would be ratified. The pro-slavery constitution was defeated in the referendum held under these rules as provided by Congress. Thus, Kansas could be admitted to the Union in 1861 after the adoption of an anti-slavery constitution by referendum "in a way prescribed by the Congress". Since then, the "Enabling Act", a federal law by which a territory is authorised to enter into the Union, "has always provided that the constitution shall in every case be ratified by the people".

Referendum has been an indispensable element for the post-Civil War readmission of Southern States to the Union. "The 'Reconstruction' bills imposed the principle of popular ratification upon all southern states without exception". It cannot be denied that the normative underpinning of consent induced the federal government to endorse the referendum as a prerequisite in this process. More importantly, referendums appeared to be the best legitimating tool of the new reconstruction era since the former slave African inhabitants had been recently enfranchised.[214]

This brief historical review shows that the American history of state creation is not far detached from referendum practice and partially refutes the historical assumption that American state practice had been anti-referendum regarding territorial issues. This assertion is, however, of historical value. Our subject of interest in this section comprises the overseas territories that have diverse relationships with the U.S., the problems regarding their contemporary status in international and constitutional laws and the mapping of the referendums held or to be held in this context.

According to their status in international law, we may divide the US-related entities into three groups. The first group of territories includes Puerto Rico and the Commonwealth of Northern Mariana Islands (CNMI), which are part of the U.S. under the Territorial Clause of the US Constitution and by a Commonwealth agreement with each territory. These entities are not considered as American states within the spheres of the Constitution, but they are not foreign or independent states either. They have distinct identity and control over internal affairs, but the U.S. assumes responsibility for their foreign relations, including security and defence. Federal law is directly applicable in these territories, and the local courts are tied to the judicial system by means of a federal district court. These territories are considered, by the UN General Assembly, as self-governing. Nevertheless, serious controversy exists in international and national forums in this respect.

The second group involves the Freely Associated States (FAS): the Republic of the Marshall Islands, and the Federated States of Micronesia and Palau. The fundamental difference between the Commonwealth and the FAS is that, while according to American law the Commonwealth entities are constitutionally a part of the US, the FAS are deemed to be foreign states. Accordingly, with respect to international law, in contrast to the territories of Commonwealth, the FAS are independent states. They are members of the UN, pursue their own foreign relations

[214] Borgeaud ([1895] 1989), pp. 178–179.

and issue their own travel documents. They are tied to the US by means of bilateral agreements called "Compacts of Free Association", which delegate the competence of international security and defence of these states to the US.

In the third group, there are three other territories under the direct administration of the US: Guam, Virgin Islands and American Samoa. These territories are considered as non-self-governing by the UN, according to Article 73 of the UN charter. Therefore, the ultimate resolution of their sovereignty status is deemed as pending by the international community, and they are under the close review of the UN. [215]

6.2.7.1 Puerto Rico

Puerto Rico has been under U.S. sovereignty for more than a century. It is one of the territorial acquisitions (the others being Guam and the Philippines) taken by the US in the Spanish-American War and the concluding Paris Treaty of 1898. The dispute about the sovereignty status of Puerto Rico has not been resolved since then.[216] Puerto Rico's present commonwealth status was established in 1952 via two consecutive referendums. Since that date, there have been local efforts to change the island's political status through five referendums held respectively in 1967, 1991, 1993, 1998 and 2012. All these referendums have been inconclusive, mainly because the US government has ignored the outcomes of the referendums.

After a short military regime, Congress enacted "the Foraker Act" in 1900, which established a civilian colonial government. The Act granted the Puerto Rican people the right to elect their legislature. But still political power was practically held by a governor, an executive cabinet, and a supreme court, all of which were directly appointed by the US President. The US Congress also retained the power to annul any law enacted by the local government. In 1917, a new law, "the Jones Act", conferred Puerto Ricans with US citizenship and gave them more autonomy, including the right to elect a local senate, whose members until then had been appointed by the President. However, the power of the US Congress to repeal the laws enacted by the Puerto Rican legislature remained, and the governor was still to be appointed by the President until 1947, when federal legislation allowed the Puerto Ricans to elect their own governor. [217]

---

[215] See, for example, *Report of the Special Committee on the Situation with regard to the Implementation of the Declaration on the Granting of Independence to Colonial Countries and Peoples for 2010*. General Assembly Official Records 65th Session Supplement No. 23, New York, 2010; The United Nations General Assembly Resolution, of 20 January 2011, No 65/115 on "Questions of American Samoa, Anguilla, Bermuda, the British Virgin Islands, the Cayman Islands, Guam, Montserrat, Pitcairn, Saint Helena, the Turks and Caicos Islands and the United States Virgin Islands" (A/RES/65/115 A-B).

[216] LeDuc (2003), p. 116.

[217] Roman (2006), pp. 127–132.

The post-WWII anti-colonial movement urged the United States to revise the status of the island. The US, as an avid defender of self-determination and anti-colonialism during the foundation of the United Nations, could not ignore international pressure over its overseas possessions. The same trend also generated an overwhelming will among the Puerto Ricans to end the colonial relationship with the US. Subsequent to these developments, the US Congress adopted "Public Law 600" in 1950, which conferred more autonomy to the island, including the right to adopt a constitution. [218]

This law coined the "Commonwealth status", built by a "compact" between the US and Puerto Rico. It conferred to Puerto Rico a "considerable autonomy while remaining under American sovereignty".[219] Two successive referendums were held according to this law, the first one in 1951 for its approval and the second one for the adoption of the Puerto Rican Constitution. Following these two referendums, on March 1952, the Congress enacted "Public Law 447", by which it approved the Puerto Rican Constitution and amended the Jones Act to comply with it. This new regime, however, still remained problematic regarding the island's sovereignty status: the autonomy remained limited and revocable. Along with this, Congress still maintained the unilateral authority to make any law to be applied in Puerto Rico and annul any law made by the Puerto Rican legislature; thus, there was no real improvement to the second-class US citizenship of the Puerto Ricans.

Moreover, the process of the making of the Puerto Rican Constitution and the creation of the new Commonwealth status was defective according to the international requisites of democracy and self-determination. First, the referendum on the adoption of Public Law 600 did not provide two other legitimate options, independence and integration as a new state to the US. The status of commonwealth was imposed in a yes-or-no referendum. Second, the result of the referendum on the constitution would not be binding on the US. Public Law 600 stipulated that after its approval in the referendum, the President would submit the constitution to the Congress if he "found that such constitution conformed with the applicable provisions of Public Law 600 and of the Constitution of the United States". Congress had the ultimate word in the adoption of the constitution.

This structure did not satisfy the "Committee of twenty four", which reinstated Puerto Rico in its list of non-self-governing territories in 1972. The issue still remains problematic and under debate in international law as well as Puerto Rican politics.[220] So far, there have been five referendums concerning the US–Puerto Rican relationship: one of them being a constitutional amendment package, including the basic topics of the Puerto Rican self-determination problem. In the other referendums, three main options appeared on the ballot: independence, continuation of the commonwealth status in an enhanced version and full integration to the US as the 51st state. Referendums held so far in Puerto Rico have always

[218] Roman (2006), pp. 144–145.

[219] LeDuc (2003), p. 117.

[220] Roman (2006), pp. 145–148.

been on the initiative of the local legislature. Certain bills have been proposed to Congress, intended to effectuate a federally sanctioned referendum. Yet these federal initiatives have always failed. The US Congress so far has never been directly involved in the referendums, and this is one of the chief reasons why these referendums have always been "inconclusive".[221]

Referendums Held to Resolve the Question of Puerto Rico The first referendum after the establishment of the Commonwealth status was held in 1967. In 1966, the legislature of Puerto Rico enacted a law, requesting Congress to allow a binding "plebiscite or referendum" in Puerto Rico to decide on its political status. When Congress remained inactive, Puerto Rico then held its own non-binding referendum in 1967. The outcome was for the "enhanced status", that is, more autonomy in its internal and international affairs. Despite an intervention by Congress to create a committee for implementing the results, this call for more autonomy was left unanswered by the US.[222]

Referendum of 1991 On 8 December 1991, a project for amendment of the Constitution of Puerto Rico was put to referendum, which sought to resolve the sovereignty issue through a local constitution. The proposed amendment included, among others, the right of Puerto Rico to determine its status without being subject to the plenary powers of Congress. Yet despite the support of the Popular Democratic Party (PDP) and Popular Independence Party (PIP), the proposal was rejected in the referendum, where 53 % of the voters voted against it. [223]

Referendum of 1993 A following referendum was organised in 1993 by the Puerto Rican government. The options on the ballot appeared as decided by the political parties in the island, and the federal authorities reiterated the view that an eventual outcome would not impose any constitutional duty on the Congress to fulfil the results—since the options failed to be consistent with the relevant regulations of the U.S. Constitution. As one House report put it, "the 1993 definition of 'Commonwealth' failed to present the voters with status options consistent with full self-government and it was misleading to propose to the voters an option which was unconstitutional and unacceptable to Congress in almost every respect". In any event, the outcome of the referendum was inconclusive since no option on the ballot received the absolute majority of votes.[224]

---

[221] Medina (2009–2010), p. 1051.

[222] Roman (2006), p. 149.

[223] Medina (2009–2010), s. 1078.

[224] For the House Report: [U.S. Congress, House Committee on Resources, *United States-Puerto Rico Political Status Act*, report to accompany H.R. 3024, 104th Cong., 2nd sess., H.Rept. 104–713 Part 1 (Washington: GPO, 1996), p. 19]. Cited in Bea and Garrett (2010), p. 12; "The commonwealth option received a slightly higher percentage of votes than the statehood option did, 48.6 versus 46.4 %, respectively. The independence option received only 4.4 % of the votes" (Medina 2009–2010, p. 1079).

Referendum of 1998 On 4 March 4 1998, the House of Representatives of the US Congress adopted law H.R 856 authorising successive referendums to be held every 10 years, by which the electorate could choose one of the three following status options: (1) the current commonwealth, (2) full self-government in the form of either independence or free association, (3) statehood. On 17 September 1998, the Senate of the US Congress adopted a resolution containing the following message: "The Senate supports and recognizes the right of United States citizens residing in Puerto Rico to express democratically their views regarding their future political status through a referendum or other public forum, and to communicate those views to the President and Congress; and the Federal Government should review any such communication". Despite this declaration, no further action was fostered for H.R 856, and the project died in the Senate. [225]

The islanders responded to these developments by conducting another referendum on December 1998. Five options appeared on the ballot: (1) current commonwealth, (2) free association, (3) statehood, (4) independence and (5) none of the above. The exact legal content of these ballot options was a cause of controversy in domestic politics. For example, the Commonwealth supporters are reported to have called a vote for "none of the above". They claimed that the commonwealth definition on the ballot "failed to recognize both the constitutional protections afforded to (their) US citizenship and the fact that the relationship is based upon the mutual consent of Puerto Rico and the United States". The "none of the above" option was mostly favoured by PDP members since their prospect for an enhanced commonwealth status challenged the *status quo* and the federal government's definition of Puerto Rico as a US territory. The *status quo*, which received almost none of the votes (0.1 %), appeared on the ballot as the option of the existing commonwealth.

The majority of the electorate supported the "none of the above" option, with a slight majority (50.3 %), against the "statehood" option (46.5 %).[226] This referendum was also inconclusive: it was apparent that the pro-Commonwealth party PPD campaigned for the "none of the above" option, instead of the "current commonwealth". The outcome demonstrated that a majority of the electorate was not satisfied with the *status quo*; however, it was not clear as to a possible alternative. Besides, the pro-statehood PNP asserted that "none of the above" "was not a valid status option" and the outcome of the vote was portrayed "as an overwhelming mandate to petition the U.S. Congress for statehood".[227] In short, the outcome of the 1998 referendum was inconclusive because of the ambiguity of the legal content

[225] [S.Res. 279, 105th Cong]. Cited in Bea and Garrett (2010), p. 13.

[226] Medina (2009–2010), p. 1080.

[227] Bea and Garrett (2010), p. 13; Results of the Vote are as follows: (1) "Territorial" Commonwealth: 0.1 %; (2) Free Association: 0.3 %; Statehood: 46.5 %; Independence: 2.5 %; None of the above: 50.3 %. Source: http://electionspuertorico.org/1998/summary.html. Retrieved 01 March 2011.

of the ballot options, as well as the excessive proximity of the votes representing statehood and enhanced commonwealth options.

Referendum of 2012 The most recent referendum in Puerto Rico was held on 6 November 2012. There were two questions on the ballot: the first one asked the voters whether they wanted to retain the existing commonwealth status of Puerto Rico, and the second question, which was asked irrespective of their answer to the first question, required them to choose among three possible options: statehood, independence and a sovereign free associated state.[228]

The maintenance of the current status was rejected by a slim majority (54 %), while of those who voted on the second question, 61 % chose statehood, 33 % wanted free association and 5 % opted for independence. This result generated differing and controversial reactions. The non-voting resident commissioner of Puerto Rico, Pedro Pierluisi, sent a letter to President Barack Obama stating that "there is no reasonable way to interpret these results as anything other than a decisive rejection of the territory's current status. . .Among the three viable alternatives, statehood won a decisive victory. . .In the light of these results, I believe that the White House has a clear basis and a clear responsibility to act".[229]

However, the governor, Alejandro Garcia Padilla, who was elected by the gubernatorial elections on the same day as the referendum, also sent a letter to President Barack Obama asking him to ignore the results of the referendum and go for the convocation of a constituent assembly to resolve the status problem. In fact, the possibility of a Constituent Assembly was discussed in the Latest Report by the Presidential Task Force, which said—with a certain degree of caution, however—that "Constitutional conventions have the advantage of being able to adapt the language of the status options and to allow for a more complete consideration of a variety of subsidiary issues".[230] In the same letter, Padilla also questioned the validity of the outcome, citing the ambiguity caused by the small difference in votes between the "yes" and "no" answers to the first question.[231] Indeed, President Barack Obama had visited the island a year before the referendum ("the first such visit by a president in 50 years") and said that he would concede to the outcome on the condition that there was a clear majority for any of the options presented.[232] With only a bare majority as low as 54 % against the *status quo*, there was a general pessimism in thought as to Obama's adherence to the result. Furthermore, the initial news and comments from the press lead one to imagine that Congress would not be

[228] For a brief comment prior to the referendum, see Garrett (2012).

[229] http://pierluisi.house.gov/PDF/letters/2010/11.13.12%20Letter%20to%20President%20Obama%20Regarding%20the%20Puerto%20Rico%20Plebiscite%20Results%202.pdf. Retrieved 23 November 2012.

[230] *Report by the President's Task Force on Puerto Rico's Status* (March 2011), p. 28.

[231] http://www.scribd.com/doc/113173819/Carta-Garcia-Padilla-a-Obama-Plebiscito. Retrieved 23 November 2012.

[232] http://www.bbc.co.uk/news/world-us-canada-20238272. Retrieved 23 November 2012.

so eager to start the process of admission of the island into the Union. It was observed, for example, that "it is unclear whether the US Congress will debate the referendum results or if Obama will consider the results to be a clear enough majority".[233] As one commentator put it: "Congress is likely to respond to Puerto Rico's vote in favour of statehood with stony silence, and is not expected to undertake any effort to make Puerto Rico the 51st state".[234]

From these explanations, it may be inferred that this referendum could not easily claim a legitimate mandate for an immediate accession to the United States. Even if the contrary were the case, the reluctance of the federal government and Congress to act would slow down the process considerably. On the other hand, the choice made by the majority of the island renders the *status quo* very difficult to maintain in its present state. This leaves little room for the pro-*status quo* views and may be considered as a turning point in the history of the resolution of the island's international status.

The Problematic Status of Puerto Rico in Constitutional and International Laws The Relationship between the US and Puerto Rico (as well as Guam, American Samoa and US Virgin Islands) is basically governed by the "Territorial Clause" of the US Constitution (Article IV, Section 3, Clause 2).[235] The legal nature of the constitutional status of these territories is also elucidated by a series of US Supreme Court Decisions known as the *Insular Cases*. In these decisions, the Court interpreted the Territorial Clause with respect to the territories acquired by the US in the Spanish-American War. Particularly as regards Puerto Rico, two statutory regulations are also in force: the Puerto Rico Federal Relations Act (Federal Relations Act) and Public Law 600. Finally, the Commonwealth Constitution of Puerto Rico serves as the highest legal source, on a local level, with respect to its internal government, international competences and the other constitutional matters of the island.

Within the legal framework of its present Commonwealth status, Puerto Rico has a local self-government on domains such as tax, social policies and other local matters, while international competences such as defence, international relations and trade belongs to the United States.[236]

---

[233] http://www.cbsnews.com/8301-202_162-57546260/puerto-rico-votes-for-u.s-statehood-in-non-binding-referendum/. Retrieved 23 November 2012; http://www.usatoday.com/story/news/world/2012/11/07/puerto-rico-referendum/1689097/. Retrieved 23 November 2012.

[234] http://thehill.com/blogs/floor-action/house/266799-congress-expected-to-ignore-puerto-ricos-statehood-vote. Retrieved 23 November 2012; http://edition.cnn.com/2012/11/07/politics/election-puerto-rico/index.html. Retrieved 23 November 2012.

[235] "The Congress shall have power to dispose of and make all needful Rules and Regulations respecting the Territory or other Property belonging to the United States; and nothing in this Constitution shall be so construed as to Prejudice any Claims of the United States, or of any particular State". See Vile (1997), p. 106; Holder and Holder (1997), p. 50.

[236] Special Committee on the Situation with regard to the Implementation of the Declaration on the Granting of Independence to Colonial Countries and Peoples. "*Special Committee decision of*

The legal relationship between the U.S. and Puerto Rico still remains problematic, as regards self-government. Firstly, even after the approval of the local Constitution after 1952, federal laws pertaining to the island's relationship with the federal government remained intact via the Federal Relations Act.[237] Secondly, even though the island does not have a voting representative in Congress, federal laws are superior to local laws. Moreover, despite the existence of local courts, the legal system of Puerto Rico is incorporated into the federal judicial system of the US by means of the First Circuit of Appeals.[238] Finally, the Puerto Rican Constitution provides its own limits *vis-à-vis* the federal legislation. In this respect, the constitution says: "Any amendment or revision of this constitution shall be consistent with the resolution enacted by the applicable provisions of the Constitution of the United States, with the Puerto Rican Federal Relations Act and with Public Law 600" (Section 3 of Article VII of the Constitution of Puerto Rico).[239]

In view of this constitutional fabric, the question of the status of Puerto Rico within the US Constitution revolves around whether the US Congress has unilateral and absolute power in regulating both the government of the island and its sovereignty status. The ensuing debates also provide substantive insights into the related question of whether the current status of the island conforms to basic tenets of international law concerning self-determination.

In the years following the cession of Puerto Rico to the United States, the sovereignty status of Puerto Rico and its relationship with the US was defined by a series of US Supreme Court decisions commonly known as the Insular Cases.[240] These cases created the distinction between incorporated and unincorporated territories. Unincorporated territories are those that are considered by Congress to be under the unfettered sovereignty of the US but that are not incorporated as a state. The states on the mainland, as well as Hawaii and Alaska, are incorporated territories, whereas overseas territories such as Puerto Rico are not incorporated

9 June 2008 concerning Puerto Rico Report prepared by the Rapporteur of the Special Committee, Bashar Ja'afari (Syrian Arab Republic)". United Nations General Assembly, A/AC.109/2009/L.13, 17 March 2009. para. 5.

[237] Special Committee on the Situation with regard to the Implementation of the Declaration on the Granting of Independence to Colonial Countries and Peoples. "*Special Committee decision of 10 June 2002 concerning Puerto Rico Report prepared by the Rapporteur of the Special Committee, Mr. Fayssal Mekdad (Syrian Arab Republic)*". United Nations General Assembly, A/AC.109/2003/L.3, 12 May 2003. para. 8.

[238] *Special Committee decision of 10 June 2002 concerning Puerto Rico*, (A/AC.109/2003/L.3), 12 May 2003, para. 7.

[239] For the text of the constitution, see http://welcome.topuertorico.org/constitu.shtml; Retrieved 12 November 2012.

[240] *Delima v. Bidwell*, 182 U.S 1 (1901); *Goetze v. United States* 182 U.S. 221 (1901); *Dooley v. United States*, 182 U.S. 222 (1901); *Armstrong v. United States*, 182 U.S. 243 (1901); *Downes v. Bidwell*, 182 U.S. 244 (1901) *Balzac v. Porto Rico*, 258 U.S. 298 (1922). Cited in Roman (2006), p. 48, footnote 151.

territories since Congress has uttered no "clear declaration of purpose" in that way.[241]

Therefore, in terms of the US Constitution, Puerto Rico may be described as a "territory appurtenant and belonging to the United States, but not part of the United States within the. . .Constitution".[242] It may be argued that there is a constitutional dualism in the US, where the states enjoy full constitutional protection but the territories do not. It is observed that "the people of Puerto Rico are not full United States citizens because they do not share the same rights held by other United States citizens: They are disenfranchised citizens with limited status. This status has not changed to this date".[243]

We may summarise the legal ramifications of this status as follows: firstly, the citizenship status of Puerto Ricans is revocable by Congress. As opposed to the citizens in the mainland, the citizenship of the islanders is not governed by the 14th Amendment of the Constitution, but of statutory nature. Consequently, Congress may at any time modify or revoke the citizenship of the descendants of the island. [244]

Secondly, only "fundamental constitutional rights" apply to Puerto Rico. Unlike incorporated territories, in which residents have full constitutional rights, unincorporated territories have only basic protections from the US Constitution, such as the writ of habeas corpus, prohibition against cruel and unusual punishment and protection against unreasonable searches and seizures.[245] In this way, in 1975, the US Supreme Court asserted that Congress and the Supreme Court had the power to decide "the personal rights to be accorded to the inhabitants of Puerto Rico". Likewise, in another decision, the Court ruled that Congress "may treat Puerto Rico differently from states, so long as there is a rational basis for its actions".[246] The disenfranchised status of Puerto Rico may be best observed in the fact that Puerto Ricans do not have voting rights in the presidential and congressional elections. In fact, as US citizens, Puerto Ricans may vote so long as they reside in one of the states. Yet, according to the Constitution, a geographical entity should be a state to possess the voting right. Consequently, unincorporated territories (but not necessarily their descendants) do not have the right to vote in federal elections.

Thirdly, Puerto Rico does not enjoy the constitutional guarantee of self-government, as do the states on the mainland. American federalism is based on power sharing between the federal government and the states, in which the federal

[241] See *Balzac v. People of Porto Rico*, 258 U.S. 298 (1922): http://caselaw.lp.findlaw.com/scripts/getcase.pl?navby=case&court=us&vol=258&invol=298. Retrieved 10 August 2012.

[242] [*Downes v. Bidwell*, 182 U.S. 244 (1901)], cited in Roman (2006), pp. 50–51.

[243] Roman (2006), p. 136.

[244] [*Rogers v. Bellei*], cited in Roman (2006), p. 138; See also: Bea and Garrett (2010), p. 26.

[245] Rezvani (2007), p. 120.

[246] [*Examining Board v. Flores de Otero*, 426 U.S. 590"; "*Harris v. Rosario*, 446 U.S. 651 (1980)], cited in Bea and Garrett (2010), p. 10; this view is reiterated by the Court in 1990 in [*United States* v. *Verdugo Urquidez*], cited in Roman (2006), pp. 56 and 138.

government has the enumerated powers, whereas the residual powers are owned by the states themselves. In practice, however, the contours of federal–state relations have not been as clear as stated in the constitution, where the competences of federal government and states have waxed and waned across time according to Supreme Court decisions. This federal power-sharing pattern does not apply to non-state territories of the United States. As a matter of domestic constitutional law, Puerto Rico is subject to the Congress's plenary powers pursuant to the territorial clause of the US Constitution (Article IV, Section 3). In this framework, US federal laws are directly applicable in Puerto Rico, although Puerto Rico has no voting representative in the US Congress. Likewise, according to the Federal Relations Act of 1950, all federal laws that are "not locally inapplicable" are the law of Puerto Rico *per se*.[247]

Three theories may be listed in an attempt to explain the constitutional status of Puerto Rico: the compact theory, the territorial supremacy theory and the conventional entrenchment theory.[248] Compact theorists argue that Congress does not have an absolute legal power over Puerto Rico and whenever an alteration of the status is in question, mutual consent is indispensable. Compact theorists base this argument on the preamble to Public Law 600 and the Constitution of Puerto Rico, which refer to "government by consent" and describe the US–Puerto Rico relationship as a "compact". Therefore, according to this view, these legal instruments create a legally binding duty for Congress to avoid arbitrary intervention in the territory. This view is upheld by certain courts. In 1985, for example, the First Circuit Federal Court stated that "under the Compact between the people of Puerto Rico and the United States, Congress cannot amend the Puerto Rico Constitution unilaterally".[249]

With respect to territorial supremacy theory, which is more commonly supported than the other two described here, "Congress's plenary power is legally intact and consequently exercisable" in the face of "the overriding legal force of the territorial clause of the US Constitution". Advocates of this theory refuse to trace a hint of a constitutional limit to the unlimited power of the US Congress in the "vague phrases" of the legal instruments, other than that within the Territorial Clause of the U.S. Constitution. For them, neither any law enacted by Congress nor Puerto Rico's Constitution provides a binding legal force *vis-à-vis* the Constitution. Certain lower courts upheld this view. To give one example, in 1993, the Eleventh

[247] Rezvani (2007), p. 119.

[248] Rezvani (2007), pp. 123–139.

[249] [*United States v. Quiones* (1985), 758 F2d 40, 42], cited in Rezvani (2007), pp. 122–123. The preamble to Public Law 600 makes the following statement: "Fully recognizing the principle by consent, this Act is now adopted in the nature of compact so that the people of Puerto Rico may organize a government pursuant to a constitution of their own adoption". Similar provisions may be found in the Puerto Rico Constitution: "the Commonwealth of Puerto Rico is hereby constituted. Its political power emanates from the people and shall be exercised in accordance with their will, within the terms of the compact agreed upon between the people of Puerto Rico and the United States of America."

Circuit Court declared that "Congress may unilaterally repeal the Puerto Rican Constitution…and replace (it) with any rules or regulations of its choice".[250]

Federal authorities endorse this supremacy theory. There had been a verbal statement by a representative of the United States to the United Nations, before the submission of the official request for the removal of Puerto Rico from the list of non-self-governing territories, indicating that mutual consent would be required to make any modifications in the status of Puerto Rico. However, this statement became obsolete when the Department of Justice maintained in 1959 that Puerto Rico was a territory under the territorial clause.[251] Similarly, in 1997, the U.S. House Committee on Resources asserted that Congress, under the territorial clause, has full constitutional authority to revoke unilaterally the autonomy that Puerto Rico enjoyed.[252] The President's Task Force on Puerto Rico's Status reiterated the same view: "autonomy of Puerto Rico rests on the unilateral will of Congress. Congress could modify or abolish the current status, could pass any law directly applicable to local matters or decide on the system of government by a mere statute".[253]

The Conventional entrenchment theory is the American version of the doctrine of constitutional convention. Rezvani explains the difference between the British and American conceptions of the conventions.[254] As mentioned above in the British conception, conventions are distinct from laws as they are not legally enforceable or recognisable in courts. They are a part of the constitution, albeit as non-legal rules. In the British context, the prevalent constitutional principle of parliamentary sovereignty and the firm self-restraint of the courts in the face of this maxim render the conventions non-applicable by the courts. Conversely, in American courts, the obvious distinction between the unwritten and written rules of the Constitution is blurred. The supremacy of the constitution as the ubiquitous maxim and the consequent authority of the judiciary in the governmental system allow American judges to feel freer when resorting to the conventions in the legal reasoning of their decisions. As the decisive overseers of the constitutionality of laws and other governmental actions, courts have a greater liberty for a larger interpretation of the constitutional text. In most cases, courts use the conventions as interpretive insights to fit the existent written rules for the desired decisions. In particular, the Supreme Court has "arguably" used the conventions as "deeply held principles not

---

[250] [*United States v. Sanches* (1993), 99 2F.2.d 1143,1152-53(11th Cir.)], cited in Rezvani (2007), pp. 124–125.

[251] *Special Committee decision of 9 June 2008 concerning Puerto Rico*, (A/AC.109/2009/L.13), 17 March 2009, para. 17.

[252] Puerto Rico Status Field Hearing Before the Committee on Resources House of Representatives One Hundred Fifth Congress First Session on **H.R. 856** April 19, 1997, Retrieved from http://commdocs.house.gov/committees/resources/hii43194.000/hii43194_0.HTM on 12 November 2012.

[253] *Report by the President's Task Force on Puerto Rico's Status* (*December 2005*) p. 5; *Special Committee decision of 9 June 2008 concerning Puerto Rico*, (A/AC.109/2009/L.13), 17 March 2009, para 15.

[254] Rezvani (2007), pp. 132–134.

articulated in the explicit text of the written Constitution". When this happens, "the resulting judicial decision is a semi-legal hybrid between a non-legal-unwritten source and a legal written, common-law outcome". It may be observed that certain significant decisions of the Supreme Court—such *as Brown v. Board of Education*, *Baker v. Carr* and *Roe and Wade*—could not have found their legal support, if the underpinning constitutional provision had been interpreted within the strict confines of its text. Courts do not necessarily resort to an explicit use of the conventions, though they are discernible in such decisions where clauses such as due process or equal protection are "speciously invoked", even if they have no clear relationship to these decisions. Besides, in certain cases, the Court has simply neglected to show a constitutional basis. In *Shapiro v. Thompson*, for example, the Court openly declared that "there was no occasion to ascribe the source of this right to…a particular constitutional provision".[255]

With respect to Puerto Rico, the conventional view acknowledges the unfettered power of Congress in view of the strict textual interpretation of the written constitution. Nevertheless, legal rules that give Congress plenary powers are superseded and made non-usable by certain conventions governing the relationship between the US and Puerto Rico. Just as in the territorial supremacy theory, conventional theory asserts that Congress' legal plenary power is still present, yet the so-called conventions have practically invalidated this unilateral power. These conventions draw their sources from certain instruments such as non-binding agreements between leaders, statements by the U.S Government, decisions by the judiciary and lower court rulings that endorse the conception of mutual consent. It is argued that these instruments provide an "informal constitutional rule that renders the territorial clause of the US Constitution frozen with respect to Puerto Rico".[256] Thus, Puerto Rico's status in the US constitutional system may be described as one that is "conventionally entrenched". Unilateral revision of its allocated constitutional powers is rendered very difficult in practice because of conventional (unwritten) rather than formal legal rules.

The government of Puerto Rico offers notable evidence in support of the conventional theory. In practice it is observed that, since 1952, Congress has usually granted Puerto Rico self-government with enough *de facto* autonomy so as to fit the international obligations of the US. The theoretical plenary power of Congress is superseded by the consistent political practice of non-interference in the local affairs of Puerto Rico.[257] One may confirm this observation by subsequent

[255] [*Brown v. Board of Education* (*1954*), 347 U.S. 483; *Baker v. Carr*, (*1962*), *369 U.S. 186*; *Roe v. Wade* (1973) 410 U.S. 113,153, *Shapiro v. Thompson* (1969) U.S., 618,630]. Cited in Rezvani (2007), pp. 132–134.

[256] Rezvani (2007), p. 125.

[257] Lawson and Sloane (2009), pp. 1127 and 1158.

reports of the Freedom House, which has consistently ranked the territory as "free" during the last decade.[258]

The conventionally entrenched status of autonomy is also in harmony with the territory's status in international law. The international law of decolonisation hovers over the constitutional relationship of the United States with its overseas territories. Considering that the lawfulness of any sort of dependency status of an entity to a foreign state depends on the consent of the population concerned, US officials have had to remain silent as to the applicability of the rule of plenary power of Congress regarding Puerto Rico. In this vein, there have been constant oral and written commitments made by US Officials to the United Nations suggesting that any alteration to the legal basis of the US–Puerto Rico relationship should be made bilaterally. Therefore, the US has committed itself, in the context of international law, to the basis of the bilateral compact.[259]

In the light of these explanations, we may assume that there is very little possibility that the federal authorities would blatantly impinge on the local affairs of the territory without the consent of the Puerto Rican people and its government. Any conduct to the contrary would meet with the intense criticisms of moral opprobrium and tyranny from all parts of the domestic and international political spectrum, and no rational statesman would want to face that. "Such deeply held principles and countervailing political influences are added to the precedents of non-interference and semi-legal judicial rulings that reinforce and defend Puerto Rico's post-1952 constitutional order".[260] From these explanations, we may infer that it is not probable that the US would make any unilateral revision of the current sovereignty status of Puerto Rico against the clear wishes of the populations concerned.

The conventional theory may be resorted to explain the non-intrusion of the US into the current government of the island. This basis would be satisfactory if the contemporary problem of Puerto Rico was to preserve its current constitutional situation. Yet the existing sovereignty status is under review in municipal and international forums, and disagreement prevails as to whether the *status quo* satisfies contemporary norms of self-determination. The chief problem, in this respect, is that the present status of Puerto Rico may not be altered without the consent of the US Congress.

Under the territorial clause, federal government has the competence regarding the final decision to accept territories as new states. Indeed, in view of Article IV, Section 3 of the US Constitution, Congress has the decisive authority for the incorporation of a territory. Whenever Congress does not opt for incorporating a

[258] "As a commonwealth, Puerto Rico exercises approximately the same control over its internal affairs as do the 50 states". For the 2010 report of freedom house on Puerto Rico, http://www.freedomhouse.org/template.cfm?page=22&year=2010&country=7971. Retrieved 25 March 2011.

[259] Lawson and Sloane (2009), p. 1155.

[260] Rezvani (2007), p. 136.

territory as a state, the territory is a "mere territorial possession" under the full disposition of Congress, and this is no doubt the case for the current status of Puerto Rico. These explanations allow the US to infer that an eventual change in the sovereignty status of Puerto Rico requires a final Congressional assent, and thus "no change in the status of Puerto Rico is legally possible unless authorized by the US Congress".[261]

So what is the status of the Puerto Rican referendums that have been held so far in this legal framework? One may note two important ramifications. Firstly, as implied by the conventional theory, the absolute power of Congress to unilaterally change the current status of the island is somewhat dormant. The referendums, their non-binding status notwithstanding, prove to be an effective safeguard and a veto tool. Secondly, in addition to the veto function of the Puerto Rican referendums, they also draw the attention of US public opinion to the issue and stimulate a considerable amount of debate within US politics, within the international community and among the Puerto Ricans themselves. These referendums have revealed the fact that "the status question is far from settled".[262]

One should also be reminded that international law bestows on the Puerto Ricans the right to independence, as it was considered a territory subject to the post-WWII decolonisation norms.[263] If Congress refused this right in the face of a clear wish of the island for that option, the US would be in breach of international law. Yet the option of independence is not very popular among Puerto Ricans, as observed in past referendums and local elections. Therefore, the independence scenario is very unlikely to manifest itself in the near future, as proved unequivocally by the results of subsequent referendums in the territory. Besides all this, the Independence Party is highly invisible in the gubernatorial elections.[264]

This fact rules out the most favoured option for the former colonies in international law. The people of Puerto Rico are divided between the other two possible options: statehood and commonwealth status—albeit in an enhanced version. The requirement for the consent of Congress becomes more problematic with respect to these options. If the electorate of Puerto Rico were to opt for statehood, a possible refusal of the Congress would meet with less condemnation, if any, from international society since the annexing of a decolonised territory to the ex-coloniser has a quasi-illegitimate status. Besides, one could not blame a people, i.e. Americans in the mainland, if they refuse to alter the boundaries of their state by incorporating a new state to the US. The Americans' right to self-determination could be rightfully invoked at this point, and the Territorial Clause elucidates this right on a constitutional level. As regards commonwealth status, controversy arises when Puerto Rico wants to modify the main terms for more autonomy. The federal government either

[261] LeDuc (2003), p. 117.

[262] Diaz (2001), p. 204.

[263] Lawson and Sloane (2009), p. 1124.

[264] For the elections in Puerto Rico, see http://eleccionespuertorico.org/home_en.html; Last Accessed 15 May 2013.

refuses or remains motionless when facing such demands. Subsequently, the current commonwealth status remains controversial both in the domestic politics of Puerto Rico and within international law.

The legal framework regulating the relationship between the US and Puerto Rico is insufficient to resolve this issue. Even though, according to Puerto Rico's constitutional system (i.e., local constitution and related federal laws), self-determination is established as a right, this system does not offer a process for the implementation of that right.[265]

The difficulty arising from this legal problematic is the unwillingness of the federal government to resolve the question. Roman notes at this point that "history suggests that there seems to be little interest in the United States to change the (current) relationship". A brief historical description confirms this argument. In 1959, despite three consecutive proposals to amend the constitutional status of the island, Congress remained inactive. The US also remained silent on the result of the 1967 referendum for an enhanced commonwealth status. The same inertia continued in 1993 when a new referendum was held on the same options as presented in 1967. The result was again for an enhanced commonwealth. Yet when the Puerto Rican legislature asked the US Congress to decide whether the enhanced commonwealth status was acceptable, the Congress responded that the commonwealth status as defined on the ballot "contained expectations that were not (constitutionally) viable".[266] Indeed, federal authorities consistently maintain the view that there could be three options that are constitutionally feasible: maintaining the status quo, full integration as a new state and independence. Thus, modifying the commonwealth status is categorically rejected.[267]

As was the case for the preceding referendums, the 1998 referendum was held pursuant to the unilateral decision of the Puerto Rican Legislative Assembly. In fact, in 1997, an attempt was made in the US Congress to render the results of the planned referendum binding for the United States. The related bill—"The United States-Puerto Rico Political Status Act"—was adopted by the House of Representatives on March 1998, but it lapsed because of the inactivity of the Senate, as the congressional session terminated.[268]

Thus, Puerto Rico's status remains in limbo. While there is considerable controversy in the international community as to whether the current status conforms to the norms of international law, Puerto Rican politics is also occupied by this conundrum. Despite its removal by the UN General Assembly from its non-self-governing territories, the view that Puerto Rico is still a colony has been maintained by the Special Committee since 1972. The question is still "under continuous

[265] Camacho (2004), p. 518.

[266] *Special Committee decision of 9 June 2008 concerning Puerto Rico*, (A/AC.109/2009/L.13), 17 March 2009, para 9.

[267] *Report by the President's Task Force on Puerto Rico's Status* (December 2007) p. 6; Medina (2009–2010), p. 1082.

[268] http://www.govtrack.us/congress/bill.xpd?bill=h105-856; Retrieved 17 July 2011.

review" in its many documents (28 as of 2009). In its 2009 decision, the Committee reaffirmed the "inalienable right of the people of Puerto Rico to self determination and independence in conformity with General Assembly resolution 1514 (XV) and the applicability of the fundamental principles of that resolution to the question of Puerto Rico". In the same document, it is stated that "despite the diverse initiatives taken by the political representatives of Puerto Rico and the United States in recent years, the process of decolonization of Puerto Rico, in compliance with General Assembly resolution 1514 (XV) and the resolutions and decisions of the Special Committee on Puerto Rico, has not yet been set in motion".

From these explanations, we may infer that as the question of Puerto Rico is related to decolonisation, international law requires a certain participation of the people concerned during the relevant process. In this manner, the Special Committee held that "the principle that any initiative for the solution of the political status of Puerto Rico should originate from the people of Puerto Rico".[269]

With respect to the internal politics of Puerto Rico, it is the common assumption that the territory is disagreeably preoccupied by the status question. Shortly after the establishment of their current Commonwealth status, Puerto Rican's domestic politics developed around this divisive issue, where three popular parties arose. The Popular Democratic Party (PDP) advocates the Commonwealth status, but it contends that this status should be transformed so as to be exempted from the territorial clause. While this enhanced Commonwealth status retained US citizenship, more autonomy should be given to Puerto Rico in terms of both domestic and international affairs.[270] The New Progressive Party (NPP) wants Puerto Rico to be incorporated into the US as a state, while the Puerto Rican Independence Party (PIP) opts for independence while maintaining certain ties with the US. The three leading political parties are distinguished basically in terms of their stance regarding this sovereignty issue, and none of them is satisfied with the current status.[271] Political conflict on the future of the territory is quite bitter, and the internal politics of the island are stalemated by this troublesome issue.

---

[269] United Nations. *"Report of the Special Committee on the Situation with regard to the Implementation of the Declaration on the Granting of Independence to Colonial Countries and Peoples for 2010"*, General Assembly Official Records 65th Session Supplement No. 23, (A/65/23), 2010, para. 26. See also Special Committee on the Situation with regard to the Implementation of the Declaration on the Granting of Independence to Colonial Countries and Peoples. "*Special Committee decision of 15 June 2009 concerning Puerto Rico Report prepared by the Rapporteur of the Special Committee, Bashar Ja'afari (Syrian Arab Republic)*". United Nations General Assembly, (A/AC.109/2010/L.4), 22 April 2010; *"Special Committee decision of 11 August 1998 concerning Puerto Rico"* A/AC.109/1999/28, 7 July 1999.

[270] *Special Committee decision of 9 June 2008 concerning Puerto Rico*, (A/AC.109/2009/L.13), 17 March 2009, para. 5

[271] *Special Committee decision of 10 June 2002 concerning Puerto Rico*, (A/AC.109/2003/L.3), 12 May 2003, para. 4.

Proposed Solution: A Two-Referendum Process Thus, the case of Puerto Rico is perceived in both internal and international politics as yet to be resolved. We may briefly explain the developments concerning the resolution of this issue.

In 1999, a congressional committee report examining the 1998 referendum reiterated the necessity of a "process of enabling the people of Puerto Rico to implement a structured process of self-determination based on constitutionally valid options Congress is willing to consider". In a blunter manner, four members of the Congress chairing the committees concerning Puerto Rico asserted that the *status quo* did not enjoy the "majority consent" of the island, and the federal government had the duty to resolve this issue.[272]

The response from the executive to the 1998 referendum came without delay. President Clinton promised to collaborate with Congress and leaders in Puerto Rico to resolve the status problem. Subsequently, the President's Task Force on Puerto Rico's Status was established on 5 December 2003 and has been active until today. The Task Force is assigned with the duty to provide choices of sovereignty status for Puerto Rico, viable in terms of both constitutional and international laws.[273]

Two consequent reports by the Presidential Task Force Report proposed a two-staged process.[274] In this framework, there would be two consecutive referendums (federally sanctioned plebiscite) in the island. The first vote would be held to ask the people whether they wanted to change the *status quo*. To this end, the ballot would have two options: "remaining a United States territory subject to the will of Congress or pursuing a constitutionally viable path towards a permanent non-territorial status with the United States". In case of a pro-*status quo* result, the Task Force recommended that future referendums be held periodically, to ensure that the *status quo* remained popular in the island. If the result were to change in the *status quo*, there would be an additional referendum for the final decision to resolve the issue. The Puerto Ricans would vote to choose between two constitutionally viable permanent non-territorial options: statehood or independence. [275]

This template was endorsed by subsequent bills submitted to Congress. On 7 February 2007, the Puerto Rico Democracy Act of 2007 (H.R. 900) was proposed to the House of Representatives: "to provide for a federally sanctioned self-determination process for the people of Puerto Rico". The bill provided that the first referendum to decide on whether the *status quo* should remain be held not later than December 31, 2009. If the result were for the *status quo*, subsequent referendums

[272] [U.S. Congress, House Committee on Resources, *The Results of the 1998 Puerto Rico Plebiscite*, Serial No. 106-A, 106th Cong., 1st sess. (Washington: GPO, 1999), p. 7]. Cited in Bea and Garrett (2010), p. 14.

[273] *Special Committee decision of 9 June 2008 concerning Puerto Rico*, (A/AC.109/2009/L.13), 17 March 2009.

[274] *Special Committee decision of 9 June 2008 concerning Puerto Rico*, (A/AC.109/2009/L.13), 17 March 2009, para. 15.

[275] *Report by the President's Task Force on Puerto Rico's Status* (December 2005), p. 10.

would be held periodically after every 8 years. If the result were for the non-territorial status, three options would be presented to the voters in a final referendum to be held no later than 31 December 2011: statehood, independence or free association. Following this referendum, the United States Congress would have 6 months to implement the result. However, the bill lapsed in the Congress as the Congressional session expired before the House Vote occurred.[276] A new version of the bill was introduced during the 111th Congress, entitled "the Puerto Rico Democracy Act of 2009" (H.R. 2499). This bill providing for the same two-staged plan also lapsed when no action was taken in the Senate before the session expired.[277] On the other hand, the two-staged approach [(1) decision on ending the *status quo*, (2) decision on alternative options] was resonated in the latest referendum held in 2012. Right after the lapse of the H.R. 2499, the then Resident Commissioner Luis Fortuño had returned to Puerto Rico to urge the local legislative assembly to authorise a referendum. The relevant legislation was enacted on 16 December 2011. Based on this legislation, the 2012 referendum endorsed the two-staged approach, albeit not by consecutive referendums but by two complementary questions on the same ballot.[278]

6.2.7.2 Former Trust Territory of the Pacific Islands (TTPI)

TTPI were the Japanese mandates handed over to the US after WWII under its capacity of administering authority pursuant to the Trusteeship Agreements. These territories were subject to the Security Council, where the US had the veto power in the final decision of their status. The TTPI comprises the Caroline Islands, the Marshall Islands, and the Northern Mariana Islands, situated in an area between the Philippines and the northeast of Indonesia in the North Pacific Ocean. The term "Micronesia" was also used to define these islands. Today, the Federated States of Micronesia consists of the Caroline Islands, with the exception of Palau.

There were two main issues during the negotiations in the process of settlement of sovereignty status of these territories. The first one was about the nuclear-testing activities carried out by the US in the area.[279] The procrastination of the resolution of the status of Palau until 1994 was due especially to the controversy regarding the use of nuclear material in the territory. The second problem involved the question of whether the TTPI should be treated as a single territory. The U.S. was inclined to

---

[276] http://www.govtrack.us/congress/bill.xpd?bill=h110-900. Retrieved 12 November 2012; *Special Committee decision of 9 June 2008 concerning Puerto Rico*, (A/AC.109/2009/L.13), 17 March 2009, p. 22.

[277] http://www.govtrack.us/congress/bill.xpd?bill=h111-2499. Retrieved 10 November 2012.

[278] See Sect. 6.2.7.1 in this chapter.

[279] As the US is entitled for the military use, notwithstanding their independence in international law, these territories became a nuclear testing area of the US. They have suffered from undesired results of nuclear testing on public health and environment. Palau, for instance, responded to this situation by prohibiting nuclear weapons in its constitution.

treat the territory as a whole and aspired to form one state. The same tendency existed in the UN.[280]

As an initial development, in 1965, the Congress of Micronesia was established to decide on a future sovereignty status of the TTPI. In 1969, the United States began negotiations with the Micronesian Congress. Soon after the beginning of these negotiations, it became evident that the sovereignty prospects of the different districts were disparate. The Marianas wanted a more inclusive relationship with the US, and to this end, a referendum was held in the region, on November 9, 1969, in favour of integration with Guam. The US rejected this attempt, and in turn, the Marianas legislature adopted a resolution declaring their intention to end their relationship with the US as provided for by the Trusteeship Agreement. These events ended up with the commencement of separate negotiations between Marianas and the US. At the end of these negotiations, the US signed a Covenant establishing the US Commonwealth of Northern Mariana Islands in 1975. In a referendum held in the Northern Marianas, the Covenant was approved by a 78 % majority in favour of commonwealth status. On July 1975, a constitution was made for the rest of Micronesia and voted for in a referendum. The Marshall Islands and Palau rejected the constitution, which opened the way for the beginning of separate negotiations with the United States.[281]

After a number of separate status negotiations, the TTPI ended up with the creation of a Commonwealth of the Northern Mariana Islands and three Freely Associated States—the Federated States of Micronesia (Pohnpei, Truk, Yap and Kosrae), the Republic of the Marshall Islands and the Republic of Palau. In 1990, the UN Security Council declared that the Commonwealth of Northern Mariana Islands (CNMI), the Federated States of Micronesia (FSM) and the Marshall Islands had become "fully self-governing", after a process in which each of the entities "freely exercised their right to self-determination in approving their respective new status agreements in plebiscites observed by visiting missions of the Trusteeship Council..."[282] The same decision was made for Palau in 1994.

Commonwealth of Northern Mariana Islands (CNMI) The status of the CNMI is similar to that of Puerto Rico in many respects, regulated by a Covenant signed between the US and Northern Mariana Islands. The Covenant entered into force by a federal law of 1976 following a non-binding referendum in 1975.[283] The Covenant is portrayed as a "pre-constitutional act by which the people of Northern Marianas exercised their right of self-determination".[284] In this way, it specifies

[280] Roman (2006), p. 219; Keitner and Reisman (2003), p. 37.

[281] Roman (2006), pp. 218–219; Keitner and Reisman (2003), pp. 36–37.

[282] [S.C. Res. 683, U.N SCOR, 45th Sess., 2972nd mtg. at 29, U.N. Doc. S/res 683 (1990)], cited in Keitner and Reisman (2003), pp. 38 and 44.

[283] The Covenant received 55 % of the votes cast; see http://www.c2d.ch/detailed_display.php?lname=votes&table=votes&page=1&parent_id=&sublinkname=results&id=38889. Retrieved 01 April 2011.

[284] Willens and Siemer (1977) cited in Keitner and Reisman (2003), p. 39.

certain requirements for the CNMI constitution, such as republican government, popular election of the governor and the inclusion of a bill of rights. Following the effectuation of this Covenant, a constitution was adopted by the assembly of Northern Marianas, and this constitution was approved in a referendum on 6 March 1977 with a 93 % affirmative vote.[285]

As to the substantive aspects of its sovereignty status, CNMI is defined as "a self governing commonwealth under the sovereignty of the United States of America". The inhabitants of the territory are US citizens. Northern Mariana has control over its internal affairs, while the US has plenary competence in international relations and defence. The relevant provisions of the US Constitution and its treaties and laws are applicable in the territory, along with the Covenant and the judiciary system that is integrated into that of the US via a federal district court.[286]

The federal authorities define the sovereignty status of the CNMI in the same way as they do for Puerto Rico. The United States maintains that it has the plenary power to govern the Commonwealth under the territorial clause of the US Constitution.[287] Thus, the CNMI is not an independent state, and, as is the case with Puerto Rico, international attention on the territory still persists. "The contours of the relationship between the CNMI and its former administering authority remain in a state of evolution".[288] In short, it is apparent that the sovereignty status of the CNMI is open to reappraisal, both in international law and in the municipal laws of the CNMI and the U.S.

Republic of the Marshall Islands, Federated States of Micronesia and Palau The remaining territories of the TTPI emerged as three different independent states having a Compact of Free Association with the US. They are the Republic of Marshall Islands (population: 70,000), the Federated States of Micronesia (population: 136,000) and Palau (population: 20,000).

The Republic of Marshall Islands adopted a constitution that entered into force on May 1, 1979. The following step was the signature of the Compact of Free Association (COFA) between the Marshall Islands and the US. This Compact was approved in a UN-observed referendum on September 7, 1983,[289] The Compact was approved as law with "minor modifications" by the US Congress and entered into force on October 21, 1986.[290]

---

285 Keitner and Reisman (2003), p. 39.

286 Keitner and Reisman (2003), p. 43.

287 Keitner and Reisman (2003), p. 41. See, for the official site of the Office of Insular Affairs, http://www.doi.gov/oia/. Retrieved 01 April 2011.

288 Keitner and Reisman (2003), p. 44.

289 This referendum was mandatory pursuant to Chapter XIII Art. 6 of the Marshallese Constitution. http://www.c2d.ch/detailed_display.php?lname=votes&table=votes&id=130720&continent=Australia/Oceania&countrygeo=11699&stategeo=&citygeo=&level=1&recent=1. Retrieved 12 November 2012.

290 Keitner and Reisman (2003), p. 48.

The Federated States of Micronesia (FSM) was formed out of four states, Chuuk, Pohnpei, Yap and Kosrae, when they respectively ratified the founding Constitution in a UN-monitored referendum on July 12, 1978.[291] After this, the FSM negotiated a COFA with the United States and signed the Compact on October 1, 1982. On June 1983, the Compact was submitted to voters in the FSM, where it was approved by 79.00 % of the votes cast.[292]

The constitutional referendum establishing the FSM was also put to referendum in Palau, yet it was rejected by a 55–45 % margin. Staying out of the FSM, Palau adopted its own constitution on July 9, 1979.[293] In this constitution, a mandatory referendum is specified for the bilateral or multilateral treaties that provide transfer of sovereignty (Art. II, Sec. 3). In this framework, a minimum "majority of the votes cast in a nationwide referendum" is required "to delegate Major governmental powers including but not limited to defence, security, or foreign affairs", "by treaty, compact, or other agreement between the sovereign Republic of Palau and another sovereign nation or international organization". In addition, the Constitution requires an enhanced majority of 3/4 of the votes cast to approve any bilateral agreement that authorises the "use, testing, storage or disposal of nuclear, toxic chemical, gas or biological weapons intended for use in warfare".

This provision resulted in the delayed resolution of the sovereignty status of Palau. In *Gibbons v. Salii*, the Supreme Court of Palau decided that the nuclear provision of the Constitution "prohibit(ed) transit of nuclear powered vessels or vessels equipped with nuclear missiles".[294] This interpretation implied that the Compact between the USA and Palau had to be approved by 75 % of the votes cast since the US insisted on a privilege to nuclear transit to be inserted in the Compact. Consequently, several successive referendums were held to reach the required 75 %. In 1987, Palauans attempted to overcome this obstacle by a constitutional amendment, intending to lower the required majority to a simple majority. Yet the Palauan Supreme Court nullified this amendment, arguing that constitutional procedures had not been observed. Finally, a similar amendment was adopted on November 9th of 1993; the Supreme Court did not annul the amendment this time. In the amendment, it is provided that the required majority for nuclear substances "shall not apply to votes to approve the Compact of Free Association and its subsidiary agreements".[295] Consequently, Palauan voters approved the Compact by 68–32 % in the eighth referendum.[296]

---

[291] Keitner and Reisman (2003), p. 49.

[292] For the referendum results: http://www.c2d.ch/detailed_display.php?lname=votes&table=votes&id=130713&continent=Australia/Oceania&countrygeo=11693&stategeo=&citygeo=&level=1&recent=1. Retrieved 01 April 2011.

[293] Keitner and Reisman (2003), p. 50.

[294] [*Gibbons v. Salii, 1 ROP Intrm. 333, 348 (Palau 1986)*], cited in Keitner and Reisman (2003), p. 50. See Also: Hinck (1990), pp. 931–932.

[295] This amendment was adopted through a mandatory constitutional referendum: http://www.c2d.ch/detailed_display.php?lname=votes&table=votes&id=37986&continent=Australia/Oceania&countrygeo=11685&stategeo=&citygeo=&level=1&recent=1. Retrieved 01 April 2011.

[296] Keitner and Reisman (2003), p. 51.

6.2.7.3 Non-Self-Governing Territories: Guam, Virgin Islands and American Samoa

Guam Guam is a Non-Self-Governing Territory administered by the United States of America. It is the southernmost and the largest of the Mariana Islands in the Pacific Ocean with a population of approximately 178,000. The United States has maintained absolute and plenary power over Guam under the territorial clause of the United States Constitution. Guam's constitutional status is an organised unincorporated territory of the United States.[297] In 1950, the Congress enacted the Organic Act of Guam, providing for a local government. The territory is under the administration of the Department of the Interior, and as "an unincorporated Territory, Guam is a possession of the United States but not part of the United States".[298]

The quest for self-determination and the future status of the island in the last three decades has been the "overriding theme" in Guamanian politics.[299] The island has been a scene of constant attempts to resolve the island's sovereignty status. Yet little has been achieved so far. In 1976, a referendum was held, after which the Guamanians decided to maintain a close relationship with the US. They also started negotiations to resolve the territory's status. In 1979, a draft constitution was rejected in a referendum "on the grounds that the question of political status had to be resolved before a meaningful constitution could be drafted".[300] Another referendum was held in 1982, in which 73 % of the voters chose a Commonwealth status. Following this result, the Commission on Self-Determination, established in 1984, prepared a draft of Commonwealth Act in 1986, according to which "Guam would become a fully self-governing Commonwealth of the United States under a locally adopted constitution".[301] This draft was submitted to a referendum on 8 August 1987, on an article-by-article basis. The basics of the proposal were approved by the voters while rejecting the article "granting the indigenous Chamorro people the right to determine the future political status of the Territory". In an additional referendum on November 1987, this was also approved after having been passed through an amendment.[302]

---

[297] Roman (2006), p. 161.

[298] Special Committee on the Situation with regard to the Implementation of the Declaration on the Granting of Independence to Colonial Countries and Peoples. "*Guam: Working paper prepared by the Secretariat*" (A/AC.109/2011/15), 11 March 2011. para. 3.

[299] Roman (2006), p. 167.

[300] *Guam: Working paper prepared by the Secretariat* (A/AC.109/2011/15), 11 March 2011, paras. 9–10.

[301] Special Committee on the Situation with regard to the Implementation of the Declaration on the Granting of Independence to Colonial Countries and Peoples. "*Guam: Working paper prepared by the Secretariat*" United Nations General Assembly, (A/AC.109/1192), 19 May 1994. paras. 19–22.

[302] "*Guam: Working paper prepared by the Secretariat*" (A/AC.109/2011/15), 11 March 2011, para. 10.

Between 1988 and 1995, the Draft Commonwealth Act was, at different intervals, submitted to the United States House of Representatives as a bill, but it could not attain any serious attention. Guam's scheme for its renewal of sovereignty status contained a provision for "mutual consent" in the changing of laws and treaties, which would be a legal guarantee against Congress' discretionary interference in the laws or treaties of Guam. Yet this proposal was declined by the first Bush administration, on the ground that it was not in compliance with the territorial clause of the US constitution.[303]

The process of resolution of sovereignty in Guam is deeply troubled by the conflict between the indigenous ethnic groups of the island, the Chamorros and other Gumanians.[304] The identification of eligible voters is one of the chief reasons that procrastinates the process of the resolution of Guam's status. In 1997, "the Commission on Decolonization for the Implementation and Exercise of Chamorro Self-Determination" was established by virtue of the Guam Public Law 23-147. This Commission was authorised to "oversee the conduct of a vote with regard to the status preferences of the Chamorro people (independence, integration or free association), in accordance with international standards". It would collaborate with the Guam Election Commission, which is entitled to identify the eligible voters.[305]

In 2000, the Guam Election Commission was empowered by the local legislature with the authority to set "the date of the decolonisation plebiscite", where the islanders would be given the triple options of statehood, independence and free association with the United States. The foreseen referendum would have been non-binding but would have initiated the process of future negotiations with the US. The vote was set to take place on 2 November 2004. However, it was postponed due to the conflict over the identification of the eligible voters. Until today, there has been no other action in the Island. On October 2010, a law was signed by President Barack Obama, which provides the Secretary of the Interior with the authority and obligation to provide federal funding for political education to "inform the people of Guam of their constitutionally viable political options".[306]

Virgin Islands Another organised and unincorporated territory of the United States is the United States Virgin Islands with a population over 108,000. It became a US territory when in 1917 it was purchased from Denmark. The first referendum ever held on the island's status was in 1867. Denmark and the US agreed by means of a treaty for the cession of St. Thomas and St. John, and it was put to a referendum among the qualified voters in the island. This first attempt failed when the treaty of cession lapsed in the US Congress. In 1917, the sale of the islands was completed.

---

303 Roman (2006), p. 170.

304 Roman (2006), p. 170.

305 *Guam*: *Working paper prepared by the Secretariat* (A/AC.109/2011/15), 11 March 2011, para. 11.

306 *Guam*: *Working paper prepared by the Secretariat* (A/AC.109/2011/15), 11 March 2011, para. 12.

This time, however, only the Danish voters were consulted on the issue, while the islanders were not.[307]

The territory was organised under the Organic Act of the Virgin Islands and subsequent amendments of the Revised Organic Act of 1954. Since the revision of the Organic Act in 1954, there have been four unsuccessful attempts to establish a local constitution. On 26 May 2009, a local Constitutional Convention adopted a proposal of "the Constitution of the United States Virgin Islands". The current proposal includes a procedure for the resolution of the island's sovereignty status. In this framework, after the adoption of the proposed constitution, a referendum would be held following one year of public education. The right to vote in this referendum would be granted to "ancestral native" and "native" Virgin Islanders, as defined in Article III of the proposed Constitution, "whether residing within or outside the Territory".[308]

The definition of the voters in a future sovereignty referendum has been a "source of contention" among others. The Governor of the island initially refused to submit to the draft to the US, asserting that the provision "is inconsistent with basic tenets of equal protection and fairness". The draft was sent to the US following a decision of the Supreme Court of the Territory. The proposition was submitted to Congress on 26 February 2010 by the President of the United States, indicating, however, that "provisions conferring legal advantages on certain groups, defined by place and timing of birth, timing of residency or ancestry" required further "analysis and comment".[309]

American Samoa American Samoa, with a population of 66,500, is the third Non-Self-Governing Territory administered by the United States of America under the Department of the Interior. American Samoa is an "unincorporated and unorganized" territory according to the Constitution of the United States. Roman observed that "it exists under a classic form of colonialism with virtually no form of local autonomy: . . .the United States government has unfettered control over this territory, as the Secretary of the Interior has plenary power over every aspect of Samoan governmental life".[310] The secretary is empowered to remove laws and overrule court decisions. The election of the local governor is subject to the final approval of the Secretary of Interior. Besides, there is no appeal or judicial review to the

[307] Roman (2006), pp. 191–196.

[308] "Article III of the proposed Constitution states that an 'ancestral native' Virgin Islander is a person or a descendant of such a person who was born or lived in the Territory on or before 28 June 1932 and was not a citizen of any other country; a 'native' Virgin Islander is a person or descendant born in the Territory after 28 June 1932" (Special Committee on the Situation with regard to the Implementation of the Declaration on the Granting of Independence to Colonial Countries and Peoples, "*United States Virgin Islands*: *Working paper prepared by the Secretariat*", (A/AC.109/2011/9), 25 February 2011, Para. 9).

[309] "*United States Virgin Islands*: *Working paper prepared by the Secretariat*", (A/AC.109/2011/9), 25 February 2011 (para 12).

[310] Roman (2006), p. 190.

decisions of the Secretary on the federal level. The territory has a local Constitution adopted in 1960. Any amendment or modification to this Constitution requires an Act of the United States Congress following a preliminary approval of the Secretary of the Interior.[311]

References

Allen, M. J., & Thompson, B. (2005). *Cases and materials on constitutional and administrative law* (8th ed.). Oxford: Oxford University Press.

Alley, R. (2003). Ethnosecession in Papua New Guinea: The Bougainville case. In R. Ganguly & I. Macduff (Eds.), *Ethnic conflict and secessionism in South and South East Asia: Causes dynamics and solutions* (pp. 225–256). New Delhi: Sage Publications.

Amiel, H. (1976). La pratique française des plébiscites internationaux. *Revue générale de droit international public*, 425–501.

Anckar, D. (2004). Finland. In B. Kaufmann & M. Dane Waters (Eds.), *Direct democracy in Europe: A comprehensive guide to the initiative and referendum process in Europe* (pp. 59–61). Durham, NC: Carolina Academic Press.

Ardant, P. (2005). *Institutions politiques & droit constitutionnel* (17th ed.). Paris: L.G.D.J.

Auer, A. (1996). Le référendum constitutionnel. In A. Auer (Ed.), *Les Origines de la Démocratie Directe en Suisse* (pp. 79–101). Bale, e.t.c.: Helbing et Lichtenhahn.

Auer, A. (2007). La démocratie directe comme piège et comme chance pour l'Union européenne. In A. Flücgiker, A. Auer, & M. Hottelier (Eds.), *Etudes en l'honneur du Professeur Giorgio Malinverni Les droits de l'homme et la constitution* (pp. 57–75). Genève: Schulthess.

Barany, E., Brhlikova, R., & Colotka, P. (2001). Slovakia. In A. Auer & M. Bützer (Eds.), *Direct democracy: The eastern and central European experience* (pp. 170–191). Aldershot, e.t.c.: Ashgate.

Barnett, H. (2006). *Constitutional & administrative law* (6th ed.). London: Routledge.

Bea, K., & Garrett, R. S. (2010). Political status of Puerto Rico: Options for congress, May 19, 2010. http://www.hsdl.org/?view&did=24445. Retrieved 13 July 2012.

Beaud, O. (1994). *Puissance de l'Etat*. Paris: PUF.

Beaud, O. (1997). Propos sceptiques sur la légitimité d'un référendum Européen ou plaidoyer pour plus de réalisme constitutionnel. In A. Auer & J. F. Flauss (Eds.), *Le Référendum Européen* (pp. 125–180). Bruxelles: Bruylant.

Björklund, T. (2004). Norway. In B. Kaufmann & M. Dane Waters (Eds.), *Direct democracy in Europe: A comprehensive guide to the initiative and referendum process in Europe* (pp. 98–101). Durham, NC: Carolina Academic Press.

Bogdanor, V. (1998). Devolution: The constitutional aspects. In J. Beatson, C. Forsyth, & I. Hare (Eds.), *Constitutional reform in the United Kingdom: Practices and principles* (pp. 9–19). Oxford: Hart Publishing.

Bogdanor, V. (2003a). Introduction. In V. Bogdanor (Ed.), *The British constitution in the twentieth century* (pp. 1–28). Oxford: Oxford University Press.

Bogdanor, V. (2003b). Conclusion. In V. Bogdanor (Ed.), *The British constitution in the twentieth century* (pp. 689–720). Oxford: Oxford University Press.

Borgeaud, C. ([1895] 1989). *Adoption and amendment of constitutions in Europe and America* (trans: Hazen C. D.). Littleton, CO: F.B. Rothman.

---

[311] Special Committee on the Situation with regard to the Implementation of the Declaration on the Granting of Independence to Colonial Countries and Peoples. "*American Samoa*: *Working Paper Prepared by the Secretariat*", (A/AC.109/2011/12), 7 March 2011. para. 6.

Bortwick, R. L. (1997). What has happened to the sovereignty of parliament? In L. Brace & J. Hoffman (Eds.), *Reclaiming sovereignty* (pp. 26–41). London: Pinter.

Burdeau, G. (1943). *Cours de droit constitutionnel* (2nd ed.). Paris: R. Pichan et R. Durand-Auzias.

Cadoux, C. (1980). *Droit constitutionnel et institutions politiques. Vol 1: Théorie générale des institutions politiques*. Paris: Cujas.

Camacho, K. (2004). The United States–Puerto Rico relationship: Incomplete decolonization. *Howard Law Journal, 48*(1), 491–523.

Carcassonne, G. (2007). *La Constitution* (8th ed.). Paris: Éditions du Seuil.

Carroll, A. (2003). *Constitutional administrative law* (3rd ed.). Harlow: Pearson-Longman.

Chander, A. (1991). Sovereignty, referenda, and the entrenchment of a United Kingdom bill of rights. *Yale Law Journal, 101*, 457–480.

Chantebout, B. (1991). *Droit constitutionnel et science politique* (10th ed.). Paris: Armand Colin.

Christakis, T. (1999). *Le droit a l'autodétermination en dehors des situations de décolonisation*. Paris: La Documentation Française.

Conac, G. (1987). Article 11. In F. Luchaire & G. Conac (Eds.), *La Constitution de la République française* (pp. 409–505). Paris: Economica.

Dahl, R. A. (1989). *Democracy and its critics*. New Haven: Yale University Press.

Debbasch, C., Pontier, J. -M., Bourdon, J., & Ricci, J. -C. (1986). *Droit constitutionnel et institutions politiques* (2). Paris: Economica.

Diaz, J. O. (2001). Puerto Rico, The United States, and the 1993 referendum on political status. *Latin American Research Review, 30*, 203–211.

Dicey, A. V. (2010). *Introduction to the law of the constitution* (6th ed.). Lexington: Elibron Classics [1902].

Dobelle, J.-F. (1996). Référendum et droit à l'autodétermination. *Pouvoirs, 77*, 41–60.

Ellis, E. (2004). The legislative supremacy of parliament and its limits. In D. Feldman (Ed.), *English public law* (pp. 142–172). Oxford: Oxford University Press.

Favoreau, L. (1976). La décision du 30 Décembre 1975 dans l'affaire des Comores. *Revue du droit public et de la science politique en France et à l'étranger*, 557–579.

Feldhune, G. (2004). Latvia. In B. Kaufmann & M. Dane Waters (Eds.), *Direct democracy in Europe: A comprehensive guide to the initiative and referendum process in Europe* (pp. 77–82). Durham, NC: Carolina Academic Press.

Formery, S.-L. (2011). *La constitution commentée: article par article* (14th ed.). Paris: Hachette Superieur.

Freedman, J. (2004). Comoros–France (Mayotte). In P. Calvert (Ed.), *Border and territorial disputes of the world* (pp. 12–18). London: John Harper Publishing.

Gallagher, M. (1996). Ireland: Referendum as a conservative device. In M. Gallagher & P. V. Uleri (Eds.), *The referendum experience in Europe*. Houndmills, e.t.c.: Macmillan Press Ltd.

Garrett, R. S. (2012). Puerto Rico's political status and the 2012 plebiscite: Background and key questions congressional research service report. 2 October 2012. http://www.fas.org/sgp/crs/row/RL32933.pdf. Retrieved 23 Nov 2012.

Gawenda, J. A. B. (1946). *Le plébiscite en droit international*. Fribourg: Imprimerie St. Paul.

Gebethner, S. (2001). Poland. In A. Auer & M. Bützer (Eds.), *Direct democracy: The eastern and central European experience* (pp. 129–140). Aldershot, e.t.c.: Ashgate.

Gillis, M. (2001). Czech Republic. In A. Auer & M. Bützer (Eds.), *Direct democracy:The eastern and central European experience* (pp. 39–46). Aldershot (e.t.c): Ashgate.

Goldmann, M. (2004). Sweden. In B. Kaufmann & M. Dane Waters (Eds.), *Direct democracy in Europe: A comprehensive guide to the initiative and referendum process in Europe* (pp. 115–118). Durham, NC: Carolina Academic Press.

Gözler, K. (1992). Le Pouvoir Constituant Originaire:Mémoire du D.E.A. de Droit public, Directeur de recherches: Prof. Dmitri Georges Lavroff, Université de Bordeaux I, Faculté de droit, des sciences sociales et politiques. www.anayasa.gen.tr/gozler/memoire.htm. Retrieved 11 November 2012.

Gözler, K. (1997). *Le pouvoir de révision constitutionnelle*. Villeneuve d'Ascq: Presses universitaires du Septentrion.

Gözler, K. (1999). *Pouvoir constituant*. Bursa: Ekin.

Gözler, K. (2011). *Anayasa Hukukunun Genel Teorisi* (Vol. I, II vols.). Bursa: Ekin.

Hadfield, B. (2003). The United Kingdom as a territorial state. In V. Bogdanor (Ed.), *The British constitution in the twentieth century* (pp. 585–630). Oxford: Oxford University Press.

Hamon, F. (1995). *Le référendum: étude comparative*. Paris: L.G.D.J.

Hamon, F., & Troper, M. (2005). *Droit Constitutionnel* (29th ed.). Paris: L.G.D.J.

Hinck, J. (1990, July). The Republic of Palau and the United States: Self-determination becomes the price of free association. *California Law Review, 78*(4), 915–971.

Holder, A. R., & Holder, J. T. R. (1997). *The meaning of the constitution*. New York: Barron's.

Jennings, I. W. (1959). *The law and the Constitution 136* (5th ed.).

Jennings, I. (1963). *The law and the constitution*. London: University of London Press.

Johari, J. C. (2006). *New comparative government*. New Delhi: Lotus Press.

Kjaerulff-Schmidt, S. (2004). Denmark. In B. Kaufmann & M. Dane Waters (Eds.), *Direct democracy in Europe: A comprehensive guide to the initiative and referendum process in Europe* (pp. 51–54). Durham, NC: Carolina Academic Press.

Keitner, I. C., & Reisman, W. M. (2003). Free association: The United States experience. *Texas International Law Journal, 39*, 1–64.

Klein, C. (1996). *Théorie et pratique du pouvoir constituant*. Paris: PUF.

Lawson, G., & Sloane, R. D. (2009). The constitutionality of decolonization by associated statehood: Puerto Rico's legal status reconsidered. *Boston College Law Review, 50*, 1123–1193.

LeDuc, L. (2003). *The politics of direct democracy: Referendums in global perspective*. Ontario, e.t.c.: Broadview Press.

Lindahl, H. (2007). Constituent power and reflexive identity: Towards an ontology of collective selfhood. In M. Loughlin & N. Walker (Eds.), *The paradox of constitutionalism: Constituent power and constituent form* (pp. 9–24). Oxford: Oxford University Press.

Linz, J. J., & Stepan, A. (1996). *Problems of democratic transition and consolidation: Southern Europe, South America, and post-communist Europe*. Baltimore, MD: Johns Hopkins University Press.

Loveland, I. (2003). Britain and Europe. In V. Bogdanor (Ed.), *The British constitution in the twentieth century* (pp. 663–688). Oxford: Oxford University Press.

Maestre, J.-C. (1976). L'Indivisibilité de la République Française et l'exercice du droit a l'autodétermination. *Revue du droit public et de la science politique en France et à l'étranger*, 2, 431–461.

Malberg, R. (1920). *Carré de Contribution à la théorie générale de l'Etat* (Vol. II, II vols). Paris: Librairie Recueil Sirey.

Marrani, D. (2006). Principle of indivisibility of the French Republic and the people's right to self-determination: The "New Caledonia Test". *Journal of Academic Legal Studies, 2*, 16–29.

Marshall, G. (2003). The constitution: Its theory and interpretation. In V. Bogdanor (Ed.), *The British constitution in the twentieth century* (pp. 29–68). Oxford: Oxford University Press.

McCorquodale, R. (1995). Negotiating sovereignty: The practice of United Kingdom in regard to the right of self-determination. *The British Yearbook of International Law, 66*, 283–331.

McWhinney, E. (2007). *Self-determination of peoples and plural-ethnic states, in contemporary international law*. Leiden: Martinus Nijhoff.

Medina, L. E. (2009–2010). An unsatisfactory case of self-determination: Resolving Puerto Rico's political status. *Fordham International Law Journal, 33*, 1048–1100.

Morel, L. (2001). The rise of government initiated referendums. In M. Mendelsohn & A. Parkin (Eds.), *Referendum democracy: Citizens, elites and deliberation in referendum campaigns* (pp. 47–66). Houndmills: Palgrave.

Morel, L. (2007, November). The rise of politically obligatory referendums: The 2005 French referendum in comparative perspective. *West European Politics, 30*(5), 1041–1067.

Negri, A. (1999). *Insurgencies: Constituent power and the modern state*. Minneapolis, MN: University of Minnesota Press.

Offe, C. (2004, Fall). Capitalism by democratic design? Democratic theory facing the triple transition in East Central Europe. *Social Research, 71*(3), 501–528.

Palayret, G. (2003). Overseas France and minority and indigenous rights: Dream or reality? *International Journal on Minority and Group Rights, 10*, 221–252.

Parpworth, N., & Padfield, N. (2002). *Constitutional and administrative law* (2nd ed.). London, e.t.c.: Butterworths/Lexis Nexis.

Pavia, M.-L. (1989). Le Référendum du 6 Novembre. *Revue de droit Public, 4*, 1697–1734.

Pavkovic, A., & Radan, P. (2007). *Creating new states*. Aldershot: Ashgate.

Pellet, A. (1987). Commentaire de l'Article 53. In F. Luchaire & G. Conac (Eds.), *La Constitution de la République Française* (pp. 1005–1058). Paris: Economica.

Philips, O. H. (1962). *Constitutional and administrative law* (3rd ed.). London: Maxwell & Sweet.

Phillips, O. H., Jackson, P., & Leopold, P. (2001). *Constitutional and administrative law* (8th ed.). London: Sweet & Maxwell.

Poggi, G. (1978). *The development of the modern state: A sociological introduction*. Stanford, CA: Stanford University Press.

Preuss, U. K. (1994). Constitutional power-making for the new polity: Some deliberations on the relations between constituent power and the constitution. In M. Rosenfeld (Ed.), *Constitutionalism, identity, difference, and legitimacy: Theoretical perspectives* (pp. 143–164). Durham: Duke University Press.

Preuss, U. K. (2007). The exercise of constituent power in central and eastern Europe. In M. Loughlin & N. Walker (Eds.), *The paradox of constitutionalism: Constituent power and constituent form* (pp. 212–228). Oxford: Oxford University Press.

Qvortrup, M. A. (2005). *A comparative study of referendums: Government by the people* (2nd ed.). Manchester: Manchester University Press.

Reti, P. (2004). Hungary. In B. Kaufmann & M. Dane Waters (Eds.), *Direct democracy in Europe: A comprehensive guide to the initiative and referendum process in Europe* (pp. 67–69). Durham, NC: Carolina Academic Press.

Rezvani, D. A. (2007, Spring). The basis of Puerto Rico's constitutional status: Colony, compact or "Federacy"? *Political Science Quarterly, 122*(1), 115–140.

Rideau, J. (1997). Les référendums nationaux dans le contexte de l'intégration européenne. In A. Auer & J.-F. Flauss (Eds.), *Le référendum européen: actes du colloque international de strasbourg, 21–22 février 1997* (pp. 81–113). Bruxelles: E. Bruylant.

Roman, E. (2006). *The other American colonies*. Durham: Caroline Academic Press.

Rosenfeld, M. (1994). Modern constitutionalism as interplay between identity and diversity. In M. Rosenfeld (Ed.), *Constitutionalism, identity, difference, and legitimacy: Theoretical perspectives* (pp. 3–35). Durham: Duke University Press.

Rourke, J. T., Hiskes, R. P., & Zirakzadeh, C. E. (1992). *Direct democracy and international politics: Deciding international issues through referendums*. London: Lynne Rienner Publ.

Roussillon, H. (1996, April). Contre le référendum! *Pouvoirs, 77*, 184–190.

Ruin, O. (1996). Sweden: The referendum as an instrument for defusing political issues. In M. Gallagher & P. V. Uleri (Eds.), *The referendum experience in Europe* (pp. 171–184). London: Macmillan.

Ruus, J. (2001). Estonia. In A. Auer & M. Bützer (Eds.), *Direct democracy: The eastern and central European experience* (pp. 47–62). Aldershot, e.t.c.: Ashgate.

Ruus, J. (2004). Estonia. In B. Kaufmann & M. Dane Waters (Eds.), *Direct democracy in Europe: A comprehensive guide to the initiative and referendum process in Europe* (pp. 54–58). Durham, NC: Carolina Academic Press.

Schmitt, C. ([1928] 2008). In J. Seitzer (Ed.), *Constitutional theory* (trans: Seitzer, J.]. Durham, NC: Duke University Press.

Schwarze, J. (2001). The birth of a European constitutional order. In J. Schwarze (Ed.), *The birth of a European constitutional order: The interaction of national and European constitutional law* (pp.463-568). Baden-Baden: Nomos.

Seaward, P., & Silk, P. (2003). The house of commons. In V. Bogdanor (Ed.), *The British constitution in the twentieth century* (pp. 139–237). Oxford: Oxford University Press.

Sparrow, B. H. (2006). *The insular cases and the emergence of the American Empire*. Lawrence, Kansas: University Press of Kansas.

Suksi, M. (1993). *Bringing in the people*. Dordrecht: Kluwer.

Suksi, M. (1996). Finland: Referendum as a dormant feature. In M. Gallagher & P. V. Uleri (Eds.), *The referendum experience in Europe*. Macmillan/Stjames: London/New York.

Svensson, P. (1996). Denmark: The referendum as minority protection. In M. Gallagher & P. V. Uleri (Eds.), *The referendum experience in Europe* (pp. 33–50). Houndmills, e.t.c.: Macmillan Press.

Taaffe, D. (2004). Ireland. In B. Kaufmann & M. Dane Waters (Eds.), *Direct democracy in Europe: A comprehensive guide to the initiative and referendum process in Europe* (pp. 70–73). Durham, NC: Carolina Academic Press.

Tierney, S. (2007). 'We the Peoples': Constituent power and constitutionalism in plurinational states in the paradox of constitutionalism. In M. Loughlin & N. Walker (Eds.), *Constituent power and constituent form*. Oxford: Oxford University Press.

Usacka, A. (2001). Techniques and procedures for popular votes. In A. Auer & M. Bützer (Eds.), *Direct democracy: The eastern and central European experience* (pp. 255–263). Aldershot, e.t.c.: Ashgate.

Valach, M. (2004). Czech Republic. In B. Kaufmann & M. Dane Waters (Eds.), *Direct democracy in Europe: A comprehensive guide to the initiative and referendum process in Europe* (pp. 48–51). Durham, NC: Carolina Academic Press.

Vile, J. R. (1997). *A companion to the United States constitution and its amendments*. Westport: Praeger Publishers.

Wambaugh, S. (1920). *A monograph on plebiscites (with a collection of official documents)*. New York: Oxford University Press.

Willens, H. P., & Siemer, D. C. (1977). The constitution of the Northern Mariana Islands: Constitutional principles and innovation in a Pacific setting. *The Georgetown Law Journal, 65*(6), (1373-1379).

Wyller, T. C. (1996). Norway: Six exceptions to the rule. In M. Gallagher & P. Uleri (Eds.), *The referendum experience in Europe* (pp. 139–152). London: Macmillan Press Ltd.

Chapter 7
Sovereignty Referendums: Common Legal Problems

Abstract This chapter focuses on the comparative study of the common legal problems of sovereignty referendums. Foremost, there will be an analysis of the issue of referendum administration. Then this chapter leads to an explanation on the subject of judicial review of the sovereignty referendums. Another common legal issue of the sovereignty referendums is the problem of the quorum, whether there is a need to require an enhanced majority for the final result. This issue is also under discussion in this chapter. Equally important is the question as to who should be entitled to vote. This problem lies at the heart of almost all sovereignty referendums. This question will be assessed within the framework of cases, most particularly those of Western Sahara, Puerto Rico, South Sudan and New Caledonia. Moreover, in this chapter, the question of the designation of the voting units will be tackled. Finally, this chapter handles the issue of formulation of the ballot question, which is of crucial importance in ensuring a legitimate and credible referendum.

7.1 Administration of Sovereignty Referendums

Referendum administration involves the body of rules for the organisation and implementation of the vote. This concept has a particular implication for the post-war or post-conflict situations where the trait of internationality can be clearly seen. Thus the issue of administration of the referendum is mainly a question of international law. In this perspective, the administration of a referendum comprises every action necessary to ensure a fair, accurate and democratic vote. These actions might include census; preparation of electors list through the registration of the voters; guaranteeing of the freedom of speech, the freedom of assembly, and the right to vote; counting of votes; declaration of results; resolution of legal disputes; and the daily administration of the referendum area during a fixed period before and after the poll. The procedural accuracy and fairness of these actions are vital conditions for the legitimacy and future viability of a referendum and its result.

İ.G. Şen, *Sovereignty Referendums in International and Constitutional Law*,
DOI 10.1007/978-3-319-11647-1_7

7.1.1 In General

The international nature of sovereignty referendums brings about the involvement of the international community. In sovereignty referendums that take place during politically unstable times, such as in a post-revolution or post-war period or in the presence of foreign military powers, there is always some concern about the respect of the rule of law and respect for basic rights and freedoms. In most of these cases, like the post-WWI referendums, conflicting interests of rival countries may also enter the equation. Therefore, there is no doubt that in most international sovereignty referendums, regulating and executing the process of voting requires an impartial and neutral body to "serve as an international stamp of approval" for the process.[1]

Wambaugh's remarks and comments on the post-WWI referendums and the lessons drawn from them may be useful in this regard: [2]

1. The plebiscite must be held under the formal agreement of both parties.
2. The area must be neutralized and the agreement must clearly provide this.
3. On the signing of the agreement the area must be put at once under international control.
4. All troops of both parties must be evacuated at once.
5. A plebiscite commission of unquestioned neutrals, acceptable to both states, must be set up.
6. The commission must be supported by a police force of its own, however small.
7. The commission must have complete power over the administration of the area, itself taking the place of the highest officials.
8. It must have sufficient personnel to exercise this power effectively.
9. It must exercise this power for a sufficient time in advance of the vote to establish confidence that a change of sovereignty is possible.
10. It must remove the local key officials and replace them with its own appointees approved by both parties.
11. It must set up an effective organization for supervision of all officials, using the local administrative divisions as the bases.
12. It must immediately reorganize the police.
13. It must immediately reorganize the judicial system, cutting off the local courts from the higher courts outside the area.
14. It must set up a plebiscite tribunal to have exclusive jurisdiction over all plebiscite offenses.
15. The regulations for registration and voting must allow sufficient time for all processes of registration.
16. They must provide adequate tests of identity of the applicants for registration.
17. They must provide adequate penalties.

More recently, Beigbeder's observations on the first-generation UN missions of decolonisation referendums provide similar insights on the requisites for an effective and fair referendum regime[3]:

---

[1] Beigbeder (1994), pp. 110–117.

[2] Wambaugh (1933), p. 506

[3] Beigbeder (1994), p. 145.

1. The mission's terms of reference need to be clearly formulated by the authorizing body (Trusteeship Council, Special Committee or General Assembly), agreed to by the administering Power and communicated to all local officials.
2. The mission's composition must be really international, and be seen as impartial.
3. The mission's size must be related to the size of the territory and of the population, unless a purely symbolic presence is required, or unless the UN mission may be supplemented by a sufficient number of other international observers from other organizations and governments.
4. A mission needs to arrive in the territory well in advance of election (or plebiscite, or referendum) day: its members need time to meet the local officials, the electoral Commission if any, to familiarize themselves with the institutions, electoral law, procedures, territory and polling stations,—they need time to assess possible flaws and problems, make suggestions and see them applied; to make arrangements for liaison and cooperation with other international observers.

For Farley, "a defective plebiscite delivers a defective title to sovereignty". Against such defects, he presents a procedural scheme for a legitimate referendum by which he discerns three main stages: (1) before the referendum, (2) implementation of the vote, (3) issues after the vote. With respect to the issues before the referendum, he reaffirms the importance of a "plebiscite conference" where the parties agree on the general terms of the vote. In this perspective, the main issues are (1) the formulation of the ballot question, (2) the determination of qualified voters, (3) designation of the voting units, (4) the creation of the referendum administration and definition of its competences, (5) the approval of the method of financing the referendum, (6) the establishment of a plan and timetable for the withdrawal of the troops from the referendum zone, (7) the organisation and dispatch of neutral troops into the area and (8) a pledge by the various parties that no reprisals will be taken against any person for his democratic preference in the referendum. With respect to the vote, Farley addresses the importance of a democratic campaign and lawful assessment, registration and identification of voters, as well as protection against "electoral intimidation". Also in this context, the presence of neutral international observers, accessibility of the ballots and polling stations and the authenticity of vote counting and declaration of the results are considered to be the basic actions to be properly fulfilled. Finally, with regard to the issues after the vote, Farley discusses certain basic problems such as the "transfer of administration", the free and orderly transfer of the population if so needed and protection against reprisals.

To summarise these accounts on referendum administration, one should note the importance of an impartial administrative body along with a neutral armed force, responsible for the conduct of the referendum since the existing political institutions are, in most cases, parties to the conflict. Also, the basic terms of the referendum such as the legal framework, competences of the referendum administration, neutralisation of the area, the timetable, finance, the ballot question and the post-referendum issues should all be decided beforehand by agreement between the parties.

7.1.2 *Important Aspects of Referendum Administration*

7.1.2.1 Ensuring an Impartial and Effective Referendum Administration and Security

We may now focus on certain important aspects of referendum administration. To begin with, there should be a neutral body set up to oversee the administration of the referendum (plebiscite commission). This body is assigned the tasks of conducting the whole referendum process, administering the zone before the vote, conducting the vote and fulfilling the final task of the transfer of sovereignty after the vote is completed. Its competences should be the outcome of a compromise between the parties to the conflict. Its powers may be either "plenipotentiary" or "delegated". In the former case, the administration would have all the discretionary powers in making, interpreting and implementing the rules of the referendum regime. In the case of delegated powers, the administration has a limited authority to undertake specific tasks, and it has to consult the signatory parties or a higher organ (the UN in the contemporary context) before taking any extraordinary measures. Between these two options, plenipotentiary referendum administration is preferable, as reports on previous experiences have shown, for securing both impartiality and effectiveness.[4]

Regular daily administration of the area in question should be carried out under the strict control of the referendum administration and should be free of the politics of issues related to the upcoming referendum. The chain of command between the central decision-makers of the contending/contested state and the local administration should be cut. In cases where the personnel of the referendum regime is composed of mostly foreigners, a "local advisory board", made of local notables acting as the representatives of the conflicting parties, may provide useful local expertise.

During the administration of the referendum area, the maintenance of the neutrality of the various public institutions also gains importance. Of these, schools are the places where nationalist identities are moulded. However, control over schools can only be efficient if the referendum regime lasts for at least several years. If the time frame of a referendum is not long enough, the control of schools serves only as a symbolic affect. The church (or other sort of religious institutions and opinion leaders) is another institution that is prone to politicisation as religion is one of the main elements of national identity and its related conflicts. Religious cleavages are one of the most important reasons for territorial differentiation, and

[4] As mentioned above, Wambaugh, commenting on the post-WWI referendums, reiterated the need for a "Commission" having "complete power over the administration of the area". "Experience has shown that the powers of the commission over the political administration of the area must be absolute" (Wambaugh 1933, p. 498). When Beigbeder's report on the shortcomings of the UN's first-generation referendum mission is recalled, one may reach a similar conclusion. Likewise, Farley argued: "Most successful plebiscite commissions have been granted plenipotentiary power" (Farley 1986, p. 59).

for this reason conflicts arising in a sovereignty referendum may well have a religious aspect. In this context, religious/opinion leaders often have a decisive effect on formulating voter preferences. For example, in the Upper Silesia referendum, there were rumours of Polish priests refusing to absolve "the 'sin' of voting for Germany". In order to ensure religious impartiality, the Vatican took two measures during referendums in Upper Silesia, Allenstein and Marienwerder. One of them was "detaching the referendum area from existing dioceses or church districts", and the other was to "order the clergy in the zone to refrain from partisan pronouncements".[5]

Thus, a fair administration lies at the heart of a legitimate referendum since it involves every aspect of the voting, including the polling procedure and the daily government of the territory before, during and after the vote. In this context, *security* is a key aspect of any referendum administration. The main issue about the conduct of the referendum and administration of the area is to ensure a secure, stable and free democratic atmosphere. Therefore, the main objective of a referendum administration is to create a "plebiscitary atmosphere", "a state of readiness of the population in the referendum area", to discuss, negotiate and deliberate freely and peacefully on the issue in question, and to abide by any eventual outcome.[6] Freedoms of thought and information are the vital elements of such a plebiscitary atmosphere, so the ability of all parties to act free of intimidation and reprisal is vital. Ideally, such a setting may only be taken for granted in well-established and stable democracies, and it would be considered too optimistic to expect such standards in a region torn by violent conflicts. Therefore, the referendum administration has the arduous task of creating such an atmosphere of trust, the failure of which may possibly lead to the failure of the referendum itself. The existence of a democratic atmosphere is possible only when all parties are convinced that the referendum and its conduct are legitimate and any perturbation of the latter is a threat to the validity of the result.[7] In this context, there may be three fundamental security-related issues that a referendum administration has to deal with. Firstly, it goes without saying that everyday safety and security in the area of the referendum must be completely established in the period leading up to the referendum. Secondly, the voters in the area should be protected against any sort of electoral intimidation. This may include assuring the conditions for a free vote and the prohibition of any threat of reprisal from the parties to the conflict (i.e., guerrilla or central state). The clearing away of all such elements from the referendum area falls within the responsibility of the referendum administration. Thirdly, border control is an essential element for the security of the referendum area, so that the referendum area may be delimited clearly and rigorous border control be applied. This is vitally important in securing the area, freeing it from any interference from

[5] Farley (1986), pp. 65–66.

[6] Farley (1986), p. 83.

[7] Farley (1986), pp. 83–85.

the neighbouring countries, which have in most cases vested interests in the outcome. [8]

Disarmament of the area is the key aspect regarding security. In violent war-torn regions having experienced conflict, secessionist and nationalist turmoil, it is very likely that the military and police forces have lost their impartiality. Therefore, if a referendum is to be held in such an atmosphere, the initial measure to be taken is the neutralisation of the area from disputing armies, troops or any other armed groups that are party to the sovereignty conflict and replacement of them by neutral armed forces. "Precedent as well as justice…requires that all troops of the interested parties shall be removed."[9] It is also important that the number of neutral troops be sufficient to deal with the size of the area, the number of the population and the seriousness of the strife. One of the reasons for the failure to hold a referendum in Teschen, for example, was that the number of the troops was insufficient to seize control of the area. [10]

There are certain other important aspects as regards the new security regime. Firstly, it is important that the police force of the referendum area is not politicised in favour of any of the contesting parties. Yet in almost all cases, the tumultuous strife and conflict preceding a referendum render this requisite virtually impossible. In the case of the extreme politicisation of the police force, the most appropriate measure seems to disband the police force. But this measure is prone to cause legitimate unrest among a population who are on the same political side as that of the police. As a balancing measure, the police may be put under the control of a neutral international supervisor. Secondly, it is preferable that the new police force has a "new appearance". This may include wearing new uniforms, having no military appearance and patrolling without guns. This is necessary to ensure that the relevant population does not perceive the referendum administration as being identical with the antecedent one. [11]

7.1.2.2 Initial Survey

An initial survey is a possible preliminary phase in the implementation of a referendum. To this end, a research commission may be considered in order to conduct the initial survey. This commission may have several duties. In the first duty, local documents and records should be identified and placed under protection as they serve as a primary reference for the identification of eligible voters. In

[8] It should be reminded at this point that the failure of the plebiscites in Tacna Arica and Teschen was largely due to the lack of effective control of the border. It opened the way for the manipulation of the process by cross-border saboteurs, agents and propagandists (Farley 1986, pp. 80 and 108–109).

[9] Wambaugh (1933), p. 496.

[10] Wambaugh (1933), p. 448.

[11] Farley (1986), pp. 72–74.

highly controversial and violence-strewn cases, there is a high risk that the documents or records may be damaged or altered by the interested parties. Secondly, an assessment should be made as to whether the local administration is politicised regarding the issues of the future referendum. If so, its neutralisation should then be managed. Lastly, the ethnic, religious and economic cleavages among the population should be defined. The differentiation of the different layers of a given population and their dispersion around the referendum region is important in determining the boundary of the referendum area and the delimitation of the voting districts.[12]

7.1.2.3 Registration of the Voters

There are two methods of registration that may be distinguished. According to "Registration on Application", potential voters have to apply to be registered. The advantage of this system is that it provides complete and detailed information about each voter, enabling cross-checking of the voters in case of confusion. The disadvantage is that it may cause unfair situations: while the well-organised party may regularly register their voters, the less organised side may fail to gather enough people for registration. As to "Registration by Compilation", no application is required. Instead, registration is done by the authorities directly from available records. This method helps to overcome the unfair consequences of registration and, additionally, also prevents intimidation. Its disadvantages are the risk of registration errors and lists that are open to fraud in the hands of referendum authorities.[13]

The post-conflict or post-war character of the majority of sovereignty referendums may make voter registration practically impossible. In this context, one may refer to the term "conflict-forced migrant" to refer to "any person displaced from their home community due to a deteriorating security or human rights situation, generally as a consequence of violence. The term encompasses (particularly) those who could be categorized as refugees or internally displaced persons".[14] Conflict-forced migrants often lack the necessary documentation to verify their identity and other voter qualification requirements. Therefore, the task of the referendum administration in identifying eligible voters is much harder than that of elections and referendums under stable conditions. Grace and Fisher discern three possible mechanisms for this purpose: "(1) Verification commissions within the election management body; (2) Combined voter registration and census/civil registration programs; (3) Social documentation".[15] In the case of verification commissions, there may be "special mechanisms whereby electoral authorities perform

[12] Farley (1986), p. 52.

[13] Farley (1986), pp. 93–96.

[14] Grace and Fischer (2003), p. 4.

[15] Grace and Fischer (2003), pp. 32–40.

documentation searches and/or verifications". In this case, an individual lacking sufficient documentation may apply to the registration authority, which then on behalf of that individual applies to the local institutions to seek and investigate whether the individual's eligibility claim is true. This method was employed by the OSCE in Bosnia–Herzegovina. As regards the second option (applied by the UN/OSCE in Kosovo), the registration authority may be given the right to provide the election cards on the basis of any other document provided by the individual. In the case of a complete lack of documents, the registration authority may initiate a review process, by asking the applicant to fill out a detailed questionnaire regarding his claim to eligibility. This questionnaire may then be submitted to one of the local records offices, where the staff of the referendum administration search for evidence certifying the claim through available records such as official forms of the former state, ID cards, driving licenses and passports. Finally, the method of social documentation allows the applicants "to swear their identity, residence, and/or citizenship in front of a recognized legal authority or village/tribal notable". Obviously, this method is the most susceptible to fraud and should only be used in the most exceptional conditions, where the notables involved in the affidavit should not generate any doubts as to their integrity. Indeed, in Western Sahara, for instance, the use of social documentation has been a failure. As will be seen below, in Western Sahara, the nomadic nature of the people renders the issue of voter qualification unresolved and is the main reason for the delay of the referendum. The identification commission was established to resolve the undocumented claims for eligibility: composed of an official from the UN, an Organization of African Unity (OAU) observer, observers from each party and two sheiks (one chosen by each party). During the course of this process of identification, the sheiks' testimony had become "almost entirely predictable – each recognized all applicants presented by his party and refused those sponsored by the other. Thus, the sheik's loss of credibility removed a key element needed to substantiate or refute the oral testimony of the applicants."[16] In East Timor, social documentation was also used, but in limited cases and numbers, which prevented its abuse by the local actors. These experiences show that the social documentation method should be used in most exceptional cases or as a complementary method, along with other registration mechanisms.

7.1.2.4 Campaigning and Voter Education

In general, referendum campaigns involve two different aspects: voter education and propaganda. While the former tends to inform the voters on the legal effects of either option, the latter involves persuading the people to vote for one of the two options. This twofold nature of referendum campaigns is the fundamental

[16] Dunbar (2000). Cited in Grace and Fischer (2003), p. 38.

difference from the campaigns of parliamentary or presidential elections where the candidates are identified through their party affiliations.[17] In referendums, on the contrary, voters do not have any cognitive cues or shortcuts to understand the issue in question.[18] Thus, there are two challenges for a referendum administration in terms of the referendum campaign: (1) ensuring an effective and accurate voter education and (2) securing a democratic atmosphere for fair and equal representation of the opposing views.

There may be three reasons that make voter education crucial in a sovereignty referendum.[19] In the first place, most sovereignty referendums are held on ad hoc basis as an exceptional element of a polity. In certain cases, voters have no equivalent experience, and in this context, it is likely that a majority of the voters do not know the procedural aspects, let alone the possible ramifications of the outcome. The problem becomes even greater when the referendum is to be held in the polities without democratic experience. In the second place, the question of voter competence is more important than in any other context, considering the irreversible nature of the outcome of the vote. This problem was mentioned in several referendums held during the decolonisation. In the Northern Cameroons, for example, the UN observers expressed their feelings that the central point and importance of the question had not been understood by the voters. Instead, the attention of the voters had concentrated on regional problems that obstructed them from understanding the signification of the vote.[20] In the third place, given the great importance of the issue as an act of self-determination, maximising voter participation is of great importance as it is closely related to the legitimacy of the act. Thus, voter education in a sovereignty referendum includes (1) procedural aspects such as educating voters on how to register and vote, (2) the ramifications of the alternatives and the meaning of the ballot questions and (3) effective encouragement of the populace to participate in the vote.

As to propaganda it may be useful for the opposing groups to organise themselves under umbrella organisations. Considering that there are two possible options in most sovereignty referendums (i.e., yes–no or remaining in the state–secession), the two opposing views may be included under two umbrella organisations. This model may be the most suitable one for the parties in channelling their views in a consistent and coordinated manner. Also, this model makes it easier for the referendum administration to ensure a fair framework in terms of funding and access to the media.[21]

---

[17] Hamon(1995), pp. 34–37.

[18] For this, see Jenssen and Listhaug (2001), p. 174. *But cf.* Kriesi (2004), p. 12: "[I]f the voters do not have clear opinions, are ambivalent or ignorant about the key arguments surrounding the issues in question, they make use of heuristic shortcuts which allow them to approximate the vote of an enlightened citizen to a considerable extent."

[19] Sureda (1973), p. 315.

[20] Sureda (1973), p. 320.

[21] Hamon (1995), pp. 34–37.

The above-mentioned campaign pattern may be observed in East Timor, where the issue of voter education (information, campaign and propaganda) was clearly delimited in the New York Agreements. The task of voter education was entrusted to the UN, which was supposed to "make available the text of the main Agreement and the autonomy document to be voted on in the languages, Tetun, Bahasa Indonesia, Portuguese and English; to disseminate and explain the content of the main Agreement and the autonomy document in an impartial and factual manner inside and outside East Timor; explain to voters the process and procedure of the vote, and the implications of an 'accept' or 'reject' vote".

In addition, it was specified: "The radio stations and the newspapers in East Timor as well as other Indonesian and Portuguese media outlets will be utilized in the dissemination of this information. Other appropriate means of dissemination will be made use of as required." It is recorded by the Secretary General that the UNAMET had performed its tasks sufficiently. To this end, it has established a radio and a TV station to broadcast the education material regarding the content of the referendum and the voting process. [22]

As for propaganda, the responsibility of the opposing parties to act in "a peaceful and democratic manner" was emphasised in the Modality Agreement. To this end, the UN was authorised to issue a Code of Conduct for the campaign following a discussion between the opponents and proponents of independence. To ensure impartiality, "The United Nations (would) devise the means to provide equal opportunity for the two sides to disseminate their views to the public". Officials of the Governments of Indonesia and Portugal were barred from participating in the campaign in support of either option. The pro-independence and pro-integration groups gathered according to the umbrella organisations model: the National Council of Timorese Resistance (CNRT) was a coalition of pro-independence groups, whereas the pro-autonomy was represented under Front Bersama Pro-Otonomi Timor-Timor (UNIF).[23]

7.1.2.5 Post-referendum Issues

The post-referendum issues may include all necessary actions to provide peaceful transfer of sovereignty. Considering the fact that in cases of violent secession or post-war conditions there is no effective and impartial state authority, the referendum administration should ensure its stay for a certain period after the vote. In this framework, it may have to deal with state building and succession issues, as well as security issues, which may arise as a response to the outcome of the vote. In particular, monetary and currency, due compensation for the real property of those leaving, state rights of local officials, erecting of borders and their

[22] United Nations Security Council. "*Question of East Timor Report of the Secretary-General.*" S/1999/803, 20 July 1999. Para. 8.

[23] Teles (2002), p. 228.

control—all of these may be listed as examples related to state building. In most areas, there may arise demanding security issues as a reaction to an undesired referendum result. In this context, the protection of individuals and groups against reprisals is of utmost importance. Likewise, the reassertion of a secure and free transfer for those who wish to emigrate from the area should be remembered in this context as this is an indispensable component for a legitimate sovereignty referendum.[24]

7.1.3 Historical Evolution of Referendum Administration

Pre-WWI Referendums Compared to today's standards, the process of the voting in early referendums held after the French Revolution was far from being free and fair. The lack of secrecy of the vote and the presence of the partisan French agents and armed troops discredit any claim that these referendums were impartial.[25] Similar assertions may be made, despite a certain amount of progress, for the referendums held in the nineteenth century where the idea of neutralisation and impartial commission was "embryonic only". None of the pre-WWI treaties contained a clause prescribing withdrawal of troops from the referendum area.[26] Notwithstanding these facts, the radical effect of these referendums should not be underestimated. Many historians admit that, despite the fact that the said referendums fell short of ideal democratic principles, they were relatively free and allowed the voters to express their wishes regarding the fate of their territory.[27]

Post-WWI Referendums Given the intensity of the use of referendums in post-WWI territorial modifications, the need for a more careful regulation and administration arose. Since then, securing an impartial conduct has been the focal point of a fair referendum. Ensuring the neutrality of the area was the first measure to be taken in all of the referendums held under the Paris Treaties. The recognition of the principle of neutralisation in the post-WWI legal instruments was defined to be "a great advance".[28] Indeed, the principle of military neutralisation was recognised for

---

[24] "No plebiscite is complete unless due regard is shown to the option to emigrate" (Farley 1986, p. 133).

[25] Farley (1986), p. 31; Wambaugh (1920), p. 7.

[26] For instance, in 1857, during the referendum in Moldavia and Wallachia, upon the objection of France, Austrian troops were drawn from the referendum area. A similar situation appeared during the vote in Savoy and Nice where both the forces of France and Italy withdrew (Wambaugh 1933, pp. 443–444).

[27] Wambaugh (1920), p. 7.

[28] However, the actual state was problematic: the troops replacing those of the former sovereign (Germany and Austria) were from Great Britain, France, Italy and the United States. This "was, undeniably, far from an ideal arrangement, for although the war was over, the troops were technically neutral, actually they were from states recently at war with Germany, one of the parties to the plebiscite" (Wambaugh 1933, pp. 443–446).

the first time in the post-WWI referendums. During this period in every case, the troops of the former sovereign power of the territory were evacuated and were replaced by the troops of outside powers. Under the Treaty of Versailles, in all of the referendums, contesting states were required to withdraw their troops. The same measures were enshrined in the Treaty of St. Germain. While in the Treaty of Versailles the date for the evacuation of troops of the former state and their replacement by troops of the allied powers was fixed, in the treaty of St. Germain the decision was left to the plebiscite commission. In the case of Vilnius, despite the promise of the Polish Government, the commander of the Polish troops in the region refused to evacuate the forces under his command, arguing that these soldiers were the natives of the area and should be allowed to stay. This event and a further refusal of the Lithuanian Government to allow an international force into the territory were noted as the "chief causes" of failure to hold a referendum.[29]

As regards the referendum administration itself, the main idea was to avoid using existing authorities as they belonged to the interested parties. A new mechanism, an international referendum commission, was established to administer the referendum with complete power over the concerned area. Wambaugh noted this development as "a marked progress" and observed that all of the commissions carried out their tasks in an unbiased manner.[30] In this framework, a referendum commission had the task of conducting the whole referendum process: the administration of the area before the vote, conducting of the vote and the carrying out of final tasks concerning the transfer of sovereignty after the vote. Its powers were given as an outcome of a compromise between the parties to the conflict. One lesson learned from the post-WWI experience is that the mandate of the commission should be specified in the original agreement with which the referendum decision is taken. In Vilnius, the powers were not specified in advance, and it caused a conflict between the Polish Government and the Council on the reorganisation of the local administration. In Tacna-Arica, the commission was authorised to exercise "in general complete control over the plebiscite" by a clause in the referendum agreement ("The Arbitral Award of President Coolidge"). Yet the competences as specified by the Award merely included the registration and voting. This formulation gave the Chilean Government space for arguing that the power of the commission was limited to the period between registration and polling and that the rest of the referendum administration would fall within the competence of the Government. This controversy constituted one of the reasons for failure to hold the referendum in the area.[31] This incidence shows that each competence should be expressly specified in the referendum agreement or in any other sort of related legal document.

Under the Treaty of Versailles, in the articles regulating Schleswig, Allenstein and Marienwerder referendums, related commissions were given "the general

[29] Wambaugh (1933), pp. 445–446.

[30] Wambaugh (1933), p. 449.

[31] Wambaugh (1933), pp. 456–458.

powers of administration, task and competence to take all the measures that they think necessary to ensure the freedom, fairness and secrecy of the vote". The Upper Silesian Commission was given "all powers exercised by the German or the Prussian Governments except those of legislation or taxation". These formulations did not differ much in practice for the commissions to find the legal basis for their actions in terms of the referendum administration.[32]

There were four distinct types of commission composition. In Schleswig, representatives from two neutral states were included in the referendum commission in addition to the representatives of the Allied Forces. In Allenstein and Marienwerder, Upper Silesia and Sopron, only Allied Forces were represented. In these two types, the interested states had no members except for non-voting observers attached to the commissions. The third type of commission composition was that of Klagenfurt, in which the interested states, Austria and Yugoslavia, had observing members. This method proved to be efficient in the daily administration and conduct of the voting. Finally, in Tacna-Arica, the referendum commission was composed of an equal number of each party under a neutral chairmanship. This formula, with equal voting rights of representatives of the two interested parties, caused inefficiency in the functioning of the commission.[33] In relation to this last case, Farley argues that "attempts to balance commissions with partisans have shown poor results".[34] Indeed, given the highly sensitive nature of the issue in question, trying to balance the commission, with each of the two rival parties having the power to block the decision-making process, may result in a deadlock.

Given the lack of time and resources, it has been decided by many post-WWI referendum commissions to leave lower ranking officials in their position by supervising their actions. Referendum commissions established control commissions corresponding to the traditional unit of administration. Each commission left the daily administration of the area to existing officials while exercising control and supervision through subcommittees.[35]

In those referendums held in territories related to Germany, all the state authorities were fully subordinated to the referendum commission. The commission had the power to suspend and expel any official relying on its discretion. All the laws, regulations and taxes were made subject to the approval of the referendum commission. The commission was also endorsed with the power to abrogate any law or regulation, which it might have considered contrary to the fair operation of the referendum. Germany was compelled to provide any document and information that the commissions would ask for and provide the basic needs of the referendum areas such as food and fuel provisions.[36]

[32] Wambaugh (1933), pp. 451–454.

[33] Wambaugh (1933), pp. 450–451.

[34] Farley (1986), p. 59.

[35] Wambaugh (1933), p. 454.

[36] Wambaugh (1933), p. 453.

Post-WWII and the UN The issue of an impartial and fair referendum administration was also important in the post-WWII decolonisation referendums. The case of French Somaliland may be remembered in this context.[37] French Somaliland (Djibouti) was a colonial possession of France. France ceased sending information, as was required under Art. 73 of the UN Charter, claiming that French Somaliland became a self-governing territory after an affirmative result obtained in the referendum held on 19 March 1967. In this referendum, the inhabitants were asked whether they wanted to remain under the sovereignty of France.[38]

The administration of the referendum was deemed as unfair as a result of the policies of France in preventing the Somali people[39] from unifying with the neighbouring Somali Republic. The voting was held with the exclusion of the Somalis, where only the pro-France Afars were permitted to vote. During the referendum, France manipulated the voting constituencies to the advantage of the Afars. Furthermore, 8,000 Somalis had been expelled, while another 4,000 were kept in deportation camps before and during the vote.

The General Assembly did not accept this referendum as valid and decided to keep the region in the list of non-self-governing territories. In this context, the General Assembly stated that "considering the circumstances in which the referendum (was) organized. . .France has not cooperated with the UN" in the implementation of the people's right to self-determination in the territory. The General Assembly also called upon the administering power "to create the political conditions necessary for accelerating the implementation of the right of people to self determination and independence including the full exercise of political freedoms and allowing the return of all refugees to the territory".[40]

Thus, one of the most important challenges for the UN was to secure the fair administration of the decolonisation referendums. The UN's role, in this context, has not been consistent. "It has varied according to the circumstances of the case and the mandate established by the General Assembly, the Trusteeship Council or other appropriate organ. The ultimate objectives in all cases however, have been to ensure that the people make their choice and determine their future in complete freedom."[41]

During decolonisation, the UN has adopted various resolutions, setting the general principles of self-determination and urging states "to promote through

[37] Sureda (1973), pp. 210–212.

[38] The official question: "Do you approve of this territory, part of the French republic, being submitted to a new local government, the details of which have already been disclosed?" http://www.c2d.ch/detailed_display.php?lname=votes&table=votes&page=1&parent_id=&sublinkname=results&id=38321. Retrieved 05 October 2012.

[39] One of the ethnic groups in French Somaliland, the other being the Afars.

[40] The UN General Assembly Resolution of 19 December 1961 No: 2356: (XXII), on the "*Question of French Somaliland*".

[41] United Nations General Assembly. "*Enhancing the effectiveness of the principle of periodic and genuine elections Report of the Secretary-General.*" A/46/609, 19 November 1991. Para. 10.

joint and separate action, realization of the principle of… self-determination of peoples…to refrain from any forcible action which deprives peoples in the elaboration of the present principle of their right to self-determination, freedom, independence…(and to give) due regard to the freely expressed will of the peoples concerned".[42] Following these principles, in the cases where a referendum was envisaged, its administration has varied from case to case.

The position of the UN in decolonisation referendums may be roughly divided into two main categories. In rare cases, the UN has acted like a sovereign state over a territory. It has carried out the organisation and conduct of the voting all by itself. This role was designed particularly within the framework of second-generation operations, such as that of Western Sahara and East Timor. On the other hand, in most decolonisation referendums, the UN has just assumed a supervisory role over the administering authorities. Within these disparate cases, the UN, at times, has interacted actively with the administering power via negotiations, recommendations and the certification of each step. In others, it has limited itself to a mere certification of the freedom and fairness of the different aspects of the voting process.

In his report "Enhancing the effectiveness of the principle of periodic and genuine elections", the Secretary General set out the basic principles to guide the involvement of the UN in electoral consultations, including sovereignty referendums. One noteworthy observation is that "in the view of most Member States, electoral verification by the United Nations should remain an exceptional activity of the organization and should be undertaken only in well defined circumstances". Moreover, the UN involvement should meet certain criteria[43]:

> Requests (for the involvement of the UN in the referendums) should pertain primarily to situations with a clear international dimension, the monitoring of an election or referendum should cover the entire electoral process in order to secure conditions of fairness and impartiality, there should be a broad public support, there should be approval by the competent organ of the United Nations.

The degree and extent of involvement of the UN in referendums during the decolonisation process varied according to the special circumstances of each different case. Acting with the concern of maintaining the most appropriate administration system for varying conditions in order to ensure free and fair voting, the General Assembly, Trusteeship Council and Security Council established their mandates in each different case with UN resolutions. According to the degree of involvement, the role of the UN may be divided into three categories[44]:

[42] A/RES/2625: The UN General Assembly Resolution of 24 October 1970, on the "*Declaration on Principles of International Law Concerning Friendly Relations and Cooperation Among States in Accordance with the Charter of the United Nations*"; See also: The UN General Assembly Resolution of 9 December 1981 No A/36/103 on the "*Declaration on the Inadmissibility of Intervention and Interference in the Internal Affairs of States*".

[43] *Enhancing the Effectiveness of the Principle of Periodic and Genuine Elections*: *Report of the Secretary General*, para. 79.

[44] Beigbeder (1994), pp. 110–117.

Organisation and Conduct of an Electoral Process This category comes closer to the role adopted by the Referendum Commissions for the post-WWI referendums, which assumed almost all of the powers for both the administration of the referendum area and the regulation/conduct of the voting. Here, the UN had the role of carrying out every action related to the referendum, which would normally be carried out by the national authorities. These actions include the general administration of the area, the setting of legal norms and procedures and the conduct of the voting process and judicial adjudication of contesting allegations. The foreseen role of the UN in the administration of the referendum in Western Sahara and Kashmir and the function of UNAMET and UNTAET in East Timor fall into this category.[45]

Supervision of an Electoral Process This model was the most frequently used during the decolonisation process as seen during the referendums in British Cameroon (Southern part: 1959, Northern part: 1961), British Togoland (1956) and Western Samoa (1961). In this type of administration, while the administration of the area and regulation/conduct of the vote were carried out by the administering authority, the UN supervised and verified every aspect related to the administration of the area, the conduct of the voting and the verification of the results. During the decolonisation referendums, the term "supervision" was generally used "to describe the United Nations presence encompassing the whole process of popular consultation".[46] In these cases, the General Assembly resolution, establishing the legal basis of the referendums, also provided for the appointment of a "plebiscite commissioner", or of a mission, and specified their competences. The administering authority prepared the legal rules for the organisation and the conduct of the referendum process in consultation with the plebiscite commissioner. The wording of the question was formulated and approved by the relevant United Nations organ (General Assembly or Trusteeship Council). The results were also endorsed and approved by resolutions of the General Assembly and by referring to the report of the plebiscite commissioner.

Observation (Verification) of Electoral Process The main distinction of this third category from the former one is that, in the former, supervision is fulfilled in a territory that is not independent, such as trust territories and non-self-governing territories; in this third category, the verification operations are conducted for referendums or elections when a sovereign state, on its own initiative, requests the UN to do so. Also in this category, we may mention the role of the UN in the referendums in the Trust Territory of the Pacific Islands (TTPI).

As compared to "supervision", in the case of observation (verification), "the United Nations' role might be less encompassing". In those cases where the UN participated in the referendums in the framework of observation, its competences were

[45] Beigbeder (1994), pp. 110–117.

[46] *Enhancing the Effectiveness of the Principle of Periodic and Genuine Elections: Report of the Secretary General*; para. 12.

usually more limited in scope, and the mission was headed by a chairman appointed by the Trusteeship Council, as in the cases of elections and referendums in the trust territory of the Pacific Islands or by the Chairman of the Special Committee as in the case of Niue (1974) At the conclusion of the exercise, the mission compiled a report to the relevant organ of the Organization with an account of the visit to the territory and its observation of all the aspects and phases of consultation, together with conclusions and recommendations, as appropriate. The Report was also transmitted to the Administering Authority.[47]

As noted above, in East Timor, apart from the security, the New York Accords gave the total responsibility of the referendum administration to the UN, which charged an Independent Electoral Commission especially for this purpose. The Commission had the duty to ensure the transparency and fairness of the voting, including the judicial adjudication of the conflicts regarding the registration and other balloting activities. The Commission had the direct authority to oversee the whole referendum process, including registration, resolution of appeals against the refusal to register, the counting of votes and the certification of the results.[48]

As to security, during the period leading up to the New York Accords, the parties had acknowledged the need for an atmosphere free from violence for a fair and free referendum. The New York Accords gave the exclusive responsibility for security to the Indonesian police and the Indonesian authorities who repeatedly declared their commitments to provide effective security throughout the process. However, these commitments found no effective action in reality, and there were wide reports claiming that the Indonesian army and police had been supporting the pro-Indonesian militias.[49]

This was the major flaw in the East Timor referendum. Despite comprehensive competences regarding the other aspects of the referendum administration, the Security Agreements left the UN without adequate logistic and power resources to stop the violence effectively in the aftermath of the referendum. This was due to the politics preceding the vote. During the talks leading up to the New York Accords, Indonesia clearly reported that it would accept the holding of a referendum, on the sole condition that it had the exclusive competence to maintain the security. It was in fact a concession given to Indonesia in this regard, which would not have agreed to the resolution of the East Timor question if the UN and Portugal had insisted otherwise.[50]

---

[47] *Enhancing the Effectiveness of the Principle of Periodic and Genuine Elections* Paras. 6, 7 and 12; In some decolonization referendums, the Trusteeship Council and the Special Committee used the term "observation" in their relevant reports. This was the case of (TTPI) where the UN had less influence in the decision of their status as compared with the other trust territories (*Enhancing the Effectiveness of the Principle of Periodic and Genuine Elections*: *Report of the Secretary General*, Para. 12; *Report of the United Nations Visiting Mission to Observe the Referendum in the Trust Territory of the Pacific Islands*, 1978, Trusteeship Council Official Records Sup. No. 2, T/1795).

[48] United Nations General Assembly. "*Question of East Timor Progress report of the Secretary-General.*", A/54/654, 13 December 1999. Para. 17.

[49] Kondoch (2001), p. 248.

[50] "*Question of East Timor Progress report of the Secretary-General.*", A/54/654, 13 December 1999. Para. 11.

There were military liaison officers and civilian police allocated for the UN, but they did not have any competence or means by which they could maintain law and order. The Security Agreement clearly specified a limited role for the civilian police of UNAMET, whose only reason for being there was demoted to the role of providing advisory assistance to the Indonesian police. Likewise, the task of UNAMET's military liaison officers was defined as to "maintain contact with the Indonesian Armed Forces in order to allow the Secretary-General to discharge his responsibilities under the General Agreement and the Security Agreement".[51]

The Security Council established UNAMET against this background. The amount of civilian police and military observers were very limited in numbers (up to 280 civilian polices and 50 military observers). Besides, these forces were unarmed and not ready for immediate action in the case of an incident. Each time a deployment was authorised, the Secretary General had to ask the Governments to make available the required personnel.

The overall lesson was obvious: from the very beginning onwards, the UN had to focus on maintaining peace and order in the region rather than trying to cover all the other aspects.[52] In contrast to East Timor, in Sudan, the responsibility and competence throughout the referendum process belonged to the Sudanese authorities, particularly the Southern Sudan Referendum Commission (SSRC). UN support was limited to the necessary technical and logistical support. In the case of Sudan, the UN did not assume ownership of the whole process as it had in the case of East Timor. Rather, it opted for ensuring the neutrality and efficiency via an effective peacekeeping mission, by the good offices function provided by the Secretary General and by advice and technical assistance.

This perspective may be sensed by the assertions of the Secretary General:

> In planning the structure and deployment of the military component, a strong early warning system, mobility and expeditionary capacity have been identified as the key capacities necessary to accomplish the tasks (regarding the referendum). Emphasis would be placed on incorporating the lessons of past deployments when insufficient and inadequately equipped troops were deployed for peacekeeping duties and failed to meet the high expectations generated by their deployment. [53]

Accordingly, the Security Council, being apparently aware of the negative consequences of the lack of sufficient military personnel in East Timor, "Acknowledge(ed) the importance of drawing on best practices, past experience, and lessons learned from other missions".[54] Against this setting, the size of the armed forces of the UN in Sudan was to be considerably larger than that deployed in East Timor.

---

[51] S/RES/1246/(1999): The UN Security Council Resolution of 11 June 1999.

[52] In East Timor, the process and the organisational framework of constitution making were determined almost entirely by the United Nations as mandated by a Security Council Resolution. In substance, however, the external influence was minimal and choices were left to the indigenous actors (Dann and Al-Ali 2006, p. 462).

[53] United Nations Security Council. "*Special report of the Secretary-General on the Sudan.*" S/2011/314, 17 May 2011.

[54] S/RES/1996/2011: The UN Security Council Resolution of 8 July 2011.

With the intention of attaining full operational capacity, the military components of the UNMIS established their headquarters in Khartoum and the Joint Monitoring Coordination Office in Juba. By September 2006, the military elements of UNMIS had reached 8,727 troops, 695 military observers, 186 staff officers and 666 police officers.

Thus, a brief comparison between the cases of East Timor and South Sudan leads us to the conclusion that the issue of security had attained a much greater importance within the scope of referendum administration. In fact, it would be much more desirable if the referendum administration had the plenipotentiary power regarding all aspects of the voting and daily administration of the area. Yet given the lack of time, economic resources and political and logistical restraints, the international community may have to cooperate (and in all cases has done so) with the local actors. When this is the case, the international community should preferably focus its force and resources to maintaining exclusive control over security, while conducting other aspects by providing good offices, with mediation and supervision of the local actors.

7.2 Judicial Review of the Referendum

In a broad sense, the objective of the judicial review in the context of a referendum may have formal or material dimensions. The formal aspect may be further divided into the procedural aspects of the vote and the "formal validity" of the ballot question (i.e., unity of content and the clarity of the question). From a material point of view, "the material validity" of the issue is primarily a question of whether it is the lawful subject matter of referendum as stipulated by the relevant constitutions or other legal documents. Additionally, in more general terms, the question concerns the judicial review of the constitutionality of laws.[55]

Procedural issues may involve the general elements of the electoral process such as preparatory acts, identification and registration of electors, administration of the polling procedure, secrecy of the vote, counting of the votes and tabulation and declaration of the results. Also, there may be issues specific to the referendums. The question of whether the competent organ has initiated the referendum may be considered one such issue. Also, we may list quorum, campaigning and funding

[55] Morel (2013), p. 522; *cf.* Venice Commission: "Judicial review in the field of referendum applies first a priori and addresses the decision to submit a matter to referendum. It may also take place during the procedure, and address procedure itself or the voting rights and, after the vote, the validity of results. Finally, a posteriori control of the text adopted by referendum is conceivable." European Commission for Democracy Through Law (Venice Commission). "*Referendums in Europe—An Analysis of the Legal Rules in European States*" Study No. 287/2004, Council of Europe, Strasbourg, CDL-AD (2005)034, 2 November 2005, para. 146.

as examples of these issues typically appearing as matters of contention in front of the judiciary. [56]

In comparative constitutional law, authorities competent to fulfil the judicial review are generally courts, but occasionally political organs like the Federal Assembly in Switzerland (for matters other than procedural issues) may perform the role. To a large extent, we may subsume judicial review of referendums under the issue of the judicial review of constitutionality in a specific country. For example in the United States, having a well established tradition of judicial review of constitutionality, there are broad possibilities for judicial review concerning all aspects (formal and material) of any kind of referendum.[57]

In France, the question must be considered separately for referendums held under Article 11 and for referendums held according to Article 53/3 of the Constitution. Concerning referendums held under Article 11, the judicial review was initially identified as limited but has recently taken on a more active role following the *Hauchemaille* decision of the Constitutional Council and the constitutional amendment of 2008.

In 1962, the Council refused to decide on the constitutionality of a law approved by referendum held under Article 11 of the Constitution. The Council argued that the Constitution gave it the competence to control the laws made by parliament, but not those ones made by referendums. The Council held that the referendums were the "direct expression of national sovereignty".[58] The Council reiterated the same view in 1992 in its decision concerning the referendum on the Maastricht Treaty.[59]

This judicial restraint of the Constitutional Council took a dramatic turn with its *Hauchemaille* decision in 2000.[60] The Council recognised its competence to make a priori control over certain preparatory acts of the state organs before the referendum, including the initiative presidential decree. This would also open the way for a material control of the subject matter of the referendum. Finally, the constitutional amendment of 2008 clearly upended the 1962 and 1992 jurisprudence of the Council. The new constitutional provision says legislative proposals mentioned in Article 11 "will be referred to the Constitutional Council" prior to the referendum, "which shall rule on their conformity with the Constitution" (Art. 61). Thus, by this

---

[56] Morel (2013), p. 523.

[57] Morel (2013), p. 523.

[58] Decision n° 62-20 DC du 06 Novembre 1962 (http://www.conseil-constitutionnel.fr/conseil-constitutionnel/francais/les-decisions/acces-par-date/decisions-depuis-1959/1962/62-20-dc/decision-n-62-20-dc-du-06-novembre-1962.6398.html. Retrieved 15 August 2013).

[59] Decision n° 92-313 DC du 23 Septembre 1992 (http://www.conseil-constitutionnel.fr/conseil-constitutionnel/francais/les-decisions/acces-par-date/decisions-depuis-1959/1992/92-313-dc/decision-n-92-313-dc-du-23-septembre-1992.8822.html. Retrieved 15 August 2013). For a critical review of these decisions see; Stefanini (2004), pp. 57–61.

[60] Décision n° 2000-21 REF du 25 juillet 2000 (http://www.conseil-constitutionnel.fr/conseil-constitutionnel/francais/les-decisions/acces-par-date/decisions-depuis-1959/2000/2000-21-ref/decision-n-2000-21-ref-du-25-juillet-2000.105924.html. Retrieved 15 August 2013).

constitutional reform, the material constitutional control of the referendum laws became a priori and mandatory.[61]

In contrast to referendums held under Article 11, the Council showed no sign of judicial restraint in exercising active control over referendums held under Article 53/3. In 1987, the Council acknowledged its competence to control the ballot question of the referendum to be held in New Caledonia. In this decision, the Council coined the principle of the fairness (*loyauté*) and clarity (*clarté*) of the ballot questions of the referendums held according to Article 53/3.[62] The Council, along with Article 53/3, referred to the second paragraph of the preamble of the French Constitution dealing with the self-determination of the overseas territories.[63] For the Council, its competence to control the ballot question stemmed from the principles of the self-determination of the people and the free expression of their will for that purpose ("libre détermination des peuples et de libre manifestation de leur volonté"). In the Constitution, these principles are intended specifically for the overseas territories. The Council's reasoning thus created the supposition that its competence for judicial review was limited to the overseas territories. The Council—"presuming perhaps the ramifications that could result from the widespread recognition of this constitutional requirement"—restricted its competence of referendum control to the referendums organised within the framework of Article 53/3.[64]

It is necessary to note that electoral matters of pure procedure have not been a matter of controversy in the French context. Article 60 of the Constitution is clear: "The Constitutional Council shall ensure the proper conduct of referendum proceedings as provided for in articles 11 and 89 and in Title XV and shall proclaim the results of the referendum." This reflects the general situation in comparative constitutional law. "The study of comparative law reveals a clear tendency of attributing the control of the referendum process to the constitutional courts."[65]

The judicial review of the referendum processes in post-war/post-conflict conditions bears an extra importance. In this framework, the impartiality of the judiciary during a referendum is crucial. The neutralisation of the existing court system is an inevitable element of a fair administration, as the courts are viewed as a symbol of the authority of the state:

---

[61] Morel (2013), pp. 526–527.

[62] Décision n° 87-226 DC du 02 Juin 1987, *Loi organisant la consultation des populations intéressées de la Nouvelle-Calédonie et dépendances prévue par l'alinéa premier de l'article 1er de la loi n° 86-844 du 17 juillet 1986 relative à la Nouvelle-Calédonie*.(http://www.conseil-constitutionnel.fr/conseil-constitutionnel/francais/les-decisions/depuis-1958/decisions-par-date/1987/87-226-dc/decision-n-87-226-dc-du-02-juin-1987.8337.html. Retrieved 12 August 2013); Stefanini (2004), p. 188.

[63] Stefanini (2004), p. 188.

[64] Stefanini (2004), pp. 189–190.

[65] Stefanini (2004), p. 145; *but cf.* European Commission for Democracy Through Law (Venice Commission). "*Referendums in Europe—An Analysis of the Legal Rules in European States*" Study No. 287/2004, Council of Europe, Strasbourg, CDL-AD (2005)034, 2 November 2005, para. 150.

> To expect the courts of one country, at all times, to give justice to the party wishing to escape from its jurisdiction, is asking too much of human nature, just as it is too much to expect the people subjection to believe that they will receive justice from the courts of their rulers while engaged in a campaign to end that rule. [66]

In order to create a neutral court system, some of the basic measures may be set as follows[67]: firstly, the link between the local courts and the higher courts left over from the antecedent court system should be severed. Secondly, a new court of appeal should be established by the referendum commission composing of judges who should be appointed from neutral countries. The local judges should be put under the supervision of a neutral judge. At this point, it is of vital importance that this higher judiciary organ is known to be impartial by the relevant population.

In post-war/conflict conditions, Farley proposed establishing "Plebiscite Tribunals" to decide on the different aspects of the conduct of the referendum and have jurisdiction over all aspects of infringement and fairness in the voting process. He distinguishes three types of such tribunals: "Plebiscite Tribunals", "Voter Registration Appeal Boards" and "Vote Contest Boards". Plebiscite Tribunals may decide on actions such as "the falsification of documents relating to registration and voting, wilful interference with the work of (referendum) officials; acts of impersonation during registration or voting, voting more than once, tampering with ballot papers" and attempts to obstruct the eligible voters from voting. The Voter Registration Appeals Board may deal with cases and complaints concerning the irregularities in the preparation of electoral rolls. Thirdly, the "Vote Contest Board" is responsible for hearing allegations of fraud and cheating in the casting and counting of the ballots. It should also be in charge of deciding "whether the rules and procedures of the election have been violated or subverted". The board may also assess whether the irregularities have been "sufficient to materially alter" the result of the voting.[68]

In East Timor, the Modalities Agreement specified that appeals against voter registration to the lists "be submitted to the regional offices for a final decision by the Electoral Commission prior to polling day". There was no other regulation in the Main and Modalities Agreements specific to the judicial review of the referendum process. On the other hand, recalling UNAMET's omnipotent authority, there was no legal obstacle for the UN in creating its own system of judicial review of the referendum process. The Secretary General established a three-judge Electoral Commission to act as a referendum tribunal:

> In order to ensure complete transparency of the consultation process and provide an independent body for the adjudication of complaints from any quarter, an Independent Electoral Commission, responsible for the overall assessment of the consultation process, was constituted. The Commission consisted of three eminent jurists with extensive experience in the field of electoral processes: Patrick Bradley (United Kingdom of Great Britain and Northern Ireland; and Ireland), Johann Kriegler (South Africa) and Bong-Scuk Sohn

---

[66] Wambaugh (1933), p. 498.

[67] Farley (1986), pp. 66–68.

[68] Farley (1986), pp. 69–72.

(Republic of Korea). The Commission directly observed the entire consultation process, from the registration to the counting of votes, and certified the results.[69]

In South Sudan, the national courts were deemed competent for the judicial review. The SSRA identified two different types of courts. The first one was the "Court", which was defined to be the "National Supreme Court or Supreme Court of Southern Sudan" (SSRA, Art. 2). The second type of court was the "competent court". This term meant "the court determined by the President of the National Judiciary or the President of the Southern Sudanese Supreme Court as the case may be, being competent to rule on appeals and contraventions" (SSRA Art. 2). The competent courts had the duty to rule on "appeals against the decision of the referendum authorities on voter identification and registration". Their decisions were final (SSRA, Art. 30-31). The Court's most important competence was to rule on appeals lodged against the result of the referendum (Art. 41 al.1/f). Thus, the Court was competent to render the final decision on the "Appeals against Referendum Results" (Art. 43-2).

No major criticisms seem to have been raised against these different practices of judicial review. In East Timor, the Secretary General said: "The unequivocal result, certified by the Independent Electoral Commission following a judicial review of a number of protests and alleged irregularities, provided the basis for a clear resolution of the question of East Timor."[70] The situation in Southern Sudan is similar, though the judicial review was exercised by Sudanese authorities. As mentioned in Chap. 5, overall international and national reactions to the result of the South Sudan referendum were widely positive. Competent international observers defined the referendum as a referendum "reflect(ive) of the free will of the people of Southern Sudan".[71]

These experiences show that there may be several ways to effectuate judicial review of referendums, and each model has to be evaluated according to the specific surrounding conditions. We may still note down certain common qualities that should exist. First, in stable conditions, the Constitutional Court or an equivalent judicial organ should be competent to decide on the validity of the referendum result and other procedural contentions. In post-war/conflict conditions, the importance of the impartiality of the judiciary becomes apparent. Therefore, it is highly favoured that the organ competent to exercise judicial review should be composed of neutral persons from external countries, giving the possibility of appeal to a higher court of instance. To conclude, an effective judicial review of the referendum process is a key element in securing a fair and free vote.

[69] United Nations General Assembly. "*Question of East Timor Progress report of the Secretary-General.*", (A/54/654), 13 December 1999. Para. 31.

[70] United Nations General Assembly. "*Question of East Timor Progress report of the Secretary-General.*", (A/54/654), 13 December 1999. Para. 31.

[71] See Chap. 5, Sect. 5.4.4.

7.3 Qualified Majority (Quorum)

A qualified majority (quorum) may be secured by a "quorum of participation" (minimum turnout) or a "quorum of approval". When there is a quorum of participation, satisfying the minimum turnout requirement, the vote is only valid if a certain portion of the registered voters participates. In the case of quorum of approval, the result depends on the approval by an enhanced percentage of the electorate.

7.3.1 Quorum of Participation (Minimum Turnout)

Quorum of participation may be observed in some constitutions of European states without being necessarily limited to the sovereignty referendums. According to the report of the Venice Commission, a minimum turnout of a majority of the electorate is required in the following states: Bulgaria, Croatia, Italy and Malta, Lithuania, Russia and "the Former Yugoslav Republic of Macedonia". In Latvia, there should be a turnout of half of the voters who participated in the last election of Parliament, and in Azerbaijan, it is 25 % of the registered voters. In Poland and Portugal, if the turnout falls short of 50 %, the referendum is considered as non-binding.[72] Considering this evidence, the state of minimum turnout requirement throughout the European Constitutions is not uniform. This being the case, it appears that no clear and binding internationally recognised standard exists concerning the level of participation in referendums in general.

For issues other than those of sovereignty, a turnout requirement may impair the democratic credibility of the referendums since it enables a very small minority to render the results negative.[73] On the other hand, a minimum turnout requirement may be deemed rational in the case of sovereignty referendums. This assumption is more associated with the veto function of sovereignty referendums. Indeed, the participation quorum may serve those partisans wishing for a negative result of the referendum, e.g., for those who are against the secession for example. The advantage given to this side may be considered legitimate, given the high saliency of the question in ballot, which renders the participation of the half of the people concerned convenient.[74] In this context, the Venice Commission said that "regarding international practice, a minimum turnout of 50 % of the registered voters

---

[72] Based on the information of 33 of 48 member states of the Venice Commission (*Referendums in Europe—An Analysis of the Legal Rules in European States*. Para. 112).

[73] European Commission for Democracy Through Law (Venice Commission). "*Code of Good Practice on Referendums.*" Study No. 371/2006, 20 January 2009. CDL-AD(2007)008rev. Para. 51.

[74] Cazala (2006), p. 168.

seems appropriate for a referendum on the change of state status".[75] The Commission noted, at this point, that a minimum turnout had been required in the independence referendums of Slovenia (1991) and Macedonia (1991), as well as in the constitutions of the Freely Associated States (particularly the Palauan Constitution, which provides for a participation of 75 % of the voters). In the independence referendum of Montenegro, the Law on Referendums stipulated that "the decision in a referendum is taken by a majority vote of the citizens who have voted, provided that the majority of citizens with voting rights have voted" (Article 37).[76]

7.3.2 *Quorum of Approval*

In the case of a quorum of approval, the majority required to validate the results is qualified, that is, more than merely a simple majority. Two different types of majority requirements may be considered: (1) of the electorate actually voting, a percentage more than 50 % may be required; (2) in addition to a simple majority of those voting, a specified number of positive votes (e.g., 35, 40, 45 or 50 %) of the total number of registered electorate may be required.[77] Generally speaking, a quorum of approval may at first sight appear to be a useful tool for enforcing the legitimacy of a referendum. However, doubts may be raised in the same fashion as those raised for the quorum of participation:

> . . .an approval quorum (acceptance by a minimum percentage of registered voters) may be inconclusive. . .If a text is approved – even by a substantial margin – by a majority of voters without the quorum being reached, the political situation becomes extremely awkward, as the majority will feel that they have been deprived of victory without an adequate reason.[78]

This difficulty with the quorum results in the fact that it is not a universal value imposed on the states for the democratic soundness of referendums. If a qualified majority of approval is to be considered, a fair balance between the concerns for securing the maximum consent and practicability should be observed.

On the other hand, one may claim the expediency of the quorum of approval for the sovereignty referendums, for similar reasons stated in the context of quorum of

[75] European Commission For Democracy Through Law. (Venice Commission) "*Opinion on the Compatibility of the Existing Legislation in Montenegro Concerning The Organization of Referendums With Applicable International Standards.*" Opinion No: 343/2005, Council of Europe, Strasbourg, 19 December 2005. Para. 26.

[76] Cazala (2006), p. 169.

[77] European Commission For Democracy Through Law. (Venice Commission) "*Opinion on the Compatibility of the Existing Legislation in Montenegro Concerning The Organization of Referendums With Applicable International Standards.*" Opinion No: 343/2005, Council of Europe, Strasbourg, 19 December 2005. Para. 29.

[78] Ibid. Para. 36; European Commission for Democracy Through Law (Venice Commission). "*Code of Good Practice on Referendums.*" Study No. 371/2006, 20 January 2009. CDL-AD (2007)008rev, paras. 50–52.

participation. Besides, a quorum of approval may be preferable to a quorum of participation since the former does not have the defect of bestowing marginal minorities an excessive amount of power to obstruct decision taking.

Indeed, qualified majority requirement was common in the sovereignty referendums of the post-communist constitutions.[79] The Soviet Law on Secession of 1990 allowed secession if 66 % of eligible voters in a republic voted in favour, though this law was never applied in practice. In Lithuania, the amendment of the 1st Article of the Constitution, concerning the nature of the state as an independent democratic republic must secure a vote of 75 % of the electorate (Constitution of Lithuania, Art. 148.1); the Constitution of Macedonia says: "the decision on any change in the borders of the Republic is adopted by referendum, in so far as it is accepted by the majority of the total number of voters" (Art. 74.2). The same requirement is prescribed for "the approval of the association or dissolution of a union or community with other states" (Art. 120.3). Similarly, the Slovak constitution requires an absolute majority of the registered voters to approve union or secession with the other states (Arts. 93.1 and 97.1).

The need for an enhanced majority for the approval of a secession was also noted by the Canadian Supreme Court in its decision on Quebec. In that case, the Court cast doubt on the constitutional legitimacy of secession of Quebec through a referendum with a simple majority:

> The argument that the Constitution may be legitimately circumvented by resort to a majority vote in a province-wide referendum is superficially persuasive, in large measure because it seems to appeal to some of the same principles that underlie the legitimacy of the Constitution itself, namely, democracy and self-government. In short, it is suggested that as the notion of popular sovereignty underlies the legitimacy of existing constitutional arrangements (of Canada), so the same popular sovereignty that originally led to the present Constitution must (it is argued) also permit "the people" in their exercise of popular sovereignty to secede by majority vote alone. However, closer analysis reveals that this argument is unsound, because it misunderstands the meaning of popular sovereignty and the essence of a constitutional democracy. [80]

The Court further coined the criterion of "clear majority" yet refrained from defining what this clear majority could be. The Court said that "in this context, we refer to a 'clear majority' as a qualitative evaluation. The referendum result, if it is to be taken as an expression of the democratic will, must be free of ambiguity both in terms of the question and in terms of the support it achieves." The Court said that the quantitative aspect, i.e. the level of percentage of the required majority, had to

---

[79] "Indeed, it must be emphasized that the most stringent rules on majority apply to self-determination referendums" (European Commission For Democracy Through Law (Venice Commission) "*Opinion on the Compatibility of the Existing Legislation in Montenegro Concerning The Organization of Referendums With Applicable International Standards.*" Opinion No: 343/2005, Council of Europe, Strasbourg, 19 December 2005. Para. 33); Cazala (2006), p. 170.

[80] *Reference re Secession of Quebec*, para. 75.

be decided by the political actors, dependent on the circumstances under which a future referendum may be taken.[81]

These holdings of the court led to the enactment of the Clarity Act by the Canadian Parliament, yet no exact percentage of the required majority was specified. Section 2(3) says:

> In considering whether there has been a clear expression of will by a clear majority of the population of a province that the province ceases to be part of Canada, the House of Commons should take into account the views of all political parties represented in the legislative assembly of a province whose government proposed the referendum on secession.

Thus, we may safely conclude in this section that an enhanced majority is important in securing the legitimacy of a referendum when aimed at resolving sovereignty conflicts. In fact, one should not forget the fact that a quorum—either of participation or of approval—is not a universal rule that may be imposed on states for the democratic accuracy of referendums. Moreover, as the Venice Commission notes, it is not advisable to endorse a requirement of quorum (both the participation and the approval quorums) since they assimilate abstainers into consenting to the status quo. Both preferences (for or against an enhanced majority) are legitimate since the former protects the majority against an organised minority and secures a more consensual decision-making process, whereas the latter provides a more practical and flexible decision-taking procedure.

Therefore, the question may be resolved according to the circumstances of each case by observing a fair balance between the concerns for securing the maximum consent and the workability of the referendums. Although this may be true for referendums within the everyday politics of a country, the question of sovereignty calls for a more incontestable result to referendums, and a close proximity between the two options weakens the legitimacy of the outcome.

As mentioned in the first part, the danger of the tyranny of majority is one of the most common arguments that opponents of referendums allude to. An enhanced majority may well mitigate the divisive effect of referendums stemming from their majoritarian nature and therefore protect the minorities from ephemeral and rhetorically (or ideologically) manipulated majorities.

In also recalling that sovereignty referendums are an important element of constituent power, the inclusiveness of this process is one feature that determines the wide acceptance of the new sovereignty status by the relevant people. In the process of constituent power (the creation of the political unit and the nation), sovereignty referendums appear to be a device of political mobilisation of the

---

[81] *Reference re Secession of Quebec*, para. 87; Also quoted in: European Commission For Democracy Through Law. (Venice Commission) "*Opinion on the Compatibility of the Existing Legislation in Montenegro Concerning The Organization of Referendums With Applicable International Standards.*" Opinion No: 343/2005, Council of Europe, Strasbourg, 19 December 2005. Para. 34.

people, its self definition and self-confirmation, in which case the decision by bare majorities may have an alienating effect.

In line with these premises, a comparison of diverse practices shows that in the case of sovereignty referendums, both the quorum of participation and the quorum of approval are desirable since the issue at stake is of fundamental importance, and considering the veto function in sovereignty referendums the interests of the minority outweighs those of the majority.

7.4 Voter Qualification

The definition of voter qualification in sovereignty referendums requires the conciliation of two equally legitimate principles: universal suffrage and representation of the genuine wish of the populations concerned.

Voting in a sovereignty referendum—whether for independence, accession or status—is of crucial importance as it determines the future and fate of people. In most cases, as sovereignty referendums are acts of self-determination, the precise definition of the "self" constitutes a serious challenge.[82] Indeed, voting rights are traditionally associated with citizenship. However, in most sovereignty referendums, citizenship (definition of it or membership to it) itself may be a matter of contention.[83]

In short, in order to achieve an accurate and equitable outcome, the definition of the electoral body lies at the core of sovereignty referendum regulations. Sovereignty referendums thus have the effect of self-confirmation and self-definition of a people.[84] Here, the main objective is to give the legitimate indigenous people of a land a voice, excluding any recent artificial and controlled population flow by interested parties.

In this vein, a General Assembly resolution expressly requires the following: "to take all necessary steps to ensure that only the indigenous people of the territory participate in (a) referendum".[85] We may distinguish two criteria in order to distinguish the qualified voters: birth (nativity) and residence. Combining these two elements, four categories of voters may be pointed out.[86]

[82] Blay (1988), pp. 863–880.

[83] Carter (2011), p. 664.

[84] Héraud (1983), p. 235.

[85] A/RES/2229(XXI): The UN General Assembly Resolution of 20 December 1966 on the "*Question of Ifni and Spanish Sahara*".

[86] Wambaugh (1933), p. 478.

7.4.1 Resident Natives

The resident natives' right to vote is uncontroversial. In each of the post-WWI referendums, the registration authorities registered the resident natives automatically using existing lists and other documents.[87]

However, some parties may question the right to vote of the resident natives while expecting to shape the voters' list to the advantage of their own cause. In the case of Togo, the Togoland Congress[88] proposed that voting be limited to the persons whose fathers and grandfathers were born in Togoland. Concerning the exclusive birth and nationality criterion in the Togoland case, the United Nations Visiting Mission noted that "in the complete absence of a general register of births, marriages and deaths covering the persons directly concerned in the referendum, a birth qualification would be difficult, and in many cases impossible to prove". More important than that, according to the Mission, excluding the *bona fide* inhabitants of the territory from voting for the mere reason that their ancestors were not born there would be in violation of the principle that the "freely expressed wishes of the peoples concerned" should be taken into account in the fulfilment of the trusteeship system.[89] Similarly, in Jura, the pro-separation party *Rassemblement Jurassien* claimed that voting rights should only be given to those who had been residing in the region for at least three generations.[90]

7.4.2 Non-resident Natives

Enfranchising non-resident natives (or "outvoters", as they may be called) was a novelty that appeared during the post-WWI referendums. Outvoters may be defined as persons who have been exiled, refugees and emigrants seeking a better life outside their home country because of political and economic turmoil, instability and violence resulting from conflicts of sovereignty. In the Schleswig, Allenstein, Marienwerder, Upper Silesia and Sopron referendums, those who were born in the area were qualified to vote, regardless of their residence status.[91]

Giving the right to vote to non-resident natives may be closely associated with the right of return. According to the Universal Declaration of Human Rights (UDHR), "everyone has the right to freedom...to return to his country" (Art. 13). In the same way, the International Covenant on Civil and Political Rights (ICCPR) stipulates that "no one shall be arbitrarily deprived of the right to enter his own

[87] Wambaugh (1933), p. 478.

[88] One of the parties to the referendum that favoured unification with French Togoland.

[89] Special Report on the Togoland Unification Problem and the Future of the Trust Territory of Togoland Under British Administration, T/1218, paras. 148–149.

[90] Laponce (2001), p. 51.

[91] Wambaugh (1933), p. 477; Farley (1986), p. 97.

country" (Art. 12.4). In this framework, granting the right to vote to non-resident natives gains importance when there has been a mass expulsion of the native people of a territory. In this context, the return of these exiles is another important issue to be implemented efficiently. According to the UN, for example, the return of exiles to a territory constitutes one of the conditions for creating "a favourable climate for a referendum to be conducted on an entirely free, democratic and impartial basis".[92] Thus, it may be legitimately argued that "those displaced by conflict have an inherent right to electoral inclusion".[93]

In East Timor, persons having reached the age of 17 could vote in the independence referendum of 1999 if they belonged to one of the following groups:

1. persons born in East Timor;
2. persons born outside East Timor but with at least one parent having been born in East Timor;
3. persons whose spouses fall under either of the two categories above.

In fact, in the case of East Timor, one could not refer to a record of mass migration of refugees or internally displaced persons. The UNCHR noted no refugee issues in East Timor in the period of Indonesian occupation running up to the referendum. However, "given the many instances of violence known to have been committed by the Indonesian Army during the 25-year period in which Indonesia controlled East Timor, it is inevitable that people fled the country in fear of persecution".[94] Thus, despite its relatively non-violent nature, an occupation of an entity, which is deemed illegitimate by international law, creates a *prima facie* case for the enfranchisement of non-resident natives. Also, it should be remembered that East Timor was a non-self-governing territory prior to the referendum. In light of the contemporary legal instruments, it may be well argued that "in non-self-governing territories, citizenship for the purposes of electoral participation should be linked to historical attachment to that territory".[95]

The effect of widespread displacement may be sensed in the voter qualification criteria of South Sudan—torn by a violent civil war. The South Sudan Referendum Act (SSRA) specified the conditions for eligible voters as follows:

> Born to parents both or either of whom belongs to any of the indigenous communities residing in Southern Sudan on or before the 1st of January 1956, or whose ancestry is traceable to one of the ethnic communities in Southern Sudan, or,
>
> Permanently residing, without interruption, or whose parents or grandparents are residing permanently, without interruption, in Southern Sudan since 1 January 1956.

It is apparent that the voter qualification was regulated to include the southern Sudanese people residing in South Sudan and elsewhere in the most comprehensive

[92] A/RES/2229(XXI): The UN General Assembly Resolution of 20 December 1966 on the "*Question of Ifni and Spanish Sahara*".

[93] Grace and Fischer (2003), p. 19.

[94] Carter (2011), p. 670.

[95] Grace and Fischer (2003), p. 27.

possible way. This was done as an acknowledgement of the massive displacements that occurred during the civil war and violence preceding the vote. One difficulty with these broad criteria, however, was that it was rather ambiguous since the SSRA did not define what constituted an ethnic or indigenous community. Against this, a list of southern ethnic communities was put forward to be agreed upon, to serve as a qualified electoral body. The Southern Sudan Referendum Commission refused this proposal, however, which was an opportune decision on its part. In the face of the ongoing inter-communal violence in the region, a definition of voter qualification on the basis of membership to an ethnic group could have generated further conflict and strife. Alongside this, there would be two additional difficulties that could arise from such a system of compilation arising from the nomadic, migrant and displaced nature of the several tribes: (1) it would have been difficult to decide on the exact definition of an ethnic group; (2) verification of a person's claim of affiliation with any ethnic group could have been similarly difficult.[96]

On the other hand, in more congenial conditions, one may argue that it is neither rational nor equitable even to franchise the members of a dominant group who left the territory by their own choice. For example, in the Schleswig referendum, the Polish population complained that German outvoters were included in the electoral body.[97]

When there is no record of forced migration of exiles or refugees in the pre-referendum history of a region, one may have recourse to the internationally recognised standards and practices of democratic states regarding the residency requirements for the use of electoral rights. It may be noted in this context that there is no universal value imposed on states to enfranchise non-resident natives. In this vein, it is argued that "there is no binding international standard requiring that expatriates should have the right to vote".[98] Moreover, there is an implicit acceptance on the part of the European Court of Human Rights that states may disenfranchise their own nationals who reside outside the country.[99] Indeed, the case law of the European Court of Human Rights points to the view that "...having to satisfy a residence or length-of-residence requirement in order to have or exercise the right to vote in elections is not, in principle, an arbitrary restriction of the right to vote and is therefore not incompatible with Article 3 of Protocol No. 1".[100]

---

[96] Curless (2011), pp. 3–4.

[97] Laponce (2001), p. 51.

[98] European Commission For Democracy Through Law. "*Opinion on the Compatibility of the Existing Legislation in Montenegro Concerning The Organization of Referendums With Applicable International Standards.*" Opinion No: 343/2005, Council of Europe, Strasbourg, 19 December 2005, para. 53.

[99] Cazala (2006), p. 168; "...The position is not analogous to that of persons who are unable to take part in elections because they live outside the jurisdiction, as such individuals have weakened the link between themselves and the jurisdiction." (*Matthews v. United Kingdom*, no. 24833/941999-I, ECtHR, para. 64).

[100] *Py v. France*, no 66289/01, ECtHR, 11 January 2005, para. 48; "the residence requirement (is justified) on the legitimate concern the legislature may have to limit the influence of citizens

Diverse state practices may be mentioned in this respect. In the United Kingdom, devolution referendums in Scotland and Wales and referendums on the status of Northern Ireland, residency and registration of the existing electoral register were the sole criterion for the right to vote in the relevant regions. In this context, for example, neither the Scottish people living outside Scotland were given the right to vote on devolution, nor were the Englishmen residing in Scotland disenfranchised.[101]

It is also worth mentioning the referendums held in the process of establishment of the canton of Jura in this context. In Switzerland, there is the concept of municipal citizenship, along with that of the cantons and the Federal Government. During the referendums held for the creation of the canton of Jura, only the residents in the municipalities were allowed to vote, irrespective of their cantonal citizenship, whereas the municipal citizens residing outside the canton were not. No residence period was required. This was contested by radical separatists arguing that "recent residents were akin to visitors if not occupiers and should not be party to a sovereignty decision".[102]

Therefore, in the foregoing context, it is apparent that residency criterion is more important than that of ethnic or geographical origin. Still, the length of residency requirement may be a subject of debate. In this case, contrary to the territories in the context of post-violence, occupation or decolonisation, one may not deem that 10–20 years of residence is a legitimate period. For instance, in the case of the referendum for the independence of Montenegro, the Venice Commission found the condition of 24 months of residence "excessive". According to the Commission and considering the international standards, the residency requirement should not exceed 6 months or, at most, 12 months in the case of a justifiable reason.[103]

During the process of the independence referendum in Montenegro on June 2005, the right to vote of the Montenegrin citizens living in Serbia was defended by the Government of Serbia. The government presented a list including more than 260,000 people in this respect, which was an extremely high number in proportion to the total number of registered voters (about 460,000). The applicable legislation of the independence referendum did not confer any voting rights to the Montenegrins residing in Serbia. The Venice Commission upheld this restriction indicating the tolerance to such a restriction in comparative constitutional law and

living abroad in elections on issues which, while admittedly fundamental, primarily affect persons living in the country." *Hilbe v. Liechtenstein* (dec.), no. 31981/96, 1999-VI, ECtHR.

[101] European Commission For Democracy Through Law. "*Opinion on the Compatibility of the Existing Legislation in Montenegro Concerning The Organization of Referendums With Applicable International Standards.*" Opinion No: 343/2005, Council of Europe, Strasbourg, 19 December 2005, para. 52.

[102] Laponce (2001), p. 51.

[103] Cazala (2006), p. 166; European Commission For Democracy Through Law. "*Opinion on the Compatibility of the Existing Legislation in Montenegro Concerning The Organization of Referendums With Applicable International Standards.*" Opinion No: 343/2005, Council of Europe, Strasbourg, 19 December 2005. Para. 63.

international law and, in particular, the holdings of the ECtHR. Moreover, the Commission recalled the foregoing debate about the eventual referendum and the question surrounding voter qualification in Montenegro since 2001. In such conditions, any change in the voter list would have been seen as a gerrymandering tactic and undermined the reliability of the referendum.[104]

In parallel to the exclusion of non-resident citizens in contexts where international law does not recognise the right to return, the right to vote of the non-native residents is recognised. The Venice Commission upheld the voting right of the Serbians residing in Montenegro, which "would correspond to the standard practice in federal states and in the former Yugoslavia and also to previous practice in Montenegro".[105]

The case of Puerto Rico has an instructive background. Here, controversy over voter qualification revolves around the question as to whether the Puerto Ricans residing in the mainland should be entitled to vote.[106] As in other cases, the debate on voter qualification in the Puerto Rican referendums originated from the controversy over who actually are the members of the Puerto Rican people. Nevertheless, and differing from other similar cases, the controversy as to what constitutes the "self" of Puerto Rico is not ethnic based but between the Puerto Ricans who chose to stay on the island and those who moved to the mainland.[107]

The issue of voter qualification is also intimately linked to the problem of whether the descendants of Puerto Rico constitute a people as distinct from the rest of the United States. The suggestion that the Puerto Ricans are not different from the rest of the US implies that the voting rights on issues pertaining to the island should be limited to the residents, as is the case in most of the states. The argument to the contrary assumes that the Puerto Ricans residing outside the island constitute a "diaspora", having the inherent right to vote on the future of the territory of their origin.[108] As examined previously, the question as to whether the Puerto Ricans have a distinct national identity has been unequivocally resolved by international law since the island has been identified as having been a subject of decolonisation.

However, in previous referendums, Puerto Rican citizenship has solely depended on being resident on the island, and consequently non-resident Puerto Ricans have been excluded. It is argued that this conception is akin to the residency

---

[104] European Commission For Democracy Through Law. "*Opinion on the Compatibility of the Existing Legislation in Montenegro Concerning The Organization of Referendums With Applicable International Standards*." Opinion No: 343/2005, Council of Europe, Strasbourg, 19 December 2005. Para. 60.

[105] European Commission For Democracy Through Law. "*Opinion on the Compatibility of the Existing Legislation in Montenegro Concerning The Organization of Referendums With Applicable International Standards*." Opinion No: 343/2005, Council of Europe, Strasbourg, 19 December 2005, para. 62.

[106] Napoli (1998), p. 167.

[107] Napoli (1998), p. 167.

[108] Napoli (1998), p. 167.

requirements of a state and the eligibility to vote on issues concerning that state.[109] In the proceedings *Sola v. Sanchez Vilella* before the US District Court for the District of Puerto Rico, this residency requirement was claimed to be unconstitutional and the court upheld the limitation.[110]

In this particular case, 15 citizens of New York, New Jersey and Massachusetts, who had emigrated from Puerto Rico, challenged a law barring them from voting in the referendum of 1967 due to a 1-year residency requirement. The plaintiffs alleged to have an interest, in that they would be affected by the outcome of the referendum, because they were taxpayers of Puerto Rico and had properties there. Their exclusion from the referendum violated the equal protection clause of the US Constitution.

The view of the court, judged on the merits of the case, was in disagreement with the plaintiffs, as it held that Puerto Rico should be treated like a state for the purposes of voting on questions of local interest:

> Plaintiffs are in no different position than a citizen and resident of New York, or New Jersey, or Massachusetts, who was born, for example, in Missouri, and to economically better himself moved to another state and became a citizen and resident of this state, and who, although owning property in Missouri and having nostalgia for Missouri, cannot meet the citizenship and the residential requirements for voting in a Missouri held election, even though the Missouri election may be on such fundamental matters as amending the State Constitution or adopting a new one.[111]

Following these arguments, the court found the 1-year residency requirement constitutional[112]:

> Plaintiffs who were not citizens or residents of Puerto Rico, but of mainland states, did not have standing to challenge constitutionality of statute providing for plebiscite in Puerto Rico, and requiring one year's residence of voters, although they claimed an interest in solution of political status of Puerto Rico and had property there.

This decision was upheld and affirmed by the United States Court of Appeals for the First Circuit. The court said that "simply being born in Puerto Rico gave plaintiffs no federally protected right to require the Legislature to solicit their views".[113]

In short, according to this case, the legislature of Puerto Rico could legitimately limit the voting rights to those who were resident just as any other state in the mainland might do. However, these assumptions of the courts are problematic from both aspects of constitutional and international laws.

---

[109] Napoli (1998), p. 167.

[110] [270 F. Supp. 459 (D.P.R. 1967), *af'd,390* F.2d 160 (1st Cir. 1968)]. Cited in Napoli (1998), p. 170.

[111] Cited in Napoli (1998), p. 170.

[112] *Sola v. Sanchez Vilella* 270 F. Supp. 459 (D.P.R. 1967), *af'd,390* F.2d 160 (1st Cir. 1968). at 464.

[113] *Sola v. Sánchez Vilella* 390 F.2d 160 (1968) 390 F.2d 160 (1st Cir. 1968). No. 6990. March 7, 1968.

First of all, the courts treated Puerto Rico like a state. This supposition is mistaken since from the perspective of constitutional law, the United States courts have considered Puerto Rico as an "unincorporated territory". This awkward status for Puerto Rico in American Constitutional Law renders doubtful the upholding of the residency requirement by analogy to the states on the mainland.[114]

Second, it seems that the courts, in this case, underestimated the fundamental importance of the status referendums in Puerto Rico and demoted them to mere legislative elections or everyday political referendums[115]:

> Technically, the interest of these plaintiffs in the plebiscite is purely personal rather than legal, and can be expressed by their corresponding with their own states' particular senators or representatives in Congress, who in turn can bring plaintiffs' views to the attention of Congress just as the results of the plebiscite would advise Congress of the views of those who vote in it.

On the other hand, it may also be argued that the court realised that the issue at stake might have been "such (a) fundamental matter as the amending the State Constitution or adopting a new one".[116] Yet, even if this were the case, the court thought that there was still nothing refuting the legitimacy of a residency requirement. Thus, whatever the level of importance of the question was, a non-resident would not prove a "sufficient interest" to be entitled to vote in Puerto Rico. This syllogism with reference to the state constitutions shows that the court was somewhat disinterested in the international aspect of the Puerto Rican question. The referendums in Puerto Rico were not pure products of municipal constitutional law; rather, they were held as a "necessary component of Puerto Rico's exercise of the right to self-determination under international law".[117] Considering this, one may conclude that as a territory subject to the law of decolonisation, such a strict analogy to state constitutional law may hinder the securing of the "freely expressed wishes of the peoples concerned".

Thus, referendum practices in Puerto Rico and the pursuant court decisions show that the question of voter qualification was problematic in terms of self-determination. Earlier US bills for status referendum also endorsed this approach.[118]

As an alternative view, the right to self-determination of the Puerto Rican people as "a whole" has been invoked. Declet holds that Puerto Rico has been included within the sphere of continental European civil law system throughout its history. In contrast to the common law doctrine of *jus soli*, which rests nationality on the place of birth, civil law *jus sanguinis*, confers a person the nationality of his parents. Consequently, all persons of Puerto Rican descent naturally assume the nationality

---

[114] Napoli (1998), p. 171.

[115] *Sola v. Sanchez Vilella* 270 F. Supp. 459 (D.P.R. 1967), *af'd,390* F.2d 160 (1st Cir. 1968). at 464.

[116] *Sola v. Sanchez Vilella* 270 F. Supp. 459 (D.P.R. 1967), *af'd,390* F.2d 160 (1st Cir. 1968). at 464.

[117] Napoli (1998), p. 172.

[118] [472, 105th Cong. § 2(b)(1) (1997)]. Cited in Napoli (1998), p. 172.

of Puerto Rico, regardless of their place of birth. In addition, referendums on the island's sovereignty status "are mandated by international law"[119]:

> Under international law, non-residence in the voting territory at the time of the plebiscite is not a bar to participation; but, rather, an individual's historic ties to the territory, such as by nationality, may be controlling factors. Moreover when the homeland is a colony, it is entirely proper for non-resident nationals to have a say in the resolution of the homeland's political status., since their ability to return to the homeland may be affected by the outcome of the vote.

Declet's view is more convincing, considering the fact that Puerto Rico is a territory subject to decolonisation law and because its status as a self-governing territory is controversial. On the other hand, the relatively stable political system of the territory, in comparison to that of New Caledonia for example, generates doubts as to the convenience of automatically conferring the voting right to all persons of Puerto Rican descent who (or whose parents) left the territory purely on their consent. A similar case may provide insights in this respect. In Tokelau, in the UN-observed referendum of 2006, the General Fono (the national representative body) decided that Tokelauans living overseas be excluded from the status referendum. Two justifications were suggested for this decision. The first was that it would be logistically difficult to organise voting in other countries, and the second was that the estimated number of Tokelauans living abroad was 12,000, while the active population of the island was 1,500. Consequently, the vote of the former would override those who actively resided in the island. This practice did not raise any disapproval from the United Nations monitoring team, which deemed the overall process "credible and reflective of the will of the people".[120] The same arguments have been put forward by those who opposed the granting of voting rights to the Puerto Ricans of the mainland.[121] Thus, considering a reasonable criterion as a prerequisite to enfranchising the mainland Puerto Ricans may be deemed legitimate in terms of international law.

Recent developments show that federal actors tend to enfranchise the mainland Puerto Ricans. Two competing views may be deducted from two different bills. The Democracy Act would have enfranchised the residents of the mainland on the criterion of birth. Section 3 subsection c of the bill, "...makes eligible those born in Puerto Rico but not those of Puerto Rican descent who were not born in Puerto Rico, and thereby chooses place of birth rather than ethnic identity as the eligibility criterion." On the other hand, the Self-Determination Act would have further bestowed voting rights to those US citizens residing in the mainland with at least one parent born in Puerto Rico.

---

[119] Declet (2001), p. 47.

[120] Report of the United Nations Mission to Observe the Referendum on Self-Determination of Tokelau, February 2006, A/AC.109/2006/20, para. 9.

[121] Medina (2010), p. 1090.

7.4.3 Non-native Residents

In the case of the non-native residents and acting with the concern of avoiding any possible artificial demographic manipulation by interested parties, many regulations provide a minimum period of residence within the territory prior to being given voting rights. This residency period serves as a presumption that migrants have had adequate time to develop an interest in the future of the territory. It also serves to prevent any eventual cross-border voters and/or civil-military servants of the parental state from voting:

> In referenda concerning self-determination, the residency requirement ought to be sufficiently stringent to prove a "demonstrable link" to the territory holding the ballot. In addition, electoral actors should avoid writing criteria that have the effect of discriminating against persons based on their race or ethnicity. However, criteria that disenfranchise settler populations who migrated to the territory after an agreed date are acceptable, even if this disenfranchisement has the effect of discriminating against persons based on their race or other criteria.[122]

A residency requirement is often associated with decolonisation or occupation. In both cases, there may be a manipulative move from parent states to the related territory. In this vein, the UN General Assembly labels the "systematic influx of foreigners towards the colonial territories" as a major obstacle to the right of self-determination.[123] Also as regards occupation, the Fourth Geneva Convention says: "The Occupying Power shall not deport or transfer parts of its own civilian population into the territory it occupies."[124]

In the post-WWI referendums, minimum periods for continuous residence from 6 to 20 years were prescribed for the non-native residents before the referendums were held in 1920. The cut-off points for the beginning of habitual residence were as follows: Schleswig—1 January 1900; Allenstein—5 January 1905; Marienwerder—January 1, 1914; Upper Silesia—January 1, 1914; Klagenfurt—1 January 1912.[125]

In Togo, the mission found 6 months of continuous residence too short a period to qualify as a voter, but on the other hand a longer period such as 20 years was found to be too long and presenting difficulties in proving residence. The mission concluded that a 2-year period would constitute "a sufficiently long qualifying period to constitute a *bona fide* residence and would at the same time be short enough to be reasonably easy of proof in the event of claims and objections". The mission also asserted that a short period of absence, which did not cover more than half of that period of 2 years, would not be construed as non-residence. [126]

---

[122] Grace and Fischer (2003), p. 32.

[123] Dobelle (1996), p. 53.

[124] "Convention (IV) relative to the Protection of Civilian Persons in Time of War. Geneva, 12 August 1949." http://www.icrc.org/ihl.nsf/full/380. Retrieved 11 November 2012.

[125] Wambaugh (1933), pp. 474–475; Farley (1986), pp. 92–93.

[126] Special Report on the Togoland Unification Problem and the Future of the Trust Territory of Togoland Under British Administration, T/1218, para. 152.

In Western Sahara, the dispute about the definition of the electoral body was one of the chief reasons that slowed down the referendum process since the settlement plan between Morocco and Polisario first came into existence in 1988.[127] The main reason for the dispute about voter identification is that the inhabitants of the area are mostly nomadic, and consequently there is a lack of written records related to the demographic changes. The first assessment related to voter qualification in the area was the census carried out in 1974 by Spain. While Polisario suggested that voting rights should be given to those persons who were counted in the census of 1974 and their descendants, Morocco argued that given the nomadic nature of the inhabitants of the territory, the census could not have been accurate since many tribes were not in the region and not counted when the census was made. The "Green March", initiated by the King of Morocco in 1975, exacerbated the deadlock: 350,000 Moroccans entered Western Sahara and settled in the territory. Since then, their right to vote in an eventual referendum has been contested by Polisario.

Under the settlement plan of 1988, an Identification Commission was established within MINURSO: its mandate to determine the eligible voters for the referendum. The Identification Commission started its task in order to update the 1974 census, to determine deaths and to consider applications made by persons claiming they had been excluded from the census, despite being inhabitants of the region. [128]

In 1991, Morocco claimed that a number of tribes that were normally inhabitants of the area were excluded from the census because they were temporarily absent. A number of 120,000 voters were included, and King Hassan spoke of moving 170,000 habitants into the region. A report issued after this claim by the Secretary General set out five criteria to be used for qualifying voters[129]:

1. persons whose names are included in the revised 1974 census list;
2. persons who were living in the territory as members of Saharan tribe at the time of 1974 but could not be counted;
3. members of the immediate family of the first two groups;
4. persons born of a Saharan father born in the territory;
5. persons who are members of a Saharan tribe belonging to the territory and who have resided in the territory for six consecutive years or intermittently 12 years prior to 1 December 1974.

This formulation was contested by both parties, and despite an attempt to reach agreement, the obstinate stance of the two parties, in their attempt to control the formation of an electoral body to their advantage, blocked the process. The prolongation of the problem caused a vicious circle: the longer it took for the territorial dispute to be resolved, the more the settlers identified themselves with the territory and coalesced with the original inhabitants, making the human aspect of the

[127] Castellino (2000), p. 180.

[128] Castellino (2000), p. 181.

[129] UN Doc. S/23999.

legitimacy of the sovereignty of the conflicting parties more complicated. As there was no agreement between the parties, in March 1994 the Security Council decided to set a deadline for the identification commission to finish the determination of the electoral body as 30 June 1994. This task was not as simple as predicted, primarily because the people of the region are nomadic, moving across the Sahara Desert during the year, crossing the borders of several countries. Deriving from these unresolved problems of voter qualification, neither argument was entirely satisfactory in serving the legitimacy in relation to the principle of self-determination. If, as Polisario suggested, the eligibility criterion had been limited to those who were counted in the 1974 census, it would have resulted in the exclusion of the tribes that were absent at the time of census and no less legitimate inhabitants than those who were counted. On the other hand, if voter eligibility had been extended to all nomadic tribes wandering in and around the region, this would have meant favouring the infusion policy of the Moroccan Government. While practically it became more difficult to distinguish original inhabitants from settlers, uprooting a population that had become akin to natives of the region over 25 years was also questionable in terms of self-determination. On the other hand, this is not to say that Morocco was right in its policy of altering the demographic structure of the region, given UN's condemnation of settler infusion policies and the clear prohibition by the Fourth Geneva Convention "to deport or transfer parts of its own civilian population into the territory it occupies" (Article 49). However, the practice of maintaining the *status quo* in order to preserve peace, and the limited capability of the Security Council in its use of force, obstructs the ability to prevent the introduction of new populations against the will of the related state. Due to this fact, the only solution relating to voter qualification could be worked out through an agreement between the parties. Indeed, it was finally through an agreement reached between Morocco and Polisario that the ongoing dispute was resolved. In July 1997, at the end of the London talks, the parties agreed that they would not "directly or indirectly sponsor or present for identification of any one" from the disputed tribal groupings. On the other hand, in the same agreement it was agreed that "the parties shall not be obligated to actively prevent individuals from such tribal groupings from presenting themselves. The parties agree that the identification of any such individuals who may present themselves shall proceed as soon as possible."[130]

Even after this agreement, the question of voter identification has not been an easy task. The identification process restarted in 1999 and has been unable to be completed since then because of the large number of applications, one of the "outstanding problems" the Identification Commission had to deal with.[131] The situation is still pending.[132]

---

[130] *Results of the Second Round of Direct Talks London, 19 and July 1997* Annex I, Report of the Secretary-General on the Situation Concerning Western Sahara S/1997/742.

[131] Castellino (2000), p. 210; S/2000/131 paras. 6–8 and 15–29; S/2004/39.

[132] See, for the latest update of news concerning the territory, http://www.un.org/en/peacekeeping/missions/minurso/ Last Accessed 6 October 2013.

The question of voter qualification in the decolonisation referendums may be tackled by examining the case of New Caledonia. This case dramatically illustrates the tension between the descendants of the ex-coloniser and the indigenous inhabitants of a territory. In New Caledonia, there are two main ethnic groups: the Kanaks are the original indigenous inhabitants, and the Caldoche are the descendants of French settlers. As a result of continuous immigration by French settlers to the Island, the indigenous inhabitants have become a minority in their original homelands. While the Kanaks demand independence, the Caldoche are in favour of remaining a part of France with an autonomous status. In the referendum (1987) held to solve this conflict, the matter of voter qualification was hotly contested by the two parties. While the pro-France Caldoche believed that a residency period of 3 years should be enough to qualify for voting rights, the Kanaks considered that being indigenous or at least having one parent born in the area would suffice. The referendum was held by the French authorities adopting the Caldoche version of voter qualification rules. The Kanaks responded to this by boycotting the referendum. The outcome of a vote was in favour of remaining a part of France, but as a result of the boycott, the turnout was only 58 %.[133] These events, among others, caused the referendum to be discredited in the eyes of the international community. In a subsequent resolution, the UN decided to keep New Caledonia in the list of non-self-governing territories.[134] This conflict could potentially be resolved by the Nouméa Accord and a subsequent French law that legalised rigorous rules for voter qualification in accordance with Kanak demands.

For any future referendum, Article 218 Law No. 99-209 stated;

> Persons registered on the electoral roll on the date of the referendum and fulfilling one of the following conditions shall be eligible to vote:
> They must have been eligible to participate in the referendum of 8 November 1998;
> They were not registered on the electoral roll for the referendum of 8 November 1998, but fulfilled the residence requirement for that referendum;
> They were not registered on the electoral roll for the 8 November 1998 referendum owing to non-fulfilment of the residence requirement, but must be able to prove that their absence was due to family, professional or medical reasons;
> They must enjoy customary civil status or, having been born in New Caledonia, they must have their main moral and material interests in the territory;
> Having one parent born in New Caledonia, they must have their main moral and material interests in the territory;
> They must be able to prove 20 years' continuous residence in New Caledonia on the date of the referendum or by 31 December 2014 at the latest;
> Having been born before 1 January 1989, they must have been resident in New Caledonia from 1988 to 1998;
> Having been born on or after 1 January 1989, they must have reached voting age on the date of the referendum and have one parent who fulfilled the conditions for participation in the referendum of 8 November 1998.

[133] Blay (1988), pp. 863–865.

[134] A/RES/42/79, *Question of New Caledonia* 4 December 1987.

By this legislation, the question of the non-Kanak residents of New Caledonia has been resolved through residency requirements. All inhabitants of Kanak ethnic origin have been automatically enfranchised (alineas d and e), as the concept of "customary civil status" refers to the Kanak people. For the Caldoche and other non-Kanak residents, residency requirements of 10 and 20 years, respectively, have been imposed.

If any voter can prove to have resided in New Caledonia between 1988 and 1998, he will be eligible to vote in any future referendum. This is specified for two groups of people. For those who were old enough to vote in the referendum for the Nouméa Accord, the eligibility in this referendum is re-imposed (alineas a and b). The legal basis for the first referendum on the approval of the Nouméa Accord, 8 November 1998, was provided by Article 76 of the French Constitution, which determined the electorate by referring to Article 2 of Law No. 88-1028 of 9 November 1988 (also determined in Article 6.3 of the Nouméa Accord). The article stated that "persons registered on the electoral rolls for the territory on that date and resident in New Caledonia since 6 November 1988 shall be eligible to vote". The people in this group are exempted from this residency requirement if their absence was due to family, professional or medical reasons.

For younger persons, those who had not reached the voting age by 8 November 1998, a continuous residency between 1988 and 1998 was specified as a condition. For the youngest group, those who were born after 1 January 1989, a requirement of having at least one parent fulfilling the conditions to vote in the referendum of 1998 was imposed.

In addition, if a potential voter's status does not fit any of the above-said possibilities, he may still vote in any future referendum if he can prove 20 years of continuous residence in New Caledonia on the date of the referendum or by 31 December 2014 at the latest.

This legislation was contested in the Constitutional Council of France, but the foregoing requirements were upheld. The Council stated that "there is nothing to preclude the constituent authority from introducing new provisions in the text of the Constitution which, in the situations to which they refer, derogate from constitutional rules or principles". The possibility of a restricted ballot was provided by Article 77 of the Constitution. The residency requirements and other criteria as provided by Article 218 of the Law "merely gave effect" to this provision. For the Council, therefore, derogation from the principle of universal suffrage would be justified in specific circumstances, to the extent that formal procedures for constitutional amendment are observed.[135]

In fact, the international law of human rights guarantees the right to universal suffrage. For instance, the ICCPR says:

[135] Decision 99-410 DC of 15 MARCH 1999 Institutional Act concerning New Caledonia (Official Translation of *Décision n° 99-410 DC du 15 mars 1999*: *Loi organique relative à la Nouvelle-Calé donie*) (http://www.conseil-constitutionnel.fr/conseil-constitutionnel/root/bank_mm/anglais/a99410dc.pdf. Retrieved 15 August 2013).

> Every citizen shall have the right and the opportunity, without any of the distinctions mentioned in article 2 and without *unreasonable restrictions* ... (b) to vote and to be elected at genuine periodic elections which shall be by universal and equal suffrage and shall be held by secret ballot, guaranteeing the free expression of the will of the electors (Art. 25).

The residency requirement in New Caledonia was claimed to be in violation of this provision in *Gillot et al.*[136] However, the United Nations Human Rights Committee upheld the residency requirements: Law No. 99-209 was challenged on the ground, *inter alia*, that the residency requirement to vote in the New Caledonian referendums was a "discriminatory treatment between French citizens in terms of the right to vote".[137] The applicants also claimed that the 10 and 20 years of residency requirements for the 1998 and 2014 referendums were "excessive".

France invoked Article 53/3 of its Constitution and maintained that the referendums held in New Caledonia "should be limited to eliciting the opinion of, not the whole of the national population, but the persons 'concerned' with the future of a limited territory who prove that they possess certain specific characteristics".[138]

The Committee held;

> the criteria for the determination of the electorates for the referendums of 1998 and 2014 or thereafter are not discriminatory, but are based on objective grounds for differentiation that are reasonable and compatible with the provisions of the Covenant....The criteria treated differently persons in objectively different situations as regards their ties to New Caledonia.[139]

Therefore, the committee found the criteria "reasonable" since the concrete case involved the right to self-determination of the peoples. For the Committee, it was reasonable to limit the voting right to the persons "concerned". In short, the Committee found no discriminatory elements in the criteria to vote in New Caledonian referendums.

Finally, the Committee also decided on whether the 10 and 20 years of residency requirements were excessive in length. In this vein, the Committee said[140]:

> The cut-off points set for the referendum of 1998 and referendums from 2014 onwards are not excessive inasmuch as they are in keeping with the nature and purpose of these ballots, namely a self-determination process involving the participation of persons able to prove sufficiently strong ties to the territory whose future is being decided. This being the case, these cut-off points do not appear to be disproportionate with respect to a decolonization process involving the participation of residents who, over and above their ethnic origin or political affiliation, have helped, and continue to help, build New Caledonia through their sufficiently strong ties to the territory.

---

[136] *Gillot et al. v. France*, Communication No. 932/2000, Views of 15 July 2002 U.N. Doc. A/57/40 at 270 (2002).

[137] *Gillot et al. v. France*, para. 3.3.

[138] *Gillot et al. v. France*, para. 8.3.

[139] *Gillot et al. v. France*, para. 13.16.

[140] *Gillot et al.* para. 14.7.

The foregoing decision was referred to and upheld by the European Court of Human Rights in *Py v. France*.[141] In this case, the same law was alleged to be in violation of Article 3 of Protocol No. 1.[142] In its defense, France submitted that "The residence criterion pursued a legitimate aim and was not disproportionate. The ballots should reflect the will of the population 'concerned' and that their results should not be affected by mass voting by recent arrivals in the territory who did not have strong ties with it."[143] The Court upheld this argument. The Court also observed that the 10-year residence requirement for the 1998 referendum had proved to be functional in alleviating the violent dispute in the territory. This being the case and considering also it was in "a transitional phase prior to the acquisition of full sovereignty", it was held that restrictions on the voting rights were justifiable in terms of "local requirements" as provided by Article 56 of the European Convention of Human Rights. Considering these factors, the Court found that the residence requirement pursued a "legitimate aim".[144]

7.4.4 Non-native, Non-residents

In most cases, sovereignty referendums inherently prohibit the franchising of non-native and non-residents. On some occasions, though, the voting rights of non-natives and non-residents come legitimately into question. There may be two situations related to this argument. The first is for populations who have lived for a certain period of time in the related area and claim interest in the future of it. For example, among the post-WWI referendums in Schleswig and Upper Silesia, non-natives who had lost their residence in the referendum area were conferred the right to vote, if loss of residence had been due to expulsion.[145]

The second situation is where voting rights of a population outside of the referendum area concerns people who reside in an adjacent territory. This argument appears mostly during the regional articulation of autonomy or secession demands. From this point of view, the question of the voting rights of the people, who were neither born nor resident in the area, is closely related to the delimitation of the outer borders of the referendum area. From the territorial point of view, the question deals with whether the inhabitants of one territory are entitled to vote in the sovereignty referendum of another territory. In other words, whether voting rights should be limited only to the inhabitants of a concerned region or be extended to the

[141] *Py. v. France*, no. 66289/01, 2005-I, ECtHR.

[142] "The High Contracting Parties undertake to hold free elections at reasonable intervals by secret ballot, under conditions that will ensure the free expression of the opinion of the people in the choice of the legislature".

[143] *Py. v. France*, para. 21.

[144] *Py. v. France*, paras. 52 and 61–64.

[145] Wambaugh (1933), p. 477.

population of the rest of a nation state or historically established territory. However, from a human point of view, the question of whether the right to vote may be conferred upon people who were not born, have never resided or have never been to the territory in question is pertinent. In France, the French electorate, according to Article 11 of the French Constitution, voted for the law following the Evian Agreements granting self-determination to Algeria. This was explained by the fact that Algeria was a French *département* and therefore an integral part of the Republic of France. Since the secession of a constituent part of French soil meant a constitutional change, it required the consent of the whole French people. [146] In Northern Ireland, the argument was this time in favour of the whole nation outside of the border of the country to which Northern Ireland belonged. Here, while the political branch of the IRA known as Sinn Fein claimed that all the inhabitants of Ireland should vote, Northern Ireland Unionists and the British Government asserted that only the inhabitants of Northern Ireland should have that right.[147]

From the above, it may be inferred that the theoretical basis of the practice of consulting the people who have no natal or residential connections with the related territory is the doctrine of territorial inviolability.[148] Its roots may be traced back to 1359, when in an agreement about the cession of Guayenne to England it was required that not only the representatives of the region but also the representatives of all of France be called upon to decide.

In a similar perspective, we may refer to the social contract theories regarding the constitutional change of a country. Whenever there is a change to a state's territory, including both separation and adhesion, there is also a change in the social contract, and therefore the consent of all interested people should be obtained.[149] This approach may be seen in the Quebec Secession Reference, which held that an eventual secession of Quebec may only be realised through a formal amendment to the Federal Constitution:

> Quebec could not, despite a clear referendum result, purport to invoke a right to self-determination to dictate the terms of the proposed secession to the other parties to the federation. The democratic vote, by however strong a majority, would have no legal effect on its own and could not push aside the principles of federalism and the rule of law, the rights of individuals and minorities, or the operation of democracy in the other provinces or in Canada as a whole.[150]

[146] Dobelle (1996), pp. 54–59.

[147] He (2002), p. 89.

[148] Rudrakumaran (1990), p. 50.

[149] Rudrakumaran (1990), p. 50.

[150] Reference re Secession of Quebec, [1998] 2 S.C.R. 217–244.

7.5 Designation of the Voting Units

There are two main issues relating to the designation of voting units. The first concerns the plausibility of dividing the referendum area into numerous districts or constituencies. Such a division may be necessary in cases of ethnic heterogeneity within the referendum area, where corresponding voting may provide clues for the referendum administration regarding preferences about the sovereignty issue under debate. If districts are too small, however, it may carry with it the risk of undermining the secrecy of the vote, thus inviting reprisals.[151]

The second question is whether the territory should be treated as a single entity or be divided into more than one zone. This problem appears in those territories where there is an interpenetration of rival nations and/or ethnic groups and each ethnic group claims a majority in its respective regions, but where one ethnic group is inevitably in the majority within the referendum area as a whole. In this situation, defining the voting units may ultimately determine the results. In such cases, there should be a fair balance between the concerns for territorial integrity and minority rights. For example, in the case of Upper Silesia, the region was a territory under German rule but with a majority Polish population at the time of the referendum in 1921. Two sequential votes were realised in this context. In the first vote, the people were asked which country they wanted to join. The result was 60 % for Germany and 40 % for Poland. Taking into account the results, the League of Nations proposed a border, and this was put to a second vote. In the Schleswig Referendum, the contested area was divided into two zones. While the first zone was overwhelmingly Danish, the second had a considerable German population. The vote was firstly held in the pro-Danish zone 1 and then the pro-German zone 2. These zones decided to join Denmark and Germany, respectively.[152]

In British Togoland, the Visiting Mission dispatched by the General Assembly proposed that the region should be divided into four units from north to south "in order to ensure the greatest possible measure of satisfaction for the aspirations of the populations" and that in each region the international status should be decided by a majority vote. The Mission argued that this division met the racial and linguistic characteristics as well as the current opinions of the territory, in that each unit presented a certain degree of unity in ethnicity and opinion. However, the firm intention of the UK to unify the territory with the Gold Coast prevailed, and the General Assembly decided to hold the referendum as a single unit. In the referendum, the voters were asked whether they wanted to unify with the Gold Coast or continue being part of the trusteeship. The result was 63 % in favour of Gold Coast, which later became Ghana. However, detailed counts of the votes showed that in the southern districts the unification proposition received only 44 %.

[151] Farley (1986), p. 86.

[152] Laponce (2001), pp. 41–47.

Notwithstanding this clear regional difference in preferences, the General Assembly approved the unification of the territory as a whole to the Gold Coast.[153]

In British Cameroons, during the British Mandate, the territory was administered under two subunits within Nigeria. While Southern Cameroon was an autonomous unit under the Federal System of Nigeria, Northern Cameroon was a mere administrative unit in another Nigerian region. The report of the Visiting Mission concerning the voting units stated that given the contending regional, linguistic and cultural preferences of the people of Northern and Southern Cameroons, separate referendums should be held in each territory. This view was endorsed by the General Assembly and endorsed in its resolution.[154] The General Assembly also decided that the referendum would be held on different dates and that different choices would be offered. While the inhabitants of Southern Cameroons would be asked whether they wanted to join Nigeria or Cameroon, the Northerners were asked to decide between joining Nigeria and continuing their trusteeship status.[155] However, the General Assembly was not satisfied with the first referendum that was held in the North, resulting in a bare majority in favour of continuing trusteeship. A second referendum was held in both parts of the territory, this time asking the same question (Nigeria or Cameroon?). In the North, the result was in favour of Nigeria, whereas in the South it was in favour of Republic of Cameroon.[156]

Comparing the two opposing practices in designating voter units in the Cameroons and Togo, the importance of the determination of voter districts is clearly visible. In the case of Togo, the creation of a single unit resulted in the whole entity joining Ghana, despite the clear majority of the South for the opposite option, whereas in British Cameroon, the division of the territory according to the heterogeneous population configuration allowed a more consensual way of deciding the future of the territory. This shows that in cases of ethnically differentiated and concentrated regions within a referendum zone, it is essential to fairly take this into account and create voting units accordingly.

Moreover, one may also find the legal basis of such a configuration in international law. This may be observed by referring to simultaneous referendums held in the case of Cyprus, where in the face of distinct and internationally recognised ethnic groups international law required a majority of the voters within each community for the referendum to be valid. Additionally, in the case of Western Sahara, the International Court of Justice "implicitly" acknowledged the need for the consent of each ethnic group to determine the international status of the territory.

---

[153] Sureda (1973), pp. 154–163; A/RES/1044 (XI): The UN General Assembly Resolution of 13 December 1956, on "*The future of* Togoland *under British administration*".

[154] A/RES/1350(XIII): The UN General Assembly Resolution of 13 March 1959 "*The future of the Trust Territory of the Cameroons under United Kingdom administration*".

[155] The question for North Cameroon was included in Resolution No: 1350 (XIII), whereas the question for South was included in the General Assembly Resolution of No: 1352(XIV).

[156] Sureda (1973), pp. 163–168; General Assembly Resolution of 12 December 1959, No.: 1473 (XIV).

On the other hand, in the context of decolonisation, there may be attempts by the metropolitan states to arbitrarily zone territories at the expense of the territorial integrity of a self-determination unit. This method may be used as a gerrymandering tactic to obtain the desired results of the metropolitan states. It is worth making the point at this juncture that in international law it is the *prima facie* rule that a distinct self-determination unit should be granted statehood as a whole. In this context, the General Assembly "Reaffirm(ed) the necessity of scrupulously respecting the national unity and territorial integrity of a colonial territory at the time of its accession of independence".[157]

Therefore, in a decolonisation process, the potential impairment of the territorial integrity of a self-determination unit has always met with the distrust of the international community—disapproving any separation of the territory into self-determination units unless there is a clear expression of the local population.[158] This situation may be illustrated by the case of Mayotte, which is the subject of a long-standing territorial dispute between France and Union of the Comoros. Still, insisting on the treatment of a given territory as a whole may undermine the principle of self-determination. Indeed, forcing a bunch of disparate people to become a nation may well be contrary to the principle of self-determination. This problem arose during the decolonisation of the Trust Territories of the Pacific Islands. The dispute concerned whether the TTPI should have been treated as a single territory. The US and the UN tended to treat the territory as a whole and wished to constitute one state. Yet, as shown in the previous chapter, the wish of the inhabitants of the territory prevailed, and four different states were created in the region.[159]

7.6 Formulation of the Ballot Question

Formulation of the ballot question is of crucial importance in ensuring the accuracy and the credibility of the referendum.[160] The ballot should be constructed so as to enable voters to make a choice that truly reflects their personal preference. For a referendum to be a genuine expression of the wishes of the people, the questions posed in the referendum should accurately express the opposing views of the different tendencies in the territory.[161] The ballot paper and the question have to be as clear and unequivocal as possible for voters. "The propositions or questions should seek to achieve a balance between brevity, clarity and simplicity on the one

[157] A/RES 34/91: The UN General Assembly Resolution of 12 December 1979 on the "*Question of the islands of Glorieuses, Juan de Nova, Europa and Basses de India*".

[158] Crawford (2006), pp. 333–336.

[159] Roman (2006), p. 219; Keitner and Reisman (2003), p. 37.

[160] Héraud (1983), p. 241.

[161] Sureda (1973), p. 306.

hand, and full and accurate descriptions of the issue(s), in order that voters can make an informed choice."[162] As Moore suggests, "a clear question is justifiable both in terms of democratic accountability and requirement of fairness".[163] At the individual level, "micro fairness" may refer to the true reflection of an individual's preference about the issue in question. The "macro fairness" implies producing "a final result which translates, with minimum distortion, the aggregation of individual choices".[164]

The problem of the formulation of the question to be presented to voters may display three interrelated issues. Firstly, the wording should be clear and free of ambiguity:

> The clarity of the question is a crucial aspect of voters' freedom to form an opinion. The question must not be misleading; it must not suggest an answer, particularly by mentioning the presumed consequences of approving or rejecting the proposal; voters must be able to answer the questions asked solely by yes, no or a blank vote; and it must not ask an open question necessitating a more detailed answer.[165]

Secondly, the voters should not be forced to vote for more than one option, which are disparately included in a single question. This is the rule of unity of content (or "single subject rule", as called in the United States): "...there must be an intrinsic connection between the various parts of each question put to the vote, in order to guarantee the free suffrage of the voter, who must not be called to accept or refuse as a whole provision without an intrinsic link". [166]

Finally, the ballot should not be formulated in a manner that favours the *status quo*. This problem may be observed in ballots where there are more than two options, e.g., A, B and C, where option A favours the *status quo* and B and C refer to two differing options against the *status quo*. Such a formulation of the ballot question inherently favours the *status quo* since the anti-status quo votes are divided.[167] This is the case in Puerto Rico, where despite several referendums the issue of sovereignty remains unresolved.

According to the method used in post-WWI referendums, there were two separate ballot papers, each of which contained the name of the alternative countries. The voters were given both of these papers and were told to put both of them into envelopes; the ballot of their preferred country was untouched and the other ripped up. There were no pens or pencils used in this process, preventing any

---

162 Gay (1999), p. 24.

163 Moore (2000), p. 247.

164 Gay (1999), p. 25.

165 European Commission for Democracy Through Law (Venice Commission). "*Code of Good Practice on Referendums.*" Study No. 371/2006, 20 January 2009. CDL-AD(2007)008rev. Para. 15.

166 European Commission for Democracy Through Law. (Venice Commission). "*Code of Good Practice on Referendums.*" Study No. 371/2006, 20 January 2009. CDL-AD(2007)008rev. Para. 15.

167 Héraud (1983), p. 241.

controversy as to whether the voter's mark was clear or not. This system was also useful, considering the large numbers of illiterate voters, since the ballot papers included the flags, colours or symbols indicating the countries of option. Overall, this method proved to be effective by providing clarity and by preventing any potential electoral fraud by persons waiting outside the polling office asking for ballot papers by bribing and intimidating voters.[168]

In decolonisation referendums where the UN was decisive, UN resolutions have generally formulated the wording of questions, by considering the views of the major groups in the relevant territory.[169] In British Cameroons, the Visiting Mission, after having met the leaders of the different political parties, discovered the presence of two groups with diametrically opposed views. On the one side, there were those who wanted to be a region in an independent Nigeria, and the other side wanted union with independent French Cameroons. The contending parties, however, could not agree on the subsequent wording of their views.[170] The General Assembly asked the parties to agree on alternatives to put forward in the referendum.[171] The parties agreed on a wording and agreed to put off the referendum in Southern Cameroon to 1962. Notwithstanding this agreement, the UN decided to hold the referendum in both parts of the territory, endorsing its own version of the ballot question.[172]

A short question, set on a Yes/No basis, may often be considered appropriate as it provides brevity, simplicity and clarity. However, in some cases, such a framing reflects only the most extreme views and would thus be in violation of the rule of unity of content, potentially forcing those with "diametrically opposed views" to vote the same way. Putting a set of rules concerning sovereignty under a treaty or legislation poses such a problem. For example, the referendum on devolution in the UK presented such a feature. The question was formulated as "Do you want the provisions of the Scotland Act 1978 to be put into effect?" The supporters of independence and supporters of a different version of autonomy, differing from that of the government, were forced to choose between an alternative they did not want and the *status quo*. Similarly, in the referendum in Northern Ireland in 1998, voters were asked to vote on the Belfast Agreement where both communities were protesting against different aspects of it.[173]

---

[168] Farley (1986), pp. 115–116.

[169] Beigbeder (1994), p. 144.

[170] While one party wanted the question to be "between separation from Nigeria or Remaining in it", the other one wanted the choice to be between "continued association with Nigeria or Unity with an independent French Cameroons". Sureda (1973), p. 305.

[171] General Assembly Resolution of 13 March 1959, No: 1350 (XIII).

[172] Official options: "a) Do you wish to achieve independence by joining the independent Federation of Nigeria or b) Do you wish to achieve independence by joining the independent Republic of Cameroon?" A/RES/1352/(XIV): The UN General Assembly Resolution of 16 October 1959, on "*The future of the Trust Territory of the Cameroons under United Kingdom administration: organization of the plebiscite in the southern part of the Territory*".

[173] Gay (1999), p. 25.

Another problem, common to the framing of propositions in sovereignty referendums, is the style of wording of a specific proposition. In Quebec, the wording was strategic in that secessionist politicians worded the ballot proposals ambiguously in order to appeal to all segments of society. Despite the outspoken separatist agenda of Parti Quebecois, both referendums in 1980 and 1995 avoided a clear statement of secession or independence. The ballot question of the 1980 referendum was as follows[174]:

> The Government of Quebec has made public its proposal to negotiate a new agreement with the rest of Canada based on the equality of nations; this agreement would enable Quebec to acquire the exclusive power to make its laws, levy its taxes and establish relations abroad – in other words, sovereignty- and at the same time to maintain with Canada an economic association including a common currency; no change in political status resulting from these negotiations will be effected without approval by the people through another referendum; on these terms, do you give the Government of Quebec the mandate to negotiate the proposed agreement between Quebec and Canada?

This formulation of the 1980 referendum was considered by many observers as "a potentially winning formula", as it ensured "maintaining an economic association including a common currency" and it only asked for "a mandate to negotiate an agreement with the rest of Canada", instead of a straight forward declaration of independence.[175]

As to the 1995 referendum, the question was fairly short but no less confusing than the previous referendum of 1980:[176]

> Do you agree that Quebec should become sovereign after having made a formal offer to Canada for a new economic and political partnership within the scope of the bill respecting the future of Quebec and of the agreement reached on June 12 1995?

Monahan notes that this question was misleading because it linked sovereignty with a new political partnership with Canada.[177] Also, the term "sovereign" was not as clear as, for example, "independent", "independence", "secession", etc. "The formal offer" is also a vague concept erroneously implying a last offer given by the Quebec government before gaining independence, which would not have been constitutionally or politically possible.[178] Thus, this proposition of Quebec sovereignty with an offer of political and economic partnership with Canada was prone to

---

[174] http://www.c2d.ch/detailed_display.php?lname=votes&table=votes&page=1&parent_id=&sublinkname=results&id=39152. Retrieved 11 November 2012.

[175] LeDuc (2003), p. 104.

[176] http://www.c2d.ch/detailed_display.php?lname=votes&table=votes&page=1&parent_id=&sublinkname=results&id=39218. Retrieved 11 November 2012.

[177] Monahan (2000), p. 15.

[178] Globus (1996), pp. 148–151.

be a “nebulous project”.[179] “The question was as near meaningless as one could get.” There was “no clarification”, and it was “too abstract”.[180]

Consequently, there was a great degree of confusion among the Quebec voters as to the content and possible future outcome of the results. Many knew that the winning of a “Yes” vote would result in the independence of Quebec, while a “No” would mean a change, albeit a change that was vague in content concerning the relationship between Quebec and the Federal Government. In the eye of Quebec voters, the government “deliberately obfuscated the question to hide its separatist agenda”. In an opinion poll of August 1999, 61 % of Quebecois considered the question to be unclear. The same poll also pointed out that 93 % of the participants thought that the wording of the future referendum should be clearer.[181]

The strategic wording of the Quebec Government met with continuous objections by the Federal Authorities. The Canadian Supreme Court ruled in 1998 that if in a province of Canada the people demonstrated a will of secession via referendum, the central government and other provinces of the federation would have the obligation to negotiate that question only if the question of the referendum is free of ambiguity.[182] Following this decision, the Federal Assembly adopted the Clarity Act, laying down the basic rules for a future Quebec referendum. The Quebec National Assembly responded to that by legislation Bill 99: “to reaffirm the right of the Quebec people to exercise self determination on their own”.[183]

Regarding the question asked, the aim of the Clarity Act was to ensure a clear question on a future referendum about secession. It prescribed that in the case of referendum in Quebec, the question excludes “other possibilities in addition to the secession of the province from Canada, such as economic or political arrangements with Canada, *that obscure direct expression* of the will of the population of that province, on whether the province should cease to be a part of Canada”. Thus, according to the Clarity Act, “Clarity quite simply meant secession and nothing else”.[184] It is apparent that the Clarity Act was a strategic manoeuvre of the Federal Assembly to block the Quebec movement on its way to secession. It is clearly visible from the wording that the Act with a retrospective view to the past two referendums tries to overcome any possible strategic wording in a future referendum. In addition to this, “these requirements go beyond the principles mandated by the Supreme Court”.[185] There is no doubt that by defining the clarity in such a

[179] “Stephane Dion, Referendums on Secession and Requirement for Clarity: Examples From Northern Europe, Reykjavik, Iceland, 5 August, 1999”, (http://www.pco-bcp.gc.ca/aia/index.asp?lang=eng&page=archive&sub=speeches-discours&doc=19990805-eng.htm. Retrieved 11 November 2012).

[180] Globus (1996), p. 151.

[181] Globus (1996), p. 150.

[182] *Reference re Secession of Quebec*, *[1998] 2 S.C.R. 217*; Bienvenu (1999), pp. 1–66.

[183] Lynch (2005), p. 507.

[184] Lynch (2005), p. 507.

[185] Monahan (2000), p. 30.

rigorous way, the Federal Assembly sought to "circumscribe efforts of the PQ to appeal to 'soft' sovereignists through ambiguous questions that maintained some links with Canada".[186]

A similar pattern of vague wording to appeal to volatile or moderate voters may be noted in the Tatar Referendum (1992). Before the vote, the formulation of the question was subject to lengthy debates between different political camps in the Tatar Assembly. The block that advocated remaining in Russia proposed a straightforward question—"Are you in favour of Tatarstan seceding from the Russian Federation?"—expecting that such a question would lead to rejection. At the end, the indirect question prevailed, which was framed as, "Do you agree that the republic of Tatarstan is a sovereign state, a subject of international law, building its relations with the Russian Federation and other republics and states on the basis of treaties between equal partners?" The vague wording was a part of Tatar Leader Shamiev's strategy to gain the support of both the Tatar and Russian communities. The referendum was accepted, undoubtedly thanks to this vague wording securing votes from all parties subject to the question. The Tatar Nationalists thought they had voted for independence. The consent of pro-autonomy Russians and Tatars, on the other hand, was largely due to the fact that they were convinced that they were voting for greater local control.[187]

Another question that was criticised because of its unclear wording was that of the USSR's all-union referendum stating, "Do you consider necessary the preservation of the Union of Soviet Socialist Republics as a renewed federation of equal sovereign republics, in which the rights and freedoms of the individual and of the nationality will be guaranteed?"[188]

One contradiction, for example, was the term "renewed federation", which proved difficult for the voters to understand and moreover was confusing by asking for the "preservation" of something that had been "renewed". Furthermore, no mechanism was made known as to how this so-called renewal could be accomplished. The term "equal sovereign republics" was also open to misunderstandings concerning the status of the republics and the power ceded to them in relation to the Union. Finally, the last clause about guaranteeing the rights and freedoms of individuals of any nationality did not have a concrete legal meaning.[189] Some republics found the wording of the question so unsatisfactory that they modified its application on their territory. Most of them emphasised the sovereignty of their respective republics. In local application, the question was reshaped or changed to protect regional interests. Only Azerbaijan, Belorussia, Tadjikistan and

[186] Lynch (2005), pp. 507–508.

[187] Giuliano (2000), p. 311.

[188] "Do you consider necessary the preservation of the Union of Soviet Socialist Republics as a renewed federation of equal sovereign republics, in which the rights and freedoms of the individual and of the nationality will be guaranteed?" (http://soviethistory.org/index.php?page=subject&SubjectID=1991march&Year=1991. Retrieved 15 September 2013).

[189] Brady and Kaplan (1994), p. 187.

Turkmenistan presented the referendum question to their citizens in its original version. Brady and Kaplan suggest that the "referendum question provided plenty of ambiguity, and it seems that Gorbachev wanted it that way".[190] Therefore, it could be argued that this style of wording was deliberately preferred by Gorbachev amidst the political turbulence wherein the USSR itself was in the ewe of dissolution.

In New Caledonia, the wording of the question, as specified by Law no. 86-844 of 17 July 1986, was brought before the Constitutional Council.[191] Article I of the law under consideration formulated the ballot question as follows: "Voulez–vous que la Nouvelle–Calédonie accède à l'indépendance ou demeure au sein de la République française avec un statut dont les éléments essentiels ont été portés à votre connaissance?" Two options were offered to the electorate: (1) "Je veux que la Nouvelle–Calédonie accède à l'indépendance" and (2) "Je veux que la Nouvelle–Calédonie demeure au sein de la République française".

The applicants alleged that the foregoing formulation was unconstitutional, given the ambiguity of the question. Firstly, the wording of the question was misleading since contrary to what it implied, the so-called basic elements of the law had not yet been determined. Therefore, citizens were being called upon to vote on a situation that had not yet been finalised. Secondly, it was also alleged that the question was contrary to the rule of unity of content. Indeed, for the applicants, a referendum could be deemed constitutional if and only if it included a pure and simple question: whether New Caledonia should be independent. The "yes" would lead to independence while the "no" vote would maintain the *status quo*. On the contrary, the formulation of the question under review would force the voters who wanted to remain in France to show assent to an ambiguous new status. This would disenfranchise those who wanted to maintain the *status quo*. Likewise, the same question included two separate subject matters under two different constitutional provisions. On the one hand, the question pertained to the accession to independence under Article 53/3 of the French Constitution, while on the other hand, a negative response to the option of independence involved the definition of the status of the territory pursuant to Article 74 of the Constitution. The applicants asserted that there was no provision in the Constitution that would permit the patchwork jumble of these two clearly different procedures.

Following these arguments, the Constitutional Council considered the case in the light of the second paragraph of the Preamble to the Constitution of 1958, which specifies the self-determination of the peoples of the overseas territories and their freely expressed wishes, as well as the aforementioned Article 53/3 of the Constitution. The Council coined two principles that should be observed in self-

[190] Brady and Kaplan (1994), p. 187.

[191] *Décision n° 87-226 DC du 02 juin 1987 Loi organisant la consultation des populations intéressées de la Nouvelle-Calédonie et dépendances prévue par l'alinéa premier de l'article 1er de la loi n° 86-844 du 17 juillet 1986 relative à la Nouvelle-Calédonie*. (http://www.conseil-constitutionnel.fr/conseil-constitutionnel/francais/les-decisions/depuis-1958/decisions-par-date/1987/87-226-dc/decision-n-87-226-dc-du-02-juin-1987.8337.html. Retrieved 18 January 2013).

determination referendums in overseas territories: the fairness (*loyauté*) and clarity (*clarté*) of the referendum question. In this way, the Council noted that "…la question posée aux populations intéressées doit satisfaire à la double exigence de loyauté et de clarté de la consultation…la question posée aux votants ne doit pas comporter d'équivoque, notamment en ce qui concerne la portée de ces indications". In the light of these prerequisites, the Council held that the formulation of the ballot question was ambiguous, as it was prone to mislead the voters into the false idea that the content of the proposed law of New Caledonia had already been determined. For these reasons, the Council found the following phrase in the proposed ballot question unconstitutional: "avec un statut dont les éléments essentiels ont été portés à votre connaissance".

In Puerto Rico, the question of the wording of the ballot is a matter of political controversy. The discussion revolves around the possible options to be included, along with statehood and independence. This may be sensed by reviewing two alternative federal bills on the issue: the Self-Determination Act and the Puerto Rico Democracy Act.

The inclusion of a "new or modified commonwealth" option was promoted by the Self-Determination Act.[192] The Act did not specify the legal nature of this option. Nevertheless, it may be deduced from the past and current status debates of Puerto Rico that this status implies a modification of the current status, with an increased autonomy of Puerto Rico as exempted from the territorial clause of the U.S. Constitution.[193]

The pro-commonwealth NPP and its supporters maintain that the enhanced commonwealth status would accommodate the independence and statehood and thus "avoids the hard choice that the people of Puerto Rico ultimately need to make between US statehood and independence". The NPP highlights the importance of preserving a realistic and convenient relationship between the United States and Puerto Rico and maintains that inclusion of the modified commonwealth status in a future status referendum would "offer a fair, democratic and inclusive means for the people of Puerto Rico to Express their voice and exercise their right of self-determination".[194]

Alternatively, the first version of the Puerto Rico Democracy Act of 2007 (H.R 900) provided two options on the ballot after an initial referendum on the change of the *status quo*: "statehood" and "sovereign nation". The statehood option was accompanied by the following explanation: "Puerto Rico should be admitted as a State of the Union, on equal footing with the other States." The option of "sovereign nation" would allow "Puerto Rico (to) become a sovereign nation, either fully independent from or in free association with the United States under an

---

[192] *H.R. 1230 (110th)*: *Puerto Rico Self-Determination Act of 2007*, (http://www.gpo.gov/fdsys/search/pagedetails.action?packageId=BILLS-110hr1230ih. Retrieved 12 July 2011). Medina (2009–2010), p. 1086.

[193] Bea and Garrett (2010), p. 24; Medina (2009–2010), p. 1087.

[194] Medina (2009–2010), pp. 1087–1088.

international agreement that preserves the right of each nation to terminate the association".[195]

A changed version of the Democracy Act (of 2009-H.R. 2499) proposed three options in the second referendum, which would ensue after changing the *status quo*.[196] According to this bill, the options would appear as follows:

(1) Independence: Puerto Rico should become fully independent from the United States.
(2) Sovereignty in Association with the United States: Puerto Rico and the United States should form a political association between sovereign nations that will not be subject to the Territorial Clause of the United States Constitution.
(3) Statehood: Puerto Rico should be admitted as a State of the Union.

This version of the bill was contested during the hearings in the House of Representatives, as it did not contain the option of current status, Commonwealth.[197] An amendment for this purpose was put forward by Congresswoman Ms. Foxx. For her, the absence of the Commonwealth would disenfranchise a significant portion of Puerto Ricans since the majority opts for retaining that status, albeit in a modified version.[198] Congresswoman Ms. Velázquez, in support of the amendment, invoked past referendums in Puerto Rico to purport that Commonwealth status was the preferred status in Puerto Rico.[199] It was considered in this train of thought that it would be "grossly unfair" to exclude the Commonwealth option.[200]

A second critical statement during the hearings in the House about the configuration of the ballot question was that it was "designed to push the statehood agenda". It would "create artificial conditions that will enable statehood to win a popular vote in Puerto Rico" and thus "a manipulation of the process".[201] Regarding the Freely Associated States, Congressman Mr. Rangel said, "hardly anyone here knows what it means, especially the people of Puerto Rico".[202] In the face of the absence of Commonwealth as the most popular option and its replacement by an ambiguous "Freely Associated State", the wording of the ballot would unfairly favour the second most popular option: statehood.

---

[195] Medina (2009–2010), p. 1087.

[196] The text of the Act may be found at http://www.govtrack.us/congress/bills/111/hr2499/text. Retrieved 12 October 2013.

[197] *CONGRESSIONAL RECORD—HOUSE*, April 29, 2010 (http://www.gpo.gov/fdsys/pkg/CREC-2010-04-29/pdf/CREC-2010-04-29-pt1-PgH3029-3.pdf#page=1. Retrieved 12 October 2012).

[198] *CONGRESSIONAL RECORD—HOUSE*, April 29, 2010, H3029.

[199] *CONGRESSIONAL RECORD—HOUSE*, April 29, 2010, H3049.

[200] *CONGRESSIONAL RECORD—HOUSE*, April 29, 2010, H3042.

[201] *CONGRESSIONAL RECORD—HOUSE*, April 29, 2010, H3030, H3031 and H3033. The former Governor of Puerto Rico, Aníbal Acevedo-Vilá, had also denounced the Democracy Act (of 2007), as it was "biased toward US statehood and called for a process that would have distorted the will of the people of Puerto Rico" (Medina 2009–2010, p. 1087).

[202] *CONGRESSIONAL RECORD—HOUSE*, April 29, 2010, H3033.

In response to these criticisms, the sponsor of the act, Congressman Mr. Pierluisi asserted that the proposed method of two successive referendums would be "fair" and the first referendum to ask voters whether they wanted to retain the current relationship would be a "threshold question". It would resolve the long-lasting problem of "whether a majority consents to an arrangement that denies 4 million U.S. citizens the right to have a meaningful voice in making the laws that govern their lives". With respect to the triple configuration of the second ballot, he said that the options that were presented were

> only three non-territorial options that we can offer or include in this plebiscite in accordance with both U.S. law and international law. Those options are crystal clear. We don't need studies. We don't need to define them further than necessary: Statehood, independence, and free association. And for anybody who is concerned about the concept of free association, we've done it before. Marshall Islands, Micronesia, the Republic of Palau, those are free associated states with a relationship with the U.S.[203]

Congressman Mr. Rahall argued that adding to the second ballot the option of Commonwealth would "contradict the bill's intent". Giving the voters the choice of retaining *status quo* status soon after its rejection would serve to do nothing but confuse "the process and would likely cause an inconclusive outcome".[204]

Indeed, since its adoption in Puerto Rico, the legal content of the Commonwealth status has been a source of contention among Puerto Ricans. One of the most significant problems in this regard was the terminology used by several political actors. The Spanish term used in the Constitution of Puerto Rico is *Estado Libre Asociado*. It may be literally translated into English as "Associated Free State". This term is prone to confusion as it may erroneously imply the Freely Associated State under international law, where there are two sovereign nations. As previously mentioned, such a relationship exists between the United States and the former Trust Territories of the Pacific Islands, Micronesia, the Marshall Islands and Palau. The case of Puerto Rico does not fit in this framework, as it is considered to be a territory of the United States. Since the formation of Puerto Rico's current status, the translation of this term into English has been a source of contention. The PPD favoured the term *Estado Libre Asociado* (ELA) as it had a strong connotation of sovereignty and autonomy, whereas Federal Authorities felt uncomfortable with the direct translation of it into English because of the reasons mentioned above. Eventually, a compromise was reached by retaining the Spanish term ELA while using the term Commonwealth as its English version.[205]

On the other hand, the term "Commonwealth" is itself ambiguous. It is used in the formal names of four US States (Massachusetts, Pennsylvania, Virginia and

---

[203] *CONGRESSIONAL RECORD—HOUSE*, April 29, 2010, H3031.

[204] *CONGRESSIONAL RECORD—HOUSE*, April 29, 2010, H3042.

[205] Declet (2001), p. 33; *Puerto Rico Democracy Act of 2007*, (*Report by Mr RAHALL from the Committee on Natural Resources*), House of Representatives, 110th Congress 2nd Session, Report 110-597, April 22, 2008. (http://www.gpo.gov/fdsys/pkg/CRPT-110hrpt597/pdf/CRPT-110hrpt597pdf. Retrieved 15 July 2011).

Kentucky). Also, there is a "British Commonwealth" denoting the international organisation of former British colonies.[206] This term therefore does not signify a particular international status, but rather it is used in different contexts to connote different patterns of sovereignty relationships. Thus, the use of Commonwealth to define the status of Puerto Rico may be quite confusing. This indistinctness around the meaning is worsened when the PDP used the term to refer to its enhanced autonomy proposals. Consequently, the "Use of the word 'commonwealth' obscures the issue for many Puerto Ricans, who ask, is 'Commonwealth' a territorial status or something different? Does it refer to the status quo or to the PDP's enhanced autonomy proposal?" It is argued that this confusion over the connotation and importance of the term "commonwealth" has been a major factor in the current conundrum leading to the stalemate in resolution of the sovereignty status, both in Puerto Rico and the Congress.[207]

In fact, this problem may be described as a mere "symptom"[208] of the fundamental issue of whether the current status of Puerto Rico conforms to the international norms of self-determination, the substantive aspect of which issue has been dealt with previously. However, the confusion that it generates should not be overlooked. The controversy over the terminology and the legal content interactively contributes to the current problem. D'Estafano underlined this point: "ELA which aside from unconstitutional. . .and therefore not feasible in practice is ambiguous, written in extremely flexible language, without any clear content, full of phraseology".[209]

Another important lesson to be drawn from the experience of Puerto Rico may be that including more than one option in the ballot along with the *status quo* results in the obstruction of the process; the "No" votes always surpass the divided "Yes" votes, and thus the *status quo* wins. This problem may be overcome by two alternative methods. In the first method, the possibility of casting a vote of "double yes" may be provided to the voters. In this method, voters are asked three questions in the same ballot; the first two are the main questions and the third a subsidiary. The main questions ask whether the voters are in favour of the two options against the *status quo*. The voters may cast a yes vote for both options (first two questions) against the *status quo*. Then the voters may mark their preferences between the two options in the subsidiary question, this only being taken into consideration when both the first two questions gain the required majority. If both main questions fall

[206] Declet (2001), p. 34; *Puerto Rico Democracy Act of 2007* (*Report by Mr RAHALL from the Committee on Natural Resources*), House of Representatives, 110th Congress 2nd Session, Report 110-597, April 22, 2008. Retrieved on 15 July 2011 from http://www.gpo.gov/fdsys/pkg/CRPT-110hrpt597/pdf/CRPT-110hrpt597.pdf.

[207] *Puerto Rico Democracy Act of 2007*, (*Report by Mr RAHALL from the Committee on Natural Resources*), p. 5.

[208] Declet (2001), p. 35.

[209] d'Estefano (1968), pp. 55 and 107.

short of the required majority, the status quo wins.[210] The second method involves two separate questions in the same ballot (or in two separate referendums). The first question is on whether to change the status quo. This is the question of principle. In the second question, the voters may mark their preference between choices against the status quo. The second question may be either included in the same ballot, or two subsequent referendums may be held to his end.[211] As mentioned above, in the most recent referendum held in Puerto Rico on 6 November 2012, this method was applied. The voters were asked two questions on the same ballot. In the first question, the voters were asked whether they agreed "that Puerto Rico should continue to have its present form of territorial status" with the options of "yes" or "no". The second question asked regardless of their answer to the first question was to choose from three possible options: Statehood, Independence or a Sovereign Free Associated State. This triple formulation concurred with the above-stated proposal of Congressman Mr. Pierluisi by offering three different statuses in accordance with both US law and international law.[212]

References

Auer, A., Malinverni, G., & Hottelier, M. (2000). *Droit constitutionnel suisse: L'Etat* (Vol. I, II vols.). Berne: Staempfli Editions SA.

Bea, K., & Sam Garrett, R. (2010, May 19). *Political status of Puerto Rico: Options for congress.* http://www.hsdl.org/?view&did=24445. Retrieved 13 July 2012.

Beigbeder, Y. (1994). *International monitoring of plebiscites, referenda and national elections: Self-determination and transition to democracy.* Dordrecht/Boston: Martinus Nijhoff.

Bienvenu, P. (1999). Secession by constitutional means: Decision of the Supreme Court of Canada in the Quebec secession reference. *Journal of Public Law and Policy, 21*, 1–66.

Blay, S. K. N. (1988, August). Self-determination and the crisis in New Caledonia: The search for a legitimate self. *Asian Survey, 28*(8), 863–880.

Brady, H. E., & Kaplan, C. S. (1994). Eastern Europe and the former Soviet Union. In D. Butler & A. Ranney (Eds.), *Referendums around the world: The growing use of direct democracy* (pp. 174–218). New York: Macmillan.

Carter, C. (2011). The right to vote for non-resident citizens: Considered through the example of East Timor. *Texas International Law Journal, 46*, 655–674.

[210] This method is used in Switzerland to overcome a similar problem in popular initiatives due to the division of the yes votes between the original proposal and the counter-proposal offered by the Federal Assembly (Constitution of Switzerland Art 139 al.6); (Auer et al. 2000, p. 243).

[211] As mentioned in the previous chapter, in Puerto Rico, this latter is endorsed by the latest federal law proposals in the Congress.

[212] By way of contrast, the most recent president task force report (March 2011) had said that "removing the Commonwealth option would raise real questions about the vote's legitimacy". Nevertheless, the Task Force still retained the view that "the proposals that would establish a relationship between Puerto Rico and the Federal Government that could not be altered except by mutual consent... ..remain(ed) constitutionally problematic" *Report by the President's Task Force on Puerto Rico's Status* (March 2011), p. 26.

Castellino, J. (2000). *International law and self-determination: The interplay of the politics of territorial possession with formulations of post-colonial "National" identity*. The Hague: Martinus Nijhoff.
Cazala, J. (2006). L'Accession du Monténégro à L'indépendance. *Annuaire Français de Droit International, 52*, 160–177.
Crawford, J. (2006). *The creation of states in international law* (2nd ed.). Oxford: Clarendon Press.
Curless, G. (2011, February). Sudan's 2011 referendum on southern secession. *Ethnopolitics Papers*, 7, 1–24.
d'Estefano, M. A. (1968). *Puerto Rico: Analysis of a plebiscite*. La Habana: Tricontinental.
Dann, P., & Al-Ali, Z. (2006). The internationalized pouvoir constituant – Constitution-making under external influence in Iraq, Sudan and East Timor. *Max Planck Yearbook of United Nations Law, 10*, 423–463.
Declet, R. A. (2001). The mandate under international law for a self executing plebiscite on Puerto Rico's political status, and the right of U.S. resident Puerto Ricans to participate. *Syracuse Journal of International Law and Commerce, 28*, 19–60.
Dobelle, J.-F. (1996). Référendum et droit à l'autodétermination. *Pouvoirs, 77*, 41–60.
Dunbar, C. (2000). Saharan stasis: Status and future prospects of the Western Sahara conflict. *The Middle East Journal, 54*, i4.
Farley, L. T. (1986). *Plebiscites and sovereignty: The crisis of political illegitimacy*. London: Westview Press.
Gay, O. (1999). *Referendums: Recent developments research paper 99/30*. Official website of the UK Parliament, 16 March 1999. http://www.parliament.uk/commons/lib/research/rp99/rp99-030.pdf. Retrieved 05 May 2007.
Giuliano, E. (2000, April). Who determines the self in the politics of self determination?: Identity and preference formation in Tatarstan's nationalist mobilization. *Comparative Politics, 32*(3), 295–316.
Globus, P. (1996, Summer). Questioning the question: The Quebec referendum. *Et Cetera*, 148–151.
Grace, J., & Fischer, J. (2003). Enfranchising conflict-forced migrants: Issues, standards, and best practices participatory elections project (PEP) discussion paper No. 2. International Organization for Migration, 2003. http://www.geneseo.edu/~iompress/Archive/Outputs/Standards_Final.pdf. Retrieved 12 Aug 2012.
Hamon, F. (1995). *Le référendum: étude comparative*. Paris: L.G.D.J.
He, B. (2002). Referenda as a solution to the national-identity/boundary question: An empirical critique of the theoretical literature. *Alternatives, 27*, 67–97.
Héraud, G. (1983). Démocratie et autodétermination. In G. Héraud (Ed.), *Rechtsvergleichung, Europarecht und Staatenintegration: Gedächtnisschrift für Léontin-Jean Constantinesco*. Berlin, etc.: C. Heymann, cop.
Jenssen, A. T., & Listhaug, O. (2001). Voters' decisions in the Nordic EU referendums. In M. Mendelsohn & A. Parkin (Eds.), *Referendum democracy: Citizens, elites and deliberation in referendum campaigns içinde, düzenleyen*. Houndmills: Palgrave.
Keitner, C. I., & Reisman, W. M. (2003). Free association: The United States experience. *Texas International Law Journal, 39*, 1–64.
Kondoch, B. (2001). The United Nations administration of East Timor. *Journal of Conflict and Security Law, 6*(2), 245–265.
Kriesi, H. P. (2004). How citizens decide in direct-democratic votes: Experiences from Switzerland. *Portuguese Journal of Social Science, 3*(1), 3–13.
Laponce, J. A. (2001). National self-determination and referendums: The case for territorial revisionism. *Nationalism and Ethnic Politics, 7*(2), 33–56.
LeDuc, L. (2003). *The politics of direct democracy: referendums in global perspective*. Ontario, e.t.c.: Broadview Press.
Lynch, P. (2005). Scottish independence, the Quebec model of secession and the political future of the Scottish national party. *Nationalism and Ethnic Politics, 11*(4), 503–532.

Medina, L. E. (2010). An unsatisfactory case of self-determination: Resolving Puerto Rico's political status. *Fordham International Law Journal, 33*, 1048–1100.

Monahan, P. J. (2000, February). *Doing the rules an assessment of the Federal Clarity Act in light of the Quebec secession reference*, C.D Howe Institute. http://www.cdhowe.org/pdf/monahan-2.pdf. Accessed 01 Feb 2011.

Moore, M. (2000). The ethics of secession and a normative theory of nationalism. *Canadian Journal of Law and Jurisprudence, 13*(2), 225–250.

Morel, L. (2013). Referendum". In M. Rosenfeld & A. Sajo (Eds.), *The Oxford handbook of comparative constitutional law* (pp. 501–528). Oxford: Oxford University Press.

Napoli, L. (1998). The legal recognition of the national identity of a colonized people: The case of Puerto Rico. *Boston College Third World Law Journal, 18*, 159–194.

Roman, E. (2006). *The other American colonies*. Durham: Caroline Academic Press.

Rudrakumaran, V. (1990). The "Requirement" of plebiscite in territorial rapprochement. *Houston Journal of International Law, 12*, 23–54.

Stefanini, M. F.-R. (2004). *Le controle du référendum par la justice constitutionnelle*. Paris: Economica.

Sureda, A. R. (1973). *The evolution of the right of self-determination. A study of United Nations practice*. Leiden: Sijthoff.

Teles, P. G. (2002). *East Timor and international law: A contribution to the study of how the international legal order deals with the violations infringed upon it* (Non-published Ph.D. thesis presented to the University of Geneva, Geneva).

Wambaugh, S. (1920). *A monograph on plebiscites (with a collection of official documents)*. New York: Oxford University Press.

Wambaugh, S. (1933). *Plebiscites since the world war: With a collection of official documents*. Washington: Carnegie Endowment for International Peace.

Chapter 8
Conclusion

Abstract This chapter includes the conclusions reached in this study. These may be summarised as follows: first, the prestige of referendums in the resolutions of sovereignty issues both in international and national settings is in a constant state of growth. The common subject matters include independence, European integration, membership of North Atlantic Treaty Organization and devolution. This study on international law and comparative constitutional law shows that referendums have now become crucial elements of state creation and constitutional change that involve sovereignty disputes.

Wambaugh's seminal work on the post-WWI referendums starts with the following: "In its scant century and a half of history, the plebiscite as a means of determination of questions of sovereignty has suffered great fluctuations of fortune".[1] Today, one thing is for certain that such a vague and random view of the merit of sovereignty referendums, in both international and national forums, is now out of date. Referendums are increasingly used in modern politics, and the issue of sovereignty is no exception to this. Moreover, because they require a high degree of legitimacy, sovereignty questions tend more commonly to be the subject of referendum when compared to secondary political issues. In Europe, for example, leaving Italy and Switzerland aside, more than half of the total number of *de jure* and *de facto* referendums held so far have been related to the issue of sovereignty in some way. The subject matters have included independence, European integration, membership of NATO and devolution.

The use of referendums in the resolution of sovereignty disputes has evolved and improved in a consistent way from their initial use during the French Revolution. Indeed, after having consolidated their prestige following WWI, referendums have been the key elements during decolonisation and post-communist state creation. In addition to new democracies and colonial peoples that have been utilising referendums, the old Western democracies have been using them too while dealing with the questions of European integration and regional autonomy and secessionist

[1] Wambaugh (1933), p. 3.

İ.G. Şen, *Sovereignty Referendums in International and Constitutional Law*,
DOI 10.1007/978-3-319-11647-1_8

demands from the 1970s onwards. This shows us the peerless legitimating power of referendums whenever issues such as territorial change, independence of states and transfer of central state powers to supranational organisations or to regions are to be tackled. A properly held referendum, in these contexts, not only secures the present and future support of the relevant people to the resolution of any territorial or sovereignty conflict, but it also helps to ease the international tension, assuring recognition of the new international status of a given territory by the international community. Today we may see the referendum as an appropriate tool within both the national and the international domains and from both a sociological and moral perspective.

From this perspective, *pace* Luhmann, we may see the law as being cognitively open to its environment and having the capability of self-updating (i.e., creating new legal rules) when encountering new situations.[2] As a response to the ongoing demands from its environment (i.e., politics), the law has been quick to adopt the referendum into its toolbox for the resolution of territorial and sovereignty conflicts.

Historical evidence shows that initial *de jure* experiences of sovereignty referendums in international law were based on the bilateral treaties between two states on the cession of a territory from one party to another. The first bilateral treaty in this respect was between France and the Kingdom of Sardinia (predecessor of modern Italy), the treaty of Turin. Referendums were held in Savoy and Nice before their cession to France. Thereafter, bilateral treaties became the common legal documents that served as the legal base in the nineteenth century territorial alterations. Following on, multilateral treaties were used as the legal bases of the post-WWI referendums. The Paris Peace Treaties (Treaty of Versailles and Treaty of Saint-Germain) concluding the War stipulated the use of referendums in the reconfiguration of the borders of Germany, Poland, Denmark, Austria and Yugoslavia. After the Second World War, the UN Charter provided the legal base of referendums, to be decided upon by the General Assembly or other relevant body.

There are also newer actors in international law that may be party to a treaty or agreement stipulating the resolution of a territorial conflict and the relevant referendum. These non-state international personalities include the representatives of the non-self-governing territories and belligerent or separatist groups. To the former, we may give the example of the *Front de libération nationale kanak et socialiste* (FLNKS) in New Caledonia, which concluded the Nouméa Accord with France on the future referendum about the territory's fate. Belligerent groups outside the context of decolonisation may also be in play when an attempt at secession proves to be irreversible, and the international community and states are forced into the situation of having to recognise and accept these groups. This is the case in the Comprehensive Peace Agreement signed by the Government of Sudan and the Sudan People's Liberation Movement/Army.

Another important conclusion of our study is that recent developments in international law challenge the traditional view assuming that referendums are

[2] Salter (1997), p. 297; Habermas (1996), pp. XXII and 447.

not part of customary law. This may be discussed by considering, firstly, the decolonisation and then, secondly, the territorial changes in other contexts. In fact, one could legitimately argue that the concept of decolonisation was just an issue of the immediate period following WWII, the significance of which barely lasted until the 1960s or 1970s and might therefore be too old a topic to be relevantly discussed today. Yet the relics of this colonialism survive up until today with a list of 16 entities still retaining the status of non-self-governing territories. Furthermore, according to international law on decolonisation, the freely expressed wishes of the peoples concerned should be secured, if at least anything other than full-fledged independence is an option. Moreover, even if the relevant people opt for a dependent status, they still retain their right to self-determination, in which case international law requires a periodical and ongoing evaluation at different intervals. This is the case for the Republic of the Marshall Islands and the Federated States of Micronesia and Palau, each of which has the Compact of Free Association with the US.

There has also been some procrastination regarding the final resolution of the international status of certain territories since WWII. The case of East Timor, having been resolved as late as 2000 by referendum, is a significant example. Moreover, in Western Sahara, the question is still pending due to the controversy over the determination of the electoral body. To this general overview, one can also add the cases of Cyprus and Puerto Rico, both unresolved decolonisation issues where the formerly accepted international status has been challenged either by domestic or international actors. Today, these territories are waiting for a final resolution, and these processes will definitely include the need for referendum. Most recently, in a referendum held on the 6th of November 2012, the people of Puerto Rico chose to be recognised as a state of the United States. However, this referendum, as in others on the island, is a non-binding one and the question of statehood may only be concluded after the final decision of the US Congress, which has the final right to admit new states to the Union.

In short, the question of decolonisation is still a current issue, and the relevant international legal and political documents clearly show that it is now a customary rule that whenever there is a legal or political dispute on the international status of a decolonisation-related territory, legalising an international status other than independence requires some democratic decision process. The use of the referendum is thus a common state practice to ensure this democratic decision.

The same conclusion may be reached, not without argument but albeit with some very robust reasoning, for cases other than pure decolonisation such as cases of cession, secession, dissolution and recognition of states. The legally nihilist truism of effectiveness is still valid, obscuring the answer to the question as to whether a dissident region (in a nation state) has an inherent right to secede. Yet whenever there is the so-called effective power (which achieves the secession by mere force), it tends to clash with a very explicit *jus cogens* norm: the banning of an illegitimate attack upon the territorial integrity of states. Therefore, in this case, the referendum appears to be the chief element for resolution in international law. It gives the people the power of veto over dissolution, secession and cession of their state or territory, thus ensuring the negative right of self-determination.

Not only the legal status of sovereignty referendums but also the role and extent of the international community in the decision and administration process have been evolving and improving throughout history. The referendum's pre-eminence, as well as the accompanying principles for legitimacy, may now be revealed in both international politics and the ensuing legal and political documents. The progressive development of the role and function of the international community in the overcoming of territorial conflicts in general and in the referendums held in this context in particular may be observed, from the initial experiences to more recent and sophisticated cases such as in Western Sahara, East Timor, South Sudan, Cyprus and Montenegro.

Thus, referendums today constitute a vital element in the procedural framework of state creation in international law. It may be argued that democratic norms (and namely the doctrine of the consent of the governed) as the legitimate source of state creation have become the dominant maxims in international and national legal orders. This has resulted, firstly, in the hegemonic pro-referendum argument in the rhetoric of international politics; secondly, in its widespread presence in practice and in international and national legal documents; and, finally, in the firm pledge and commitment by states and other international actors to hold a referendum whenever the international status of a territory is in question.

It can be seen that, particularly in law, the doctrinal dichotomy of monist and dualist theories on the rapport between international law and constitutional law are now rendered obsolete. From this perspective, one may argue that there is a degree of co-ordination between international and constitutional laws.[3] For this reason, sovereignty referendums in constitutional law may be considered to be in a state of constant interaction with international law. Indeed, the current state of sovereignty referendums in contemporary constitutional law must be read in the light of the state-centred approach prevalent in international law and the tendency of states to internalise the referendum within the confines of their own national legal systems. The state practice element of international law (particularly in terms of decolonisation) turns out here to be a rich source of legal bases of referendums in comparative constitutional law.

The conclusion in this respect is that sovereignty referendums have essentially become widespread and indispensable elements in all of the countries, with their differing constitutional traditions, examined in this study. Almost all of the post-communist constitutions include some sort of the sovereignty referendum. In older democracies, France implemented this with its flexible wording of Articles 11 and 53 of its constitution. The implementations were not made without debate, however. The arbitrary use of Article 11 by the President and the decision of the Constitutional Council on Comoros that construed Article 53 as the legal base of decolonisation referendums divided the doctrine and caused a significant

[3] Brownlie (2003), pp. 33–34.

controversy. The constitutional reforms of 2003 regulating the status of the overseas territories of France and the prior special provision on New Caledonia in the French Constitution seem to aim, among other reasons, at an unequivocal legal base for all future referendums to be held in the process.

In the UK, the doctrine is in consensus about the political value of referendums as a new constitutional convention. Its legal value, however, remains indistinct since the principle of sovereignty of parliament still remains intact, and if one day parliament decides to ignore this convention it is by no means certain that a court could overrule such an act. On the other hand, this discussion seems pointless, given the fact that no majority in parliament would dare to undo the political mandate of a referendum.

The Quebec case shows that there may indeed be unwritten rules of the constitution and referendums may be subsumed under them. The significance of the Quebec case is that constitutional conventions became a concept, something more than just the subject of political or doctrinal debate. On the contrary, the key constitutional actor, the Federal Supreme Court of Canada, conferred referendums with a significant legal value. Indeed, one of the landmark outcomes of the secession reference on the possibility of secession of Quebec from Canada was this. Still, to remember the merits of the case, the referendum that had been unilaterally held by the Quebec Government was only taken as an initiating element of the negotiation process towards an eventual secession.

As to the lessons that may be drawn from the historical legacy of sovereignty referendums, we may loosely discern the ones that political wisdom imposes and the others, including the legal axioms, that may be sketched from comparative constitutional law and international law. Regarding the former, particularly, it may be recognised that referendums should be a complementary and finalising element of a more complex pattern of conflict resolution, including patient negotiations, agreement on an elite level and transitory phases. Indeed, experience shows that referendums carried out hastily have caused instability and a deepening of conflict. One may be reminded of the case of East Timor in this regard and the violence that erupted after the referendum, in which a progressive phase of autonomy was rejected by international actors. Also today, the unresolved status of Cyprus is due to the then Secretary General Kofi Annan's persistent move to hold a referendum in 2004, before key issues could be resolved at an elite level.

Parties should agree foremost on the holding of a referendum itself and then on the key issues to be resolved, such as the legal framework, the competences of the referendum administration, the neutralisation of the area, the timetable, finances, the ballot question and the post-referendum issues in an original agreement. Any region prior to a referendum should attain a consolidated state of peace and security before, during and after the referendum. Since the referendums held after WWI, including the most recent experiences such as East Timor and South Sudan, the neutralisation of the referendum area from the armed forces of the parties to the conflict has proved to be of the utmost importance. Also in this context, the formation of a neutral security force, an international impartial administrative body and a sufficient number of other international observers from other organisations and governments proves to be decisive. The body of the referendum administration should be adequately staffed with regard to its size and resources by considering the size of the population and geographical area concerned.

Of all the post-conflict and post-war referendums, the issue of security appears to be the most important criteria to be tackled. While the risk of intimidation and violence is always present across the whole referendum spectrum, the issue of security becomes particularly important after the proclamation of results, when individuals and groups are very vulnerable to reprisals. In addition, the secure and free transfer of emigrants becomes a delicate undertaking. The lessons drawn from the East Timor and South Sudan experiences show that the management of security should be exclusively carried out by an international peace force having plenipotentiary power over the area, disarming forces that are parties to the conflict.

Voter qualification is another common problem in all sovereignty referendums. The attitude and attempts by the parties to shape the electoral body to their advantage is fairly typical behaviour, and corresponding patterns of dispute are quite common. Against this setting, international law confers non-resident natives the right to vote, particularly in the post-war/post-violence situations assuming and/or observing a mass persecution or expulsion of the relevant peoples. In such cases, being born in the territory or having a parent born there suffices to bestow the right to vote, no matter how many years the relevant persons have lived elsewhere.

In more benign conditions, international law is less stringent and comparative constitutional law tends to bestow voting rights upon a residency requirement. However, in the case of former trust territories and non-self-governing territories, it could still be argued that non-resident natives have an inherent right to vote. As to non-native residents, the question gains importance in the context of post-violence, decolonisation or occupation. In this case, international law requires stringent residency requirements for non-native residents. This is mainly due to the assumption that parent states may attempt to manipulate the electoral body by creating an artificial demographic change. In the post-WWI referendums, minimum periods for continuous residence, from 6 to 20 years, were required. As a more recent example in the case of New Caledonia, the European Court of Human Rights found residency requirement ranging from 10 to 20 years permissible. However, if the case is outside of the context of decolonisation or occupation, international law is less rigorous. The case of Montenegro may be cited in this context, where the Venice Commission found the condition of 24 months of continuous residence excessive.

Designation of voting units should also be included as another typical issue arising in sovereignty referendums. Basically, the question pertains as to whether the territory should be treated as a single entity or be divided into two or more zones. The chosen preference in this respect may affect the result considerably, if there is a minority within the whole territory that is a majority in a certain region. In the context of decolonisation, international law requires that the territory should be treated as a whole. This is mainly due to the concern against any gerrymandering moves by the metropolitan states, as may be seen in the case of Mayotte.

However, in cases of a stark inter-ethnic strife, it would be much more reasonable to consider the ethnically differentiated and concentrated areas within a referendum zone and create voting units accordingly. This is plausible and desirable both from a political and a moral point of view, contributing to the potential future stability of the new territorial configuration. In Bosnia, for example, the Serbian boycott of the independence referendum was disregarded by the international community, adding fuel to fire leading to the Bosnian War. In Cyprus, the simultaneous referendums in the Turkish and Greek communities were based not on pure political decisions but on the preceding international legal documents. Therefore, the Cyprus case may be taken as a precedent that in the case of distinct and internationally recognised ethnic groups, a majority requirement from both communities should be secured.

Finally, we should consider the formulation of the ballot question. To start with, the wording should be clear and free of ambiguity and should not be deceptive or confusing. It must not give the voters wrong or ambivalent impressions about the legal consequences of their preferences. Also in this context, the voters should be able to answer the question by yes, no or a blank vote. The ballot should not include an open question requiring a further detailed answer. Common sense here says that the longer the ballot question is, the more prone it is to cause confusion. A fair balance between the necessity of giving an instructive explanation of each option and avoiding overly worded phraseology should be observed. Next, the universal democratic values impose that the ballot should observe the rule of unity of content: the voters should not be forced to vote on more than one option disparately included in the same ballot question. Finally, the ballot should not be formed in a manner favouring the *status quo*. This is a risk where the pro-*status quo* actors may include more than two options in the ballot, one for the *status quo* and the other covering different options against the *status quo*. By dividing the anti-*status quo* votes, the "No" votes always beat the divided "Yes" votes, thus the *status quo* wins. To avoid such an inconvenience, the questions as to whether to change the *status quo* and the options in case of a change should be asked separately. This may be done either by doing separate referendums or by separate questions on the same ballot, the first asking whether the electorate feels the need to change the *status quo* and the second giving the options available in the case of change.

To sum up this research, we may conclude by reflecting on two centuries worth of experience of sovereignty referendums. These referendums have consolidated their position as an imperative component in the politics and law of state creation. A regular and continuing pattern of political practice has led the way not just to the acceptance of referendum but likewise to the requirement of it by diverse international and national actors. Such ample experience and practice have created their own precedents, legal instruments and case laws in both comparative and international laws.

References

Brownlie, I. (2003). *Principles of public international law* (6th ed.). Oxford: Oxford University Press.

Habermas, J. (1996). *Between facts and norms: Contributions to a discourse theory of law and democracy* (trans: Rehg, W.) Cambridge, MA: MIT Press.

Salter, M. (1997, June). Review: Habermas's new contribution to legal scholarship. *Journal of Law and Society, 24*(2), 285–305.

Wambaugh, S. (1933). *Plebiscites since the world war: With a collection of official documents.* Washington: Carnegie Endowment for International Peace.

Reports by International Organisations

European Commission For Democracy Through Law (Venice Commission). "*Opinion on the Compatibility of the Existing Legislation in Montenegro Concerning The Organization of Referendums With Applicable International Standards.*" Opinion No: 343/2005, Council of Europe, Strasbourg, 19 December 2005.

European Commission for Democracy Through Law (Venice Commission). "*Referendums in Europe – An Analysis of the Legal Rules in European States*" Study No. 287/2004, Council of Europe, Strasbourg, CDL-AD (2005)034, 2 November 2005.

European Commission for Democracy Through Law (Venice Commission). "*Code of Good Practice on Referendums.*" Study No. 371/2006, 20 January 2009. CDL-AD(2007)008rev.

OSCE/ODIHR Referendum Observation Mission. "*Republic of Montenegro Referendum on State-Status: 21 May 2006 Final Report.*" Warsaw, 4 August 2006.

OSCE/ODIHR. "*Republic of Montenegro (Serbia and Montenegro) Referendum 21 May 2006 Needs Assessment Mission Report.*" Warsaw, 14 March 2006.

OSCE/ODIHR. "*Republic of Montenegro (Serbia and Montenegro) Referendum 21 May 2006 Needs Assessment Mission Report.*" Warsaw, 17 March 2006.

Report of the Special Committee on the Situation with regard to the Implementation of the Declaration on the Granting of Independence to Colonial Countries and Peoples for 2010. General Assembly Official Records Sixty-fifth Session Supplement No. 23, New York, 2010.

United Nations General Assembly. "*Question of East Timor Progress report of the Secretary-General.*", (A/54/654), 13 December 1999.

Special Committee on the Situation with regard to the Implementation of the Declaration on the Granting of Independence to Colonial Countries and Peoples. "*American Samoa: Working Paper Prepared by the Secretariat*", (A/AC.109/2011/12), 7 March 2011.

Special Committee on the Situation with regard to the Implementation of the Declaration on the Granting of Independence to Colonial Countries and Peoples.

İ.G. Şen, *Sovereignty Referendums in International and Constitutional Law*,
DOI 10.1007/978-3-319-11647-1

"*Guam*: *Working paper prepared by the Secretariat*" (A/AC.109/2011/15), 11 March 2011.

Special Committee on the Situation with regard to the Implementation of the Declaration on the Granting of Independence to Colonial Countries and Peoples. "*New Caledonia*: *Working paper prepared by the Secretariat*." The United Nations General Assembly, (A/AC.109/2011/16), 21 March 2011.

Special Committee on the Situation with regard to the Implementation of the Declaration on the Granting of Independence to Colonial Countries and Peoples. "*Resolution adopted by the Special Committee at its 12th meeting, on 6 July 1999*" "*Special Committee decision of 11 August 1998 concerning Puerto Rico*" A/AC.109/1999/28, 7 July 1999.

Special Committee on the Situation with regard to the Implementation of the Declaration on the Granting of Independence to Colonial Countries and Peoples. "*Guam*: *Working paper prepared by the Secretariat*." United Nations General Assembly, A/AC.109/1192, 19 May 1994.

Special Committee on the Situation with regard to the Implementation of the Declaration on the Granting of Independence to Colonial Countries and Peoples. "*Special Committee decision of 10 June 2002 concerning Puerto Rico Report prepared by the Rapporteur of the Special Committee, Mr. Fayssal Mekdad* (*Syrian Arab Republic*)." United Nations General Assembly, A/AC.109/2003/L.3, 12 May 2003.

Special Committee on the Situation with regard to the Implementation of the Declaration on the Granting of Independence to Colonial Countries and Peoples. "*Special Committee decision of 9 June 2008 concerning Puerto Rico Report prepared by the Rapporteur of the Special Committee, Bashar Ja'afari* (*Syrian Arab Republic*)." United Nations General Assembly, (A/AC.109/2009/L.13), 17 March 2009.

Special Committee on the Situation with regard to the Implementation of the Declaration on the Granting of Independence to Colonial Countries and Peoples. "*Guam*: *Working paper prepared by the Secretariat*" United Nations General Assembly, (A/AC.109/1192), 19 May 1994.

Special Committee on the Situation with regard to the Implementation of the Declaration on the Granting of Independence to Colonial Countries and Peoples. "*Guam*: *Working paper prepared by the Secretariat*" A/AC.109/2011/15, 11 March 2011.

Special Committee on the Situation with regard to the Implementation of the Declaration on the Granting of Independence to Colonial Countries and Peoples, "*United States Virgin Islands*: *Working paper prepared by the Secretariat*", (A/AC.109/2011/9), 25 February 2011.

United Nations General Assembly. "*Enhancing the effectiveness of the principle of periodic and genuine elections Report of the Secretary-General*." A/46/609, 19 November 1991.

United Nations Security Council. "*Question of East Timor Report of the Secretary-General*." S/1999/803, 20 July 1999.

United Nations Security Council. "*Question of East Timor Report of the Secretary-General.*" S/1999/595, 22 May 1999.

United Nations General Assembly-Security Council. "*Question of East Timor Report of the Secretary-General.*" S/1999/513-A/53/951, 5 May 1999.

United Nations Security Council. "*Special report of the Secretary-General on the Sudan.*" S/2011/314, 17 May 2011.

United Nations Security Council. "*Report of the Secretary-General on the Sudan.*" S/2011/239, 12 April 2011.

United Nations. "*Report of the Special Committee on the Situation with regard to the Implementation of the Declaration on the Granting of Independence to Colonial Countries and Peoples for 2010*", General Assembly Official Records Sixty-fifth Session Supplement No. 23, A/65/23, 2010.

The United Nations Integrated Referendum and Electoral Division (UNIRED) Fact Sheet: Frequently Asked Questions, (2010) unmis.unmissions.org/Portals/UNMIS/Referendum/UNIRED.pdf; Retrieved on 12 September 2011 from the Official Website of United Nations Mission in Sudan.

Special Committee on the Situation with regard to the Implementation of the Declaration on the Granting of Independence to Colonial Countries and Peoples. "Report of the United Nations Mission to Observe a Referendum on Self-Determination of Tokelau", A/AC.109/2006/20 February 2006.

The Southern Sudan Referendum Act: Frequently Asked Questions, (2010) http://unmis.unmissions.org/Portals/UNMIS/Referendum/The%20Southern%20Sudan%20Referendum%20Act%20FAQ.pdf Retrieved on 12 September 2011 from the Official Website of United Nations Mission in Sudan.

Reports by National Institutions

CONGRESSIONAL RECORD—HOUSE, April 29, 2010 Retrieved on 12 October 2012 from http://www.gpo.gov/fdsys/pkg/CREC-2010-04-29/pdf/CREC-2010-04-29-pt1-PgH3029-3.pdf#page=1.

Puerto Rico Status Field Hearing Before the Committee on Resources House of Representatives One Hundred Fifth Congress First Session on ***H.R. 856*** *April 19, 1997, Retrieved from: http://commdocs.house.gov/committees/resources/hii43194.000/hii43194_0.HTM, on* 12 November 2012.

Puerto Rico Democracy Act of 2007, (*Report by Mr RAHALL from the Committee on Natural Resources*), House of Representatives, 110th Congress 2nd Session, Report 110-597, April 22, 2008. Retrieved on 15 July 2011 from http://www.gpo.gov/fdsys/pkg/CRPT-110hrpt597/pdf/CRPT-110hrpt597.pdf.

Report by the President's Task Force on Puerto Rico's Status (December 2005) http://charma.uprm.edu/~angel/Puerto_Rico/reporte_status.pdf (Accessed November 23, 2012).

Report by the President's Task Force on Puerto Rico's Status (December 2007) http://www.justice.gov/opa/documents/2007-report-by-the-president-task-force-on-puerto rico-status.pdf (Accessed November 23, 2012).

Report by the President's Task Force on Puerto Rico's Status (March 2011) http://www.whitehouse.gov/sites/default/files/uploads/Puerto_Rico_Task_Force_Report.pdf (Accessed November 23, 2012).

İ.G. Şen, *Sovereignty Referendums in International and Constitutional Law*,
DOI 10.1007/978-3-319-11647-1

The UN General Assembly Resolutions

A/RES/57/3: The UN General Assembly Resolution of 27 September 2002, on the "*Admission of the Democratic Republic of Timor-Leste to membership in the United Nations*"

A/RES/42/79: The UN General Assembly Resolution of 4 December 1987, on the "*Question of New Caledonia*"

A/RES/41/30: The UN General Assembly Resolution of 3 November 1986, on the "*Question of the Comorian island of Mayotte*",

A/RES/40/50: The UN General Assembly Resolution of 2 December 1985 on the "*Resolution of Question of Western Sahara*"

A/RES/37/253: The UN General Assembly Resolution of 13 May 1983 on the "*Question of Cyprus*"

A/RES/36/105: The UN General Assembly Resolution of 10 December 1981 on the "*Question of the Comorian island of Mayotte*",

A/RES/36/103: The UN General Assembly Resolution of 9 December 1981, on the "*Declaration on the Inadmissibility of Intervention and Interference in the Internal Affairs of States*"

A/RES/35/42: The UN General Assembly Resolution of 28 November 1980, on the "*Question of the Comorian island of Mayotte*"

A/RES 34/91: The UN General Assembly Resolution of 12 December 1979 on the "*Question of the islands of Glorieuses, Juan de Nova, Europa and Basses de India*"

A/RES/33/15: The UN General Assembly Resolution of 9 November 1978 on the "*Question of Cyprus*"

A/RES/32/15: The UN General Assembly Resolution of 9 November 1977 on the "*Question of Cyprus*"

A/RES/32/7: The UN General Assembly Resolution of 1 November 1977 on the "*Question of the Comorian island of Mayotte*"

A/RES/31/4: The UN General Assembly Resolution of 21 October 1976, on the "*Question of the Comorian island of Mayotte*"

İ.G. Şen, *Sovereignty Referendums in International and Constitutional Law*,
DOI 10.1007/978-3-319-11647-1

A/RES/3485 (XXX): The UN General Assembly Resolution of 12 December 1975 on the "*Question of Timor*"

A/RES/3291 (XXIX): The UN General Assembly Resolution of 13 December 1974 on the "*Question of Comoro Archipelago*"

A/RES/3395(XXX): The UN General Assembly Resolution of 20 November 1975 on the "*Question of Cyprus*"

A/RES/3212(XXIX): The UN General Assembly Resolution of 1 November 1974 on, the "*Question of Cyprus*"

A/RES/3162(XXVIII): The UN General Assembly Resolution of 14 December 1973, on the "*Question of Spanish Sahara*"

A/RES/2983 (XXVII): The UN General Assembly Resolution of 14 December 1972, on the "*Question of Spanish Sahara*"

A/RES/2625: The UN General Assembly Resolution of 24 October 1970, on the "*Declaration on Principles of International Law Concerning Friendly Relations and Cooperation Among States in Accordance with the Charter of the United Nations*"

A/RES/2353(XXII): The UN General Assembly Resolution of 19 December 1967, on the "*Question of Gibraltar*"

A/RES/2228(XXI): The UN General Assembly Resolution of 20 December 1966 on the "*Question of French Somaliland*"

A/RES/2229(XXI): The UN General Assembly Resolution of 20 December 1966 on the "*Question of Ifni and Spanish Sahara*"

A/RES/2072(XX): The UN General Assembly Resolution of 16 December 1965, on the "*Question of Ifni and Spanish Sahara*"

A/RES/1747(XVI): The UN General Assembly Resolution of 28 June 1962 on "*The question of Southern Rhodesia*"

A/RES/1744(XVI): The UN General Assembly Resolution of 23 February 1962 on the "*Question of Mwami of Ruanda*"

A/RES/2356 (XXII): The UN General Assembly Resolution of 19 December 1961, on the "*Question of French Somaliland*"

A/RES/1626 (XVI): The UN General Assembly Resolution of 6 November 1961, on "*The Future of Western Samoa*"

A/RES/1608(XV): The UN General Assembly Resolution of 21 April 1961, on "*The future of the Trust Territory of the Cameroons under United Kingdom administration*"

A/RES/1569(XV): The UN General Assembly Resolution of 18 December 1960, on "The Future of Western Samoa"

A/RES/1541: The UN General Assembly Resolution of 15 December 1960, on "*Principles which should guide members in determining whether or nor an obligation exists to transmit the information called for under Article 73 e of the Charter*"

A/RES/1514 (XV): The UN General Assembly Resolution of 14 December 1960, on the "*Declaration, on the Granting of Independence to Colonial Countries and Peoples*".

A/RES/860(IX): The UN General Assembly Resolution, of 14 December 1959, on "*The Togoland unification problem and the future of the Trust Territory of Togoland under British administration*"

A/RES/1473 (XIV): The UN General Assembly Resolution of 12 December 1959, on "*The future of the Trust Territory of the Cameroons under United Kingdom administration: organization of a further plebiscite in the northern part of the Territory*"

A/RES/1416 (XIV): The UN General Assembly Resolution of 5 December 1959 on the "*Date of the independence of the Trust Territory of Togoland under French administration*"

A/RES/1352/(XIV): The UN General Assembly Resolution of 16 October 1959, on "*The future of the Trust Territory of the Cameroons under United Kingdom administration: organization of the plebiscite in the southern part of the Territory*"

A/RES/1350(XIII): The UN General Assembly Resolution of 13 March 1959 "*The future of the Trust Territory of the Cameroons under United Kingdom administration*"

A/RES/1349 (XIII): The UN General Assembly Resolution of 13 March 1959 on the "*The future of the Trust Territory of the Cameroons under French Administration*"

A/RES/1046 (XI): The UN General Assembly Resolution of 23 Jan. 1957 on "*The future of Togoland under French administration*"

A/RES/1044 (XI): The UN General Assembly Resolution of 13 December 1956, on "*The future of Togoland under British administration*"

A/RES/944(X): The UN General Assembly Resolution of 15 December 1955, on "*The Togoland unification problem and the future of the Trust Territory of Togoland under British administration*"

The UN Security Council Resolutions

S/RES/2046 (2012): The UN Security Council Resolution of 2 May 2012
S/RES/1996/2011: The UN Security Council Resolution of 8 July 2011
S/RES/1990 (2011): The UN Security Council Resolution of 27 June 2011
S/RES/1986 (2011): The UN Security Council Resolution of 13 June 2011
S/RES/1953(2010): The UN Security Council Resolution of 14 December 2010
S/RES/1475(2003) The UN Security Council Resolution of 14 April 2003
S/RES/1250 (1999): The UN Security Council Resolution of 22 December 1999.
S/RES/1272 (1999): The UN Security Council Resolution of, 25 October 1999
S/RES/1246/(1999): The UN Security Council Resolution of 11 June 1999
S/RES/1179 (1998): The UN Security Council Resolution of 29 June 1998
S/RES/716 (1991): The UN Security Council Resolution of 11 October 1991
S/RES/649 (1990): The UN Security Council Resolution of 12 March 1990
S/RES/422 (1977): The UN Security Council Resolution of 15 December 1977
S/RES/384(1975): The UN Security Council Resolution of 22 December 1975
S/RES/367 (1975): The UN Security Council Resolution of 12 March 1975

İ.G. Şen, *Sovereignty Referendums in International and Constitutional Law*,
DOI 10.1007/978-3-319-11647-1

Table of Cases

ICJ Cases

Western Sahara, Advisory Opinion of 16 October 1975, ICJ Reports (1975), p. 12

ECtHR Cases

Matthews v. United Kingdom, no. 24833/941999-I, ECtHR
Hilbe v. Liechtenstein (dec.), no. 31981/96, 1999-VI, ECtHR
Py. v. France, no. 66289/01, 2005-I, ECtHR

International Arbitration and Other Cases

"Report of the International Committee of Jurists entrusted by the Council of the League of Nations with the task of giving an advisory opinion upon the legal aspects of the Aaland Islands question." http://www.ilsa.org/jessup/jessup10/basicmats/aaland1.pdf; Retrieved: 12.09.2012

Gillot et al. v. France, Communication No. 932/2000, Views of 15 July 2002, Seventy-fifth session, The UN General Assembly Official Records Fifty-seventh session, Supplement No. A/57/40 (Vol. I) (2002)

İ.G. Şen, *Sovereignty Referendums in International and Constitutional Law*,
DOI 10.1007/978-3-319-11647-1

Domestic Case Law

Canada

Reference re Secession of Quebec, [1998] 2 S.C.R. 217

France

Décision n° 62-20 DC du 06 novembre 1962
Decision n° 92-313 DC du 23 Septembre 1992
Décision n° 2000-21 REF du 25 juillet 2000
Décision n° 75-59 DC du 30 décembre 1975 "Loi relative aux conséquences de l'autodétermination des îles des Comores"
Décision n° 87-226 DC du 02 juin 1987 Loi organisant la consultation des populations intéressées de la Nouvelle-Calédonie et dépendances prévue par l'alinéa premier de l'article 1er de la loi n° 86-844 du 17 juillet 1986 relative à la Nouvelle-Calédonie.
Decision 99-410 DC of 15 MARCH 1999 Institutional Act concerning New Caledonia (Official Translation of *Décision n° 99-410 DC du 15 mars 1999: Loi organique relative à la Nouvelle-Calédonie*)

The United States of America

Delima v. Bidwell, 182 U.S. 1 (1901)
Goetze v. United States 182 U.S. 221 (1901)
Dooley v. United States, 182 U.S. 222 (1901)
Armstrong v. United States, 182 U.S. 243 (1901)
Downes v. Bidwell, 182 U.S. 244 (1901)
Balzac v. Porto Rico, 258 U.S. 298 (1922)
United States v. Sanches (1993), 99 2F.2.d 1143,1152-53(11th Cir.)
270 F. Supp.459 (D.P.R. 1967), 390 F.2d. 160 (1st. Circuit 1968)

Regularly Visited Web Sites

http://www.c2d.ch
http://www.un.org/en/documents/index.shtml
http://www.gpo.gov
http://www.servat.unibe.ch/icl/
http://www.legifrance.gouv.fr/
www.conseil-constitutionnel.fr

İ.G. Şen, *Sovereignty Referendums in International and Constitutional Law*,
DOI 10.1007/978-3-319-11647-1

Index

İ.G. Şen, *Sovereignty Referendums in International and Constitutional Law*,
DOI 10.1007/978-3-319-11647-1

MIX
Papier aus verantwortungsvollen Quellen
Paper from responsible sources
FSC® C105338

If you have any concerns about our products,
you can contact us on
ProductSafety@springernature.com

In case Publisher is established outside the EU,
the EU authorized representative is:
Springer Nature Customer Service Center GmbH
Europaplatz 3, 69115 Heidelberg, Germany

Printed by Libri Plureos GmbH
in Hamburg, Germany